CONSIGNED INDIFFERENCE

THE MILITARY CAREERS OF SIX CIVIL WAR GENERALS WITH TENUOUS FAME

By Ron V. Killian

HERITAGE BOOKS
2009

HERITAGE BOOKS
AN IMPRINT OF HERITAGE BOOKS, INC.

Books, CDs, and more—Worldwide

For our listing of thousands of titles see our website
at
www.HeritageBooks.com

Published 2009 by
HERITAGE BOOKS, INC.
Publishing Division
100 Railroad Ave. #104
Westminster, Maryland 21157

Copyright © 2009 Ron V. Killian

Other books by the author:

*A History of the North Carolina Third Mounted
Infantry Volunteers: March 1864 to August 1865*

All rights reserved. No part of this book may be reproduced or transmitted in any form or by any means, electronic or mechanical, including photocopying, recording or by any information storage and retrieval system without written permission from the author, except for the inclusion of brief quotations in a review.

International Standard Book Numbers
Paperbound: 978-0-7884-4516-3
Clothbound: 978-0-7884-8217-5

TABLE OF CONTENTS

v   Illustrations
vii   Acknowledgements
xi   Introduction

1   Generalship as it existed in the Civil War
21   Gen. Charles P. Stone, U.S
93   Gen. Charles Smith Hamilton, U.S.
135 Gen. Lloyd Tilghman, CSA
175 Gen. George Stoneman, U.S.
249 Gen. Evander McIvor Law, CSA
339 Gen. Charles Garrison Harker, U.S
377 Epitaphs and Notes

ILLUSTRATIONS

Gen. Charles Stone
- 20-B   Photograph of Gen. Charles Stone
- 54-A   Bull Run as it looked in 1861
- 54-B   Death of Colonel Baker
- 54-C   Photograph of Secretary of War Simon Cameron
- 54-D   Photograph of Secretary of War Edwin Stanton
- 54-E   Photograph of Benjamin Wade, member of Congress and the Committee on the Conduct of the War
- 54-F   Statue of Liberty

Gen. Charles Hamilton
- 92-B   Photograph of Gen. Charles Smith Hamilton
- 112-A Cavalry Charge
- 112-B Supplies Issued
- 112-C Photograph of Gen. Stephen Hurlbut

Gen. Lloyd Tilghman
- 134-B Photograph of Gen. Lloyd Tilghman
- 152-A The Bombardment of Ft. Henry
- 152-B Monument of Gen. Lloyd Tilghman at Vicksburg National Military Park
- 152-C Historic Marker indicating the battle at Champion Hill

Gen. George Stoneman
- 174-B Photograph of Gen. George Stoneman
- 210-A Fredericksburg Pontoon Bridge
- 210-B Photograph of General John Schofield
- 210-C Photograph of General Stoneman and his Staff

210-D Photograph of Gen, James Martin's grave in Asheville, NC

Gen. Evander Law
248-B Photograph of Gen. Evander Law
292-A Outline of the "Mule Shoe" at the battle of Spotsylvania
292-B The Infamous" mud slides" at the battle of the Wilderness and the Virginia battlefields of 1864

Gen. Charles Harker
338-B Photograph of Gen. Charles Harker
356-A "Cracker Line" at Chattanooga
356-B Photograph of Gen. Wood
356-C The Battle of Kenesaw, GA
356-D Kenesaw as it looked in 1864
356-E Photograph of Gen. John Newton

ACKNOWLEDGEMENTS

The University of Michigan, Amherst College, University of Wisconsin, The United States Military Academy at West Point, The Citadel, in Charleston, South Carolina and the University of North Carolina are notable institutions of higher learning that offered their benefaction in the writing of this manuscript by way of source materials. Other institutions: particularly The Spartanburg County, South Carolina Public Library, The Darlington County, South Carolina Historical Commission, Polk County, Florida Historical and Genealogy Library, Vicksburg National Military Park, Baltimore Public Library, the Swedesboro, New Jersey Historical Society, the Pack Library in Asheville, North Carolina, and the Fenton Historical Center at Jamestown, New York supplied precise and accurate information which would have been difficult to locate, if not unobtainable, elsewhere.

Individuals also were helpful in many aspects relating to this manuscript. Betsy Tolley of the Spartanburg County, South Carolina Public Library procured materials that are indispensable and seemingly unavailable regarding several of the individuals discussed in this manuscript. Mr. Joe Spann of the Polk County, Florida Historical and Genealogy Library supplied his expertise on Gen. Evander Law's life that is probably not available from any other source. All of the employees of the Fenton Historical Center in Jamestown, New York gave their time and knowledge on the life and career of General Stoneman that is exceedingly applicable. Members of the Swedesboro Historical Society supplied information on General Harker of an exceedingly concise nature.

In conclusion, it would be fair to say this manuscript would not have been completed without the help and services of the above listed persons and institutions. Appreciation is hereby expressed to them for their assistance.

INTRODUCTION

The question "why are these particular six generals included in this work" might occur to anyone who reads this volume and it is a fair question. Each one of the generals included depicts a specific aspect or stylized prefigured opinion that has evolved over the past 150 years. For example, the *Commission on the Conduct of the War* in the 1860s labeled Gen. Charles Stone a traitor. This was not true, yet his life was ruined and he never determined the cause for this hyperbole. The public became indifferent to the man who was in charge of President Lincoln's safety when Lincoln made his way to Washington for the Inauguration.

The circumstances leading to Gen. Lloyd Tilghman's suffered indifference in the post war years are of another variety. General Tilghman was given an assignment by the Confederate high command concerning the river forts that was predetermined to be indefensible. The river forts had many problems and a number of competent generals had expressed these problems to the command of the Army of Tennessee. While nothing was done to allay the problems much was done to compound them, all at the expense of Tilghman's reputation, which was trashed, and he was labeled an expendable general.

The young Gen. Charles Harker is an expression of all that is right in the history of this nation. Hard working, struggling against life's adversities, and prevailing, defines his life. The young Harker made a slow but steady rise in the western Union army. He was in no small measure a factor in Gen. George Thomas fame as the "Rock of Chickamauga". In a haughty attempt by Sherman to defeat the entrenched

Confederate forces at Kenesaw, General Harker's life was ended before he was an established person in the public's thoughts.

If one examines the career of Gen. George Stoneman, a myriad of commands will be found. Stoneman made mistakes in his career, but when an individual gives much to a cause, mistakes occur. Weigh this against an individual who makes a single outstanding contribution, laced with little else and mistakes as well, and the situation becomes clear. Stoneman is remembered for the battle of Chancellorsville and the attempt to free Union prisoners at Andersonville prisoner of war camp in Georgia, both unsuccessful. The failure of the venture to Andersonville must be laid entirely on Stoneman, but the Chancellorsville failure goes to the apex of the Army of the Potomac command. No general held more command positions than Stoneman, but unfortunately the indifference regarding his career rest upon these two blunders while much of his overall service is unrecalled.

The military service of Gen. Charles Smith Hamilton was cut short because of his resignation from the army in April of 1863. General Hamilton was an extremely complicated person surrounded by individuals who were equally complicated and pompous. Hamilton wanted an independent command or better yet, a corps command. He lacked the prerequisites for either of these positions, and thus resorted to a personal attack against those that he felt stood in his way to acquire them. Hamilton's wrath spared no one, and even included General Grant. General Hamilton's fate was somewhat deserved yet surprisingly his career has escaped most Civil War works, which is another form of indifference.

Evander Law has acquired a measure of fame for his military service but it falls short of what he actually deserves. Law was a brilliant student at the Citadel in South Carolina and, along with the future Confederate general,

Micah Jenkins, established a military school after graduation. Law took part in most of the important battles involving the Army of Northern Virginia and along the way an interesting scenario began to develop. Law became a favorite of General Hood and his former friend and business partner General Jenkins, also in Gen. James Longstreet's corps, became Longstreet protégé. Hood's unfortunate battle wounds took him away from the command of his division. Law acquired the division command for a time and the struggle between Jenkins and Law for the command of Hood's division began to take shape. To a degree, Longstreet seems to have maligned Law in favor of Jenkins. Toward the end of the war, Law transferred to the cavalry command of Gen. Wade Hampton. Add to this mixture the fact that Law left a dearth of information about his service while <u>in the Confederate Army</u>, little attention has been given to this important Confederate officer.

    The military saga of the generals discussed in this manuscript represents only six of the nearly 1,000 notable individuals who held the exalted rank of general during what is perhaps America's most important conflict. While many of these individuals have received their just attention, one can only hope that future historians will investigate the lives of those who have not.

GENERALSHIP AS IT EXISTED IN THE CIVIL WAR

Who could become a general in the armies of the Civil War? The long answer short is that well nigh any adult male qualified for the position. A casual perusal of men who became generals will bear out this statement. The age of candidates for this position of command covered the entire conceivable contingency. Confederate general David E. Twiggs was born in 1790 and became a general in 1861, while Union general Galusha Pennypacker was promoted to brigadier general in 1865 at the tender age of twenty.[1] These two men are examples and by no means extreme exceptions to the absence of any age requirement for generalship during the Civil War. The average age of the six generals discussed in this work is thirty-five, the oldest being Gen. Lloyd Tilghman at forty-five and the two youngest are Gen. Evander Law and Gen. Charles Harker at twenty-five.

    The background of the candidates for this exalted command position appears to have covered a broad spectrum. For the sake of discussion and reasonable brevity, the candidates essentially came from three sectors of antebellum life. Of the 1,000 plus generals discussed in Ezra Warner's two volume work on Civil War generals, 526 of these men were either West Point graduates, attended West Point but did not graduate, or attended another military school such as the Citadel or Virginia Military Institute. The

---

[1]Anne Bailey," David E. Twiggs" , *The Confederate General (Harrisburg*: National Historical Society, 1991), Vol. VI, p.64-65; hereinafter cited as The General; Ezra J. Warner, *Generals in Blue* (Baton Rouge: Louisiana State University Press, 1994), p. 365; hereinafter cited as Warner Gray and Blue

remainder had some other type of limited military experience, although others had no military experience whatsoever. [2] Many of the generals with military backgrounds were volunteers in the Mexican War of 1846. All six of the generals discussed here had military backgrounds, five were West Point graduates and one was a graduate of the Citadel. A second sector, which accounted for a large number of generals, was that of business and finance, supplying some 236 generals. This area includes plantation owners in the South as well as the owners of large farms in the North. The remaining 300 plus generals came from a variety of positions such as the law, education, medicine, religious work, newspaper editors, to mention a few of the varied occupations. [3]

The final category embraces an overlap of the previously discussed sectors. While some generals were businessmen, or had some unqualified amount of military training, they became generals for a quite incongruous reason-they were politicians. This was not unheard of in previous wars, nor will it be excluded in future wars in which this nation is involved. To quote an old slang, "money and influence don't talk, they scream."

The Union made no concerted effort to mix the regular army officers and the volunteers coming into service. In addition, Union regiments were allowed to select and elect their officers. The result of this practice was that many experienced officers were neglected or quite often overlooked. An example of the extent of these omissions can be seen in the obviate acceptance of General Grant, who contacted the War Department in 1861 but never received a reply. West Point and military school graduates were often relegated to minor unimportant positions while men with no military experienced frequently commanded regiments and divisions. Military records show that the Union put 142

---

[2] Ezra Warner, *Gray and Blue*, see the introduction in either volume
[3] Ezra Warner, Gray and Blue, see introduction

generals from the Old Army [51 major generals and ninety-one brigadiers] into service, which accounted for less than half of the available number.[4] The Confederacy used the opposite tact, making it easy for the old Army officers to become part of the Confederate army with more or less the same rank. Of the 250 officers who joined the Confederate army, 182 became generals. The Confederacy took advantage of *every* trained potential military officer available. The experienced officers and soldiers were mixed together, which created cohesion that seems to have been lacking in the Union Army until 1863.[5] The military policies of the Union and Confederate armies differed in many other practices as well. Union officers were frequently degraded and dismissed by both President Lincoln and Secretary of War Stanton and neither had any significant military training. The Confederacy's President Jefferson Davis, a graduate of West Point, never dismissed a general for lack of success with the exception of Gen. Joseph Johnston in 1864. However, in the Union Army not until General Grant's appointment as Commander-in-Chief of the Army in March of 1864, did this practice end. The result was a steady increase in the performance of Union troops and successful outcomes in more battles.[6] Gen. Charles Stone, covered in this work, was driven out of the service, place in military confinement for months, never charged, and was given no explanation as to why this occurred. The probable reason was General Stone's loss at the battle of Ball's Bluff in 1861, leading to the death of President Lincoln's close friend, General Edward Baker. This treatment of Union officers was not an uncommon occurrence prior to Grant's take over of the Union forces in March of 1864.

---

[4] Walter Geer, *Campaigns of the Civil War* (Saybrook, CT: Konecky & Konecky, 1926 { reprint of the original}, p. 432; hereinafter cited as Geer
[5] Geer, p. 433
[6] G.F.R. Henderson, *The Art of War*, (London: publisher not given, 1919), p. 239-240

If one considers the time, events, and reasons leading to the Civil War, it is not difficult to conclude that if you were of age, and especially in the South, the chance of active participation in this conflict was very high. With this consideration in mind, what were the advantages of fighting the war as an officer, and especially as a general? The Union Army allowed for only three levels of general officers. From lowest to highest rank the order is brigadier, major general, and finally, General Grant was promoted to Lieutenant General, a rank reserved for him alone so that no other general could outrank him. The Confederate army had a very similar arrangement for ranking general officers, but used the rank of Lieutenant General frequently. Also, the rank of General [referred to as Full General] was a part of the Confederate ranking structure, but reserved for a very select few, such as Gen. R. E. Lee, Gen. Braxton Bragg, Gen. Edmund Kirby Smith, and Gen. John Bell Hood, to mention a few of the men who held this rank.

The ratio of officers killed in battle was one officer per sixteen enlisted men, but death due to disease presents different odds: one officer for every seventy-two enlisted men. This is not difficult to believe in that officers had better quarters and a much better opportunity to obtain proper food. However, during a campaign, the food, quarters, and other needs were satisfied at about the same level for both officers and enlisted men. A final qualification of the death rate for officers and enlisted men must be stated. Only thirty-five Union generals died of disease during the war, and a total of fifty-one officers died in battlefield situations. Records of Confederate general officers who died of diseases are very limited, but existing records list seventy-three Confederate officers who died in battle. It stands to reason that the fatality rate would be about the same in both armies for deaths due to disease. The Confederacy's losses in battlefield situations are probably accurate but the loss due to disease is uncertain. Both the Union and the Confederacy lost commanders of armies; the Union lost Gen.James B. McPherson, commander of the Army of the Tennessee and the Confederacy lost Gen. Albert Sidney Johnston, commander of the western Confederate troops at the battle of Shiloh. Both armies lost Corps commanders; the Union losses were Gen. Joseph K. Mansfield, Gen. John Reynolds, and Gen. John Sedgwick. The Confederacy lost Gen. Thomas Jackson, Gen. Leonidas Polk, and Gen. A. P. Hill. The Union lost fourteen Division commanders and the Confederacy suffered the loss of seven Division commanders. Brigade commanders were lost at many of the significant battles by both armies. Of the six generals discussed in this work, General Tilghman was killed at the battle of Champion Hill, and General Harker died at the battle of Kenesaw.[7]

It is clear that generals died in battle at a much lower rate, when compared to enlisted men, had better food and provisions, and doubtless received much better pay. Upon a more complete analysis the fact emerges that generals on both sides of the conflict exposed themselves to great danger when it was necessary and did not hesitate to lead their regiments, divisions, etc when the need occurred, completely at the mercy of enemy fire. One need but consult the number of generals killed in battle, a total of 124, to verify this statement.[8]

The fact cannot be overlooked that fame and glory can be driving forces in the actions taken by individuals in and out of the military, and the Civil War was certainly no exception. Many generals were extremely popular with their troops, but never obtained any real success on the battlefield. Gen. George McClellan is a prime example of this allegation. McClellan received all types of slurs and put downs, even from President Lincoln who said he had the "slows" when it came to offensive battle. Nevertheless,

---

[7] For a complete analysis of these numbers and individual deaths see William F. Fox, *Regimental Losses in the American Civil War: 1861-1865* (Albany, NY: Augustus S. Brandow publishers, 1898), p. 40-41; 571-573; hereinafter cited as Fox

[8] Fox, 42,43; 571-573

many of his men loved and respected him as their leader. An example to point up this fact is a statement by Captain Francis A. Donaldson of the 71st Pennsylvania Vols. , Army of the Potomac in 1862, concerning General McClellan's rumored dismissal as the commanding general of the Army of the Potomac, " As to the replacement of Genl. McClellan, I give no credence to the report, as it would be a hazardous undertaking to remove so renowned & competent a General upon the eve of a campaign. Certainly the men who love him dearly would resent such an outrage. I do not believe that any living man can handle this army successfully were he removed."[9] Major Harry L. Abbott of the 20th Massachusetts, Army of the Potomac expresses another example of McClellan's popularity among his men in a letter to his father in 1864, " ... to show McClellan's.... sagacity &insight, both political & military, wonderful comprehensiveness, energy, tenacity & directness of purpose, & above all his *pluck*, never to be ruffled by any danger or suffering, even when every body else knock under."[10] Major Abbott states elsewhere in a letter to his brother in September of 1863, that McClellan's slowness was simply a matter of impatience on the part of Washington officials, because McClellan was invading the most difficult country in the world with an army that was too small for such an invasion.[11] Popular Confederate generals also faced this problem of limited battlefield success. A cardinal example is that of Gen. Maxcy Gregg, a brigade commander in Gen. A.P. Hill's Light Division, Army of Northern Virginia. General Gregg was born in Columbia, was never married, viewed by most associates as an intellectual, and

---

[9] *Inside the Army of the Potomac: The Civil War Experience of Captain Francis A. Donalson* , edited by J. Gregory Acken, *(Mechaniscburg, PA:Stackpole Books, 1998)*, p. 49

[10] *Fallen Leaves: The Civil War Letters of Major Harry Livermore Abbott,* edited by Robert G. Scott, (Kent, Ohio: Kent State University Press1991), p.239; hereinafter cited as Fallen Leaves

[11] Fallen Leaves, p. 213

was practically deaf, which contributed to his death at Fredericksburg. General Gregg's greatest glory occurred at Gaines' Mill and Second Manassas. The general died in 1862, yet when facing the icy hand of death at the Yerby House near Fredericksburg, Gen. Thomas "Stonewall" Jackson visited Gregg, talked about religious matters and with high emotion. Gen. A. P. Hill was probably General Gregg's last visitor. Hill said his good byes to General Gregg and left with tears in his eyes after placing an *agape* kiss on the dying general's forehead.[12] General Gregg was unable to achieve greatness in the Civil War due to an early death yet he is remembered in his home city with both a street and a public park named in his honor.

Generals on occasion made decisions that caused them lifelong grief and remorse, even beyond the scope of the war. An example of this can be found in *The History of the 61st Ohio Vol. Infantry*, by 1st Lt. John Arbuckle in reference to Gen. O. O. Howard, commander of the XI Corps and his actions at the battle of Chancellorsville, "Fitzhugh Lee's brigade of cavalry.... when he got good and ready made his charge. The result was he doubled up Howard's right and again doubled and redoubled the XI Corps of only ten thousand to his twenty-two thousand men; but instead of taking any steps to check Jackson's continual flank movements, Howard must needs rush among his own men, swing his revolver and whine, 'I am ruined.' No, the XI Corps did not ruin General Howard, but he ruined the reputation of the XI Corps forever."[13] Arbuckle goes on to state that the shame of this event followed the XI Corps for twenty-eight years, and will never be forgotten.

Many articles and books have been written to show exactly how a general comes to the point of making the mistakes made by Howard, McClellan, etc. Steven E.

---

[12] Robert K. Krick, "Maxcy Gregg", The General, Vol. III, p. 41-43

[13] *From Freeman's Ford to Bentonville: The 61st Ohio Volunteer Infantry,* edited by Robert C. Carroon,(Shippensburg, PA: Burd Street Press, 1998), p. 45

Woodworth, in his book *Civil War Generals in Defeat*[14] offers a superior discussion of the reasons this might occur. Woodworth states that often the defeated general lost to the best general the opposing side had to offer, using Grant's defeat of Pemberton in the Vicksburg campaign as an example. A second factor stated is the difficulties faced in dealing with both superiors and subordinates. Woodworth states that Gen. Lloyd Tilghman was slow to follow orders and this had an effect upon the outcome of Gen. Albert S. Johnston's loss at Shiloh. Another explanation however, might be possible in this case. The *authority* on the Confederate Army of Tennessee, Thomas L. Connelly, states in his book, *Army of the Heartland*:

> ... in late January a reconnaissance force moved up the Tennessee in order to test the defenses of Fort Henry, which Polk knew, were in poor condition. On the morning of January 14, three federal vessels shelled Henry, while three transports landed a reconnaissance party on the west bank of the Tennessee. Tilghman estimated the force At about 5, 500 and asked Polk and Johnston for assistance. [15]

Connelly goes on to state that even though Tilghman repeatedly asked for infantry, none was supplied. He concludes, "Polk sent no help and, after a courageous defense by Tilghman, Fort Henry fell on February 6. The Kentuckian in charge of the fort's defense [Tilghman] did not have a chance to hold the position."[16] One could reasonably conclude that instead of Tilghman being slow to obey orders, Gen. Leonidas Polk *refused* to obey orders, as Woodworth contends in his analysis, [Polk, Jefferson Davis,

---

[14] Steven L. Woodworth, *Civil War Generals in Defeat* (Lawrence, Kansas: University Press of Kansas, 1999), p. 192; hereinafter cited as Woodworth

[15] Thomas L. Connelly, *Army of the Heartland: The Army of Tennessee, 1861-1862* (Baton Rouge: Louisiana State University Press, 1967), p.106; hereinafter cited as Connelly

[16] Connelly, p.107

and Johnston were close friends at West Point which might account for Polk's disregard for Johnston's orders and Tilghman's request for infantry] and ignored Tilghman's pleas for assistance, even though infantry was available. General Tilghman's situation at Fort Henry is much like the yard dog challenged by the Bengal tiger: sometimes the best defense is no action whatsoever [brigadiers do not challenge Corps commanders]. Woodworth continues his excellent discussion of the failure of generals by stating that many times a losing general simply could not adapt to conditions and there is little doubt that this is a major factor in the loss of a battle in any war.

Civil War generals, much like corporate executive officers of today, developed a style of command that could often seem somewhat unique with each individual. One of the styles can be identified as a sort of singularity or an anomaly, or a quirk This style of command worked for only a limited few commanders, mainly because it is difficult to carry out a command when the command is not specified or conveyed until the very last minute. General Thomas "Stonewall" Jackson is most frequently identified with this command style.

A second style most frequently involves the group of generals mentioned earlier and referred to as political generals. Because of their lack of knowledge about military tactics, a sense of inadequacy pervaded their every decision; people who feel inadequate and beyond their expertise make mistakes--- and frequently. Many generals in both armies fall into this category; some examples are Ben Butler, John Floyd, and Stephen G. Burbridge. General Burbridge was the grandson of a Revolutionary War hero, which may account for his military position. Burbridge was detested in Kentucky for the policies he developed and for all intents and purposes forced to leave the state of Kentucky as a result of these policies even though in control of portions of the state in 1864. After the war he was never able to live in Kentucky again because of his conduct during the war. General

Burbridge also had a command dispute with Gen. George Stoneman [discussed in this work] when Stoneman was placed in command of East Tennessee at the time of his final raid in that area in 1865. Burbridge attempted to use high level political friends to have Stoneman removed, but to no avail *only* because of the intervention of Gen. John Schofield. John Floyd was a former Secretary of War appointed by President Buchanan. His incompetent decisions are too numerous to name and discuss; suffice it to say that he never should have been commissioned. Ben Butler was so atrocious that the people of New Orleans gave him the title of "the beast".

A <u>third</u> command style is that exemplified by Gen. William S. Rosecrans. Rosecrans was a straight forward leader who explained, noted and denoted every detail of every plan in a campaign to everyone involved, but frequently had difficulty understanding why other staff members did not carry out their assignments as explained to them. A prime example of this problem occurred with Gen. Charles Hamilton [discussed in this work] at the battle of Chickamauga. Hamilton claimed he did not understand what he was expected to do with his division after receiving written orders from Rosecrans as well as a verbal discussion the evening before the battle occurred. Rosecrans then sent his adjutant to Hamilton for additional explanation and clarity. Again, Hamilton then claimed the order could not be executed as written. Hamilton claimed and insisted that statements were made for which no records exist and no one present at the meeting could confirm. No final resolution occurred concerning this incident before Rosecrans was moved to another command.

A <u>fourth</u> and final command style is that of the rigid, uptight, and anal retentive individual who has a value system which he expects others to immediately adhere to, which brings about a wave of contested wills against him by his subordinates. This type of leadership can be successful, but only at the lowest levels. It is much like the famed psychologist B. F. Skinner stated, "punishment or negative reinforcement never works to bring about the desired learning". Braxton Bragg fits this style of command, and in a sense, Gen. John Pope as well, in that he consistently laid blame for his ineptness on the shoulders of his subordinates and sometimes had them court-martialed when his plan of action failed.[17] A statement made concerning Braxton Bragg by his biographer Grady McWhiney gives a clear vision of Bragg's thought patterns, " Handicapped by poor health, he had no real taste for combat.... Nor did he have the ability to inspire confidence in his subordinates. Notoriously inept at getting along with people he disliked, he simply could not win the loyalty of his lieutenants. He lacked what has been called the common touch."[18]

One often hears the comment, "oh, you have the personality to be a fine physician", or some such statement connecting one's personality with a given occupation or other lifelong endeavor. Could a personality inventory to determine an individual's qualifications to be a successful Civil War general have existed in 1861? If we look at the life and career of some of the best-known and most successful generals perhaps some delineation of traits will emerge.

General William Sherman is a personality study that is both interesting and very confusing. The general had a somewhat irregular childhood, since he grew up outside of his nuclear family. He is a West Point graduate, was married, and lived in the South for a period of his life near the beginning of the Civil War. General Sherman suffered from what some historians might refer to as "enemy infantry phobia" or some such label. Sherman suffered what would today be termed a "nervous breakdown" in 1861, and was driven to the point of thoughts of suicide and resignation

---

[17] W.J. Wood, *Civil War Generalship: The Art of Command* (Westport, CT: Greenword Press, 1997), p. 236-239;Lt. Colonel Wood gives an excellent discussion and layout of the military command system

[18] Grady McWhiney, *Braxton Bragg and Confederate Defeat, Vol. I* (New York: Columbia University Press,1969), p. 390

from the army. He seems to have felt that he could not succeed no matter what he did, so why try any longer. Some studies have suggested that he developed a personality change and became unstable and began to show signs of what today would be termed a manic-depressive or bipolar personality. His wife confessed that he had a "manic elation and a strong desire to dominate", which led many people to think that he viewed himself as something akin to a Old Testament prophet on a mission. The historian Otto Eisenschiml suggest that Sherman felt he was "called "to punish the South for the existence of slavery.[19] Michael C. C. Adams in his book, *Fighting for Defeat: Union Military Failure 1861-1865* feels that Sherman was greatly influenced by General Grant and that Grant may have been the stabilizing factor which brought some degree of order and realism to Sherman's life.[20] A prime example of this "manic elation" is Sherman's order to make a frontal attack on a well entrenched Confederate force at Kenesaw in 1864. This type of attack had almost disappeared by 1864, because of the high loss of infantrymen and Sherman was discouraged by his subordinates at Kenesaw, but to no avail. General Charles Harker [discussed in this work] lost his life in this senseless show of reckless power and disregard by General Sherman.

One could garner from this information that war brings out any personality flaw that might exist in an individual. Therefore an individual's background might be a key as to how he will perform as a general. Robert E. Lee is a quite different personality, and performed his duty as a general in a different fashion. Lee also had an atypical childhood. His father, the famous "Light horse" Harry Lee was a famous Revolutionary War soldier, ["First in war, first in peace etc] but a nor-do-well in a sense. Lee's family

---

[19] Otto Eisenschiml, " Sherman: Hero or War Criminal?", *Civil War Times Illustrated*, 1964, p. 29
[20] Michael C. C. Adams, *Fighting for Defeat: Union Military Failure in the East-1861-1865* (Lincoln: University of Nebraska Press, 1992), p. 130, 161-163

always seemed to have been on the edge of disaster even though his mother was from a famous and wealthy Virginia family. Lee learned responsibility early in life and he exemplified the West Point motto of "Duty, Honor, and Country." In the minds of many people, even to this day, Gen. Robert E. Lee has all the qualities of George Washington. Few people in the history of this nation have enjoyed the respect and admiration given to General Lee. Much like Grant, Lee seemed to have instilled a sense of security and well being in the officers who served with him. General John Gordon at the battle of Spotsylvania, along with the entire Confederate forces in that battle insisting that General Lee "go to the rear" is a classical example of this respect. The mark, perhaps, of the highest respect and admiration is that respect given by an enemy. A forceful example of this is found in a statement made by Corporal Thomas H. Mann of the 18th Massachusetts on his way to Andersonville prisoner of war camp after the battle of the Wilderness in 1864 he comments," Here I saw General R. E. Lee for the first and only time in my life. He sat upon his horse carelessly, with one knee resting upon the pommel of the saddle…. He appeared a middle-sized man, with iron-gray hair and full graybeard, but not closely cut…. He remarked as we filed pass him," I am sorry to see you in this fix, boys, but you must make the best of it." His tone was kind and spoken as though he really sympathized with us, as I have no doubt he did."[21]

It is universally known that General Grant experienced a rather unpleasant childhood. His father owned a leather tanning business, which Grant detested. Grant seemed somewhat antisocial to visitors because of his lack of conservation, and his father often ushered him into a backroom, if possible, when company called. After his

---

[21] Thomas H. Mann, *Fighting with the Eighteenth Massachusetts: The Civil War Memoir of Thomas H. Mann*, edited by John J. Hennessy (Baton Rouge: Louisiana State University Press, 2000), p. 238

marriage, Grant suffered some very difficult financial times in the 1850s and actually resorted to cutting and splitting firewood just to "keep body and soul together." The Civil War was probably a true gift from heaven for Grant's advancement and success in life. The signal point in General Grant's life, like Lee and Sherman is the fact that he learned responsibility *early* in life because of the circumstance life dealt to him. This same situation confronted Gen. Thomas "Stonewall" Jackson, who lived with an uncle at a gristmill in West Virginia as opposed to the usual two-parent home and again, responsibility is the key word. Gen. Charles Harker [discussed in this work] was forced to work early in life to raise funds for his education, and impressed his employer with attention to his duties so much so that a recommendation was made on his behalf to attend West Point. Again, responsibility was the prime factor in his obtaining an education that altered this young man's life. A final example is the life of Gen. James Longstreet, born in South Carolina in 1821,but soon moved to Georgia. Longstreet's father died about 1833 and his mother moved to North Alabama with her remaining children. In 1830, Longstreet had been sent to Augusta to live with his uncle, Augustus Longstreet who was an occasional teacher at the famous Richmond Academy in Augusta where Longstreet attended to prepare for his education at West Point. His Uncle Augustus later became a member of the state legislature, and a key figure in the establishment of the University of Mississippi, yet Longstreet 's kinsman Congressman Rubin Chapman of Alabama made the request for him to attend West Point and he was admitted in 1838. Longstreet exemplifies the point that responsibility learned early in life could be a factor in successful generalship.[22]

---

[22] *Civil War Journal: The Leaders* edited by William C. Davis, Brian C. Pohanka, and Don Troiani (Nashville: Rutledge Hill Press, 1997), p. 211; another source states that Longstreet attended Westover School in Augusta – Jim Nesbitt, "Intentions of Old Pete Remain Misunderstood", Augusta *Chronicle*, date unknown

Examples are endless, and only some generals came from humble and poverty stricken backgrounds or atypical family situation. Nevertheless the factor of responsibility learned early in life seems to have been a significant ingredient in a successful general's personality make up. The ability to gain the confidence of subordinates and put them at ease by showing them a measure of respect and the meaning and the example of success in battle also seems to have played a role in the makeup of the successful general. As in all things when judgement of human qualities are concerned, there are many exceptions which could be drawn to confront this hypothesis of personality make up as a correlate to the success of the Civil War general. And it should not be forgotten that Steven Woodworth's excellent discussion concerning generals who failed should be included in this inventory as well. The successful general must be able to adapt and make changes as each situation demands. This is essential for success. While not referenced in this discussion, the reader is referred to John C. Waugh's book, *The Class of 1846* for additional information on the many famous generals who graduated from West Point in this stellar class of soldiers. General George Stoneman, discussed in this work, was the roommate of General Thomas "Stonewall" Jackson at West Point, both graduates in the class of 1846. General Charles Stone, also a part of this work was well acquainted with all of these men, graduating in 1845.

The two most notable generals who took part in the Civil War, Gen. R. E. Lee and Gen. U. S. Grant have again come to the forefront in recent times for much discussion concerning Civil War generals and who "was the greatest general in Civil War." After the war a movement was generated in the South to discredit any negative comment about General Lee. General Longstreet was smeared by this association of image keepers for over a century after the war, mainly for an article that he did for the *Annals of War* in the 1878 in which he gave his reasons as to why the Gettysburg campaign was a failure, placing some of blame on General Lee.[23] General Grant's image suffered somewhat as a result of the scandals of his presidency. Less attention was then paid to Grant in the North, and virtually none in the South. This situation has changed significantly in the past decade. A statement by Gary Gallagher in the *North & South,* the magazine of the Civil War Society gives a focus to this change, "Critics have mounted a major assault on his [Lee] reputation over the past decade, insisting that he too often took the offensive, wasted precious manpower, neglected to consider Confederate forces outside Virginia, and failed to adapt to a mid-19th century war."[24] Dr. Gallagher offers a twelve-page synopsis of the battles and a brief history of the Army of Northern Virginia's campaigns in defense of his support of Lee. In a footnote on his article Gallagher states that the historian Alan T. Nolan in an article "Historians' Perspectives on Lee", gives a different and unfavorable "estimates" on Lee's generalship.[25] The historian Thomas Connelly also blasted Lee's approach in his two-volume work on the Army of Tennessee. The historian Peter Carmichael views Lee's offensive strategy as appropriate up until Gettysburg,"but he failed thereafter to adapt to the new situation facing the Confederacy. In a review of his book, *Audacity Personified: The Generalship of Robert E. Lee,* in which Dr. Carmichael edits a book containing essays written by five historians, plus his views in an attempt to find and reassess Lee's reputation as a warrior. Carmichael 's view is

---

[23] *Annals of the War* (Philadelphia: Times Publishing Company, 1878), written by the participants in the war, North and South and published in the Philadelphia *Times Weekly*
[24] Gary Gallagher, " The Generalship of Robert E. Lee", *North & South,* Vol. 3, no. 5, June 2000, p. 10-23
[25] Alan T. Nolan, "Historians' Perspectives on Lee", *Columbiad: A Quarterly Review of the War Between the States* 2 (Winter 1999), pp27-45 [from Gallagher's article above]

that "Lee was searching for a decisive battle of annihilation, but late in the war he should have conserved manpower."[26]

In an article which occurred in the Charlotte, North Carolina Observer, "Admiring U. S. Grant More, Robert E. Lee Less" by Janny Scott from the New York *Times*, Gary Gallagher is quoted as saying that a "cottage industry" has developed in books devoted to the criticizing of General Lee, faulting him for aggressiveness, squandering manpower, and prolongation of the war. In addition, Lee's offensive actions have been discredited by these sources. Many new books in print are now reassessing General Grant and are portraying him as "an extraordinary general who gave a new dimension to American military strategy. Also appearing in many sources," Grant had fewer casualties in proportion to the size of his army than Lee's. Grant worked hard to free the slaves, save the Union, and carry out Reconstruction, bringing equality to black people," are some of the views contended by these books. Finally, "the extent of his drinking is also suspect." James McPherson is quoted as saying, "The kind of romanticized sympathy-with-the-underdog attitude to the Confederacy has been increasingly outweighed by the recognition that what the Confederacy was fighting for was a society based on slavery. And what the North was fighting for, if not initially and enthusiastically, was a society moving toward biracial democracy."[27]

From this information one can but conclude that after a century or more, the entire interpretation of the Civil War is undergoing change which is coming from many different directions. Generals are being reassessed as to their abilities, reasons for battle failures, shortsightedness, the selection of when and where to fight, and a host of other factors. The

---

[26] John David Smith, "Going into Battle with the Image of a Southern Hero", a review of Peter Carmichael's book, *Audacity Personified: The Generalship of Robert E. Lee*, Charlotte *Observer, 2004*

[27] Janny Scott, "Admiring U. S. Grant more, and Robert E. Lee less," The Charlotte *Observer* by way of the New York *Times*, date unknown

number of generals from each of the states [in the Confederacy] has also come under attack. To a degree, the selection of generals may have been influenced by the state in which they resided. Virginia had seventy-nine generals, a total greater than the combined total of generals from both North and South Carolina. This is somewhat confusing, since North Carolina supplied the largest number of troops to serve in the Confederate army. The Union Army did somewhat better concerning the number of generals per state. New York supplied the largest number of men to the Union Army and also had the largest number of general officers, 113, Pennsylvania supplied the next largest number of general officers, sixty-six, and Ohio came next with sixty-four general officers. This is essentially in sync with the number of troops from these states. One can but speculate as to why Virginia, with seventy-nine generals, is so far out of proportion to the number of men that state supplied to the Confederate army.[28] These numbers may have no significance, but this is a charge raised by several historians, of which Dr. Thomas Connelly is perhaps the most vocal.

Even so, it seems that the selection of general officers was a very haphazard process in both the Union and the Confederate armies. There were no real qualifications, politics played a significant role, some of the generals were eccentric neurotics, a segment of the generals in both armies was completely incompetent, and some were borderline precarious threats to the men under their command because of their irrational behavior and negligence. Yet, many of the generals in both armies were such an inspiration that "their hearts will live forever." The six generals covered in this work, while not the best known generals in their particular army, displayed some of the qualities both good and bad discussed in this section. With this in mind something can be

---

[28] C. E. Jones, "Confederate Officers" *Southern Historical Society Papers*, Vol. 23, p. 335; Warner Gray and Blue, p. 599-601 [Union Vol.] numbers indicate the state in which the general was born

learned from their experiences in the "Great War" of American history.

No conflict in the history of this great nation has come close to the display of respect and friendship shown by generals to *other* generals captured in battle. It was not unusual for two friends to have an emotional conversation while one was a captive of war and the other was his captor. When word crossed the battle line that a general known before the war in the old Army had been killed or mortally wounded, a show of sincere emotion frequently occurred. Such factors, as well as the previously mentioned ones insure that the study of Civil War generals will continue far into the history of this nation. As a nation, we can only hope this is the case.

All six of the generals discussed in this work had a military education, five are West Point graduates and one is a Citadel graduate. All competent generals, honed in the science of military procedure plus the fact that each one made a contribution to the war effort, yet three of these men are virtual unknowns. Additionally, two of the six generals, Tilghman and Harker paid the ultimate sacrifice for the cause that they embraced. Only Generals Stoneman and Law have any public recognition today, yet Law is credited with the formation of the public education system in Florida and Stoneman was a Governor of California. As for the remaining two, General Hamilton was the University of Wisconsin Chairman of the Board Regents, and also a very successful businessman and General Stone was the major director/engineer responsible for the final foundation for the Statue of Liberty. While some of these accomplishments are postwar, it would seem that these things alone would make these generals public figures of some note, yet this is not the case. Nonetheless, these six generals plus a legion of others who took part in the American Civil War are waiting for their deserved acknowledgement for their commitment to the cause they upheld, which is arguably one of the most important events in the history of this nation.

An attempt is made in this work to explain how one could become a general in the Civil War, the qualifications, how these qualifications were often relaxed for some individuals, the role personality in the acceptance and success of a general, the advantages of this rank, and what role, if any, education and scholarship played in the process of generalship. In the study and comparison of Civil War generals, these factors will hopefully give a degree of delineation to an investigation of the success or failure of individual generals.

General Charles P. Stone

GEN. CHARLES P. STONE, U.S.

Charles Pomeroy Stone was born in the hamlet of Greenfield, Massachusetts on September 30, 1824, both a safe and secure place for a child to reside and mature to adulthood. Stone's ancestors were of Puritan stock and played a significant role in every war in which this nation was engaged. The Stones, without doubt, had earned their place in Greenfield with their efforts and sacrifice for state and nation. Young Stone's ancestral village is located in the northwestern section of Massachusetts and was settled about 1686, originally as part of Deerfield. The village was incorporated as a separate entity in 1753, later in 1811, becoming the county seat of Franklin County. Greenfield is located on the Connecticut River, at the eastern entrance to the Mohawk Trail. As early as the 1800s, Greenfield was beginning to take shape as a manufacturing and farming village.[1] Charles Stone's birthplace was typical of many New England towns of that era, in that there was a sense of unity, protection, and belonging which prevailed in all aspects of life.

Stone was the son of Alpheus Fletcher Stone, a physician, and Fanny Cushing.[2] As a descendent of a founding New England family, Stone had a very "American" background, and the family traditions were deeply ingrained

---

[1] Ezra J. Warner, *Generals in Blue* (Baton Rouge: Louisiana State University, 1964), p. 480. Hereinafter cited as Warner Blue.
Encyclopedia Britannica, Vol. IV, p. 716, 15th edition, 1979.
[2] Edward G. Longacre, "Charles Pomeroy Stone", American National Biography Online, February, 2000, http://www.anb.org/articles05/05-00748.html. Hereinafter cited as Longacre Biography.

and totally above suspicion. Nowhere in Stone's background can one detect any flaw or precursory factor or event that could have caused the copious number of problems, both political and military, which would descend on him in a few short years. He grew up in the land of Emily Dickinson, the Puritans, Amherst College, and all of the things with which America is associated. Young Stone was an American, "through and through", and he would later have to prove it to the highest powers of the United States.

Charles Stone received what would today be considered a "good" elementary education in Greenfield.[3] New England schools in general, and Puritan influenced villages in particular, were usually very attentive to education, which they felt was needed in order to read and understand holy scripture. Around 1840, Stone began to seriously think about his future and made application to the United States Military Academy. It would take over a year to finalize this application but young Stone had some heavyweight political support for his West Point petition. Osmyn Baker, a lawyer and House member from Amherst, George Grennel, a Greenfield Congressman and Whig presidential elector, and also the president of the Troy & Greenfield RR, are examples. He also had the support of a member of the Vose family of Norfolk County, Massachusetts, who served as his military connection. Stone's application would ultimately be considered by two Secretaries of War: Joel Poinsett, a Democrat, and John Bell, also a Democrat, later to become a Whig and a presidential candidate of the Constitutional Union party.[4]

---

[3] General George W. Cullum, *Biographical Register of the Officers and Graduates of the U.S. Military Academy at West Point, Vol. II*, (Boston: Houghton, Mifflin and Company, 1891), p. 215. Hereinafter cited as Biographical Register

[4] Archival Records from the United States Military Academy, West Point, New York. Hereinafter cited as Archival Records.

Stone's acceptance to West Point was due to an alteration in the circumstances of another young man, a W. H. Smith who withdrew his application due to a change in his employment status. As a result, Congressman Baker was free to recommend Stone. In a letter dated March 23, 1841, Stone gave official acceptance of his appointment to Secretary of War, John Bell.[5] This letter is post marked as having been sent from the Leicister Academy of Leicester, Massachusetts, which would lend credence to the fact that Stone did in fact have an exceptional education, given the time in which he lived.[6]

On July 1, 1841, Stone entered the Academy as a cadet. During the time that he was a cadet, young Charles became a member of the Episcopal Church, and subsequently a member of the Roman Catholic Church. From all available information, it seems that Stone was a devout adherent to the Christian faith all of his life. The instructors at West Point respected Stone, and his fellow cadets held him in high esteem, and this was due in no small part to his forthright attitude, making him an honored man to many cadets. All people have limitations and faults, and Stone certainly had his share that often surfaced under the right conditions at very inopportune times. He was impulsive and quick to take action, often too quick in some instances. He frequently came over as tactless in his resolve to carry out his duties, which would later prove to be troublesome. He was fearless, trustworthy, and exceeding loyal to those he held as friends.[7]

Stone's classmates at West Point included such notable future generals as Fitz-John Porter, William

---

[5] Archival Records
[6] Archival Records
[7] *Eighteenth Annual Reunion of the Association Graduates of the United States Military Academy*, (Evening News Printing and Binding House, East Saginaw, 1887), p. 41. Hereinafter cited as Reunion of Graduates.

Rosecrans, Samuel French, and Gustavus W. Smith. In his first year at West Point, Stone received only three demerits and did even better his second year, only one demerit, which would lead one to conclude that he was a serious student. His final two years at the Academy were only slightly worse, five each year.[8] This was a highly focused and dedicated young man who without doubt had much to offer upon graduation, which was evident to even the casual observer.

Stone graduated number seven in a class of thirty-four cadets. His best subjects were ethics, artillery, and geology. Future generals Barnard E. Bee and William H. Whiting were also in the 1845 graduating class and both would attain great fame in the Civil War, although their views were in opposition to those of Stone.[9] This is important in that General Stone would later be accused of having excessive interest in things involving the Confederacy.

Upon graduation, Stone was assigned to the Ordnance Corps and his first duty as an officer of the United States Army was as an instructor at his alma mater. The young graduate taught classes in history, geography, and ethics, but the assignment would be short lived. Anxious to be involved in more soldierly duties, on January 13, 1846, Stone requested and received a new assignment. He was sent to the Watervliet Arsenal, and ultimately to Fort Monroe as an assistant to Captain Huger [later of the Confederate army]. Stone and Huger made their way to Vera Cruz where he was attached to a siege battery, the only such battery used in the Mexican War. Due to his excellent service with this battery, Stone ended the conflict serving on the staff of General Winfield Scott. As a result of this eventful set of circumstances, he won brevets for the battles of *Molino del*

---

[8] *Register of the Officers and Cadets of the U.S. Military Academy* (West Point, 1840-1845) p. 17 &19. Hereinafter cited as Register of Cadets.
[9] Register of Cadets, p. 7

Rey and *Chapultepec*.[10] During his service in the Mexican War, the future general won a degree of devotion and approbation from his military contingent for an act of selfless bravery. Stone was able to make the ascent of *Popocatepetl* and plant the American flag on the <u>very summit</u> of the volcano. In later years, Stone would give a personal description of this feat to the great Humboldt, who arranged for him to dine with the King of Prussia.[11]

In July of 1848, Stone was granted a leave of absence to visit Europe. The Mexican War was over but Stone had an interest in remaining in the Army beyond the usual tour of duty to satisfy his obligation for a West Point education. He wanted to increase his knowledge as to the "ins and outs" of moving large ground forces during war. He was able to observe military operations in Europe as well as Syria and Egypt. In addition, he spent about a month in Paris studying languages, making this a very profitable visit.[12]

Stone returned to the United States in January 1851, as a brevet captain. The future general made his way from Fortress Monroe, Virginia to California by way of Cape Horn for a new tour of duty. When he arrived in San Francisco, he was assigned as Chief of Ordnance on the Pacific coast and immediately made extensive tours up and down the coastal area. As was his custom, he was a stickler for details and never accepted anything at face value. This would later come back to haunt him in a ubiquitous fashion. Stone selected the site for the Pacific coast arsenal at Benicia and determined that all buildings for residences, workshops, and store houses should be constructed of stone, which was both readily available and abundant. This put Stone in a distinctly unfavorable position with the lumber interest of the Pacific coast. By command of the ranking departmental

---

[10] Biographical Register, p. 215
[11] Biographical Register, p. 215
[12] Reunion of Graduates, p. 43

officer, Stone set out to erect the buildings. Unbeknown to Captain Stone was a law that stated that certain buildings [some of those erected by Stone] could only be constructed with lumber, unless otherwise appropriated by Congress. Stone's pay was curtailed by the United States Treasury and he was forced to make high interest loans to cover this mistake. Fortunately, an obscure and forgotten law was discovered which stated that lower ranking officers were excluded from expenses incurred by orders of superior officers. Stone's pay was ultimately restored but the money he was forced to borrow and the interest on this borrowed money, was never recovered. The young officer suffered financially for some time as a result of this command fiasco.[13]

    In 1853, Captain Stone had a pleasant occurrence; he got married. Stone and Maria Louisa Clary would later become the parents of one child.[14] Captain Stone remained on duty with the Pacific Department until 1856. Before his departure, one more unpleasant emergency would crop up, to which Stone would have to react. The French Consul General at San Francisco felt that he had been insulted by the United States and hauled down the French flag, and threatened the United States with the arrival of the French fleet. Stone was charged with getting the coast in a state of high defense. He brought in heavy guns and mobile batteries to Fort Point. Fortunately the situation was shortly defused and the crisis abated.[15] After five years of incessant toil, during which time his income did not equal his necessities, Captain Stone resigned from the Army in November of 1856.[16]

---

[13] Reunion of Graduates, p. 44
[14] Longacre Biography, p. 1
[15] Reunion of Graduates, p. 44.
[16] Biographical Register, p. 216

After his resignation from the Army, Stone went into the banking profession for about a year and was an abysmal failure at this line of work. To add insult to injury, his treasurer embezzled large sums of the bank's funds,[17] yet another fiasco with which poor Stone had to deal. "How quickly nature falls into revolt when gold becomes her object."[18]

In March of 1857, Stone was selected by a private concern as chief of a scientific commission to survey and explore the State of Sonora, Mexico. The real purpose of this exploration was to determine the potential commercial developmental possibilities of Sonora. The exploration continued until about 1859 after which Stone became the acting U.S. consul at Guaymas. Due to a lack of support and the sanction of the Mexican government, Stone now faced another financial debacle. He was not compensated for his work in Mexico, and in addition, he again lost some personal funds.[19] During the summer and fall of 1860, Stone worked on the preparation of maps, charts and other assorted materials collected while he was in Mexico from 1857 to1859. The result was a well written and well-received travelogue entitled "Notes on the State of Sonora," published in 1861.[20]

Charles Stone was a student of history, and having been an instructor of history at West Point, he was well aware of what was occurring in the nation in 1860. South Carolina seceded from the Union on December 20, 1860, and other states followed their lead in short order. Captain Stone, being the patriot that he was and with a military background, felt a duty to do whatever he could to serve his country. He immediately tendered his resignation as a government

---

[17] Biographical Register, p. 216
[18] Shakespeare, King Henry in *Henry IV*, part 2
[19] Longacre Biography, p. 1; Reunion of Graduates, p. 44
[20] Longacre Biography, p. 1

employee. Gen. Winfield Scott had Stone under his command in Mexico and being aware of his talents, offered him the position of Inspector General of the Militia of the District of Columbia. This position carried the rank of Colonel. The militia was made up largely of Southern sympathizers and Colonel Stone attempted to rid the militia of this disloyal element. After purging the anti Union element, Stone whipped the remaining troops into a military force to be reckoned with. This militia force served the nation with distinction, performing a number of diverse military services, most importantly; it protected the city of Washington from military disturbances. Secondly, it rendered protection to President Lincoln during his inauguration. This volunteer military force served until the regular army forces arrived.[21] It has been purported that Stone was the first former military officer to reenlist for military service as a result of the conflict that became the Civil War.[22] Concerning the protection of the president, a final incident must be related. The president elect's railroad route was scheduled to pass through the city of Baltimore and a very ugly riot was under way there. The rioters burned bridges and severed communication lines with the North. Colonel Stone countered the rioters by seizing the Baltimore and Ohio depot and directing troops to Annapolis Junction to ensure that reinforcements could reached Washington. This action won Stone much praise, especially from President Lincoln. Stone was made a Colonel in the regular army, and three days later, a Brigadier-General of Volunteers. This promotion was followed by Stone's receiving command of the Rockville Expedition, and one month later [early July 1861] Stone was given command of a brigade in Gen. Robert Patterson's Army of the Shenandoah Valley.[23]

---

[21] Reunion of Graduates, p. 45; Biographical Register, p. 216
[22] Longacre Biography, p. 1
[23] Biographical Register, p. 216

During this unstable period from the spring of 1861 extending into the summer, many prominent people were in, and passing through, the city of Washington. One who had a major, although indirect bearing on General Stone's future was Leonard Sweet. Mr. Sweet was from Illinois and was a friend of President Lincoln, and in a very generous and complimentary fashion Mr. Sweet praised and thanked General Stone for his superb handling of the Baltimore Riot crisis. Sweet also made reference to General Scott and his exceptional work during the crisis. His final words to the General were, "He [Lincoln] will be grateful to both." As stated earlier, Stone could be rather tactless, whereby with no hesitation Stone replied, "Mr. Lincoln has no cause to be grateful to me. I was opposed to his election, and believed in advance that it would bring on what is evidently coming, a fearful war."[24] One can but speculate about the future impact this comment must have had on General Stone's military career.

Stone's adherence to trivia and minutia concerning military affairs soured many possible friends and allies. As time passed and events unfolded, he became more vocal about his opposition to the abolition of slavery. He also had no qualms about expressing his friendship with old army friends, who now served in the Confederate army. He often and openly associated with secessionist friends, and was accused of returning runaway slaves who found their way into his camp. This behavior, while in Stone's perception of events was innocent and simply good manners, was viewed by others as inappropriate and possibly treason.[25] These factors, along with Stone's dogmatic support of the Democratic Party, as well as his family's support of the party, would be a major part of his military and political problems in the near future.

---

[24] Reunion of Graduates, p. 46
[25] Longacre Biography, p. 2

General Stone was a part of the ill fated and disastrous battle of First Bull Run. Stone requested and received permission to take his command up the north bank of the Potomac River to Edward's Ferry. He was to guard the Chesapeake & Ohio Canal, as well as the Baltimore and Ohio Railroad, and in addition, he was to prevent any communication between the Confederate armies in Virginia and Maryland. He was ordered to interact with General Patterson, when and if necessary. Patterson, meanwhile, was checking General Johnston's Confederate forces at Harpers Ferry. It was the army's fear that political pressure would force General McDowell to attack the Confederate army at Manassas. Such a move by McDowell would immediately allow Johnston to move troops by rail to aid the Confederate army at Manassas. Since he would have no forces on his flank or rear to deter this movement, it would be his best option. If this happened Stone was to be joined by Patterson's forces, then cross the Potomac and join McDowell's right, and fall on the Confederate army's left at Manassas. The plan was to hold Johnston in the Shenandoah Valley, and protect the Baltimore and Ohio Railroad for Union use.[26] Patterson was recalled from Virginia, thus his entire force was rendered useless when it was most needed by McDowell. There seems to have been some command confusion concerning Patterson's recall from Virginia. The confusion occurred at the highest level: Scott, Patterson, and McDowell.[27] General Patterson was <u>forced</u>, by the events which were unfolding, to come to General Stone instead of the original plan, which was for Stone to be joined by General Patterson to check Johnston. General Patterson

---

[26] Reunion of Graduates, p. 48; Warner Blue, p. 480
[27] *Battles and Leaders of the Civil War*, edited by Clarence Buel and Robert U. Johnson. 4 vols. New York: The Century Company, 1887-88, Vol. I, p. 183(note), hereinafter cited as Battles and Leaders; Reunion of Graduates, p. 48

claimed he never received orders to attack and therefore made no move to do so. Because of this high command blunder, General Johnston joined General Beauregard, along with General Bee and General Thomas "Stonewall" Jackson.[28] As a result, the Confederate army carried the day, notwithstanding the fact that both armies were essentially "battle green" and untried. Unfortunately for General Stone, his name became imprinted, along with others, as" the generals who lost the battle of Bull Run". General Patterson was mustered out of the army on July 27, 1861, most likely due to this command blunder.[29] In the mindset of Charles Stone, the farce that was First Bull Run doomed the nation to a long and drawn out war, with many deaths and prolonged misery.

In August of 1861, General Stone was released from the command of General Banks, who had superseded General Patterson as the commander of the Army of the Shenandoah. Stone was assigned to a special service corps whose duty would be to act as an observation force on the right flank of the Army of the Potomac. He would be operating from Poolsville, and charged with the defense of Maryland from Seneca Falls to Point of Rocks. Stone, true to form, engaged these troops in extensive training and discipline. He shaped them into what was to become the crack 2nd Division of the II Corps of the Army of the Potomac.[30]

In October of 1861, General Stone commanded the division from the Maryland side of the Potomac. According to Dyer's *A Compendium of the War of the Rebellion*, an engagement occurred on October 21, 1861, which involved Ball's Bluff, Leesburg, Harrison's Island and Conrad's

---

[28] Battles and Leaders, Vol. I, p. 183(note)
[29] Mark Boatner, *The Civil War Dictionary* (New York: David McKay Company, 1959), p. 623
[30] Reunion of Graduates, p. 49

Ferry. The engagement is collectively referred to as the battle of Ball's Bluff.[31] October 21, 1861, and the events of this engagement would alter the life of Charles Stone to an extent and in avenues, which he could not have imagined. Much has been related and debated about this engagement and the ensuing political ramifications that would follow.

Stone's division was made up of the brigades of Willis A. Gorman, Frederick West Lander, and Edward Dickinson Baker. The division or "Corps of Observation" as it was often referred to, engaged in observation of the fords on the Potomac in front of Poolsville. Gen. George Archibald McCall's division, part of the Army of the Potomac, under the command of Gen. George McClellan, was located at Dranesville. McClellan telegraphed Stone directing him to observe closely events in Leesburg and attempt to determine if the operations of McCall would push the enemy away. McClellan closed his message with, "Perhaps a slight demonstration on your part would have the effect to move them."[32] This slight demonstration became the engagement referred to as Ball's Bluff.

Early in the day of October 21, General Stone gave Colonel Edward D. Baker the discretion to retire the small force at Ball's Bluff on the Virginia side of the river, or send over his brigade to support it. Colonel Baker immediately gave the order to cross the Potomac and reinforce the regiment size force on the Virginia side of the river. This was done without additional information, without reconnaissance reports, having made no plans as to how the soldiers would get across the river or having crossed the river himself. A formula for annihilation was set in motion

---

[31] Frederick Dyer, *A Compendium of the War of the Rebellion* (Dayton: Broadfoot Publishing Company & Morningside Press, 1994), Vol. I, p. 896, hereinafter cited as Dyer's Compendium
[32] Battles and Leaders, Vol. II, p. 124

when Baker gave the command to cross the river, under such conditions.

Who was Edward Baker? Much can be learned about Stone's future problems by examining this key individual and his background. Baker was born in London, and at the age of four, brought to Philadelphia, where he was apprenticed to a weaver. His family later moved to New Harmony, Indiana. The Bakers finally settled in Belleville, Illinois. Colonel Baker had little, or no formal education, nevertheless he read law and was admitted to the bar to practice law in Illinois at the young age of nineteen. He took part in the Black Hawk war and later moved to Springfield, Illinois where he became a close friend and associate of Abraham Lincoln. Of additional importance, Baker was an outstanding orator that was an incentive for him to become involved in politics. He was in the Illinois legislature, and later actually defeated Lincoln to became a member of Congress. Baker took part in the Mexican War and after the war, he was elected to Congress. He served as a presidential elector in the 1848 election. In 1852, Baker moved to California and became a prominent lawyer and speaker. At the request of the Republican Party, Baker moved to Oregon and was elected to represent that state as her senator in 1860.[33]

After the inauguration of Lincoln, Baker took part in raising the so-called "California Regiment". This regiment was nothing more than a force recruited from New York and Pennsylvania, and ultimately became the 71st Pennsylvania. Baker declined the rank of brigadier general of the 71st and instead became a colonel in May of 1861. On September 21, he was appointed major general of volunteers. Acceptance of this rank would have necessitated his resignation from the

---

[33] Warner Blue, p. 16; Stewart Sifakis, *Who was Who in the Union* (New York: Facts on File, 1988), Vol. I, p. 18-19. Hereinafter cited as Who was Who, Vol. I

Senate. As of October 21, he had neither accepted nor declined the appointment[34]

To demonstrate the close association of Abraham Lincoln and Baker, Lincoln named his second son in Baker's honor. In addition, Baker did much to keep the Pacific coast in the Republican ranks, for which Lincoln was very appreciative. It is manifestly evident that Lincoln did not view Baker as simply another Union colonel. Lincoln felt a debt of gratitude to Baker; after all, they had a considerable amount of history together.

On October 21st, part of General Stone's division [Colonel Baker's brigade] crossed the Potomac at Edward's Ferry and another segment of the division crossed at Harrison's Island, near Smart's Mill. This crossing was accomplished with great difficulty, since little thought had been given to transportation, and apart from that, only three small boats were available for use. The invaders took a position on an outcrop on the Virginia side of the river called Ball's Bluff. In the woods above and all around them, the Confederate army, giving no sign that they were leaving, and every indication that they were about to attack. The ranking officer of this force [a regiment size command from Colonel Baker's brigade already on Harrison's Island] sent word to General Stone of the situation at hand. General Stone then gave Colonel Baker the discretionary power to withdraw the force or send over additional troops.[35] There is confusion at this point as to exactly who is responsible, and for what action. The following is General Stone's account of what happened:

> Orders were sent to Colonel Devens, at Harrison's Island, 3 to 4 miles up the River and nearly east of Leesburg, to detach

---

[34] Warner Blue, p. 16 ; Who was Who, p. 18-19
[35] T. Harry Williams, " Investigation: 1862", *Civil War Chronicles*, Vol. III, no. 3, 1994, p. 30. Hereinafter cited as Chronicles

Captain Philbrick, with 20 men, to cross from the island and explore by a path through the woods, little used, in the direction of Leesburg, to see if he could find anything concerning the enemy's position in that direction, but to retire and report on discovering any of the enemy.[36]

General Stone continues his report stating the following:

As darkness came on I ordered Gorman's brigade and the Seventh Michigan Volunteers back to their respective camps, but retained the Tammany Regiment, the companies of the Fifteenth Massachusetts Volunteers, and the artillery near Conrad's Ferry in their positions, awaiting the results of Captain Philbrick's scout, remaining with my staff at Edward's Ferry. About 10 o'clock p.m. Lieutenant Howe, regimental quartermaster Fifteenth Massachusetts Volunteers, reported to me that aptain Philbrick had returned to the island after proceeding unmolested to within One mile of Leesburg, and that he had discovered, in the edge of a wood, an Encampment of about thirty tents, which he had approached to within 25 rods without being challenged, the camp having no pickets out any distance in the direction of the river.[37]

General Stone immediately sent four companies to the Virginia shore to attack and destroy the camp at daybreak, pursue the enemy as far as was practical, and return to the island. General Stone goes on to explain in his report:

Orders were dispatched to Colonel Baker to send the First California regiment to Conrad's Ferry, to arrive there at sunrise, and to have the remainder of his brigade in a state of readiness to move after an early breakfast[38].... [Stone continues]

---

[36] *The War of the Rebellion: A Compilation of the* **Official Records of the Union and Confederate Armies,** Series I, Vol. V, p. 293. Hereinafter cited as OR
[37] OR, series I, Vol. V, p. 294
[38] OR, series I, Vol. V, p. 294

Colonel Baker, having arrived at Conrad's Ferry with the First California Regiment at an early hour in the morning, reported in person to me at Edward's Ferry, stating that the regiment was at its assigned post, the remainder of his brigade under arms ready to march, and asking for orders. I decided to send him to Harrison's Island to assume command, and in a full conservation with him explained the position of things as they stood according to reports received; told him that General McCall had advanced his troops to Drainesville, and that I was extremely desirous of ascertaining the exact position and force of the enemy in our front, and exploring as far as it was safe on the right towards Leesburg and on the left towards the Leesburg and Gum Springs road....

Stone continued with an explanation of the transportation situation, the support forces that would assist Colonel Baker on his return, if that became necessary and other particulars of the military situation at hand. Then, Stone made these crucial statements to Colonel Baker:

...that I wished no advance made unless the enemy were an inferior force and under no circumstances to pass beyond Leesburg, or a strong position between it and Goose Creek, on the Gum Springs (Manassas) road.... I pointed out to him the positions of some bluffs on this side of the river from which artillery could act with effect on the other, leaving the matter of crossing more troops or retiring what were already over to his discretion, gave him entire control of operations on the right.[39]

General Stones elaborated that Colonel Baker departed between 9 and 9:30 A.M. and proceeded up the river to carry out his orders. Messengers from Harrison's Island informed Stone that Colonel Baker had arrived and was moving his entire force across the river with great haste. In addition, Colonel Baker had secured a flat boat from the

---

[39] OR, series I, Vol. V, p. 296

canal, had it placed in the river with a line provided to allow the boats to cross the river more rapidly.[40]

During the morning of the October 21st, an intense skirmish occurred between two of the advanced companies of the Massachusetts 15th and a force of about 100 Mississippi Riflemen [Gen. William Barksdale]. As the skirmish progressed, a Mississippi cavalry unit appeared. Colonel Devens of the Massachusetts 15^{th,} then fell back to a more secure position, with backup from Colonel Lee's position. Colonel Devens continued the advance-retreat-advance for a time. The Massachusetts 15th was ultimately overwhelmed and forced to withdraw.[41]

After Colonel Deven's second advance, Stone states in his account of the engagement that Colonel Baker then moved to the field in person. General Stone purports that he was unable to ascertain who Baker placed in charge of the boats to insure the crossing of the troops. The entire situation was utter chaos and a prime example of poor command procedure. The reinforcements sent to Colonel Baker by General Stone were unnecessarily delayed and hindered in the completion of their assignment. Added to this delay was the fact that the artillery was crossed before the infantry force, even though artillery transport is by nature a slow process. In Stone's view, the transport of the infantry prior to the artillery would have made a significant difference in the outcome of the engagement. [42]

Colonel Charles Devens, who would later serve as Attorney General under President Hayes, gives his account of the battle scene:

> About 12o'clock Sunday night, October 20th, I crossed the Potomac by your (Stone) order from Harrison's Island to the

---

[40] OR, series I, Vol. V, p. 296
[41] OR, series V, p. 296
[42] OR, series V, p. 297

Virginia shore with five companies, numbering about 300 men, of my regiment, with the intention of taking a rebel camp, reported by scouts to be situated at the distance of about a mile from the river, of destroying the same, of observing the country around, and of returning to the river, or of waiting and reporting if I thought myself able to remain for reinforcements, or if I found a position capable of being defended against a largely superior force.... We passed down the river about sixty rods by a path discovered by the scouts, and then up the bluff known as Ball's Bluff, where we found an open field surrounded by woods. At that point, we halted until daybreak....[43]

Colonel Devens explains the report of the "Confederate tents" made by scouts to General Stone. The "tents" were simply a line of trees that presented uncertain light, giving the appearance of tents. After a reasonable exploration and search of the area, Colonel Devens determined that no sizable Confederate force was in the area, and then sent word to General Stone at Edward's Ferry that he felt that it was prudent for him [Devens] to remain until he could be reinforced.[44] At about 6:30 A.M. Quartermaster Howe left the Virginia shore to relay this communication to General Stone. At about 8 A.M. he returned with instruction from the general specifying that Colonel Devens should remain in place and await reinforcements, while the remainder of the regiment under Lieutenant-Colonel Ward would proceed to Smart's Mill. Ten cavalrymen would report to Colonel Devens for the purpose of reconnoitering. Colonel Devens further states that the ten cavalrymen never arrived. General Stone's position is that Colonel Baker allowed this cavalry force to return and did not replace it, even though he had ample cavalry at his disposal.[45] In the period of time from 8 A.M. until 10 o'clock, Quartermaster Howe made a second trip to

---

[43] Battles and Leaders, Vol. II, p. 125
[44] Battles and Leaders, Vol. II, p. 125
[45] Battles and Leaders, Vol. II, p. 125; also see the footnote on p. 125 in which General Stone's comments on the cavalry appear

Edward's Ferry and arrived back at Colonel Deven's position. Colonel Devens was informed that Colonel Baker would shortly arrive with his brigade and take command. In the interim period, Lieutenant-Colonel Ward arrived at Harrison's Island with the remainder of the 15th Massachusetts. The force under Colonel Devens command now numbered about 625 men. About 12 o'clock a report was given to Colonel Devens that an extensive Confederate force was massing on his left, and around 12: 30 P.M., a strong attack was made on Devens' position. Devens was forced to retreat back into a wooded area. This encounter with the Confederates continued for nearly two hours. Around 2:15 P.M. Colonel Baker arrived at the bluff and took command of the forces.[46]

It appears that the account of General Stone and that of Colonel Devens are in reasonable compliance. The time fame is in sync as well as the troop movement. General Stone continues his account of the engagement:

> Colonel Baker immediately formed his line and awaited the attack of the enemy, which came upon him with great vigor about 3 o'clock p.m., and was met with admirable spirit by our troops, who, though evidently struggling against largely superior numbers [nearly if not quite three to one], maintained their ground and a most destructive fire on the enemy.[47]

General Stone continues with praise for various members of his division (Colonel Cogswell & Lieutenant Baronial). At this point of the engagement Colonel Baker's death occurs. General Stone's account relates:

> At about 4 p.m. Colonel Baker, pierced by a number of bullets, fell at the front of his command while cheering his men, and by his own example sustaining the obstinate resistance they were

---

[46] Battles and Leaders, Vol. II, p. 126
[47] OR, series I, Vol. 5, p. 297

making.... Colonel Lee then took command (20th Massachusetts) and prepared to commence to throwing our forces to the rear, but Colonel Cogswell, of the Tammany regiment, being found senior in rank, assumed the command, and ordered dispositions to be made immediately for marching to the left and cutting a way through to Edward's Ferry.[48]

From this point in the engagement, confusion seems to have reigned over the troops under Colonel Cogswell command. Stone relates that an enemy officer suddenly appeared in front of the Tammany Regiment and beckoned them towards the enemy. The only conclusion that seems logical is that the Tammany Regiment mistakenly identified the enemy officer as one of their officers. The men responded and charged forward, carrying with them the entire line. All received a murderous fire from the enemy at close range, according to General Stone. Attempts were made to recall the men, but with no success. The order to retire was then finally given by Colonel Cogswell. The enemy pursued the Union forces to the edge of the bluff over the landing place, and then pounded the men with heavy fire, as they attempted to cross to the Island. (Harrison's Island)[49]

The accounts of the engagement and Colonel Baker's arrival on the Virginia side of the river are at odds. Colonel Cogswell of the Tammany Regiment (42nd New York) states, in his report dated September 22nd, 1862:

> Arrived at the landing opposite Harrison's Island, I found the greatest confusion existing. No one seemed to be in charge, nor anyone superintending the passage of the troops, and no order was maintained in their crossing.[50]

Colonel Cogswell continues, stating that Colonel Baker welcomed him on the field seeming very confident of a

---

[48] OR, Vol. V, p. 297
[49] OR, Vol. V, p. 297
[50] Battles and Leaders, Vol. II, p. 127

successful day, and in good spirits. Baker asked if Colonel Cogswell thought the battle line would be effective. He states that he informed Colonel Baker that it would not be effective. No attention was given to this advice, and Cogswell was ordered to take charge of the artillery.

Colonel Cogswell says, in conclusion:

> I deem it my duty as commander of the field during the last part of the action to state my convictions as to the principal causes of the untoward results of the day: first. the transportation of the troops across the two branches of the river was in no way guarded or organized. There were no guards at any of the landings. No boat crews had been detailed and each command as it arrived was obliged to organize its own. No guns were placed in position either on the Maryland side or on the island to protect the passage, although several pieces were disposable on the Maryland shore near the landing. Had the full capacity of the boats been employed, more than twice as many men might have been crossed in time to take part in the action. Second. The dispositions on the field were faulty, according to my judgment.[51]

Captain Francis J. Young, assistant quartermaster of Colonel Baker's staff gives a different picture of the situation on the Virginia side:

> ...Colonel Baker apprised Colonel Devens that he had been placed in command and learned that the 15th Massachusetts, after having advanced for a mile in the direction of Leesburg, had been attacked and fallen back to the position they then occupied, just in the edge of the woods on the right. The other forces were lying under the brow of the hill; and with the exception of an occasional rifle shot all was quiet, and no sight of the enemy...there was no regularity or order in the movement of the boats.

---

[51] Battles and Leaders, Vol. II, p. 129-130 (see footnote at the bottom of page 129

General Stone's reply to Captain Young's report is of interest:

> This extraordinary production of a fertile imagination is respectfully forwarded. I have no time to notice its misstatements, but simply call attention to the last clause in the communication, which I am informed is true. 'There is no regularity or order in the movement of the boats.' Had there been, there would have been no disaster....[52]

General Stone's division, at least the segment that was on the Virginia side of the Potomac River, was in a very desperate situation. They had no where to go except into the river. General Stone stated that the small boats had disappeared, but no one knows why, or how this occurred. The larger boat was too heavily loaded and was swamped about fifteen feet from shore. Men were seen stripping and discarding their arms, jumping into the river, holding on to logs hiding in bushes or whatever they could find. Many perished attempting to swim to the Maryland shore.

Where was General Stone while this melee was in progress? In his report of the battle, Stone states that," while these scenes were being enacted on the right, I was preparing on the left for a rapid push forward to the road by which the enemy would retreat if driven, and entirely unsuspicious of the perilous condition of our troops on the right".[53]

At about 4 P.M. Stone telegraphed General Banks requesting a brigade from his division to assist with the control of Harrison's Island on the Maryland side of the river. Stone also telegraphed General Banks and General McClellan of the death of Colonel Baker and then made a rapid approach to assume command.

Orders arrived from the Headquarters of the Army of the Potomac to hold the island and the Virginia shore at

---

[52] OR, series I, Vol. V, p. 328 & General Stone's reply is on p. 330
[53] OR, series I, Vol. V, p. 297

Edward's Ferry at all cost, with the promise of reinforcements. At about 3:00 A.M. General Banks arrived and assumed command. General Stone had high praise for all the troops involved in the engagement. He also seemed very remorseful about the entire situation, especially concerning the wounded and captured. [54]

What is known about General Stone's Confederate adversary at the engagement of Ball's Bluff? Gen. Nathan George Evans, commonly known as "Shanks" was born in Marion County, South Carolina in 1824. Evans graduated from Randolph-Macon College before he was eighteen, and from the United States Military Academy in 1848. Since General Stone graduated in 1845, for a short while, the two men were at the Academy together. Evans received his Academy appointment from John C. Calhoun. After graduation, Evans served in the West and developed a career as an Indian fighter. Evans was present at the bombardment of Fort Sumter and he had a command at the battle of First Bull Run under General Beauregard. At First Bull Run, Evans was in command of a small brigade when he detected General McDowell's turning movement in time to re-deploy his troops, which did much to bring about the final outcome of the battle. Evans received praise and honor from General Beauregard and the Legislature of South Carolina. Not until the engagement at Ball's Bluff did Evans receive promotion to the rank of brigadier-general.[55] After this battle, his presence was requested in South Carolina by the governor. His new command came to be called the "Tramp Brigade". By the end of 1863, Evans' career had reached its pediment. He was brought up on charges of intoxication and disobedience, but was acquitted by a court martial yet still

---

[54] OR, series I, Vol. V, p. 299
[55] The Confederate Military History, Vol. VI, South Carolina,(Wilmington: Broadfoot Publishing Company, reprinted in 1987),p. 392-393

lost his brigade command. He returned to duty in the spring of 1864, however, an accidental fall from his horse all but ended his career for any command purposes. [56]

It would seem that the engagement known, as Ball's Bluff was a disaster for General Stone, but not so for General Evans. Both generals would suffer great calamity during the course of the war, but for different reasons. General Stone would ultimately serve as one of many "fall guys" for those in command. General Evans created his problems with constant drinking and failure to comply with orders. About these two men, Shakespeare said it well, "Reputation, reputation, reputation! O, I have lost my reputation! I have lost the immortal part of myself and what remains is bestial". [57]

How bad was the "disaster" at Ball's Bluff? One of the leading source books on Civil War losses, *Regimental Losses in the Civil War*, by William F. Fox states that the Union deaths were 49; wounded, 158; missing/captured, 714 for a total of 921 men. The Confederates casualties numbered less than eighty-five [dead, missing or captured].[58] The Confederate losses were about 9% of the Union losses. These totals were viewed with alarm and vexation in the North. Since many people felt the war would be over in a few months, this "huge defeat" was difficult to tolerate. Americans in the North lost sight of the fact that this was only the second or third eastern engagement of the war. The

---

[56] Ezra Warner, *Generals in Gray* (Baton Rouge: Louisiana State University Press, 1964), p. 84. Hereinafter cited as Warner Gray; Jeffrey Wert, "Nathan George Evans", The *Confederate General* (Harrisburg: National Historical Society, 1991) Vol. II, edited by William Davis, p. 108; Stewart Sifakis, *Who was Who in the Confederacy* (New York: Facts on File, 1988), Vol. II, p. 88. Hereinafter cited as Who Was Who, Vol. II

[57] William Shakespeare, Cassio speaking in *Othello*

[58] William F. Fox, *Regimental Losses in the American Civil War: 1861-1865* (Dayton: Moringside Press, 1985), p. 543 & 560

troops on both sides were certainly not veterans, in fact for the most part, they were untrained and undisciplined troops.

Had the engagement at Ball's Bluff occurred in 1862 or 1863, it most probably would have received little attention. After all, Shiloh and many of Gen. Robert E. Lee's victories would already have taken place. Radical Republican Senators such as Ben Wade and Charles Sumner were the leading critics of the methods and techniques used by the Union generals. Given the position held by Colonel Edward Baker in the Senate before the war, and with the President and members of the Senate, there was absolutely no way he was going to be blamed for this fiasco.[59] If not Colonel Baker, then who was responsible? It did not take the political legion of Washington very long to point the finger at Colonel Baker's commanding officer: Gen. Charles P. Stone.

As early as November 2, 1861, General Stone penned the following to Assistant Adjutant General Williams:

> General: the persistent attacks made upon me by the friends (so called), of the lamented late Colonel Baker, through the newspaper press, have made it my duty to call the attention of the major-general commanding to distinct violations of my orders and instructions to that officer in the affair of October 21st ultimo, more pointedly than it has been my wish to do in an official report concerning one who is no more. Painful as it may be to censure the acts of one who has gallantly died on the field of battle, justice to myself and to those who served under me requires that the full truth should be made to appear.... I have been fiercely attacked in some newspapers, which have not waited for official reports, but have seized upon every word of any friend of the late colonel who might choose to invent or color a description of the disaster. Every false statement has been pronounced to be true, unless denied by myself, who have

---

[59] Edward G. Longacre, " Charles P. Stone and the 'Crime of Unlucky Generals', (Gettysburg: *Civil War Times Illustrated*) Vol. XIII, no. 7, November 1974, p. 4-5. Hereinafter cited as Unlucky Generals

had too many and too important duties to permit me to write to the public prints, even were such a course allowable to a soldier.[60]

General Stone elaborates in his report by bringing to light what was stated in the letter given to Colonel Baker. The press, and others, implied General Stone had stated that the letter commanded the colonel to attack Leesburg on Sunday, the 20th of October. Stone denies such a letter was ever sent, stating the very mention of such a document was absurd. He further iterated that no order of any kind was sent to Colonel Baker until 2:00 A.M. Monday, October 21. This order instructed the colonel to send one regiment to Conrad's Ferry and to hold the remainder of his brigade in readiness to march.[61] General Stone enclosed a copy of the order with his report to Assistant Adjutant-General Williams. The order asserted the following:

> Colonel: You will send the California regiment (less camp guard) to Conrad's Ferry, to arrive there at sunrise and await orders. The men will take with them blankets and overcoats and forty rounds of ammunition in boxes, and will be followed by one day's rations in wagons. The remainder of the brigade will be held in readiness for marching orders (leaving camp guards) at 7o'clock a.m. to-morrow, and will all have breakfasted before that hour....[62]

General Stone avows that Colonel Baker's associates claim the colonel said, on receiving the order, " I will obey General Stone's order, but it is my death- warrant." [63] Needless to say, General Stone had nothing but abhorrence for this promulgation, which he felt, maligned his ability as a commanding general.

---

[60] OR, series I, Vol. V, p. 300
[61] OR, series I, Vol. V, p. 301
[62] OR, series I, Vol. V, p. 302-303
[63] OR, series I, Vol. V. p. 301

General Stone ends the report to General Williams with a discussion of the battlefield placement of the brigade. This placement was mentioned by Colonel Cogswell and to a degree, by Colonel Devens. According to General Stone, Colonel Baker had between 1,600 and 1,700 troops. He was confronted with a steep bluff in his rear, a valley on his left, and opposite the valley, a wooded hill. A reserve force could only have been of value if it was placed on the edge of the bluff, yet Colonel Baker saw fit to place four companies near the center of the battlefield. Thus, they could have added nothing to the success of the battle at hand, plus they were in a position to receive very heavy enemy fire. Only two companies of skirmishers were placed out to the left flank, and these two companies were able to hold off an enemy regiment for twenty minutes. Stone's contention is that Colonel Baker should have placed the reserves in a position to extend the line of fire. In this scenario, General Stone felt that victory would have been assured. Stone felt the reserves could have charged while the two companies of the California regiment held the enemy regiment's charge to a halt.[64] In a word, the outcome of the battle would have been victory for Colonel Baker and his brigade, in General Stone's opinion.

What was the position of General McClellan, the Commanding-General of the Army of the Potomac, concerning General Stone's handling of the engagement at Ball's Bluff? On November 1, 1861, McClellan sent a letter to Secretary of War Cameron. The Greenfield Gazette and Courier of Greenfield, Massachusetts, Stone's hometown, reprinted the letter. McClellan states:

> ...My dispatch did not contemplate the making an attack upon the enemy, or the crossing of the river in force by any portion of General Stone's command, and not anticipating such movement

---

[64] OR, series I, Vol. V, p. 302

> I had upon the 20th directed Major General McCall to return with his division on the forenoon of the 21st from Drainesville, to the camp from which he had advanced, provided the reconnaissance entrusted to him should have been then completed.[65]

This statement by McClellan is critical to the engagement at Ball's Bluff, in that McClellan simple never made it clear to Stone that McCall might be called back to the Washington lines. Stone acted accordingly, and directed Colonel Baker to use his discretion in the sending or withdrawing of troops from the Virginia side of the Potomac. Stone was under the assumption McCall was still at Dranesville on October 21. McClellan had withdrawn McCall and had failed to inform General Stone of this very imperative fact.[66] In another attempt to clear up personal blame, McClellan states:

> ...I sent to him (Stone) at Edward's Ferry, the following dispatch at half past 10 p.m.: 'Intrench yourself on the Virginia side, and await reinforcements, if necessary.' I immediately telegraphed Major General Banks to proceed with three brigades of his division to the support of General Stone; and advising the latter he would be so supported, I directed him to hold his position at all hazards.[67]

Military men of the Stone and McClellan vintage viewed war and its procedures quite differently from the soldier of later years. It was their maxim that war was the realm of the soldier, and it was his domain exclusively. They did not realize that war has many ramifications, not the least of which is politics. Stone was a political neonate, an infant, seemingly uninformed; in addition, General Stone held very

---

[65] Greenfield, Massachusetts *Gazette and Courier*, Monday, November 11, 1861. Hereinafter cited as Gazette and Courier
[66] Stephen W. Sears, *George B. McClellan: The Young Napoleon* (New York: Ticknor& Fields, 1988), p. 121. Hereinafter cited as McClellan
[67] Gazette and Courier

conservative views about slavery. An illustration of this fact is his order that denied fugitive slaves the right of asylum when they entered his lines, moreover, he often returned them to their owners. An incident which was to spark this situation into a major problem for General Stone occurred when two fugitives slaves made their way into the lines of the 20th Massachusetts in September of 1861. When word reached the Governor of Massachusetts, John A. Andrew, he immediately leveled a severe reprimand on the Lieutenant of the 20th who had carried out the return. Governor Andrew made the following accusations in a letter to Secretary of War Simon Cameron:

> ...I wish to call your attention to the inclosed copy of a recent letter from a reliable source in relation to the use to which Massachusetts soldiers are being put (as is alleged) by Brigadier General Stone.... Massachusetts does not send her citizens forth to become the hunters of men or engage in the seizure and return to captivity of persons claimed to be fugitive slaves without any recognition or even the forms of law... (A)

A sub-enclosure details:

> On Saturday last an order came down from General Stone giving a description of two fugitive slaves and directing their return (in case they should enter our camp) to their owners whoever they might be. This order it appears was handed by Lieutenant-Colonel Palfrey to the officer of the day, Mr. Macy, of Company I. On Sunday morning several negroes came into our camp as usual for the purpose of selling cakes, pies, & etc., to the soldiers.... Lieutenant Macy espied the negroes ...and then immediately detailed a file of soldiers under a sergeant with loaded muskets to escort them to their supposed owners and deliver them up. (B)[68]

---

[68] OR, series II, Vol. I, p. 784-85

This return of the fugitive slaves was in accord with the national policy of Congress, the President, and the Government of the United States at that point in history. Both General Stone and General McClellan viewed this action by Governor Andrew as interference with the war effort and as a hindrance to discipline. The correspondence was sent to Senator Sumner, who denounced Stone with vehemence. This incident and the Ball's Bluff disaster came to public attention at about same point in time. The specter of suspicion was now on General Stone. The nation was in a state of paranoia and a situation resembling McCarthyism of the 1950s had developed. Everyone had to establish and reestablish his loyalty and faith in the American system to the point that the very definition of loyalty was blurred. Who was and was not loyal became a matter of an individual's point of view, derived from opinion rather than facts in many instances.[69]

General Stone, by mid December, was a victim of the Washington rumor mill. In the interim, Stone had written a very hostile and trenchant letter to Senator Sumner. This letter, as well as a letter penned to Governor Andrew, was ultimately given to the eight members of the Joint Committee on the Conduct of the War. Unfortunately, General Stone was now in the proverbial "hatchet fight without a hatchet".[70] General McClellan privately supported General Stone, but did little else to assist him in restoring his good reputation. One of Stone's officers related to Attorney General Edward Bates a discussion which he had with General McClellan concerning General Stone's plight, "They want a victim," McClellan remarked. "Yes," the officer replied, "and when they have once tasted blood, got

---

[69] Chronicles, p. 34; Battles and Leaders, Vol. II, p. 132
[70] Unlucky Generals, p. 38

one victim, no one can tell who will be the next victim!"[71] McClellan would soon have his own problems with government officials, and he may well have been thinking that he could be the next victim.

The Committee on the Conduct of the War was a joint committee of Congress. It was organized on December 20th, 1861, to inquire into the management of the Civil War. The Committee existed until ninety days after the close of the Thirty-eighth Congress, June 1865, and Senator Benjamin Wade of Ohio served as the chairman of the Committee. Other members were: Zachariah Chandler, Senator from Michigan, Andrew Johnson, Senator from Tennessee, D.W. Gooch, House Member from Massachusetts, John Covode, House Member from Pennsylvania, George W. Julian, House Member from Indiana, M. F. Odell, House Member from New York. Andrew Johnson was appointed Military Governor of Tennessee on March 4th, 1862. His position on the Committee was filled temporarily by Joseph A. Wright of Indiana. Most of the Committee members were from the radical segment of the Republican Party. This Committee would ultimately investigate every commander of the Army of the Potomac with the exception of General Grant. The Committee also delved into the competency of many commanding officers, military campaigns, and expenditures of the armies. It seems to have been all encompassing.[72]

General Stone, being the politically unwitting person that he was, paid little attention to the rumors, and seems to have had no real concerns that he was in any political danger. Stone was called by the Committee on the Conduct

---

[71] McClellan, p. 145; a quote from the diary of Attorney General Edward Bates, used by Sears

[72] *Dictionary of American History*, James Truslow Adams, editor (New York: Charles Scribner's Sons,1961) , p. 436-37; Battles and Leaders, Vol. II, p. 134 (see footnote)

of the War to give testimony on January 5, 1862, which was less than three months after the engagement at Ball's Bluff. Stone would subsequently be charged with the following counts of malfeasance: misbehavior at the battle of Ball's Bluff; holding correspondence with enemy before and since the battle of Ball's Bluff, receiving visits from rebel officers in his camp; allowing the enemy to build a fort or strong work, since the battle of Ball's Bluff, under his guns without molestation; exposing his forces to capture and destruction by the enemy, under pretense of orders for a movement from the commanding general which had not been given.[73]

General Stone's testimony before the Joint Committee was laced and tempered with the idea that he could not compromise any military tactics, past or present, nor divulge any military secrets. This point was conveyed and stressed to Stone over and over by McClellan. Since McClellan labored under a certain amount of hostile opinion by many in the government, this was a form of self-protection as well as military policy. Stone, being the loyal soldier and artless political realist that he was, followed McClellan's advice.

The first questions asked of General Stone were by Benjamin Wade. Wade attempted to deceive Stone and "set him up" for the kill. Wade asked questions about troop movements, possible obstacles to movement, positioning of various types of troops, etc. After ten to fifteen questions of this type, Wade asked: "I would ask you your own plan. What in your judgment would be the best place to move?" Stone replied by saying, "If I had plans, I should not wish to tell them, even to my aide-de-camp," to which a parenthetical reply was given by Wade. Stone continued: "Or anybody else; certainly to no one outside of him." (Aide-de-camp) If I had any plans of operations, I would not

---

[73] Battles and Leaders, Vol. II, p. 131-32 (see the footnote)

confide them to my own staff, to have them discussed by them, until the moment came to put them in action."[74] This was exactly the type of answer the Committee was seeking. Stone had not given Colonel Baker adequate instructions as to what he was expected to do or not to do, they reasoned. Chairman Wade proceeded with the question as to what troops made the demonstration at Edward's Ferry. General Stone gave a very detailed answer, reiterating many of his reports presented earlier. Stone ends his lengthy answer with: "...Colonel Baker choose to bring on a battle. He brought it on, and I am sorry to say, handled his troops unskillfully in it, and a disaster occurred which ought not to have...." Chairman Wade then posed the question to Stone as to whether or not he had intended for Baker to cross the Potomac. Stone gave the same reply that he had stated in his report, that it was a discretionary decision, to be determined by Colonel Baker.

    Congressman Gooch asked Stone to continue with his assessment of Colonel Baker's decision to cross the river. Stone replied, "Colonel Baker came to the point of crossing, and there occupied himself more than an hour and a half in personally superintending the getting of the boat from the canal into the river." Gooch made a transitional comment and Stone continued: "That work ought to have been done by a junior officer, while Colonel Baker ought to have used that time in looking at the field he was sent to look at. Colonel Devens was a mile and a half in front of the river with a small force. He was instructed in the morning from me to receive his orders from Colonel Baker; but he received no orders from Colonel Baker until a quarter past two o'clock in

---

[74] *Report of the Joint Committee on the Conduct of the War* (Washington: Government Printing Office, 1863), Vol. II, p. 266-67. Hereinafter cited as Joint Committee Report; (The 1977 edition of the Kraus Reprint Company of Millwood, New York is the source used for these notes)

the afternoon, when he had been forced by the enemy back to Colonel Baker's position on the bluff."[75]

Stone advanced more information concerning Colonel Baker's incorrect transport of artillery pieces across the river with horses, as opposed to infantry. This led into a discussion by Stone, concerning the lack of boats for the infantry's use, and the poor use made of those available due to Colonel Baker's incompetence as a military leader.[76] General Stone was again asked by Chairman Wade if he gave Colonel Baker the order to cross the river, and Stone stated he gave no such order. He added that a written order was found in the Colonel's hat, which stated that the crossing was discretionary. Much has been said about this discretionary order. A Mr. J.T. Eason, a veteran of the Seventeenth Mississippi regiment, Company I, claims that the man who killed Colonel Baker (a John Fitzgerald) found a large envelope containing a message from General Stone inquiring as to whether Colonel Baker needed reinforcements, and stated that the message was given to Colonel Featherstone, CSA. This dispatch was sent by General Beauregard to the Joint Committee, under flags of truce via the Federal commander.[77]

Stone was questioned by Representative Gooch and asked if he had any additional points to make concerning the use of the forces at Ball's Bluff. The general replied that he did and then proceeded to explain the poor choice of the battlefield. He felt that the artillery was placed in an open field, unsupported by infantry. Representative Gooch followed with the question as to who was responsible for the Massachusetts regiments involved at this point. Stone replied, "The commanding officer." Gooch then retorted,

---

[75] Joint Committee Report, Vol. II, p. 268-69
[76] Joint Committee Report, Vol. II, p. 270
[77] J.T. Eason, "Ball's Bluff Battle", *The Confederate Veteran Magazine*, 1902, p. 23; Hereinafter cited as Confederate Veteran

Library of Congress

Bull Run Battlefield as it looked in 1861

Death of Colonel Baker, Ball's Bluff, October 21, 1861

Library of Congress

Simon Cameron, Secretary of War

Library of Congress

Edwin Stanton, Secretary of War

Benjamin Wade, member of Congress and
the Committee on the Conduct of the War

General Stone designed the base of the Statue of Liberty within close view of the detention center where he was detained for no actual crime

"Colonel Baker?" Stone's reply was, "Undoubtedly; he was the commanding officer." [78] While this is an honest answer, it was exactly the wrong answer, as far as Stone's position was concerned. He had established that Baker was incompetent, and that the Colonel was in command, as opposed to Stone himself. The Committee viewed this, no doubt, as a "cope out" to shift blame from Stone to Baker. Even more damning was the fact that Baker was an intimate friend of the President, a fellow member of Congress and a hero in the eyes of many Americans. Most disastrously of all, Colonel Baker was dead and could not speak for himself. This was truly a mixture for calamity, mishap, and failure for General Stone.

Representative Julian from Indiana questioned Stone as to the sufficiency of the boats to transport the infantry under Colonel Baker's command. General Stone rejoined:" I do not think a careful commander would have attempted that crossing so heedlessly. I think any careful commander would have himself gone on the field and attempted to look before him, before he attempted to cross 2,000 men in the face of the enemy. One of the chief faults is, that he commenced crossing the troops, remaining himself on this side, before he had received one single distinct report from the front."[79]

The questioning continued in the direction of transportation for Colonel Baker's troops, battlefield selection, and positions of the various regiments. Representative Gooch and Chairman Wade seemed more interested in this aspect of the Ball's Bluff engagement than the other Committee members did. Finally the questioning shifted to a crucial area, the degree of Stone's responsibility for the failure. Chairman Wade asked if General Stone had received an order to make a reconnaissance from General McClellan, whereon Stone responded that he had not

---

[78] Joint Committee Report, Vol. II, p. 270
[79] Joint Committee Report, Vol. II, p. 271

received an order to reconnoiter the Virginia side of the river. Wade then asked if General Stone had received an order to make a demonstration and Stone replied that in fact he had received such an order. He was then asked to explain the significance of the order. General Stone retorted: "It was something in this form, by telegraph; it was received by me, I think, about 11o'clock in the day of the 20th. That 'General McCall occupied Drainesville yesterday; will send out reconnoitering parties in all directions today. It is made for the effort to drive the enemy from Leesburg. And a slight demonstration on your part might produce the same effect.' On the evening of the 20th, the demonstration was made."[80] Wade replied by asking how a demonstration could be made without crossing the river, instantly General Stone's response was: "It is the easiest thing in the world to make a demonstration. Simply to show your troops; to make a feint of going across. Boats were filled with men, a cannon fire was opened on the ground to clear a space around the point of landing, and boat loads of men were sent off." Wade questioned how this technique would induce the enemy to give battle. Stone replied that if the enemy was foolish, or had no other options, "he would not meet us with the chances in our favor."[81] The Committee did not seem content with this answer. Stone seemed to "stonewall" the Committee at this point, by refusing to second-guess the General-in-Chief, saying that, "I have no right to."

    Senator Chandler questioned General Stone as to what hour the first order was given to Colonel Baker to cross the river. Stone had repeatedly stated that no such order was ever given to the Colonel and again reiterated that no such order was given. Chandler pressed on with this line of questioning, asking "At what hour was the order given?" General Stone then gave a listing of the various orders,

---

[80] Report of the Joint Committee, Vol. II, p. 274
[81] Joint Committee Report, Vol. II, p. 274

previously stated in his reports to General McClellan and others. The hour at which any order was received by Colonel Baker was finally established to have been between, "eight and half-past nine in the morning."[82] Stone continued with his testimony stating that he received word from Colonel Baker that he was crossing his whole force at about 11 o'clock. General Stone then testified that, "I then at once commenced crossing over Gorman's brigade, pushing them over much more rapidly than I had been doing before. The number that was over there at the time this action was going on the right was some 1,500 or 1,600 infantry, thirty cavalry, and a section of howitzers, with their horses and equipment."[83] Senator Chandler requested clarification that the troops were in fact across the river prior to Colonel Baker's death. Chandler seemed to think that a force of that magnitude should have been able to overthrow the Confederate forces that were present. General Stone explained that to do so would have been too great a risk. Chandler persisted that a force could have come to the Confederate artillery entrenchment's rear, since Colonel Baker was facing them, forcing the Confederate artillery from their entrenchment. General Stone said he felt that 4,000 infantrymen probably could have taken the entire Confederate force but Chandler was still not satisfied with the answer he received. He felt that a flanking movement of any kind should have been enough to capture the Confederates. Stone explained that the flanking force would have been required to march eight to nine miles over unknown ground to engage an unknown force. The fatigue factor alone would have been overwhelmingly in favor of the Confederate army.[84]

---

[82] Joint Committee Report, Vol. II, p. 275
[83] Joint Committee Report, Vol. II, p. 276
[84] Joint Committee Report, Vol. II, p 277

Additional questions were raised concerning the availability of boats; in addition Senator Chandler raised questions as to the possibility of a pontoon bridge at Ball's Bluff, or Edward's Ferry. General Stone explained the various problems this would have entailed, and the impracticality of such a plan. Representative Odell again raised questions about the boats and what became of them, and once again General Stone made a sincere attempt to give an honest answer, but again, played right into the hands of the Committee. He replied, "... I was not there, had no charge of the matter at all, and do not know exactly about it."[85] A very incriminating statement, but typical of Stone's blunt and curt directness.

A large segment of the remainder of General Stone's testimony given on January 5 concerned the return of fugitive slaves. The opening question was posed by Chairman Wade. Stone was asked to explain the return of slaves to their secessionist masters. Stone was aghast but his reply however, was ordered and logical:

> ... I was sent with a military force into a certain county in Maryland. I was told when I was sent there that I was to give full and complete protection to that county. I have tried to obey every order of the War Department I have every received; and, upon the other hand, I have insisted upon my troops obeying every law of the state of Maryland. I do not allow them to harbor the slaves, or the free employed negroes, or the apprentices, or the sons and daughters of the farmers in that neighborhood in my camps... The slaves that run away from the enemy and come over are got to my headquarters as rapidly as possible; they are then questioned carefully, and all the information I can get out of them is taken... I am not aware of any slaves coming over from the enemy's lines having been given up to any claimant. There is but one case where one has been claimed that has come in. In that one case I stated to the owner, or the son of the owner rather, who came to claim him, that it was not a matter that I had

---

[85] Joint Committee Report, Vol. II, p. 278

anything to do with at all, that of deciding whether he was his negro or not.[86]

General Stone, after a few intervening statements from the Committee, gave a rather stern reprimand to the Committee about the entire situation:

> …And we cannot call into question the actions of a senator or a member of Congress on the floor of the Senate or House. But I have had in my own camps soldiers discussing in their tents the conduct of their general and the senator from their State, not knowing anything about the original circumstances, but simply discussing what their senator says of their commanding general. This is not a healthy state of discipline at all.[87]

Wade denied any knowledge of this claim by General Stone, nonetheless, given other statements made by Senator Wade and the other Committee members; this denial is somewhat suspect. Representative Julian again asked what amounts to the same question that Stone had already answered concerning the return of slaves to claimants. General Stone gave an exact and a rather terse reply, "Until you gentlemen change the laws, I am bound to let any civil magistrate order a search of my premises, under the laws of the state in which I am serving."[88]

At that point, the Committee interjected questions that would not be allowed in any court of law in any state or the federal courts. Representative Julian asked: "Suppose you know the claimant is a rebel slaveholder, although he has a civil process and a constable there, would you feel it your duty to give up the fugitive?" General Stone hesitated and asked," Let me understand you. You say a 'rebel slaveholder'. Julian responds, "I mean a disloyal man. I am supposing that you know him to be a disloyal man." Stone

---

[86] Joint Committee Report, Vol. II, p. 279
[87] Joint Committee Report, Vol. II, p. 280
[88] Joint Committee Report, Vol. II, p. 280

asked, "In arms against the United States?" Julian replied, "Yes, sir; on the side of the rebels, giving them aid and comfort." Stone replied, in a very disconcerted and mercurial fashion, "I will state this, that if the slave of a man whom I know to be in rebellion [Stone is very "rattled" at this point] is this being taken down?" He was informed that it was in fact being recorded by a reporter. The general continued, "I can hardly imagine that I am obliged to swear to what I would do". Stone then repeated his earlier testimony concerning the slave and the slave owner's son who came to claim the slave. He concluded with the statement that, "... I refused on the ground that I had no jurisdiction over the man." [89]

A final series of questions were posed to General Stone. The purpose of these questions seemed to have been an attempt to ascertain the degree of communication among division, brigade, and regimental officers. There also seems to have been a hidden intent in these questions. The Committee was searching for some weakness, some "slip up" made by General Stone, concerning Colonel Baker's instructions, transportation, orders, when, and if they were received---- anything to vilify General Stone and reinvent Colonel Baker as a military genius.

General Stone may, or may not have felt he was exonerated after his testimony on January 5, 1862. The claim has been made that he felt that he was being questioned about procedures, troop movements, etc. and that he had no conception of the actual intent of the Committee. General Stone was a perceptive man and he must have quickly realized that this was not a simple fact finding inquiry. He certainly seems to have been irascible and vehement with much of his testimony, and with good reason. The general did not have legal counsel, nor any other legal advisor with

---

[89] Joint Committee Report, Vol. II, p. 280

which to consult, while most of the Committee members were either lawyers, or men with a long association with Congress and the law making process. General Stone must have felt very intimidated by this austere Committee. Unfortunately for the general, this Committee was not finished with him and the worst was not yet in sight for Gen. Charles Stone.

The testimony of Col. George W.B. Tompkins of the 2nd New York Militia Regiment turned this investigation into a modern day "witch hunt" by the Committee. Of interest is the fact that Colonel Tompkins' regiment was not present at Ball's Bluff. In September of 1861, Stone had processed charges against Tompkins for intentionally padding a muster report with the intent to receive pay for soldiers not present, which he intended to pocket. In addition, he displayed cowardice in battle at Bull Run. The government pressured Tompkins to resign from the military during the time period the Committee inquiry was taking place.[90] Tompkins had grievances against General Stone and he wanted vengeance. This was just the kind of juicy half-truths and gossip that the Committee was seeking. Tompkins stated that the officers of the division were very uncomplimentary of General Stone and that they questioned his integrity as a Union man. The question was then posed, "What do they accuse him of?"[91] Colonel Tompkins replied:

> It is said he receives and sends communications back and forth across the river. In fact, my officers have told me that they have sent, by his orders, letters across the river--- sealed letters---- and have received sealed letters from the other side, directed to him; that they have received men from the other side, purporting to be his spies; that he had ordered women to be sent across, and

---

[90] Stephen W. Sears, *Controversies and Commanders: Dispatches from the Army of the Potomac* (New York: Houghton Mifflin, 1999), p. 40. Hereinafter cited as Commanders
[91] Joint Committee Report, Vol. II, p. 295

has sent flags of truce across for others to come over on this side. Officers have mentioned these things to me... I presumed he had his spies. Indeed, he told me he had, and that he knew everything that was going on over there, and I have been told so by other officers[92]

It is patently preposterous that any elected group of lawmakers could have given any credence to Colonel Tompkins' testimony, given the relationship that existed between the two men. It should have been unequivocally clear to any observant person that this inquiry was a sham. If this was not enough, Tompkins continued to malign General Stone's name. He stated that," not a man in my regiment will fight under him, if they can avoid it, not one. In fact they all want to get up a petition to be removed from his division, and I was going down to the hotel this afternoon to see General Dix, to see if we cannot get out of General Stone's division into General Dix's division." [93] Tompkins testified that the men in his regiment did not have faith in General Stone's ability and skills as an officer. He also claimed that he personally questioned General Stone's loyalty.[94] Senators Chandler and Wade, Representatives Odell and Gooch, stalked the idea that General Stone fraternized with the rebels, both military and civilians, with their questions. Tompkins even testified that this view extended to the Rhode Island Regiment, as well as the 34th New York Regiment.[95] Ten of the witnesses testifying in the Joint Committee hearings concerning Ball's Bluff were from the 2nd New York Militia Regiment. Yet there were only thirty-six witnesses who actual gave testomony. That should have been a legal revelation to the Committee. If this was not sufficient to raise concern, two of the 2nd New York Regiment

---

[92] Joint Committee Report, Vol. II p. 295
[93] Joint Committee Report, Vol. II, p. 295
[94] Joint Committee Report, Vol. II, p. 295
[95] Joint Committee Report, Vol. II, p. 296

witnesses, in addition to Colonel Tompkins, had charges pending against them by General Stone, and they, in point of fact, had to be released from confinement to give testimony![96]

Captain Dennis De Courcy of the 2nd New York Regiment gave very damaging testimony to the Committee. De Courcy's testimony followed the same general design as that given by Tompkins. He claimed that General Stone did not have the confidence of the officers and men of the regiment. The messages from across the river were also a part of his testimony. Again, Stone's loyalty was impugned by a member of the 2nd New York Militia Regiment. De Courcy admitted that he was not present at Ball's Bluff, yet he had no hesitation about condemning Stone's battle plan and troop movement. De Courcy additionally testified that General Stone did not appear on the Virginia side of the river until Wednesday, after the battle on Monday.[97]

Captain James Brady, also of the 2nd New York Militia Regiment, gave testimony similar to that given by Tompkins and De Courcy. Brady claimed that letters were sent across the river to General Stone. Captain Brady admitted that he read the letters before they were passed to Stone. Senator Johnson asked, "You say you read the letters, and then sent them to General Stone"? Brady answered yes. Johnson then asked the "drift and purport" of the letters. Brady answered," they were letters very disgusting for us Union soldiers to read: blackguard letters about our defeat at Bull Run, etc.". Representative Gooch asked if Brady remembered who had written the letters. Brady answered, " There were different names. I do not remember them; but I think one name was Chichester. I had all the names and all

---

[96] Commanders, p. 40 (Sears does not specify the names of these soldiers)
[97] Joint Committee Report, Vol. II, p. 303-305

the dates, but when I left the army, I threw away all I had relating to military matters?"[98]

Another member of the 2nd New York gave testimony in much the same vein as was previously given. Captain Clinton Berry stated that letters crossed the river both ways. He claimed that he was instructed to inform the Confederates on the Virginia side that Stone ordered the exchange to stop immediately, under penalty of death. He also claimed that General Stone went out of his way to protect the local people, referred to as secessionists by many of the troops.[99] This witness gave extraordinarily confusing testimony in many ways. He seems to have implied that the local people were not disloyal to the government of the United States, yet he suggest that General Stone has protected them because they were disloyal, or secessionists. He seemed to have been attempting to discredit the general by innuendo or allusion. In addition he had an audience that required very little convincing.

At least one private citizen was questioned by the Committee; a Mr. Philip Hagner gave testimony on January 18, 1862. Hagner was a resident of Edward's Ferry. He testified that he was a grain merchant and was not connected with the military in any way. Hagner stated that he was not present at Ball's Bluff, and that his home was about two and one half miles above the area. The purpose of this testimony was to determine why a flourmill owned by a John P. Smart of Leesburg was allowed to remain in operation. Hagner testified that Smart was a Confederate sympathizer and had no business dealings with the Union. Chairman Wade questioned Hagner as to the distance from the Maryland shore of the Potomac to the mill, and if artillery fire could reach it. Hagner responded that it could, and in fact it could be reached with small arms. Wade continued to question

---

[98] Joint Committee Report, Vol. II, p. 335
[99] Joint Committee Report, Vol. II, p. 361

Hagner, asking about a person by the name of Young. Hagner stated that he knew Young well and that his son was in the Confederate army. Hagner claimed that Young and his son were given passes to cross the river at will. According to Hagner, these men were allowed to take items of their choice across the river and were never searched or questioned in any manner. The Committee's questioning included some testimony about the boats used by the troops. In addition, Hagner stated that Maryland secessionists praised General Stone above all other Union officers.[100]

This testimony was very damaging to General Stone and very compelling to the Joint Committee. In their view, General Stone quite simply allowed a rebel supply mill of the Confederate army to operate within his area of disposition without interference. To the Committee, this was proof positive that Stone was a rebel sympathizer and, therefore, disloyal to the Union cause. It never occurred to them to look beyond this suspicion.

At least one other New York regiment offered testimony against General Stone. Major Byron Laflin of the 34th New York Regiment gave testimony to the Committee much like that of the 2nd New York. Laflin in essence, accused General Stone of treason. Captain Francis Young of the 71st Pennsylvania regiment, or the "California Regiment" also testified. This testimony, taken in mid January, was a virtual aping of that given by the New York regiments. Young even claimed that General Stone refused to fly the American flag.[101]

A very important deposition was given toward the end of January of 1862. This testimony was heard very shortly before General Stone's second appearance before the Joint Committee on January 31, 1862. Gen. Nathaniel Banks

---

[100] Joint Committee Report, Vol. II, p. 345-350
[101] Joint Committee Report, Vol. II, p. 370; Captain Young's testimony, p. 328

gave testimony which confirmed much of what General Stone had previously stated to the Committee. When asked about Colonel Baker's orders on crossing the Potomac to the Virginia side, Banks replied, "...Colonel Baker therefore crossed, under the direction of General Stone, as speedily as he could, and with instructions to act according to his own discretion upon the statement of facts they had received. He did not relate to me what Colonel Baker's purpose and actions were, but that he crossed about 2 o'clock in the afternoon, and the enemy in great force was immediately upon him.[102] General Banks was then asked if it was his impression that Stone had directed Colonel Baker to cross the river and given him powers of discretion to act after he got there. Banks answered, "My impression was that Colonel Baker desired to cross, and General Stone gave him authority to act pretty much within his own discretion, considering the statement of facts which had been made to them in regard to the position and strength of the enemy, which was very different from what it afterwards turned out to be." Banks also affirmed that General Gorman also felt that this was to be a reconnaissance mission only, and never suspected it would be an engagement with the enemy in force.[103]

Much of the testimony taken by the Committee during the month of January would never have been allowed in any court of law. The witnesses testified under the constraints of pressure and subjugation, fearing both legal and military repercussions. As any person who undertakes to gain an understanding of historical events is aware, truth often comes from very strange places. In the case of General Stone's dilemma, it came from the Confederate army. Major James W. Ratchford was Adjutant General for Confederate Gen. Daniel H. Hill at Leesburg. Major Ratchford states:

---

[102] Joint Committee Report, Vol. II, p. 420
[103] Joint Committee Report, Vol. II, p. 420

>...one of my jobs was to arrange for the exchange of letters at nearby Edward's Ferry, under a flag of truce. I was also responsible for reading all the mail before allowing it to pass, in order that no contraband news was sent...At first I found this mail reading quite amusing, but in time it became monotonous. I came to know the Federal officers I met under the flag of truce and had many friendly chats with them...
>
>As Adjutant-General of the department, I carried every flag of truce, and inspected every communication that passed across the lines, and though there was nothing in any of the correspondence unbecoming an officer in Stone's position, it worked much evil to him. He was a Democrat, and hence viewed with suspicion by his superiors in Washington, and when they learned of his personal friendship with General Hill, they lost no time in attempting to ruin him....[104]

It would appear that Tompkins and the other members of the 2nd New York Militia Regiment, along with Captain Young of the 71st Pennsylvania, and Captain Laflin of the 34th New York gave the Committee testimony which is at extreme variance with the statements of Major James Ratchford, CSA. Ratchford's comments about General Stone in his memoirs are made under no constraints, and certainly with no hope or expectation of reward. One must draw his own conclusions as to the actual facts of the situation.

On January 28, 1862, Secretary of War, Edwin Stanton ordered General McClellan to relieve General Stone of command of his division. He also directed McClellan to place Stone under arrest and that he be "kept in close custody until further orders."[105]. The timing of Stanton's order is unusual. He had taken office as Secretary of War on January 15, 1862, upon the resignation of Simon Cameron. Less than two weeks later, he called for the arrest of General

---

[104] James W. Ratchford, *Memoirs of a Confederate Staff Officer: From Bethel to Bentonville*, Edited by Evelyn Sieburg (Shippensburg: White Mane Books, 1998) p. 10-11
[105] OR, series I, vol., V, p. 341

Stone. In fact, Stanton did not actually take control of the Office of Secretary of War until January 20th, 1862--- a mere eight days before the order for the arrest of General Stone. Stanton held the position of Attorney General under James Buchanan. Could Secretary Stanton have been that close to the Committee hearings in such a short period of time? To order the arrest of a general in command of an infantry division in the Union army was a serious measure.

General McClellan refused to carry out Stanton's arrest order, instead he approached the Committee and requested that Stone be allowed to again testify, and state his case concerning the events under consideration. The Committee agreed, but with conditions. He, Stone, could not confront any witness, read any testimony to the Committee, have legal council or advice, or call witnesses in his defense.[106] On January 31, 1862, Chairman Wade summarized the findings against General Stone to the Committee and others present. Chairman Wade said:

> In the course of our investigation here there has come out in evidence matters which may be said to impeach you. I do not know that I can enumerate all the points, but I think I can. In the first place, is your conduct in the Ball's Bluff affair-your ordering forces over without sufficient means of transportation, and in that way, of course, endangering your army...We deem the testimony tends, also to impeach you for not reinforcing those troops when they went over there in the face of the enemy...The evidence tends to prove that you had undue communication with the enemy by letters that have passed back and forth, by intercourse with officers of the other side, and by permitting packages to go over unexamined to known Secessionists...you have suffered the enemy to erect fortifications or batteries on the opposite side of the river, within reach of your guns, and that you could have easily have prevented[107]

---

[106] Commanders, p. 41
[107] Reunion of Graduates, p. 50

On a motion by Representative Gooch, Chairman Wade was asked to notify General Stone that the Committee was ready to hear his testimony. General Stone stated that he was informed that testimony had been given to the Committee that he felt should be addressed. Chairman Wade then begin to lay out the four major charges against General Stone. Wade set forth the first charge, " In the first place is your conduct in the Ball's Bluff affair---your ordering your forces over without sufficient transportation, and, in that way, of course endangering your army, in case of a check, by not being able to reinforce them...." General Stone replied:

> ...I do not know how far the committee may have conceived that I risked the troops there. I certainly did risk the first party sent over; but I think that to any military eye I explained very clearly how I arranged for their return. I gave discretion to the next officer, who had command of a sufficient number of troops---discretionary power, he being the judge of the propriety of passing over and the means he had to do so---whether he should retire what troops were over there or whether he should advance more. That officer took the responsibility of making a passage of more troops, with a full knowledge of the facts.[108]

General Stone went on to specify that when Colonel Baker determined to cross the river, the responsible of the engagement, the troops, and the transportation of the troops became the responsibility of Colonel Baker. Wade begged off saying that he and the Committeemen were not military men. Yet, he persisted in the belief that Stone was responsible because he did not reinforce the troops on the Virginia side of the river. General Stone then asked at what point the troops should have been reinforced. Wade responded maybe from Edward's Ferry or even at Ball's Bluff. General Stone purposed that Colonel Baker had a

---

[108] Joint Committee Report, Vol. II, p. 426

vastly superior force at his disposal compared to that of the enemy. Wade seemed to have become defensive and stressed that he was stating "heads" and did not want to discuss these "heads". General Stone then invited the Committee to go to Ball's Bluff and see for themselves the impracticality of doing what they were suggesting: passing troops from Edward's Island to the right at that time.[109] Wade continued to stress that the Committeemen were not military men and Stone replied, "But you judge military men." Wade consistently used the term impeached to define all the "charges" against General Stone. Wade then went from the ridiculous to the sublime with the statement, " The evidence tends to *prove* that you had undue communications with the enemy by letters that have passed back and forth, by intercourse with officers from the other side, and by permitting packages to go over unexamined to known secessionists". In effect, the general was being accused of treason--- giving aid and comfort to the enemy in the presence of two or more witnesses during times of war (see Article III, Section II, of the United States Constitution). General Stone emotionally enunciated:

> That is one humiliation I had hoped I never should be subjected to. I thought there was one calumny that should not be brought against me. Any other calumny that anybody can raise I should expect, after what I have received; but that one I should have supposed that you personally, Mr. Chairman, would have rejected at once. You remember last winter when this government had so few friends, who had this city, I might almost say, in his power. I raised all the volunteer troops that were here during the seven dark days of last winter. I disciplined and posted those troops. I commanded them, and those troops were the first to invade the soil of Virginia, and I led them.[110]

---

[109] Joint Committee Report, Vol. II, p. 427(this exchange between Stone and Wade is contained on this page)
[110] Joint Committee Report, Vol. II, p. 427

Chairman Wade proclaimed that he was not so unjust, and that he had mentioned this to the Committee. General Stone reiterated that he could have surrendered the city of Washington and also stressed and restated his devotion and loyalty to the United States. He explained that the packages were goods and comfort items sent to Union prisoners of war held by the Confederate army in Virginia. Items such as blankets, tea, and money, were sent. The Confederates asked for the same consideration, Stone declared, and rightly so, that he felt obliged to comply. Some daguerreotypes were also sent over, after proper examination. General Stone stressed that all materials were properly screened for information, so that nothing that might be helpful to the Confederates would fall into their hands. Nothing untoward was allowed to pass over to the Confederates and neither were the Confederates allowed to send anything of significance to their captive and wounded on the Maryland side of the river.[111] General Stone gave explanation that the flags of truce were sent over and accepted only after Washington was telegraphed and gave their consent, stating that Stone could use his discretion in the matter. (See footnote 104, Major James Ratchford's statements from his memoirs)

The final "impeachment" was the so-called erection of formidable fortifications within range of federal artillery, which could easily have been destroyed. General Stone explained that these fortifications were empty and of no consequence. He informed the Committee that he had passed over the works in a hot air balloon and had more than casual knowledge of the fortifications, furthermore, a few pickets occupied only one of the fortifications. The Confederates had only three field guns, which were moved around the fortifications from time to time. Stone stressed the expense

---

[111] Joint Committee Report, Vol. II, p. 428

to the government of useless shelling and he also felt that he would be needlessly exposing the extreme firepower at his command to the Confederates. He wanted to use that power when it could be of greatest advantage to the army. General Stone inquired as to the source of this allegation of his failure to destroy fortifications. "Were they artillery officers", Stone inquired? Stone then informed the Committee that he had only two artillery officers in his command, and neither of these men had testified.[112]

Stone made several comments about Smoot's mill. This was a flourmill from which the Confederates were obtaining much needed flour. He informed the Committee that he could have easily destroyed it on any day. It was Stone's contention that if the mill were destroyed, the Confederates would simply go a few miles down river and purchase flour. The end result of the destruction would be a needless denial of private property to the owner of the mill. All of this suggested activity would have made no substantial difference, continuing he also explained that the local people were allowed to harvest crops on the islands in the river. This was allowed because his men could hardly be expected to stay on the islands all the time. This suggested occupation would have been dangerous and counterproductive, since he could have taken the islands at any time.[113]

This ended General Stone's testimony of January 31, 1862. He would not have an opportunity to speak to this Committee again until February 27, 1863. Much humiliation, emotional pain, anger, and the entire range of human feelings would be constant companions of Gen. Charles Stone for most of his remaining life. Yet, little did he know when he left the Committee on January 31st what was in store for him: Gen. Charles Stone's fate was sealed.

---

[112] Joint Committee Report, Vol. II, p. 432
[113] Joint Committee Report, Vol. II, p. 433

After giving testimony to the Committee, General Stone was, for a time, "out from under the gun". As his friend, General Fitz- John Porter set forth, "He was assured February 7th, by the Secretary [of War] that his explanation was satisfactory, his exculpation complete, no charges were being entertained, and that arrangements were being considered how to increase his command and responsibilities."[114] However, on February 8th, a vexing situation began to take shape. Allan Pinkerton, the detective-operative of the government during this period of history, informed General McClellan that he had questioned a Negro refugee. The man's name was Jacob Shorb, and the identity of Shorb is still unclear, but at any rate, Shorb claims to have overheard very complimentary remarks made by the Confederate command praising General Stone. General Nathan Evans is supposed to have said that, " General Stone was a brave man and a gentleman." Much of this was second and third hand information and even Pinkerton was somewhat suspicious of the report. When this information came to McClellan's attention he was on a short limb concerning the Stone situation. This report offered a possible way out for him and McClellan quickly passed the information to Secretary of War Stanton. Stanton viewed this as an extreme covert situation that had to be extinguished as rapidly as possible. [115]

The January 28th arrest warrant was activated and carried out. General McClellan sent the following message to General Andrew Porter, Provost-Marshal:

> You will please at once arrest Brig. Gen. Charles P. Stone, U.S. volunteers, retain him in close custody, sending him under suitable escort by the first train to Fort Lafayette, where he will

---

[114] Reunion of Graduates, p. 51
[115] Commanders, p. 42; Chronicles, p. 36; Longacre, p. 3

be placed in charge of the commanding officer. See that he has no communication with any one from the time of his arrest.[116]

This arrest warrant has a very strange command, given the person, the reason for the arrest, and the person issuing the warrant. Why would McClellan forbid General Stone communication, in light of the fact that McClellan had previously stated that Stone was an innocent man, a friend, and fellow officer? Did McClellan have something to hide? As T. Harry Williams puts it, "If the Radicals wanted a sacrifice, McClellan preferred that it be Stone."[117]

About 11 P.M., a detachment of about twenty soldiers from the 3rd U.S. Infantry came to General Stone's house on Seventeenth street, in Washington. The detail was under the command of Gen. George Sykes, the commander of the city guard. General Stone was informed that he was under arrest. He was livid with anger and rage and asked Sykes for the charge against him. Sykes of course could give no answer. The enlisted detail flanked General Stone and the return march began. The cadre past Lafayette Park, and then on to the Chain Building where Stone was placed in a solitary room, with an armed guard outside.[118] This, indeed, was strange treatment for a man who, less than a week prior to February 8th, was virtually cleared of any wrongdoing. On February 9th, A.M., General Stone was allowed to write a note to General McClellan requesting a copy of the charges against him:

> This morning about 1o'clock I was arrested by Brigadier-General Sykes, commanding city guard, and made a close prisoner by order, as I was informed, of the Major-General Commanding-in-Chief.

---

[116] OR, series I, Vol. V, p. 341
[117] Chronicles, p. 36
[118] Commanders, p. 30

Conscious of being and having been at all times a faithful soldier of the United States, I most respectfully request that I may be furnished, at as early a moment as practicable, with a copy of whatever charges may have been preferred against me and the opportunity of promptly meeting them.

Very respectfully, I am, general, your most obedient servant....[119]

Paradoxically, Stone held on to the expectation that McClellan would save him from this revolting turn of events. This simply was not going to happen. In an article published by the Milwaukee *Sentinel*, concerning the *Report on the Conduct of the War*, General McClellan was characterized in the following fashion: "General McClellan's evidence occupies a large number of pages, but the questions make two pages and the answers will make up one. His style of answering questions is amusing. He hesitates, and when he does give an answer, it is not of the character that will harm himself or anyone else."* Influential members of Congress attempted to get at the Joint Committee's role in this case, with the hope of freeing General Stone. Winfield Scott expressed complete outrage at the suspicion and arrest of General Stone. Members of Congress from Massachusetts, the aldermen from Boston, and many influential families sent letters to the President, to no avail. Senator McDougall from California requested a Court of Inquiry concerning the charges against the General, but Lincoln refused. Wade insisted that Stone was a traitor, and as a further insult, he attempted to use the Constitution to cover up the lack of evidence, claiming that in times of war, conclusive proof was not necessarily demanded for conviction. [120]

While being held at Fort Lafayette, General Stone was confined to a small room. After about a month and a half, Stone's health was noticeably in a state of decline. At

---

[119] OR, series I, Vol. V, p. 342
[120] Chronicles, p. 36; * Milwaukee *Sentinel*, April 4th, 1863

the request of his doctors and family, he was transferred to Fort Hamilton; a land based fort, where he could have fresh air and exercise. During this period of time, his family life deteriorated, and his marriage ended in divorce. For all intents and purposes, his life was in shambles. [121]

General Stone repeatedly requested copies of the charges, confinement orders, and letters that had passed between any authorities in Washington concerning his case, all to no avail. Typical of the request is Stone's letter of April 5th, 1862, "Colonel: I respectfully request of you a copy of the order by authority of which, on the 10th of February last, I was confined in Fort Lafayette." The request was addressed to Lt.-Col. Martin Burke, at Fort Hamilton. [122]

This "Kafka" like ordeal continued for another five months. Finally, Senator McDougall of California sponsored a rider to a military pay and allotments bill that addressed military officers in confinement. The bill was simple: charges must be made, in writing, within eight days, and a trial must take place within thirty days. The bill became law on July 17, 1862.[123] On August 16, 1862, 29 days after the bill became law Stone was released from Fort Hamilton, a free man. The Committee and Chairman Wade made no concessions, even when it was evident they had made a grievous error of fact and judgment.

After General Stone was released from Fort Hamilton, he spent some weeks with friends and family. Following a period of relaxation and reorientation, Stone began his quest to determine who was responsible for this assault against his career and character. No official would admit any involvement or responsibility. He was never granted a Court of Inquiry or anything close to a disclosure of evidence and charges. The only concession made to

---

[121] Chronicles, p. 36-37; Commanders, p. 44-45; Longacre, p. 3
[122] OR, series I, Vol. V, p. 343
[123] The bill was passed by the 37th Congress, 2nd Session

General Stone by the United States government and the Joint Committee was a third appearance before the Joint Committee.

On February 27th, 1863, General Stone appeared before the Committee and was asked if there was anything more he cared to tell the Committee. Stone expressed to the Committee that he was aware that he had been blamed for the entire situation at Ball's Bluff. He explained that he had sent an officer to the Virginia side of the river at about 5 P.M. to ascertain the situation of Colonel Baker. At this point, Colonel Baker's body, in the custody of a man claiming to be his nephew appeared. Stone then made his way to the crossing, where he encountered larger and larger numbers of men, wet and without weapons. Stone states that he came upon the chaplain of the 15th Massachusetts who was aiding the wounded. He inquired of the chaplain as to what had occurred on the Virginia side of the river. The chaplain replied that all the command was either killed or captured. General Stone revealed that he had concerns about Colonel Gorman's command, and the possibility that it would be overwhelmed. Furthermore, he did not know if General McCall would be there to assist Gorman. McClellan was notified of the situation and Stone's command on the Virginia shore and Edward's Ferry was withdrawn as rapidly as possible. Stone claims he then received a message from General McClellan to hold any territory on the Virginia side that he possibly could, if his men would fight. [124] Stone went on to say that he thought McClellan could, and would send immediate reinforcements.

When Colonel Baker's death was reported to General Stone, he then telegraphed General Banks for reinforcements. A dispatch was received from General McClellan that was in cipher. Stone relates that he did not

---

[124] Joint Committee Report, Vol. II, p. 488

have the key, since neither McClellan nor his chief of staff had relayed it to Stone's command, for this reason, much time was lost on this message. A second message was sent to McClellan requesting that reinforcements be sent to Goose Creek on the Virginia side. Stone continued by stating that all the while he thought McCall was near at hand. At 11P.M. General Stone testified that he received a telegraph dispatch informing him that McCall was not near his command during much of this time, and that reinforcements could not reach him on the Virginia side. General Banks, he was told, would probably reinforce him on the Maryland side of the river.[125] Stone was questioned about the reinforcement: did McClellan mean that Banks would be the reinforcement? Stone replied that he thought perhaps that he did, but that it was his conception [Stone's] that McCall was near and would supply the reinforcements. A dispatch "foul up" occurred at this point. The dispatched message asked if there was a good road from Dranesville to Edward's Ferry?[126] Stone felt the dispatcher meant Drainesville and sent a return dispatch stating that a good road existed. Later, he states that he realized that the dispatcher probably meant Darnestown, Maryland. This was disclosed to point out to the Committee how errors occur during the furor of battle. Stone was questioned as to why he had not mentioned this fact on January 31, 1862. He replied that he felt it improper, since McClellan had not authorized the release of these dispatches. He informed the Committee that General McClellan had

---

[125] Joint Committee Report, Vol. II, p. 488-489
[126] See Frederick H. Dyer, *A Compendium of the War of the Rebellion*, Vol. 1 (Dayton: Moringside Press, 1994, p. 896; also see Battles and Leaders, Vol. II, p. 124[map]; both sources list the spelling as Dranesville, General Stone consistently spelled the location as Drainesville

79

instructed him not to disclose any information concerning troop positions, orders, etc.[127]

The Committee asked a number of questions relevant to General McClellan's feelings about troops crossing from Edward's Ferry to Ball's Bluff. General Stone replied that he felt McClellan in fact, did approve of the crossing. Stone cited a reply to a telegram he had sent to McClellan, " I congratulate you and your command." Stone confirmed that he felt this congratulation signified McClellan's approval of the crossing.[128] The transportation question again arose and Stone said that he felt McClellan might have believed the boats were larger than was actually the case. He continued by saying that the dispatch sent to the McClellan was given after a trial run at Edward's Ferry on Sunday. In that trial, he was able to cross 250 men in ten minutes, however, completed under optimal conditions. The Committee then asked the logical question: why were more troops not sent over? Stone explained that Baker had a large part of the command, and there simply were no more available men to send.[129]

The question of General McCall's location, and his overall role and significance in this engagement was again brought to the forefront by the Committee. This was one of the four points at issue in the Committee's questioning of General Stone. The question was posed as to why Stone believed McCall was near his command. Stone expressed that he had received a dispatch stating that McCall was at Drainesville. This was received at 11 o'clock on Sunday. The dispatch continued, saying that McCall would send out reconnaissance in all directions. Stones furthered stated that this reconnaissance would have been in view to any observer from a high hill on Edward's Ferry. He maintained a lookout

---

[127] Joint Committee Report, Vol. II, p. 489
[128] Joint Committee Report, Vol. II, p. 489
[129] Joint Committee Report, Vol. II, p. 489

until late Sunday afternoon, expecting to see General McCall coming up on the Leesburg side of Goose Creek. Stone finished this segment of his testimony by stating, "As I was never advised of the withdrawal of General McCall, I supposed him to be near us, until late Monday night, when I was informed that no reinforcements would come from that direction."[130]

The questions of the Committee covered the same ground endlessly, over and over again. The question of discretion concerning Colonel Baker, the transportation and reinforcement problems, and next, the culpability question: was General Stone alone responsible for the Ball's Bluff defeat? Stone states that McClellan showed him a telegram he had sent to President Lincoln, to the end that he (McClellan) had examined the entire situation, and that General Stone was blameless in the whole affair. Stone confirmed that he felt with such support from his commanding officer, he saw no need to ask for a Court of Inquiry. Later, Representative Roscoe Conkling made an attack on General Stone on the floor of the House. Stone asked McClellan's advice about requesting a Court of Inquiry. General McClellan replied, "Write nothing; say nothing; keep quiet." [131] General Stone, on this advice, did not seek a Court of Inquiry.

A series of questions were asked about communications with the enemy, sending over persons with packages, and other items. General Stone called the Committee's attention to the testimony given previously by members of the 2nd New York Militia, and then explained the matter. He responded that he had communications with a Mrs. Mason, of Chestnut Hill, Loudon County, Virginia. Stone explained that he had received a "safeguard", or pass from the adjutant general of the army for Mrs. Betsey C.

---

[130] Joint Committee Report, Vol. II, p. 490
[131] Joint Committee Report, Vol. II, p. 492

Mason, and one for her daughter Caroline, and for their property, with orders to respect their persons and property. The safeguard or pass was signed by General Scott, and countersigned by one of the assistant adjutants general. The pass was sent to Mrs. Mason and she returned several letters to General Stone, which he answered. Mrs. Mason inquired as to how she could use the pass. She also informed the general that some of her livestock had been killed by pickets, and that they (pickets) had fired upon her overseer. Additional requests were made about the pass, trips to Washington, etc. A Mrs. Price also received a pass or safeguard from General McClellan, according to General Stone. Colonel Tompkins searched her baggage before she went over the river. A Mrs. White, whose husband was in the Confederate army, was allowed to go over to Virginia, after some debate, by General Stone. It was decided that she might signal the Confederates, or communicate in some way if she was held in Union lines. Of interest, Colonel Tompkins' family was boarding with Mrs. White at the time of her request. In addition, Captain DeCourcey, also of the 2nd New York Militia who had been so vehemently critical of General Stone, received Mrs. White back from Virginia, without General Stone's permission. [132] This is odd, in light of the fact that these two men did all in their power to smear General Stone's reputation. Colonel Tompkins was a "walk on", or volunteer to the Joint Committee hearings. He was never requested to testify, but simply interjected himself into the hearings. Both these men seemed to have had "axes to grind" against General Stone.[133] As Shakespeare so aptly phased it, "One face, one voice, one habit, and two persons."[134]

---

[132] Joint Committee Report, Vol. II, p. 494
[133] Joint Committee Report, Vol. II, p. 496
[134] Orsino in Twelfth Night

Additional questions were asked about exchanged papers, information, packages, and other such items. General Stone answered all these inquires with factual retaliations which relegated the questions to the level of gossip and misinformation. One previously unmentioned situation was brought up by General Stone, as opposed to the Committee asking for the information. A man by the name of Young was allowed to pass to an island below Edward's Ferry. The island had a large crop of grain and Young was allowed to work the grain fields in order to allow General Stone to procure forage for his division, and to prevent the Confederates from obtaining the forage for their use. Young was illiterate and could hardly have given the enemy valuable or accurate information, even if that was his intent. Explanation was also supplied concerning the so-called "returned slaves" testimony given earlier. Stone offered as testimony that the slaves stated that they had family members in Virginia or that they simply wanted to return to Virginia. General Stone allowed them to return, with no guard. The rebel pickets refused them and they returned to Stone's command. They were given food and shelter and allowed to do as the pleased.[135]

The Committee asked a series of redundant and extremely inane questions toward the end of General Stone's testimony. He was asked who ordered his arrest and all the circumstances connected with the arrest. One cannot wonder why such questions were posed to the general. This would be much like shooting an individual with a high caliber weapon and then asking why he is in pain. At any rate, the general recounted the unpleasant circumstances to the Committee: arrested on February 8th, taken to Fort Lafayette on February 10th, for forty-nine days, transferred to Fort Hamilton, held there until August 16th, 1862. No written or vocal arrest

---

[135] Joint Committee Report, Vol. II, p. 497-498

warrant or slate of charges was ever furnished. No orders were supplied to the general and he was left in limbo as to where or when he was to report for duty. Stone related that he remained an additional day at Fort Hamilton, after sending a telegram to Army Headquarters asking for orders that were never sent. Stone left his New York address with the Fort Hamilton authorities and remained another five days in New York, after which time he returned to Washington. No orders were forthcoming. Upon returning to Washington, the general went to the adjutant-general's office, and was informed that no orders were there for him, and that they had no knowledge of his arrest. He recorded his name on the duty roster and left his address.[136]

Stone then consulted the general-in-chief of the army, General Halleck. Halleck informed Stone he knew nothing of the arrest and could supply him no orders unless the War Department assigned Stone to his command. Stone's next stop was President Lincoln. The president was unable to tell General Stone anything of substance about his arrest. Lincoln simply said it happened under his authority, but he did not personally "do it."[137] Lincoln referred him back to Halleck, who then said the Secretary of War had informed him that the arrest was done on the recommendation of General McClellan. Stone wrote to McClellan who replied that the arrest was the work of the Secretary of War, Stanton, who supplied McClellan with a handwritten letter ordering the arrest. McClellan then told Stone that Stanton claimed that the Joint Committee requested that he make the arrest. McClellan related to Stone that the testimony of the refugee from Leesburg was read to Stanton on the night of his arrest, and Stanton reiterated the arrest request. McClellan vowed that he protested, saying the evidence was too "indefinite". McClellan claimed he had a copy of the refugee's statement

---

[136] Joint Committee Report, Vol. II, p. 500
[137] Joint Committee Report, Vol. II, p. 500

and name, which he would later send to General Stone. It was never sent. Stone ends his testimony by saying, "When I was arrested the general-in-chief—General McClellan—had that power. I know I should claim that power if any man under my command was arrested."[138]

General Stone remained in Washington from August of 1862, until May of 1863, but was not on active duty, yet still in the army. On September 7th, 1862, General McClellan wrote to Secretary of War Stanton:

> Sir: I have been applied to by General Stone for permission to serve with the army during the impending movements, even as a spectator. I have no doubt as to the loyalty and devotion of General Stone, but am unwilling to use his services unless I know that it meets the approval of Government. I not only have no objection to his employment in this army, but, more than that, would be glad to avail myself of his services as soon as circumstances permit.[139]

This request by McClellan was never acted upon by Stanton. A subsequent request was made by General Hooker for Stone's service in January of 1863, to serve as Hooker's Chief of Staff, but the request was not granted. General Burnside placed Stone as President of a Court-Martial in Washington. Verbal protests were made to the President and Secretary of War. The general was given an order on his way to the courtroom relieving him of the duty to appear but no reason why was given. Even though "wronged to the core", General Stone never sought public sympathy.[140]

It is not difficult to see that General Stone's family life suffered greatly as a result of this ordeal. Stone and his wife were divorced in 1862. In 1863, Stone married Anne

---

[138] Joint Committee Report, Vol. II, p. 501-502 (the series of events leading to and following Stone's release are included on these pages)
[139] OR, series I, Vol. V, p. 342
[140] Reunion of Graduates, p. 56

Granier. The couple ultimately had five children.[141] The general's life must have been extremely trying until the war's end. It must have seemed to General Stone that this unpleasant situation would never end.

Stone, at last, received a measure of redemption. He was assigned to the Department of the Gulf on May 6, 1863, at the request of General Nathaniel Banks. Stone served with distinction at Port Hudson and in the Red River Campaign.[142] The general took part in the battles of Sabine CrossRoads and Pleasant Hill. Gen. Thomas Ransom gave his appraisal of General Stone's efforts in his official report, "I desire to bear witness to the gallantry of Brigadier General Stone, who was on the left of the line with General Lee. He used the small force of Infantry to the best advantage in bravely but unsuccessfully endeavoring to repulse the overwhelming force of the enemy."[143] At the Battle of Pleasant Hill, Stone saved the army from a sure rout, by leading part of Gen. A. J. Smith's division in the charge which changed the battle.[144]

Even though difficult to believe, General Stone was relieved from duty on April 16th, 1864, and mustered out of Volunteer service and sent to Cairo, Illinois. From there, he was reverted to his regular army rank of colonel. He was then assigned an infantry brigade in the V Corps of the Army of the Potomac. The time spent at Fort Lafayette and Fort Hamilton had taken a told on Stone's health. Add to that the stress of the past eighteen months, his health was declining. On September 13, 1864, General Stone resigned his commission and retired from the army.[145]

---

[141] Longacre Biography, p. 4
[142] Warner Blue, p. 480
[143] Reunion of Graduates, p. 58
[144] Reunion of Graduates, p. 58
[145] Reunion of Graduates, p. 58; Longacre Biography, p. 4

In 1865, Stone went to work for the Dover Mining Company where he worked as superintendent of the mines in Goochland County, Virginia. This position fell through in 1869. The company went broke and General Stone found himself again in financial difficulty. On March 30, 1870, Stone accepted a position as Chief of Staff of the Egyptian Army, with the rank of Brigadier-General, and three years later became the *Ferik-Pasha*, one rank below Field Marshall. Stone was in the good graces of the War Minister, and also of the *Khedive*, becoming his Aide-de Camp. He worked tirelessly for the Egyptian government establishing schools, geographical societies, and other such worthwhile activities. He was awarded the Grand Officer of the Order of the Medijidich award by the Egyptian government.[146]

Benson John Lossing was the editor of the *American Historical Record and Repertory of Notes and Queries* during the 1870s. Mr. Lossing made a concerted effort to determine who was responsible for the injustice General Stone suffered. Many sources were consulted, and many records examined, to no avail. Even with General Stone's assistance, and that of the government, nothing of any substance was ever uncovered concerning the plight of General Stone.[147] No written charges, no arrest records, no exact account of who ordered the arrest, this would be a nightmare for anyone caught up in such a legal quagmire.

When General Stone returned to the United States, he went to work for the Florida Ship Canal and Transit Company, in the early 1880s. This position allowed the General to make use of all his engineering skills. He also did surveys for the state of Florida which sustained Stone and his family for about three years. He was happy during this time of his life, and some of the pain from the war had dimmed,

---

[146] Biographical Register, p. 218
[147] James S. Schoff Civil War Collection, Vol. 12 Letters and Documents, Clements Library, University of Michigan.

and things seemed to have improved markedly for the Stones.[148]

On April 3rd, 1886, General Stone entered into the final phase of his life. He was appointed Engineer-in-Chief of the Committee for the Construction of the Pedestal of the Colossal "Statue of Liberty Enlightening the World" on Bedloe's Island, New York harbor. This island is in sight of the military prison where General Stone spent a six-month segment of his life for an undetermined reason that has never come to the legal "light of day."

On October 28, 1886, unpleasant weather prevailed but the ceremony went on as scheduled. General Stone, riding a fine black horse, led a parade estimated at over 20,000. The parade went through the city of New York, past the reviewing stand of President Cleveland to the New York harbor, where the presidential yacht, *Dispatch*, which had carried the president and the official guests to New York, was moored. Tall ships formed a crescent in the harbor. The president accepted the gift on behalf of the American people. This must have been recompense, in some ways, to General Stone for a debt owed to him by his nation for anachronistic treatment shown to him in 1862.[149] A comment by the great bard appropriately describes the circumstances of General Charles Stone at this instant in time, "In thy face, I see the map of honor, truth, and loyalty".[150]

Many historians of the past have given their appraisal of General Stone's unjust arrest, "kangaroo hearing", and the events which followed the hearings. Carl Sandburg makes light of Lincoln's denial of any knowledge of the arrest and Stanton's role in the whole affair after two weeks in

---

[148] Biographical Register, p. 218; Reunion of Graduates, p. 59
[149] Kimberly A. Keefer, "Rekindling the Flame of Freedom", *American History Illustrated,* Vol. XIX, no. 6, October, 1984, p. 36
[150] King Henry in Henry VI, part 2

office.[151] The great Lincoln scholar, James G. Randall discusses Stone's great care to protect Lincoln in the early days of the war. Randall, like many, if not most, historians condemned the Committee and their role in this scenario of injustice toward General Stone. Randall gives a short segment from Senator James Blaine's *Twenty Years of Congress*. It was Blaine's conclusion that: "the testimony regarding Stone was not sifted by the Committee, that the case was ' prejudiced', and that the drive against the general was conducted in an atmosphere of rumor and 'victim-hunting mania'."[152] Randall goes on to explain that the Committee had pre-selected targets which they intended to expose. These targets were Stone, McClellan, and Fitz-John Porter, among others. The Committee also had its favorites, such as Fremont and Butler. Randall exonerates Lincoln, to a degree with the position that this Committee was a pain to Lincoln. He quotes Lincoln as stating, in a conversation to Ward Hill Lamon, that this Committee was "a marplot and its greatest purpose was to hamper my actions...."[153] Randall gives a quotation about the president from Zachariah Chandler, on December 8, 1862, "the Cabinet is weak & Lincoln weaker...."[154] From this exchange one can conclude that there was no fondness between President Lincoln and the Joint Committee.

From a view back into the history of the Ball's Bluff engagement, the death of Colonel Baker, the unjust arrest of General Charles P. Stone, who is accountable for the general's embarrassing and unjust disgrace? Without doubt, General George B. McClellan must take a share of the

---

[151] Carl Sandburg, *Abraham Lincoln-The Prairie Years and the War Years* (New York: Harcourt, Brace and World, Inc.), 1966, p. 282-283
[152] J.G. Randall, *Lincoln the President (* Dodd, Mead & Company*)*, 1952, p. 133; hereinafter cited as Randall
[153] Randall, p. 134
[154] Randall, p. 134

blame. McClellan attempted to defend Stone, and actually did so in private. When McClellan realized he might be next, he rapidly began to search for a scapegoat. The refugee from Leesburg who gave McClellan information about General Stone, which was inaccurate, was McClellan's pathway to personal exoneration concerning events at Ball's Bluff. He passed completely suspect information on to Stanton, who now had his "philosopher's stone" about the conduct of the army at Ball's Bluff.

Edwin Stanton must also share in the shame of this political dissolution, which disgraced and ruined an innocent man. How could Stanton, after a mere two weeks in office have arrived at such far-reaching conclusions? It is obvious that he was influenced by the Committee long before he became Secretary of War. Add this to the fact that General Stone was a known Democrat, from an influential Democratic family of Massachusetts. Stanton was a radical who intended to remake the nation, after the war, into the image that he believed to be the "correct image". This did not included influential Democrats, in or out of the army. The thought must have occurred to him to begin the process with General Stone's "exposure and conviction" for the imagined offenses he felt Stone had committed.

The Joint Committee on the Conduct of the War must also be held accountable for their actions and contributions to the Stone calamity. While a number of these men were lawyers as well as lawmakers, they totally and completely bungled and marred the testimony and related evidence. They allowed second and third hand accounts of events, hearsay accounts, biased evidence, and evidence from men awaiting trial for crimes committed within General Stone's command. They granted credence to information that any ordinary person would have immediately discarded as tainted and bogus. In addition, they denied Charles Stone his constitutional rights, under civil as well as military law. All of this was done under the guise of searching for the truth concerning the events that occurred at the engagement of Ball's Bluff.

President Lincoln cannot escape his role of omission in this affair. As president, Lincoln had the power under Article II, Section Two, Clause One of the United States Constitution to act as commander and chief of the military, and of the militia during times of war. He could have ended this unjust attack on General Stone with little difficulty. Even after the general was released in August, Lincoln could have given him a presidential pardon to end the situation and allow Stone to return to a semblance of normal life. Granted, a pardon might imply guilt, but General Stone labored under that banner for the remainder of his military life. Lincoln was aware of Stone's loyalty and devotion to the United States, and he is purported to have stated that "General Stone could never be disloyal". Lincoln shunned his responsibility to General Stone for some goal which eludes even the informed thinkers of this day, let alone General Stone's.

General Charles Stone died on January 24, 1887. He is buried at West Point. Somehow, this seems fitting. His life was forever altered by the events of October 1861, at Ball's Bluff. Another Union general, who had problems of his own, much like those of General Stone, gives an interesting account of the final days of the general. General John Pope, in his military memoirs gives the following account:

> I saw him, indeed dined with him, in New York in the Spring of 1883, the last time I ever saw him. He talked to me fully but uncomplainingly of his unhappy life and told me that it had only been within a few days that he had found out who had been his enemy and had caused his arrest and imprisonment. The only harsh expressions he used were in regard to this man, whom he

had always regarded as his friend and to whom he had talked of this matter more than once.[155]

General Pope does not name the individual referred to by General Stone. He states that under the conditions by which he received the information, he felt he should not reveal the name in question. He gives high praise to General Stone as a soldier and a human being.

It is unfortunate fact that General Charles Stone is a mere footnote in the overall magniloquence of the Civil War. His "time on the political cross" is unknown to most Americans. His is another unknown contribution to America's saga.

---

[155] John Pope, *The Military Memoirs of General John Pope* (Chapel Hill: University of North Carolina Press) edited by Peter Cozzens and Robert I. Girardi, 1998, p. 203

General Charles Smith Hamilton

GEN. CHARLES SMITH HAMILTON, U.S.

Charles Smith Hamilton was born on November 16, 1822, ultimately becoming a creditable soldier and one of the most ambitious and enigmatic generals in the Union Army. Hamilton's father was Zane Hamilton, and his grandfather was Dr. Hosea Hamilton, a member of General Washington's staff during the Revolution. He was a direct descendent of Gallatin Hamilton, one of Connecticut's first settlers, and his mother, Sylvia Putnam, was the niece of General Israel Putnam of Revolutionary War fame. Charles Hamilton assuredly had a military heritage, and it extended all the way back to the beginning of this nation.

The Hamilton family resided in Western New York until shortly after young Hamilton's birth, and most of Hamilton's early years were spent in Aurora, New York, part of Erie County where he attended the local schools and received a reasonably good education. On January 17, 1839, Hamilton was given a recommendation to attend West Point by his uncle, House Member Harvey Putnam from the Twenty Ninth Congressional district of New York. In his acceptance letter, young Hamilton replied, "I have the pleasure to accept my conditional appointment made by His Excellency the President of the United States." This could have simply been an error on young Hamilton's part, yet it seems he must have been aware that his uncle, not the president, appointed him to attend West Point.[1]

---

[1] United States Military Academy Archives, West Point; *Twenty-second Annual Reunion of Graduates of the United States Military Academy* (Saginaw, Michigan : Seemann & Peters Printers, 1891), p. 75; hereinafter cited as Reunion of Graduates

Hamilton's academic career at West Point was somewhat atypical. He finished his first year standing at number eighteen in a class of sixty students. In his second year he dropped to number twenty-three, one number ahead of Ulysses S. Grant, who later would play a major role in his military career. Hamilton graduated number twenty-six in a class of thirty-nine students.[2] This configuration is the reverse of most student achievement, and since Hamilton was an intelligent young man, no creditable explanation can be given for this circumstance. His behavior was very much in line all four years, receiving about sixty demerits per year, and additionally he seems to have been a serious student. Hamilton had ambitions to be placed in engineering after graduation, but this was not to be, instead he was brevetted a Second Lieutenant in the 2nd Infantry. Engineering was reserved for the upper ten to fifteen percent of the graduating class, for which Hamilton had the ability but lacked the drive to achieve.

After graduation, Hamilton was sent to Buffalo, New York from 1843 until 1845 and later to Copper Harbor Michigan (Fort Wilkins) from 1845 until 1846, after which he received a promotion to Second Lieutenant in the 5th Infantry. The Mexican War was about to erupt and his new promotion took him to the Mexican border. Hamilton was engaged in the Mexican War, in the beginning, with General Taylor at *Matamoras*, but Later his regiment was part of McIntosh's brigade, Worth's division. He served extensively in rather heavy combat situations, taking part in the battle of Monterey from September 21 until September 23. Later Worth's division became part of General Scott's army, and from March 9 until the 29th, 1847, Hamilton was a participant in the Siege of *Vera Cruz*. He received a promotion to First Lieutenant on June 30, 1847, after which

---

[2] United States Military Academy Archives, West Point

he then took part in the capture of San Antonio, on August 20, 1847. He was involved in the battles of *Churubusco* and *Molino del Rey*, in August and September of 1847. As a result of gallant and meritorious service in the battles of *Contreras* and *Churubusco*, he was again promoted to brevetted Captain, August 20, 1847. During the battle of *Molino del Rey*, September 7, 1847, Hamilton was severely wounded, afterwards serving as the Quartermaster of the 5th Infantry from March 1, until September 18, 1848. From this position, he went to Pascogoula, Mississippi, a state that would have great importance later in his military career. He was assigned recruiting duty from 1848 until 1850, leading up to his final assignment before leaving the army, which was in Texas at Fort Tower and Fort Belknap fighting Indians from 1850 until May of 1853. Hamilton resigned his commission in 1853.[3]

Immediately after the Mexican War, Hamilton married Sophia Shepard, of Canandaigua, New York. After his resignation from the army, the Hamilton's moved to Fond du Lac, Wisconsin, where the future general took up farming and established a manufacturing business producing flour and linseed oil. The family would later have six sons, and continued to reside in Fond du Lac until the beginning of the Civil War.[4]

At the beginning of the Civil War, Hamilton offered his services to the Union, which was quite appropriate for a man with his military background. Governor Randall of Wisconsin commissioned him a Colonel in the 3rd Wisconsin Infantry, and a mere six days later Hamilton was made a

---

[3] General George W. Cullum, *Biographical Register of the Officers and Graduates of the U.S. Military Academy at West Point* (Boston: Houghton, Mifflin and Company, 1891), p. 181; hereinafter cited as Biographical Register; Reunion of Graduates, p. 75

[4] Milwaukee *Sentinel,* Saturday, April 18, 1891 (Hamilton's obituary notice) hereinafter cited as Obituary; Biographical Register, p. 181

Brigadier of Volunteers. His first real duty was in the Shenandoah Valley and operations on the upper Potomac, from July 1861, until March 1862. At that time, he was part of the Peninsular Campaign in Virginia, where he became the commander of the 3rd division, III Corps, commanded by General Samuel Heintzleman, Army of the Potomac. This assignment would prove to be less than rewarding for the general, moreover, it would be the beginning of a countless number of controversies in which General Hamilton would be involved.

The Army of the Potomac was immersed in the Peninsular Campaign in the spring of 1862. The campaign had two major objectives: capture the Confederate capital and prevent the Confederate army from poising any consequential threat to Washington. On March 17, Hamilton's division was given the following orders:

> ...embark at Alexandria, and proceed to Fort Monroe with the following orders: You will, on your arrival at Fort Monroe, report to General Wool, and request him to assign you ground for encamping your division. You will remain at Fort Monroe until further orders from General McClellan. Should General Wood require the services of your division in repelling an attack, you will obey his orders.[5]

A major error of reconnaissance was somehow attributed to the III Corps commander, General Heintzelman, and to what extent, if any, General Hamilton was involved in this miscalculation is uncertain. The III Corps would be a major part of the Yorktown Siege of April 1862, but unfortunately, General Heintzelman was an "old guard" Indian fighter. The general was in his late fifties and most of his service was garrison duty and Indian fighting, and as experience goes he was "new" to this type of modern warfare. He had already experienced a less than stellar performance at First Manassas

---

[5] Official Records, Vol. XI/1, p. 6; hereinafter cited as OR

and was at the end of any real usefulness to McClellan's plans. The Peninsular Campaign, and the Yorktown Siege in particular, would prove to be his undoing as a corps commanding general.

The Confederate commander at Yorktown was "Prince John" Magruder, who actually was not an outstanding field commander, but on the other hand, was quite a "slight of hand" artist. Magruder had around 12,000 men in his command. He had major misgivings about the design of his battle lines, construction of his defenses, and other aspects of his position. He decided that he had to give the impression that his forces were immense in number. He proceeded to march a few regiments into and through a clearing, in full view of the Federal army, double-quick time, out of sight, and back into the clearing--- repeated innumerable times. General Heintzelman was completely deceived, and armed with this misinformation, Heintzelman reported to McClellan that a frontal attack was too risky and out of the question. McClellan then determined that a siege was in order, after which plans were put into motion.[6] Needless to say, there were other considerations and concerns about the siege: miscalculations concerning the Warwick River [even its exact location], bad maps, and McDowell's absence, to name a few. The report of General Heintzelman concerning Magruder's forces was a major factor in the initiation of the siege, and would play a role in his demise in the Army of the Potomac.

A sample of the animosity that took place between Hamilton and Heintzelman is exemplified in a message sent by Hamilton on April 13: [A reply to the Assistant Adjuntant-General]

---

[6] Bruce Catton, *Army of the Potomac: Mr. Lincoln's Army* (New York: Doubleday & Company, 1962), p. 107-108; hereinafter cited as Catton; Ezra Warner, *Generals In Blue* (Baton Rouge: Louisiana State University Press, 1964), p. 228

> ... your communication on this date, instructing me " to report more promptly when anything occurs in your front," and that "in case the enemy makes a demonstration similar to the one of yesterday you will open immediately a fire of artillery upon him;"...
>
> In reply, I respectfully say that in a former communication I have notified the commander of the corps that he would be promptly furnished with information of everything worthy of notice... The information called for this morning was furnished as soon as received in detail from the commander in the front, Colonel Poe, and that all the information was furnished.... (to General Heintzelman) [7]

Before the Yorktown siege ended on May 4, 1862, McClellan had endured about as much of General Hamilton's haughty and arrogant attitude as he could handle. On April 30, 1862, McClellan sent out Special Order No. 129, which pronounced: "Brig. Gen. Philip Kearny is assigned to the command of the Third Division of the Third Army Corps, in place of Gen. C.S. Hamilton, relieved. By order of Major-General McClellan." [8] Hamilton sought, and received political help with the problem of the loss of his command. The situation ultimately went to President Lincoln, who sent the following correspondence to General McClellan on May 21, 1862:

> I have just been waited on by a large committee, who presented a petition signed by twenty-three Senators and eighty-four Representatives, asking me to restore General Hamilton to his division. I wish to do this, and yet I do not wish to be understood as rebuking you.
>
> Please answer at once. [9]

---

[7] OR, Vol. XI/1, p. 362
[8] OR, Vol. XI/3, p. 129, Union Correspondence No. 6
[9] OR, Vol. XI/3, p., 185

General McClellan answered the President's request the next day, May 22, 1862:

> Your dispatch just received. The discipline of the Army will not permit the restoration of General Hamilton to his division. Since the matter is pressed as it is I feel obliged to state what I did not care to before, viz, that General Hamilton is not fit to command a division. The task before me is too serious to permit me to hesitate when called upon to express an opinion. The cause of his removal from this army was ample to justify me in the course pursued. You cannot do anything better calculated to injure my army and diminish the probabilities of success in the approaching battle now imminent than to restore General Hamilton to his division. I earnestly protest against any such action, and I trust that after this statement you will not think of sending General Hamilton back to this army.[10]

"Little Mac" stood his ground, but did not actually spell out the direct cause or causes for the general's removal, although the reason for this action on the part of General McClellan later came to light. Hamilton claimed that General Magruder was commanding a small force and that he [Hamilton] could easily carry a battle against Magruder's forces. McClellan declined the offer, and later, Hamilton complained to McClellan that his division was overworked and weak from being in the trenches for too long. He asserted that Fitz John Porter's much stronger division was given duty which was less demanding. Hamilton asked McClellan to refer the complaint to the Secretary of War, and he was summarily relieved of command. From this exchange it can be concluded, for a certainty, General Hamilton had friends in high places and he had no qualms about calling on these friends for favors. This would be his operational standard for the duration of his military career.[11] Hamilton was later assigned to Harpers Ferry after Jackson's attack on Banks.

---

[10] OR, Vol. XI/3, p., 185-186
[11] The Milwaukee *Sentinel,* Vol. XXI, February 2, 1864

General Hamilton was later given an assignment in the West. In a message from Halleck to General Rosecrans dated June 18, 1862, Halleck writes, "...General C.S.H. has been ordered to report to you."[12] The area of the assignment may simply have been where Hamilton was needed, but another possibility is the friendship between Grant and Hamilton, both West Point graduates in the class of 1843. If this was the case, Grant probably never suspected how this situation would turn out. Also of interest is the designation of initials as opposed to stating Hamilton's name and rank, leaving one to conclude that perhaps his reputation had preceded him.

Upon Hamilton's arrival in Mississippi in the last weeks of June 1862, attention was demanded by the various situations in which he found himself. Communication problems with General Hamilton seemingly were a major concern of the Union army. Rosecrans, in a telegram to Halleck explains, "Brig. Gen. C.S. Hamilton will bivouac near Ripley tonight, because there is no water on the road for 15 miles beyond toward Salem." In another telegram from General Elliott, Rosecrans' Chief of Staff, Hamilton is instructed, "... Sherman has been directed to advance with Hurlbut on Holly Springs, expecting that you will be able to reach there by Wednesday morning; you will proceed accordingly... Report frequently; send efficient officers to keep up your supplies."[13] No word was received from General Hamilton concerning either these request. On June 30, 1862, Sherman telegraphed Hurlbut stating, "I will move at 2 P.M., and expect to communicate with you at Lamar ... From Lamar you could detach a small mounted party to Salem and beyond to hear of Hamilton, whose division is in

---

[12] OR, Vol. XVII/2, p. 14
[13] OR, Vol. XVII/2, p. 48 (both telegrams are on this page, both dated June 29th, 1862)

advance."[14] Hear of Hamilton--- why would division commanders send out parties to "hear about" other division commanders? In a telegram of July 1, 1862, Rosecrans informs Halleck, "Nothing new from the front save a telegraph from Asboth saying it is said Hamilton is encamped 14 miles west ... Orders have been given to send a messenger to Hamilton. We have a regiment of infantry and a section of artillery at the Hatchie Crossing",[15] and General Hamilton, again, did not respond. General Asboth, commander of reserves, informed the commanding general, "The supply train for General Hamilton is moving forward on the Ripley road, and General Hamilton is reported but not authentically, encamped 14 miles from here...."[16] If General Hamilton could receive telegrams, it would seem he could also send them, granted there probably were areas where no lines existed, but that was not a problem for the other division commanders. This pattern of *"cavalier neglect"* of orders, procedures, and cooperation would be part and parcel of General Hamilton's behavior for the duration of his military career.

After the defeat at Shiloh in April of 1862, the Confederate army under the command of General Beauregard moved into northern Mississippi in an attempt to reestablish a command location. The area around Corinth developed into a highly desirable location for both armies, primarily because Corinth was an important railroad town. The Memphis and Charleston Railroad passed through Corinth while making its way to Chattanooga, and this doubtless was the Confederacy's major East-West line. The Mobile and Ohio Railroad crossed the Memphis and Charleston line at Corinth, while the M&O linked Kentucky with the Gulf. The Union was in a constant struggle to keep

---

[14] OR, Vol. XVII/2, p. 58
[15] OR, Vol. XVII/2, p. 61
[16] OR, Vol. XVII/2, p. 63

these lines operational, and finally under General Halleck, the Union gained control of Corinth on May 30, 1862. Halleck's forces numbered 110,000, and for this reason the Confederate army, of necessity, evacuated the town in near secrecy. Evacuation, however, did not mean a final withdrawal from Corinth, only a temporary disappearance. A larger and more important showdown would occur later.

The railroad repair required many infantrymen, removing them from military positions, and in addition, many days of repair work could be destroyed in a few hours by Confederate partisans, guerrillas, civilians, and other pro Confederate forces. These guerrillas were the basis for many small skirmishes, some engagements, and a few larger confrontations. In the midst of all this conflict, requiring expense, men, and time, the railroads were often not operational.[17] Guerrilla warfare can be very unnerving, because an army is usually unable to determine when or where, or if the strike will occur. It pulls troops from areas where they are needed and allows the enemy to plan larger engagements with far reaching consequences. This was the scenario which General Hamilton and the Army of the Mississippi faced in the summer of 1862.

In early July, Rosecrans began a reorganization of his command, in which Hamilton was assigned the command of the 3rd division. Rosecrans and Hamilton did not particularly dislike each other; they simply did not get along well together. Rosecrans felt that Hamilton was antagonistic and rebellious, hard to deal with, and Hamilton felt that Rosecrans was not the field general that he, Hamilton, could be if given the opportunity.[18] Throughout the month of July

---

[17] Catton, p. 304-305; *Battles and Leaders of the Civil War*, edited by Clarence Buel and Robert U. Johnson (New York: The Century Company, 1877-78), p. 717-718; hereinafter cited as Battles and Leaders
[18] William M. Lamers, *The Edge of Glory*, (Baton Rouge: Louisiana State University Press, 1961), p. 93; hereinafter cited as Lamers

Hamilton and the remainder of Rosecrans' command were busily engaged in dealing with the Confederate guerrillas. On August 14, Hamilton's division was assigned to the area of Jacinto, a village about twenty five miles southwest of Iuka.[19] Rosecrans was not overly please with Grant's assignments, since he had already experienced a convergence plan gone bad at Rich Mountain with McClellan. He was not completely sure how Grant might respond in a similar situation.

Braxton Bragg was the commander of the Confederate Army of the Mississippi, and Bragg intended to carry the war deep into Kentucky. He wanted no interference from Rosecrans' army in Mississippi when the offensive was launched. Bragg was convinced that Rosecrans could easily reinforce Gen. James Negley's division, which was stationed in Nashville. Negley's division was part of the Army of the Ohio, commanded by General Buell. In an attempt to prevent this reinforcement, Bragg ordered Gen. Sterling Price to position his Army of the West to prevent Rosecrans from moving into Middle Tennessee. General Price had a command of about 17,000 troops, and Gen. Earl Van Dorn, his immediate superior, was positioned at Holly Springs, and his army numbered about 7,000. Van Dorn suggested to Price that the commands converge at Rienzi and plan attacks on the Union forces in the area. Price had arrived at Iuka about the second week of September. On September 19, Price received Van Dorn's request, and he also received a message from General Ord on the 19th demanding surrender due a "stunning defeat" of Lee at Antietam. In his account of the battle Price states this demand was received early in morning of the 19th of September. The day and time are significant, because Grant had devised a plan to totally

---

[19] OR, Vol. XVII/2, p. 168; see OR Vol. XVII/2, Union correspondence # 7, for an account of the guerrilla attacks taking place during the summer months in Mississippi during 1862

destroy Price's army, which required Rosecrans to leave a force at Barnet's where the road to Jacinto turns northeast. His main assault force would met Price on the Fulton Road, east of the Jacinto Road, where the Tennessee River was seven miles north, and the forces of General Ord were located to the northwest, and Rosecrans would be coming from the southwest. To the east, the bridges crossing Bear Creek were destroyed. Hopefully, Price would be overwhelmed with no where to retreat. This plan hinged on attacking Price before Van Dorn could reach him with reinforcements, which made it imperative that Rosecrans carry out his orders on time, as instructed. Therefore, Rosecrans was instructed to marched early on the 19th and ordered to use two roads, but however, he used only the Jacinto or Bay Springs Road. On the evening of the 18th, Rosecrans received instructions from Grant to move as rapidly as possible, and to stay in communication with Ord. Grant went to Burnsville immediately thereafter, and Ord's troops arrived at Burnsville at about noon on the 18th, meeting Grant who was already there. Other forces under Gen. Leonard Ross' command arrived during the afternoon, but Rosecrans, as fate would have it, was delayed due to Stanley's second division being led to the rear of the commands of both Ord and Ross. Rosecrans was informed that Stanley was more than twenty miles from Iuka, thus Rosecrans decided to halt his forces for the night in Jacinto. He notified Grant that he would move his command at 4:30 A.M., also he informed Grant that he would probably arrive at about 1 or 2 P.M. on the 19th. Grant then instructed Ord to hold any action until Rosecrans arrived, and Rosecrans was informed that the Burnsville forces would attack at 4:30 A.M. Ord would declare later that he never received this message, which is possible. Unfortunately, Rosecrans was unaware that his reinforcements were in Burnsville, and for this reason Hamilton was immediately ordered to proceed up the

Fulton and Iuka Road. By about noon on the 19th, one of Hamilton's brigades had reached Cartersville.[20]

General Price gives his account of the battle:

> During the early part of the afternoon...my pickets on the Jacinto road were driven in. About 2:30 o'clock they reported the enemy were advancing on that road in force. I ordered General Little to send Hebert's brigade to meet them and soon afterward directed Martin's brigade to follow it... The line of battle was instantly formed and the fight began, and was waged with a severity which I have never seen surpassed... Hebert and Martin's brigades carried on the unequal contest not only successfully but gloriously. They drove the enemy from every position a distance of more than 600 yards, capturing 9 pieces of artillery and taking about 50 prisoners. They were finally staid in their triumphant progress by darkness just as the First and Third Brigades of Little's division reached the field....[21]

A brief note on General Hebert might be of value in an understanding of this battle. Hebert was a native of Louisiana, born in 1820, and was a graduate of West Point, class of 1846, and he had also served in the legislature of Louisiana. At the outbreak of the war, Hebert was a member of the 3rd Louisiana Infantry; a unit composed of mostly northern Louisiana troops, having taken part in the Battle of Pea Ridge and other early battles. After General Little's death, he became the commander of the division, and was later assigned to General Pemberton's forces at Vicksburg.[22]

General Henry Little's death was perhaps the major Confederate loss in the battle of Iuka. He was loved by his troops and as well by General Price, who states in his account of the battle that he was saddened by Little's death

---

[20] Lamers, p. 104-198; see Http://Americancivilwar.com (Mississippi Civil War battles) for a brief overview of the Battle of Iuka

[21] OR Vol. XVII/1, p. 127

[22] Terry Jones, "Louis Hebert", *The Confederate General* (Harrisburg: National Historical Society, 1991), Vol. III, p. 82-83

to the point that he asked not to be disturbed until dawn the next day. Little died instantly from a minie ball to the head.[23]

William Lamers, General Rosecrans biographer, states, "Had Hebert's brigade, which was in position, opened fire immediately, Hamilton would have been routed; but a pause enabled him to throw the Fifth Iowa, which led, across the road and to the right." Hamilton's account of the battle concurs with Lamers comment, and General Hamilton states:

> The head of the column had just finished ascending a long hill, from the top of which the ground sloped in undulations toward the front. A few hundred yards ahead, in line of battle, the enemy lay concealed in the woods. Hebert's brigade of 6 regiments lay athwart the road by which we were approaching; Martin's brigade of four regiments had been divided, and 2 of these regiments were thrown on the right of the Confederate line and 2 on the left, making 10 regiments in line of battle. At the commencement of the conflict, the other 2 brigades which had been ordered up had arrived on the field, making the whole strength of Little's division, 18 regiments ready for action before a gun had been fired.[24]

In his official report of the battle, Hamilton states:

> ...The battle thus opened with but three regiments in position (Fifth Iowa, Twenty-sixth Missouri, and the Forty-eighth Indiana). The rebels were commanded by Maj. Gen. Sterling Price in person, who arrayed against us no less than 18 regiments. I saw the importance of holding the position we had assumed, and gave each regi mental commander orders to hold every inch of ground at every hazard. As the remaining regiments of the First Brigade came up the hill I threw them into position to protect the flanks of our little line of battle.... The battle at this time had become terrific. The enemy in dense

---

[23] C.W. Dudley, *The Confederate Veteran*, October 1896, p. 354, gives an account of General Little's death. Dudley was the editor of the Inka *Vidette*

[24] Battles and Leaders, Vol. II, p. 734-735; Lamers, p. 110

masses bore down in front on the right and left, showing a determined purpose to envelop and crush the little line in front.[25]

In a later report, Hamilton further explains, "The fight became an infantry duel. I never saw a hotter or more destructive engagement." General Price planned to hit Hamilton's division with a frontal strike as well as a flanking movement; hence Price ordered three separate assaults. In the first rush, the artillery fire was held to prevent friendly fire deaths, but as the Confederates neared the Federal lines, they were caught up in close fire, sent in volleys. A second rush and for a second time, the Confederates were repulsed, but however, by this time the 5th Iowa had lost about fifty percent of its strength. At about this point, Rosecrans arrived and immediately sent Stanley's First Brigade in to assist, which was much needed. A third assault occurred, which made its way to three spiked field guns, and brought about the death of a large numbers of the cannoneers. It was now very near dusk dark, but the battle simply grew more deadly. Given the dusk, the dust, and the smoke, infantrymen could not determine who was Confederate or Federal. Somewhere between 6 and 7 P.M., the Confederates withdrew, even though the troops of both armies were very close and could actually hear the conversations of the opposing forces. Rifle fire continued off and on until at least 8:00 P.M., after which Hamilton's division was sent to the rear for rest and food. They had suffered the most intense fire of the battle and were very depleted in both numbers and effort.[26]

Price intended to renew the battle at daybreak the next day and he was certain of a victory. As stated earlier, Price spent the night at a friend's house, in a state of extreme grief over the death of General Little, and left word with Colonel Thomas Snead that he was not to be disturbed until

---

[25] OR, Vol. XVII/1, p. 91
[26] Lamers, p. 110-114

dawn. About 4:A.M. an important message arrived from General Van Dorn requesting that Price speak with Van Dorn's staff officer. Later in the early morning hours, his general staff convinced him that withdrawal was the prudent thing to do in light of the oncoming Federal forces. Finally, he acquiesced and the army escaped during the early hours to Baldwyn, and by 8:00 A.M. the entire army was out of Iuka.[27]

There is a considerable amount of variance concerning number of troops involved in this battle. General Hamilton states," I say boldly that a force of not more than 2,800 men met and conquered a rebel force of 11,000 on a field chosen by Price and a position usually very strong and with its every advantage inuring to the enemy."[28] Colonel Snead, of General Price's staff states, "In the battle of Iuka only two brigades of Price's army were engaged, Hebert's and Adams's brigades of Little's division… The aggregate strength of both brigades was 3,179 officers and men." [29] General Rosecrans' report of the engagement at Iuka is interesting. He states, "I conclude with the following brief recapitulation: We move from Jacinto at 5: a.m. with 9,000 men on Price's forces at Iuka. After a march of 18 miles attacked them at 4:30 p.m., and fought them on unknown and disadvantageous ground, with less than half our forces in action, until night put a stop to the contest."[30]

During all this furious fighting, with the smoke, the blood, and the confusion, General Rosecrans must have wondered about the whereabouts of Grant, Ord, and Ross and the other notably absent reinforcements. After the brutal fighting on late September 19, Rosecrans feared that a renewed attack was certain on the 20th, consequently he was uncertain that his current strength could ward off Price's full

---

[27] Battles and Leaders, p. 733
[28] OR, Vol. XVII/1, p. 93
[29] Battles and Leaders, p. 734
[30] OR, Vol. XVII/1, p. 24

troop contingent. Therefore, Rosecrans called a midnight staff meeting of his brigade and division commanders. He is purported to have said, "Where in the name of God is Grant?", concluding that a bayonet charge at dawn was his only hope.[31] Rosecrans was in fear of a disaster at the hands of the Confederate army, but near noon on the 20th, he got his answer as to Grant's whereabouts when he suddenly heard music and looked to see Grant's column arriving at Iuka. This was his first contact with Grant in over 36 hours; nonetheless, Grant immediately assumed command and was not happy with what he saw. Grant commented, "This was the first I knew of the Fulton Road being left open to the enemy for their escape", with this statement he ordered Rosecrans to institute pursuit.[32] This battle [Iuka] had far reaching consequences for Rosecrans in that Grant questioned not only why the Fulton Road was left open, but as well Rosecrans competence as a field officer. As to Grant's whereabouts, all that was ever offered as an explanation was simply that he and Ord never heard any battle noises and therefore assumed that the battle was yet to occur, and Ord supported this statement.[33] Grant states in his *Memoirs* that, "I was disappointed at the results of the battle of Iuka ---but I had so high an opinion of General Rosecrans that I found no fault at the time."[34] This would change very soon, altering General Rosecrans' future as a commanding general.

The losses in killed, wounded, and missing in the engagement at Iuka for the Federal forces are given as 790.

---

[31] Bruce Catton, *Grant Moves South*, (New York: Little, Brown and Company, 1960), p. 311; hereinafter cited as Grant Moves South
[32] Lamers, p. 115
[33] Lamers, p. 119
[34] Ulysses S. Grant, *Personal Memoirs of U.S. Grant* (New York: Dover Publications, Inc, 1995), p. 161; hereinafter cited as Memoirs

The Confederate losses in the same categories are 693.[35] This is at considerable variance with the number given by General Rosecrans in his report. In all likelihood, General Rosecrans' source of information for the Confederate numbers came from General Hamilton, whereby Rosecrans gives Confederate losses as over 1,600. Hamilton records losses for his division at 693, which is greater than the number given by Fox, which is 490. Fox list the 5th Iowa, 48th Indiana, and the 26th Missouri as regiments having taken part in the battle.[36] Stanley's 11th Missouri recorded losses of seventy-six.[37] *Battles & Leaders* list 588 for Hamilton's 1st Brigade and eighty-six for the 2nd Brigade. Stanley's 2nd division losses are given as ninety-three, and cavalry losses as one. A concluding figure of 790 is given for total Union losses in the battle.[38] Equally confusing, *Battles &Leaders* gives Confederate losses as 535, however, Lamers feels Confederate losses exceeded 1,400.[39] One must draw his own conclusions as to the accuracy of the various numbers given by noted sources for this battle. From a low of 535, to a high of 1,600 is a considerable span for the Confederate army losses. The Union Army numbers which are reported by the various sources seem to be more in sync with each other, nevertheless, the motivation of Hamilton for such inflated numbers concerning Confederate losses could only have been to inflate *his* less than sterling performance in this battle. The account of the battle is not so much one of poor generalship on Hamilton's part but rather one of intentional

---

[35] William F. Fox, *Regimental Losses in the American Civil War: 1861-1865* (Dayton: Morningside Bookshop Press, 1985), p. 544 & 550; hereinafter cited as Fox

[36] Numbers for the remaining regiments are inconclusive in Fox's account

[37] OR, Vol. XVII/1, p. 75 & 93; Fox, p. 432

[38] Battles and Leaders, p. 736

[39] Battles and Leaders, p. 736; Lamers, p. 115

misrepresentation of the numbers and a display of blatant egotism on the part of General Hamilton.

Within two weeks, the two armies who were engaged in combat at Iuka would again find themselves in a deadly struggle. During the early morning hours of September 20, the Confederate Army of the West, commanded by General Sterling Price escaped from Iuka to Baldwyn. Within the week Price had made his way to Ripley and linked his forces with General Van Dorn's Army of West Tennessee, and by virtue of Van Dorn's seniority he therefore took command of the combined armies. The Confederate force now numbered about 22,000-23,000.[40]

Corinth was staffed with an observational force of about 15,000 Federal troops, roughly the divisions of McKean, Davies, and Hamilton, who were assigned the duty to overlook an area of about fifteen to eighteen miles around Corinth. On October 1, the Confederates marched toward Corinth with the hope to capture Corinth and then move into Tennessee. The Federal army controlled Corinth as a result of a successful siege in April and May, plus additional defensive work had been completed at Corinth since the spring takeover. Federal forces now numbered about 23,000 at Corinth.[41] On the morning of October 3, Van Dorn's army was within a few miles of the city, occupying some abandoned field cover built by the army in the spring of 1862. Combat began almost immediately upon Van Dorn's arrival. The Union army was situated on the outskirts of the defense works of the city, still Van Dorn's army pushed the Federals back steadily for several hours. Shortly after the noon hour a hole developed between two of the Federal brigades whereby Rosecrans devised a trap of a sort for Van Dorn. He ordered Hamilton's forces into the fight, and McKean would withdraw until his right met Davies' left.

---

[40] Battles and Leaders, p. 760
[41] Battles and Leaders, p. 760

Stanley would then come in closer and link up with McKean, Hamilton would then face Chewalla and move left until he touched Davies' right. It was hoped that Van Dorn would move in toward Davies, allowing Hamilton to close in on his flank and end it all. Hamilton was given detailed instructions about the plan and informed that the timing was absolutely essential. If Davies was too early, Hamilton would be out of position, and if Hamilton was too early, his division would be in great danger. Things seemingly were going according to plan. Davies carried out his assignment flawlessly.[42] Price was decimated by Davies men, then at about 3:00 P.M. a brigade of Stanley's division came to support Davies. In the process of alignment of his forces, Davies was again attacked but "toughed it out" until dark. Van Dorn thought he was facing one division and was unaware that Hamilton and Stanley were also present. At this point, plans went awry and confusion reigned. Hamilton received an order from Rosecrans informing him to," make a flanking movement, coming to the left of Davies". He was also told to hold back a few regiments, and examine and reconnoiter the ground. Hamilton refused the order claiming he could not understand it. Two additional men were sent by Rosecrans with instructions---both died in the process. Rosecrans ordered his chief of staff, Colonel Arthur C. Ducat, to go a second time to explain the order and even included a map, finally at last, Hamilton moved his troops, Sullivan's brigade, encountering fierce fire from Van Dorn army. All in all, Hamilton's delayed flanking movement had absolutely no impact on the battle, but his actions exemplified his self assurance that he knew better than those in command, regardless of the situation.[43]

Hamilton declares that at 3:30 P.M. he received an order from General Rosecrans, which stated:

---

[42] Lamers, p. 138-139
[43] Lamers, p. 140-141

A cavalry charge, much like many General Hamilton directed, depicted by Edwin Forbes

Supplies and military necessities as it might have occurred at the Battle of Iuka, Mississippi in September of 1862

Library of Congress

General Stephen A. Hurlbut

> General Hamilton: Davies appears to have fallen behind the works, his left being pressed in. If this movement continues until he gets well drawn in, you will make a flank movement, if your front is not attacked, falling to the left of Davies when the enemy gets sufficiently well in as to have full sweep, holding a couple of regiments looking well to the Purdy road...."Respectfully returned. I cannot understand it. -C.S. Hamilton, Brigadier General Rosecrans returned it to me indorsed as follows: "Ducat has been sent to explain it. W.S. Rosecrans, Major General—S.C. Lyford, Acting aide-de-camp[44]

Hamilton declared that he felt the order would have placed his division either in front or in the rear of Davies' division, destroying any chance of a flanking movement. In addition, Davies' would have been unprotected on the right and the road to Corinth left open. A second major controversy involving General Hamilton and General Rosecrans developed during the battle of Corinth. Hamilton states:

> Between 8 and 9 p.m. a staff-officer brought me the following order:
> "Place your batteries on the Purdy road at 10 p.m. and play them two hours in a north-west direction with shot and shell, where the enemy is massed, and at midnight attack them with your whole division with the bayonet. W.S. Rosecrans, Major-General"[45]

Hamilton claims that he told the staff officer [Colonel Ducat] that the order could not be carried out until he discussed it with General Rosecrans. He continues, stating, "An hour passed and the officer who brought the order returned, bringing General Rosecrans with him." He also claims that General John Sanborn and others present overheard the following conservation:

---

[44] Battles and Leaders, p. 757
[45] Battles and Leaders, p. 758 (this order does not exist in the *Officials Records*)

> General Rosecrans (savagely): General Hamilton what do you mean by disobeying my order to attack the enemy?
> General Hamilton: General Rosecrans I am ready to execute your order, but there is too much at stake here to be risked by a night attack…It is dark in the forest—too dark to distinguish friend from foe….
> General Rosecrans (after a few minutes of reflection without reply): Hamilton, you are right. Place your division as you suggest, and others shall be place accordingly.[46]

Ducat proclaims that he never carried such a message, and there is no mention of this occurrence in the reports of Hamilton, Rosecrans, Sanborn, or any other officers who might have been present in the *Official Records*.

General Rosecrans made plans for the attack that was certain to occur on October 4. Van Dorn had scheduled the attack for dawn, but delayed it until 9:00 P.M. because General Louis Hebert was ill. October 4 became an artilleryman's clinic. The Confederate Army suffered heavy losses and batteries Powell and Robinett were stormed and vicious hand to hand combat took place. Even though the battle "waxed and waned" the Confederates were ultimately pushed back and finally forced to retreat. Rosecrans delayed pursuit until October 5, and Grant was furious at this decision. In his *Memoirs*, Grant writes:

> Rosecrans did not start in pursuit till the morning of the 5th and then took the wrong road. Moving in the enemy's country he travelled with a wagon train to carry his provisions and munitions of war. His march was therefore slower than that of the enemy, who was moving toward his supplies. Two or three hours of pursuit on the day of battle, without anything except what the men carried on their persons, would have been worth more than any pursuit commenced the next day could have possibly been.[47]

---

[46] Battles and Leaders, p. 758 (there is no record of this conversation)
[47] Memoirs, p. 163

On October 27, Rosecrans took over the command of General Buell's army in middle Tennessee, which would ultimately become the Army of the Cumberland. Grant states in his *Memoirs*, "As a subordinate, I found that I could not make him [Rosecrans] do as I wished, and had determined to relieve him from duty that very day."[48] Conversely, Grant was in high praise of his old classmate Charles Hamilton and recommended his promotion to Major-General.

Hamilton seems to have emerged from the battle of Corinth as a hero of sorts, and this is somewhat odd, given his behavior. A sidelight of Hamilton's demeanor during the battle scene is given by Sylvanus Cadwallader, the newspaper reporter, and personal friend of General Grant. Cadwallader relates that he spent several days with General Hamilton, at his command headquarters. He writes, "He always entertained royally, but on that occasion the dinner service equalled the bill of fare. He had elegant ware on the table, silver plated knives and forks, some good glass ware, a set of approved champagne glasses, white table linen, and a smart contraband to wait upon the mess." *This is war?* Cadwallader continues, "It seemed like civilization to be seated at such a table, and when dinner ended and the post-prandial chat was stimulated by excellent cigars, mud, rain, and "hardtack" was forgotten."[49] Cadwallader gives an account of General Hamilton's command as to its relationship with the local people in Mississippi and Tennessee. He writes:

> Gen. Hamilton's command behaved even worse than McPherson's. Its line of march from Corinth to Grand Junction was marked nearly every mile of the way with burnt buildings and fences, and was literally shown by clouds of smoke in

---

[48] Memoirs, p. 164
[49] Sylvanus Cadwallader, *Three Years with Grant* (Lincoln: University of Nebraska Press, 1996), p. 16; hereinafter cited as Cadwallader

daylight and pillars of fire by night. It had an immense concourse of camp followers who stole horses, mules, and vehicles along the route for their own transportation, and robbed houses of everything they fancied. Many infantry regiments had scores of animals loaded with mess stores usually carried in haversacks, and with the arms and accoutrements of men in the ranks[50]

Cadwallader continues and explains that he feared Grant would be upset after reading this article in the Chicago papers. He later talked with Grant who confessed that he was powerless to stop such behavior and admitted that it was shameful. Grant contended that the regimental commanders alone were in a position to control such outlawed behavior.

The battle of Corinth was truly a major confrontation for both armies. Union losses in killed, wounded, and missing [includes prisoners] exceeded 2,300. Confederate losses in the same categories were 4,838.

On October 24, 1862, General Hamilton became the commanding officer for the District of Corinth, part of the XIII Army Corps, Army of the Tennessee. This position was short lived, in a sense, because Hamilton served in this slot for about one week. On November 1, he became the Left Wing commanding officer of the XIII Corps, and this was, of course, a position given by General Grant. Whether this promotion was given for ability, loyalty, friendship, or all of these, is difficult to determine, nevertheless, Hamilton's star was rising.

After the defeat of the Confederates at Corinth, Grant began to contemplate the possibility of a move on Vicksburg, primarily because the fall of Vicksburg would be a major step toward ending Confederate influence in the west, if not an end to the war in that area. Grant suggested to General Hamilton on October 25, to send a small force to destroy the railroad south of Rienzi all the way to Tupelo,

---

[50] Cadwallader, p. 20

and he [Grant] also intended to send cavalry in force to Tupelo. Hamilton felt, and reported to Grant, that Price intended to attack Corinth, based on information from deserters who reported that Price had been reinforced by recruits and veterans from Texas and Arkansas. On October 25, Grant telegraphed Hamilton stating that Price was moving toward Bolivar with a considerable force and was within four miles of Grand Junction.[51]

On November 1, Hamilton was instructed to move on Grand Junction, but he also was given some latitude in this movement--- if the enemy was north of Grand Junction, he could consider a move on Bolivar, in addition, McPherson was also to move toward Grand Junction. Hamilton telegraphed Grant asking for maps, claiming that, "Rosecrans carried off the maps that were most needed." Grant ordered the attack to travel by way of Pocahontas, and for this reason Hamilton was instructed to hold the bridge at Pocahantas with a cavalry force. Grant informed Hamilton that he believed Bolivar would be attacked within forty-eight hours, Hamilton therefore, was to have three divisions ready to march with three days rations.[52]

On November 2, Hamilton reported to Grant that he would reach the Tuscumbia, near Pocahontas by nightfall, and related to Grant that he would communicate with McPherson on November 3. If the Confederate army was in control at Holly Springs, Sherman's forces [McPherson] would be essential for any hope of a successful attack. On the same day, Hamilton sent three divisions toward Bolivar, reported that he was in communication with McPherson, but no enemy was in sight. In addition, on November 3 Hamilton received information that Price was, in fact, present in Holly Springs with a large force.[53]

---

[51] OR, Vol. XVII/2, p. 293
[52] OR, Vol. XVII/2, p. 312
[53] OR, Vol. XVII/2, p. 318

On November 4, Grant sent a rather detailed order to Hamilton. He was instructed to camp about two miles south of Grand Junction where he and McPherson were to connect and extend a line to Wolf River. They were to seize the bridges, and rebuild those that were destroyed, send cavalry to make reconnaissance movements toward Holly Springs, and attempt to also check any movement in Ripley. It was reported by General Halleck that a large troop movement was underway from New Orleans and that a force from Helena was moving toward Grenada.[54] Verification was needed to establish the correct movement to handle this potential problem.

Hamilton sent Quinby's division to carry out the reconnaissance, and afterwards he reported to Grant that deserters from the 5th Kentucky Infantry informed him that Price was in the process of evacuating Holly Springs. The deserters claimed that Price had confirmed information of the Federal troop movement and left Holly Springs the next day, November 5. On November 9, McPherson notified Grant that Quinby had not arrived and couriers had been sent out to find him. Hamilton telegraphed Grant that Quinby was to join McPherson at Lamar and that he had camped at Davis' Mill on November 8. He [Hamilton] appeared rather unconcerned about Quinby's whereabouts and seemed to be astonished that McPherson was concerned.

Faulty information seems to have a life of its own during a war; a case in point being that Hamilton reported to Grant that an officer came in from Jackson and said that France and England had formally recognized the Confederacy. He also implanted a little gossip to arouse Grant's suspicions, with information that he had received a letter from Wisconsin which purported that regiments from Pope's command and some Wisconsin regiments had been

---

[54] OR, Vol. XVII/2, p. 320

assigned to McClernand.⁵⁵ Grant had long felt that McClernand was incompetent and should not be given an independent command. Hamilton might have felt that this information would ensure his position in Grant's command. This seems to have been part and parcel, standard operating procedure, for General Hamilton--- if there is no news, invent some.

On November 11, Grant ordered Hamilton to draw rations and be prepared to move when ordered. Hamilton's cavalry commander, Col. Albert Lee, had been ordered to move toward Holly Springs, and frankly Colonel Lee had some apprehension about what he might find there. For that reason Grant sent five cavalry companies, and Hamilton ordered a brigade and a battery for Lee's support. Grant stressed that he only wanted an advance made to Holly Springs.⁵⁶

Grant was in a unique and unusual situation in Mississippi during November and December of 1862. He could probably have extended his lines from the Tennessee and Mississippi state line as far south as he desired. He had, however, a rather serious constraint. Grant was limited as to how far his supply lines extended. The further south he extended his lines, the thinner his supplies would be, making it was a very precarious situation. On November 9, Hamilton had expressed to Grant his concern about supplies, exclaiming that "Quinby took all the bread, there being only enough for his division."⁵⁷ Since Grant was a military realist, he felt that Oxford, at that point in time, would have to be his southern most point. ⁵⁸

---

⁵⁵ OR, Vol. XVII/2, p. 330
⁵⁶ OR, Vol. XVII/2, p. 343
⁵⁷ OR, Vol. XVII/2, p. 329
⁵⁸ Robert G. Hartje, *Van Dorn: The Life and Times of a Confederate General* (Nashville: Vanderbilt University Press, 1967), p. 253; hereinafter cited as Van Dorn

By November 29, Holly Springs was in the hands of the Union Army and Grant established his headquarters there on the 29th. On November 26, Grant had sent a message to General Hamilton [as well as to Sherman and McPherson] concerning command movements. Hamilton was to move his wing southward, using the most easterly roads available for the artillery. Quinby was to leave from Moscow, leaving nothing behind, while Sherman was ordered to leave Memphis on the 26th, and was to be southwest of Holly Springs to meet Hamilton and McPherson when they arrived. McPherson and Hamilton would be roughly following the direction of the Mobile and Ohio Railroad. As they passed near Holly Springs, Hamilton and McPherson encountered only token resistance. Grant now had all three wings of his army south of Holly Springs; in addition Oxford was in Federal hands by December 3, 1862.[59] Grant's Vicksburg plans were beginning to come into sharper focus, for this reason, he had to maintain his supply lines and find a better supply delivery system for the future. At present, materials had to be routed via Holly Springs, from Kentucky. This was very slow, dangerous, and inefficient, and if he hoped to take Vicksburg, he had to do better. Hamilton viewed himself as a major component of this future campaign. In fact, he visualized himself as a corps commander. His blind ambition would lead to major problems with Grant as well as other members of the high command very shortly.

General Hamilton's cavalry commander, Colonel Albert Lee, played a significant role in the engagement at Coffeeville, Mississippi on December 5, 1862. As early as November 4, Colonel Lee had pushed Van Dorn's pickets out of La Grange and Grand Junction. After a meeting with General Pemberton, Van Dorn promptly moved his forces across the Tallahatchie River and completely evacuated

---

[59] OR, Vol. XVII/2, p. 362; Cadwallader, p. 27; Grant Moves South, p. 330-331

Holly Springs. Lee occupied Holly Springs on November 13, and the Federals had complete control of the city by November 29. In fact, Grant established his headquarters in Holly Springs, as stated previously. Grant pushed the Confederates from Abbeville in the direction of Oxford, which pushed Van Dorn to the Coffeeville area. General Hamilton, on December 1, telegraphed Colonel Lee, "Yours received. I will send forward a brigade this p.m. and hold two more brigades in readiness to move. It looks like evacuation in earnest.... I want you with your whole force to pursue on the other side...."[60] The "other side" was a reference to the other side of the Tallahatchie River. General Van Dorn was moving his forces toward Grenada, south of Oxford, a necessary move under the circumstances he now faced.

Coffeeville is south of Oxford, on the Mississippi Central Railroad line, and it was Van Dorn's retreat route to Grenada. He had not yet evacuated all of his forces when elements of the Federal army arrived on the scene near the town. The pursuit of the Confederates began on December 2 with the 1st Cavalry Brigade, under the command of Colonel Albert Lee, along with Colonel Lyle Dickey, commander of the 4th Illinois Cavalry, and the 2nd Cavalry Brigade, under the command of Colonel Edward Hatch, comprised the contingent chasing Van Dorn's army. Colonel Lee was at Abbeville on the morning of December 2 and by late afternoon of December 2, Lee was near Oxford and in a sharp skirmish. The Confederates were driven from Oxford, and Lee occupied the town that night. On the morning of December 3, the entire Federal force pushed down the major Coffeeville road. Colonel Grierson, from General Sherman's wing of the XIII Corps was now present for duty, and by 9 P.M. on the night of December 3, Lee's command was eight

---

[60] OR, Vol. XVII/2, p. 373

miles below Oxford. Colonel Hatch reported that the Confederate army had destroyed the main Coffeeville bridge over the Tallahatchie River, and since Hatch was about eighteen miles from Oxford, couriers were dispatched ordering Hatch and Lee to combine forces and advance on the enemy. Hatch and Lee met at Water Valley, a small hamlet. Hatch had arrived there first and discovered a strong Confederate force, and he was compelled to withdraw. On Friday morning, December 5, Colonel Lee, followed by Colonels Mizner and Hatch all advanced on the same road toward the enemy.

At about 2 P.M., the Federal force came upon the rear guard of the Confederate force, a contingent which was protecting Van Dorn's retreat to Grenada. About one mile from Coffeeville, the Federal artillery threw a few shells toward the enemy. Suddenly, the Confederates opened up with at least four, and maybe even six artillery pieces. The Confederate infantry launched a hot torrent on the dismounted Federal skirmishers, almost instantly the Federals were catching severe fire from all directions. They realized they had encountered a large, well-led Confederate contingent that they were not prepared to deal with. The Federals, in sheer self-defense, withdrew to a field about one and one-half miles from the front. The fighting ceased, but by this time it was night. General Lloyd Tilghman, 1st Brigade commander in General William Loring's division, had ordered a charge into the Federal position. The 9th Arkansas and the 8th Kentucky Confederate Regiments had given the Federals a review in close quarters tactics. General Tilghman was a dedicated soldier not to be taken lightly, as Lee and the other Union troops soon found out. This short struggle was all Van Dorn needed to advance his forces to

Grenada. Van Dorn later remarked to General Pemberton, "the enemy will be careful how he comes up again."[61]

Coffeeville was not an exceptionally large battle. The Federal cavalry numbered about 2,500-3,000. General Tilghman's confederate force probably was about the same number. In his official report, Colonel Dickey gives his killed, wounded, and captured figure as one hundred and fourteen. Confederate losses in the same categories are thought to have been around fifty. This was the first Federal defeat, on this scale, in the west since Shiloh. Colonel Albert Lee had received a promotion to brigadier general on November 29, 1862. He, therefore, was the only Union general in the engagement.[62]

The Confederate army was struggling at this point, and Van Dorn could do nothing but watch Grant occupy Oxford and Coffeeville. In reality, the situation was probably worse than the Confederates envisioned. Grant immediately began to make preparations to move further south toward Vicksburg, and as part of this preparation on December 19, sent the following message to General Hamilton, "…detach two brigades from your command, one from Quinby's and one from Ross' division, to proceed to-morrow to Pontotoc, Miss., taking five days' rations…Arriving at Pontotoc, the officer in command will cause reconnaissance to be made as far to the south and east as practicable…."[63] On December 21, Grant instructed Hamilton to send the divisions of McArthur and Ross to Corinth, and to destroy all mills along the way, also they were to destroy or remove any and all means of supporting an army.[64] All of these plans had one significant

---

[61] Much of this is the account of General Lyle Dickey, Fourth Illinois Cavalry, OR, Vol. XVII/1, p.492-495; also see OR, Vol. XVII/1, p. 503 (Van Dorn's account); also see Van Dorn, p. 252
[62] OR, Vol. XVII/1, p. 492-495; also see WWW.Civilwar.lsu
[63] OR, Vol. XVII/2, p. 345
[64] OR, Vol. XVII/2, p. 451

hitch, which would impact on General Hamilton's plans for corps, or independent command in the future. General John McClernand was becoming more impatient for a command, fully expecting it to be an independent command, while Grant was equally determined that McClernand would never be awarded such a command. McClernand had immense political influence and much favor with the president, since both hailed from Illinois and McClernand was a former member of Congress. He could not be ignored. Thus, on December 18, 1862, Lincoln notified Grant, by way of the War Department, that his command was to be divided into four army corps. The XIII Corps would be commanded by McClernand; the XV Corps would go to Sherman; the XVI Corps to Hurlbut, and the XVII Corps to McPherson. Where was Hamilton's Corps, what had happened, how could Hurlbut or worse yet McClernand, a politician with no military experience, be given a corps command while he did not receive one? And McPherson, well, this simply had to be a mistake, it could not be true. On December 22, 1862, Hamilton was assigned the position of Left Wing Commander of the XVI Army Corps. For a brief period, January 10, 1863 until February 5, 1863, Hamilton was the Commander of the XVI Corps. Hurlbut, the former commander of the Corps, returned on February 5, 1863, and held the position as commander of the XVI Corps until April 17, 1864. [65] As a result of these new command assignments, confusion and contempt would prevail, and Hamilton's bitterness would continue to simmer and enlarge.

On January 15, 1863, General Hamilton was given the command known as the District of West Tennessee that included the Districts of Columbus, Jackson, Corinth, and Memphis. The command headquarters was to be Memphis;

---

[65] Frederick Dyer, *A Compendium of the War of the Rebellion*, Vol. I,(Dayton: Broadfoot Publishing Company/ Morningside Press, 1994), p. 502; hereinafter cited as Dyer

still, Hamilton was very displeased with this arrangement. He could not dare challenge Sherman as a corps commander, but he reasoned that he might have been promoted to Major-General before Hurlbut. Therefore, he began his attack for the XVI Corps position. If Hamilton was anything, he was a master at finesse, a prime example being a telegram sent to Grant on February 9, expressing his good wishes on the Vicksburg campaign. He closed the message with, "I hope it may be added to the laurels which belong to you as the most successful general of the war."[66] Unfortunately for Hamilton, it had no effect, because if there was ever any doubt about the command of the XVI Corps, it ended on February 11, with Special Orders, No. 30, which stated:

> In pursuance of Special Orders, No. 30, from Headquarters Department of the Tennessee, dated Young's Point, La., February 7, 1863, Maj. Gen S.A. Hurlbut hereby assumes command of all the forces in the Districts of Memphis, Columbus, Jackson, and Corinth, which forces are temporarily attached to the Sixteenth Corps....[67]

If this was not bad enough, on February 17, Hamilton received a message from General Hurlbut with more of what he considered demeaning news. Hurlbut ordered, "Maj. Gen. C.S. Hamilton is hereby assigned to the command of the troops in the Districts of Corinth and Jackson...."[68] His command had been severed in half. Hamilton established his command headquarters at Corinth and continued to send messages, make assignments, and fight the war, so to speak. On February 21, Hamilton reported the movement of the Confederates forces on the east side of the Black River and his suspension of cavalry movements to General Hurlbut. On February 25, a report was sent to Hurlbut concerning an

---

[66] OR, Vol. XXIV/3, p. 41
[67] OR, Vol. XXIV/3, p. 45
[68] OR, Vol. XXIV/3, p. 59

attack on Tuscumbia, but the report also contained information on the evacuation of Vicksburg, and the replacement of Bragg by General Joseph Johnston.[69] On the same day Hurlbut sent a message to Grant asking for confirmation as to whether Hamilton had been ordered to investigate the misconduct of the 7th Kansas Cavalry at Somerville. Hurlbut concluded with," Hamilton says he has received no such order," but on January 20, General Grant had sent Hamilton a message stating:

> Complaints have come in from Somerville from the few Union men of the outrageous conduct of the Seventh Kansas, and in one case of Colonel Lee's conduct where he was informed of the status of the party… If there are any further complaints, well substantiated, I wish you to arrest Colonel Lee and have him tried for incompetency and his regiment dismounted and disarmed.[70]

Hamilton had surely received General Grant's order, although granted, it is possible he simply had no recollection of having received the order. Nevertheless, Hamilton continued to carry out his duties, sending reports of various Confederate movements and activities to General Hurlbut.

March 11, 1863, was the day, after which, General Hamilton's usefulness was at an end for the Union Army. Hamilton sent a number of very threatening, abusive, and egotistical telegrams to General Hurlbut. In what was most likely the first telegram, Hamilton wrote, "I am authoritatively advised from Washington of my confirmation as major-general, to rank from September 19, 1862. Will you please advise me of date from which you are confirmed?" In short, if Hurlbut conformation was any date after September 19, Hamilton implied that he was his [Hurlbut] superior and

---

[69] OR, Vol. XXIV/3, p. 63-64
[70] OR, Vol. XXIV/3, p. 68 (Hurlbut's question); OR, Vol., XVII/2, p. 575 (Grant's order to Hamilton)

would act accordingly. Hurlbut replied, "As I cannot perceive any advantage to the public service, I decline furnishing the information desired. I command the Sixteenth Army Corps by orders from the President." Hamilton then sent a rather curt and defiant reply, "I have no intention to deprive you of the command of the Sixteenth Army Corps, but if I am the senior office, it becomes my duty to assume command of the District of West Tennessee, of which I will give you due notice." Hurlbut had reached his limit, and immediately sent a reply to Hamilton reminding him of the Special Orders, No. 30 from February 7, 1863. He closed by informing Hamilton, "…if you attempt to exercise independent authority, you will at once be arrested and sent to Vicksburg." Hurlbut then sent copies of these telegrams to Lt. Colonel Rawlins, Grant's Assistant Adjutant-General, and also requested that Hamilton be exchanged for General Prentiss. Hurlbut, in no uncertain terms, made it clear that he had reached the end of his forbearance with Hamilton. Hurlbut mentioned in his telegram to Rawlins that Hamilton was again writing confidential correspondence to people in high places [members of Congress]. It was also suggested that Hamilton's arrest was a real possibility because of his neglect concerning General Albert Lee's [then Colonel Lee] handling of the situation at Somerville, while commanding the Kansas 7th Cavalry. [71]

If this situation was not already bad enough, it soon got much worse; Hamilton was now playing all of his cards. On March 11, General Grant telegraphed General Halleck with information concerning Hamilton's attempts to remove General McPherson from command of the XVII Corps. Grant protested, "… There is no comparison between the two as to their fitness for such a command [corps command]. McPherson, from his activity, good sense, winning manners,

---

[71] OR, Vol. XXIV/3, p. 138-140 (all of the letters mentioned are in this section of the OR)

and effort to harmonize all parts of his command toward each other, and to preserve the same harmony toward all parts of this army, has made him the favorite with his men and officers and one of the most suitable corps commanders probably in any service". This was a glowing endorsement of General McPherson by Grant that clearly said he did not want Hamilton as a corps commander. Grant asked that the president be made aware of this situation.[72]

Hamilton was back to his old technique of letter writing to influential friends. In McPherson's case it was Senator James R. Doolittle, a Republican Senator from Wisconsin, who was the author of the epigram, "I believe in God Almighty, and under him, I believe in Abraham Lincoln". On February 11, 1863, Hamilton penned a letter to Doolittle saying, " Grant is a drunkard", and he went on to explain how he and General Quinby had taken Grant aside and cared for him during an intoxication episode. Hamilton claimed that Grant's wife was summoned to then care for the drunken Grant.[73] He also claimed that Hurlbut was, in fact, also a drunk, and McPherson was smeared with statements that he was incompetent and had done nothing to merit promotion to corps command. McClernand was untrustworthy, according to Hamilton, and he had written in earlier letters some very derogatory remarks about Gen. Gordon Granger and General Rosecrans. Granger was referred to as an "ignorant, drinking, blatant, obscene loafer", and Rosecrans was referred to as a "profane man and a hard drinker." [74]

---

[72] OR, Vol. XXIV/3, p. 137
[73] Doolittle Papers, letter from Hamilton to Senator Doolittle, February 11, 1863, State Historical Library, Madison, Wisconsin; hereinafter cited as Doolittle Papers
[74] Doolittle Papers, Granger & Rosecans letter October 22, 1862, Hurlbut letter, January 30, 1863; also see Grant Moves South, p. 395-396 for brief account of Hamilton's accusations

Hamilton was also busy writing telegrams to Grant. In a telegram of March 15, he informs Grant, "Hurlbut is at last confirmed, from September 17, myself from September 19, action on McPherson's case is not known." He continues, "If I am to remain in the District of West Tennesse, on duty, let me ask that the district be divided, and that I report direct to you." Hamilton then made comments to the effect that McPherson would soon be put aside as the commander of the XVII Corps, " It is altogether probable that my rank is senior to McPherson, and that I am entitled to the command of the Seventeenth Corps, but it will be some time before this can be officially known."[75] In all probability, Grant had no inkling of the slander and misrepresentations that Hamilton was so generously distributing to all that would listen, including his remarks about Grant.

Hamilton got in one more threatening telegram to Hurlbut before his departure. On March 20, he wrote, "You must be well aware that your appointment, as well as mine, as major-general, not having been confirmed, expired with the adjournment of Congress, leaving us both brigadiers, and as such I am your senior."[76] Hamilton had alienated too many people in authority; thus not even his politically important sources could patch it up for him this time. In a letter dated March 23, 1863, from the Headquarters of the XVI Corps, came the message, "Maj. Gen. C.S. Hamilton, having been ordered to report to Maj.Gen. John A. McClernand, is hereby relieved from duty in the Sixteenth Army Corps."[77] It must have been evident, even to Hamilton, that he could no longer function in the Army of the Tennessee, or for that matter, in the Union Army. In a letter dated March 28, 1863, General Grant explains to General Lorenzo Thomas, Adjutant-General of the Army:

---

[75] OR, Vol. XXIV/3, p. 139
[76] OR, Vol. XXIV/3, p. 141(part of a sub enclosure)
[77] OR, Vol. XXIV/3, p. 136

> Enclosed with this, I send you the resignation of Maj.-Gen. C.S. Hamilton... It is due that I should state that I have approved this resignation for the following reasons: ... Gen. Hamilton and Gen. Hurlbut could not get along together. For this reason, I relieved the former from duty in the District of West Tennessee and ordered him here. ...I had nothing longer in the field to give General Hamilton but a division. This he refused to accept. General Hamilton, being a capable officer, I gave him the choice between taking his old position, under General Hurlbut, a division in the field, the command of the District of East Arkansas, or to be relieved from duty in this department and ordered to report to Washington for orders. He accepted the latter, with the request that his resignation be forwarded. I think, in justice to the service, his resignation should be accepted.[78]

General Grant further explained to General Thomas that Hamilton wanted a separate division within Hurlbut's command, or two divisions, independent of any corps commander, rightfully, Grant felt neither of these was possible. On April 11, General Halleck informed Grant that Hamilton's resignation had been received, but not yet acted upon, as the president and the Secretary of War were absent. Halleck closed with the statement, "No doubt he resigns to get a higher command. This game sometimes succeeds, but it also sometimes fails."[79]

Hamilton's resignation became official on April 13, 1863. Previous to the acceptance of his resignation, an interesting release appeared in the Milwaukee *Sentinel*. The article stated that Hamilton, "arrived from Vicksburg last night. He is on his way to his home in Fond du Lac, Wisconsin for a short stay to recruit his somewhat shattered health."[80] About a month later, another article from the Milwaukee *Sentinel* stated, "... General Hamilton has

---

[78] OR, Vol. XXIV/3, p. 151
[79] Or, Vol. XXIV/1, p. 28
[80] Milwaukee *Sentinel*, April 4, 1863.

resigned and his resignation has been accepted. This is probably the case. The resignation was occasioned by the failure or refusal on the part of the authorities at Washington to assign the general to such command his rank as well as his services entitled him. We regret very much, as will every citizen of the state and country acquainted with the events and services of General Hamilton the necessity which led to this step".[81]

Hamilton returned to Wisconsin and engaged in the manufacture of linseed and colza oils, and things seemed to be going well for the general. However, Hamilton's nature was such that he never purged himself of a grudge or hatred. On February 2, 1864, an article appeared in the Milwaukee *Sentinel* that is rather exceptional. It began, " We are glad to learn that a Legislative Memorial is being prepared urging upon the President the re-appointment of Charles S. Hamilton of Fond de Lac, to the rank held by him in the Army of the United States until forced by self respect to resign it – that of Major-General."[82] The article is lengthy, and recounts all of Hamilton's war experiences with extreme embellishment and downright fiction. The article concludes with, "By a secession of wrongs, one of the ablest and best qualified officers in the army was forced out of the service, and the State of Wisconsin was slightest in his person." An abbreviated version of this article also ran in the Buffalo *Express* on February 9, 1864. No doubt, Hamilton motivated this outpouring of praise.

Hamilton continued to be a very influential person for a number of years. In 1866, he became a member of the Board of Regents of the University of Wisconsin; in fact, he served as president of the Board for much of that time. As usual, a major confrontation occurred at the University during Hamilton's tenure. Evidence is sketchy, but the

---

[81] Milwaukee *Sentinel,* May 5, 1863
[82] Milwaukee *Sentinel*, February 2, 1864

problem seems to have been Hamilton's displeasure with the enrollment of female students.

On March 31, 1869, Hamilton was appointed to the position of U.S. Marshall for the District of Wisconsin by President Grant. One would be forced to conclude that Grant never learned who circulated the drunkard accounts about him, but if he did know that Hamilton was to blame, he had the forgiveness of a saint. Hamilton held this position until March 31, 1877. In addition, Hamilton was a member of the Board of Visitors to the U.S. Military Academy in 1874. From 1878, until his death on April 17, 1891, he was president of the Hamilton Paper Company.[83]

The Saturday, April 18, 1891, edition of the Milwaukee *Sentinel* gave General Hamilton's death a large chunk of the front page.[84] The general's death was due to pneumonia, and all of Hamilton's military career was reviewed with glowing devotion. His association with General Grant was mentioned as well. The *Sentinel* gave the general credit for many things with which he was simply acquainted, certainly not the author, leader, or mainstay. Yet, this is proper in many ways. General Hamilton served his country, and certainly had the best interest of the nation at heart, despite how it may appear today.

How can General Charles S. Hamilton be assessed, and his services reviewed after more than a century since his death? Hamilton is a textbook example of the damage that one suffers from extreme self-aggrandizement. There is little doubt that Hamilton had greater than average ability as a soldier and as a thinker. He was a competent businessman and a public-spirited citizen, as evidenced by his acceptance of positions on the University of Wisconsin Board of Regents, and the Board of Visitors at West Point. He, unfortunately, had a number of fatal personality flaws. His

---

[83] Biographical Register, p. 182
[84] Milwaukee *Sentinel*, April 18, 1891

was the philosophy of "do unto others, but do it first, and if caught, blame it on someone else, preferable a friend." General Hamilton used this philosophy time and time again, and with many of his contemporaries, it was successful, even with a person of General Grant's insight. At a distance, General Hamilton was a very personable individual. It was only when one had to have close relations with Hamilton, relations which held possible gain or praise, did one encounter the true person.

When attempting to study and assess the accomplishments of General Hamilton, one is immediately struck with a rather unusual finding. The general was a division commander, an area commander, and briefly, a corps commander; yet, he is virtually an unknown to the general or ordinary student of the Civil War. Even though he did not complete service for the entire war, his fame is still very confined. Hamilton is an unknown to most people in the South, and his fame in the North is limited to his home state and a few other areas of the Midwest. Hamilton took part in two significant battles of the war. Compare this to almost any of Hamilton's associates in the Army of the Tennessee, such as Sherman, McPherson, Hurlbut, McClernard, all division and later, corps commanders. These men were in similar battles, at the same period of time and in the same places as General Hamilton. Hamilton's lack of fame can be summed up in a few words; he failed to learn how to cooperate with the inevitable. In Hamilton's view, when other officers made good and received promotions, it was because they were lucky. When the general succeeded, it was because of ability and talent. General Hamilton was a competent soldier who was unable to appreciate any point of view that was in opposition to the view that he held, and this greatly limited his effectiveness. This flaw was immediately picked up by others as intractability and doggedness. In time, this personality trait brought about aversion altogether.

General Hamilton was not, and never could have been a team player. His military peers did not trust him, and with good reason. Hamilton had disputes and disagreements with every commander under which he served. The most astounding aspect of General Hamilton's military career is the fact that he was never brought up on charges and forced to face a court of inquiry. Yet, the general was a patriot and wanted an end to the war and to reestablish the Union.

It has been said about greatness that some are born great, some achieve greatness, and some have greatness thrust upon them. In the case of General Charles Hamilton, none of these adages apply.[85]

---

[85] Shakespeare, *Twelfth Night*

General Lloyd Tilghman

GEN. LLOYD TILGHMAN, CSA

The Eastern Shore of Maryland today, as in the early 1800s, holds a unique position in the history of the United States. This area has a rich heritage, not only within the state of Maryland, but in the nation as well. Many of the nation's leaders came from families with a history rooted in the Eastern Shore area, and one such family is the Tilghmans of Talbot County. Probably the first notable Tilghman from the Eastern Shore is Matthew Tilghman, born in 1718, in Queen Anne County. Matthew is one of the truly important individuals concerning the political history of Maryland during the period from 1740-1790. Matthew Tilghman was a member of the first Continental Congress of 1774, as well as the subsequent Continental Congresses of 1775, 1776, and 1777. He did not sign the Declaration of Independence only because he was presiding over the Convention that was engaged in writing Maryland's first Constitution. This man has no equal in the political organization of the state of Maryland.[1] Matthew's wife was Ann Lloyd, great granddaughter of Colonel Edward Lloyd, the first Puritan Commander of Anne Arundel County. Lloyd Tilghman was the son of Matthew Tilghman, and was an important person in his own right. Lloyd was the father of James Tilghman, who married Ann C. Shoemaker, the parents of Lloyd Tilghman, future Confederate general, born January 30, 1816. Lloyd was named for his grandfather, who had been

---

[1] Oswald Tilghman, *History of Talbot County Maryland: 1661-1861* (Baltimore: Williams & Wilkins Company, 1967), p. 450. Hereinafter cited as History of Talbot County

given the name Lloyd in honor of his mother's maiden name, as well as his maternal ancestor's surname name.[2]

Lloyd Tilghman was born at "Rich Neck Manor" near the town of Claiborne, in Talbot County, Maryland. The young Tilghman displayed an early interest in military affairs, not unexpected in light of the fact that his family had always taken part in military actions whenever there was a need. One of Lloyd Tilghman's ancestors had served as General Washington's aide-de-camp during the Revolution. It comes as no surprise then, that Lloyd Tilghman wanted a military career.[3]

The Tilghman family made application for Lloyd to attend West Point in 1829. Of interest is the fact that Ann Tilghman, Lloyd's mother, completed most of the correspondence to the Academy on her son's behalf and expressed the fact that her son had received a liberal education, not withstanding many difficulties? She also felt that Lloyd had promise as a student, despite the fact that he was only fourteen years old. The only written correspondence to the Academy from James Tilghman concerning his son, is his approval for Lloyd to become a cadet in March of 1831.[4]

In July of 1831, Lloyd Tilghman was admitted to West Point at the age of fifteen years and six months. The academic's regimen was to prove difficult for young Tilghman, and at the end of his freshman year, he was found to be deficient and required to repeat the first year of study at West Point. He was adamant about his career in the military and with resoluteness, did what was required of him. He

---

[2] History of Talbot County, p. 450
[3] *Confederate Military History,* Vol. II, edited by General Clement A. Evans (Atlanta: Confederate Publishing Company, 1899), p. 163. Hereinafter cited as Military History
[4] Archives Holdings for Admissions to the United States Military Academy: 1829-1831

graduated in 1836, ranking number forty-six in a class of forty-nine students.[5] In each of the five years Tilghman attended West Point, he amassed more than one hundred demerits in each of the years, which seems to indicate that he was somewhat indulgent as to personal pleasures and frivolity, despite his determination to graduate from West Point.[6] This could well explain his poor ranking in the class of 1836.

Tilghman was assigned to the First Dragoons on July 1st, 1836, as a Second Lieutenant, and in the same month, he was granted a graduation leave of absence until September 30, at which time he resigned his commission from the army. Tilghman immediately took a position as a Civil Engineer for the Baltimore and Susquehanna Railroad from 1836 until 1837. A pattern of moving from one job to another, gaining no real status on any of the positions began to develop. Shortly, he then took a position with the Norfolk and Washington Canal from 1837 until1838. From this position, Tilghman went to work for the Eastern Shore Railroad until 1839, and worked for the Baltimore and Ohio Railroad until 1840.[7] In 1840, Tilghman went to work for the city of Baltimore in the Public Improvements division. This constant shifting of employment is unusual and probably would not have been typical of Tilghman's employment career had he survived the war. Perhaps he was attempting to aid in the establishment of a railroad network in the Southern United States, or for some other worthwhile reason, however, this type of behavior would seem more characteristic of life in a different time period than life in the

---

[5] Archival Records, United States Military Academy for the graduating class of 1836

[6] *Register of the Officers and Cadets of the United States Military Academy at West Point*, June 1838, p. 22, 23; Hereinafter cited as The Register

[7] History of Talbot County, p. 451

1840s. For an additional five years, Tilghman continued his work as an engineer for various and sundry organizations and companies.

On August 1, 1843, Tilghman married Augusta M. Boyd in Portland Maine and the couple ultimately became the parents of five sons and three daughters. Lloyd Tilghman was a man with a rather small frame for a person of his height. When he entered West Point he was only 4 feet and eleven inches in height, and even for a fifteen-year-old this is small. As an adult, he was six feet tall with dark auburn red hair, and he liked long hair, down to the shoulders! Tilghman was <u>always</u> immaculately dressed and groomed, plus he had a demeanor and attitude about him that made even the newest and most casual acquaintance feel like a friend of long standing. Lloyd has been described as a manly yet caring individual, and as will be revealed later, this is a very accurate description of Lloyd Tilghman.[8]

In 1846, the United States declared war on Mexico and not unlike many other West Point graduates, Tilghman re-enlisted in the army to serve his country, and became a part of Gen. David Twiggs' division. Gen. Winfield Scott, one of the two major field officers of the conflict, organized his forces into four divisions. General Twiggs commanded one of the four divisions in which Tilghman became a volunteer aide-de-camp to General Twiggs in May of 1846. This assignment had "good and bad" aspects for Tilghman's future as a military officer. General Scott is said to have had notorious feuds with his division commanders, and he said of General Twiggs, "he is not fit to command an army either in the presence or absence of the enemy." This attitude toward Twiggs certainly could not have helped Tilghman, but on the other hand, valuable military exposure and training were acquired by Tilghman for use in his role as a brigadier

---

[8] History of Talbot County, p. 455

general in the Confederate Army. Tilghman served with Twiggs at the battles of *Palo Alto* on May 8, 1846 and *Resaca de la Palma* on May 9, 1846. His Mexican War combat experience ended with the command of twenty volunteer partisans who were charged with erecting defenses at Matamoras in June of 1846. From August 14, 1847, until July 13, 1848, Tilghman served as Captain of a light artillery battalion of volunteers from Maryland and the District of Columbia.[9]

After the Mexican War, Tilghman took a position as an assistant engineer of the Panama Division of the Isthmus Railroad in 1849. As in the past, this position was short lived, and shortly Tilghman took a position as the Chief Engineer of exploration for the East Tennessee and Virginia Railroad in 1850. This employment continued until 1852, when in late in 1852, Tilghman again changed employment. He took employment with the Nashville, TN and Fulton, AK Railroad, until 1853, after which he worked with the La Grange and Bolivar Railroad from 1853, until 1854. Tilghman would take a more permanent position with the Mississippi, Ouachita, and Red River Railroad from 1854, until 1858. At some point during these four years, Tilghman took up residence in Puducah, Kentucky. The city of Puducah seems to have been to Tilghman's liking and he remained there until the outbreak of the Civil War, considering Puducah his home. This city was a logical selection in light of Tilghman's railroad experience, and the fact that he worked on a railroad from Puducah to Memphis during this time. He immediately developed an immense

---

[9] Otis A. Singletary, *The Mexican War* (Chicago: University of Chicago Press, 1960), p. 82, 135; George W. Cullum, *Biographical Register of the Officers and Graduates of the U.S. Military Academy* (Boston: Houghton, Mifflin and Company, Riverside Press, 1891), p. 1836. Hereinafter cited as Biographical Register; History of Talbot County, p. 451

fondness for the city called "Little Charleston," and as stated earlier was to become a permanent resident. The city acquired the "nickname" of "Little Charleston" because it was thought to be one of the most Southern oriented cities apart from the deep South.[10]

By 1858, the nation was moving rapidly toward disunion, during which time, Lincoln was seeking a seat in the United States Senate and his political reputation was on the increase. Emancipation was the daily fare in many newspapers, and Southerners were openly discussing secession from the Union. This was an inordinately serious period of time in the history of the United States, in frankness no greater issues have ever faced this nation than the issues of slavery, disunion, and civil war. All citizens were faced with the grave choice to either support the United States or take up arms in support of the state of their birth and heritage, if they were Southerners. This was a sobering decision if one ever existed, especially for a military man like Tilghman.

Lloyd Tilghman was born and grew up in a border state, and since that state had slavery, in the eyes of most Southerners, it was thought of as a Southern state. Maryland did not follow the other Southern states in secession from the Union, which enabled slave holders to retain ownership of their slaves and remain in the Union. This was legal under the laws of the United States during that time period. Tilghman had left Maryland and now lived in Kentucky, a state that took the exact same position as that taken by Maryland; consequently Tilghman may have taken comfort in the fact that Kentucky and Maryland were both on the same side. This comfort, if it ever existed, was to be short lived. In July of 1861, at Camp Boone, Tennessee the 3rd

---

[10] Biographical Register, p. 1836; History of Talbot County, p. 451; Ezra J. Warner, *Generals in Gray* (Baton Rouge: Louisiana State University Press, 1989), p. 306. Hereinafter cited as Warner Gray

Kentucky Infantry Regiment was organized with many members who had previous military service in the Kentucky State Guard. Lloyd Tilghman became a colonel and one of the leading field officers of this regiment, along with Gen. Simon B. Buckner who became commander of the Kentucky State Guard. Both Buckner and Tilghman remained loyal to the state of Kentucky's position on secession until early in September of 1861, when Grant occupied the city of Puducah. Governor Magoffin attempted to head off Kentucky's pro Union stand, but the state legislature raised the "Stars and Stripes" at the state capital in Frankfort over his veto and objection.[11] Kentucky had made her decision on secession and now Lloyd Tilghman had to make his choice.

How does one come to a conclusion about such a decision, what rationality could prepare a person for such a momentous and irrevocable choice? Lloyd Tilghman's life as a child and a young man can hardly be labeled as typical. He matured in a very affluent and influential family, one of the most influential families of Maryland, with wealth and power, and clout in any aspect or avenue one might care to delineate. The question then comes down to why would a person chance giving up such a situation? In 1852, Lloyd Tilghman had taken up residence in "Little Charleston," and this label would seem to indicate that the city held at least some of the views of the other Charleston, in South Carolina. This would certainly infer and entail wealth, influence, slavery, and a bellicose attitude toward anyone who challenged these things. There was also a rather negative feeling in Charleston, South Carolina toward the United States government because of the position the government had taken on many of the issues that impacted on the South in the 1850s. During Tilghman's eight years in Puducah before the Civil War, he became very involved with Simon

---

[11] Military History, p. 163

Buckner's Kentucky State Guard, and Buckner opposed secession. Furthermore, he [Buckner] did not own slaves and had lived in the North at various times in his life. His wife and her family also owned property and were influential in Chicago. President Lincoln offered Buckner a commission as a Brigadier General of Volunteers and the offer was refused. By the end of August of 1861, Buckner had severed all ties with the Union forces in Kentucky and became a Brigadier-General in the Confederate army on September 14, 1861.[12] Why did Buckner and Tilghman forsake Kentucky's position on secession? The state legislature in Kentucky had become too Union oriented for their inclinations. This estrangement of the South appeared to Buckner and Tilghman as an indication that the state's position of neutrality was at an end. When Grant established the Federal occupation of Puducah on September 6, 1861, this decisive action appeared to Tilghman as the "last straw" of neutrality. In a letter to Gen. John C. Fremont, Grant relates, "Have just returned from Puducah. Found secession flags in different parts of the city, in expectation of greeting the Southern Army, said to be 16 miles off, 3,800 strong...."[13] Grant and the Union Army now occupied his hometown, and consequently Tilghman viewed this as invasion. The entire 3rd Kentucky Regiment, along with Colonel Tilghman, became part of the Confederate army. Tilghman's commission as a Brigadier General ranks from October 18, 1861.[14] Lloyd Tilghman had made his decision.

During the early period of the war, Tilghman realized that his old regiment, now the 1st Kentucky Brigade, was

---

[12] Lawrence L. Hewitt, "Simon Bolivia Bruckner", *The Confederate General*, (National Historical Society), Vol. 1, p.140

[13] Official Records of the War of Rebellion, Series I, Vol. IV, (S#4) p. 197. Hereinafter cited as Official Records

[14] Warner Gray, p. 306

virtually unarmed, and in a letter to Gen. Albert Sidney Johnson, on September 23, 1861, he writes:

> I reached here this morning, by order of Brigadier-General Buckner, to superintend the arming of that portion of my brigade which remained at Camp Boone after the forward movement by General Buckner, but was afterwards moved here by order of General Buckner, expecting to find arms sufficient to fit them for the field. Not a single gun can be procured, of any sort, under any circumstances.
>
> The brigade numbers near 3,000 men, about one-sixth badly armed.... If anything can be done, I beg you will telegraph me as to how I shall proceed.[15]

Tilghman would soon discover that this would be the norm, not the exception, which meant that he would probably have to spend the remainder of his military career, his life, in an attempt to procure weapons, provisions, and other military necessities for his brigade. Little did he know that he was playing against a "stacked deck".

Tilghman would ultimately gain the reputation as somewhat of a "troublemaker", constantly requesting supplies, food, building materials, workers to use the materials, and a "laundry list" of war related items. It probably never occurred to him that his needs were near the bottom of the priority list in the scheme of things, as viewed by those receiving his request. In another letter to General Johnston, just two days after his September 23 request, Tilghman explains:

> ...I have instructed Major Boyd, brigade quartermaster, now *en route* for Memphis, to call at Columbus (Kentucky) and ascertain something definite as to the arms for my brigade ... I would request, if compatible with the public service, that you

---

[15] Official Records, Series I, Vol. IV, (S# 4), p. 424

give Major Boyd an order to receive 2,500 stand from the first arrival at Nashville.[16]

While this is a very legitimate request, it probably had little if any impact on General Johnston. Johnston certainly would have desired to fully equip every brigade and regiment in the Confederate Army, but conditions, funds, and politics prevented that from occurring. This was a reality Lloyd Tilghman had not yet learned, but soon would fully comprehend.

On September 27, 1861, Colonel Tilghman was ordered to report to Camp Trousdale and General Buckner. At this point, the decision had been made to promote Tilghman to Brigadier General. There may have been more to this promotion than at first appears. Since Tilghman lived in Kentucky his interest obviously would have gravitated to what was good for Kentucky, and for that reason Tilghman was being considered for the command of the river forts as early as late September. To have this command, he had to be a brigadier. The decision was made and Tilghman was promoted to Brigadier General on October 18, 1861, and assigned the command of the troops at Hopkinsville, Kentucky on October 23, 1861.[17]

Less than ten days before leaving his command at Clarksville, Tennessee Tilghman had written a message to be hand delivered to General Johnston at Bowling Green. This message was passed to General Johnston by a civilian, a Mr. Hillman. In this letter Tilghman pronounced:

> This will be handed to you by Mr. Hillman, with whom I have talked freely on points of great interest to us all. He will give you facts connected with events now thickening fast around us that I am sure will be of service. ...I am sorry to also hear of

---

[16] Official Records, Series I, Vol. IV, (S# 4), p. 426
[17] Official Records, Series I, Vol. IV, (S# 4), p. 430; Official Records, Series I, Vol. IV, (S# 4), p.472

the inefficient condition of things at Fort Donelson. I fear our interests there are well-nigh beyond our control.[18]

One cannot but wonder how General Johnston must have received this message. This letter clearly demonstrates at least two important points. First, General Tilghman was a political neophyte, and Johnston, in all likelihood, did not have the slightest idea as to the identity of Hillman. He must have also been puzzled about the prospect of a brigadier general in his command discussing military matters with a civilian. Secondly, the thought must have crossed his mind, if it had not already done so, that General Tilghman was a perfect prospect for command at Fort Donelson. Since he was so concerned about Fort Donelson and its lack of preparedness, why not place him in command and let him attempt to improve the situation.

On October 31, Tilghman telegraphed a letter to Colonel Mackall, Assistant Adjutant-General. This letter contained some of the same requests and an overly optimistic attitude about the military supply situation as it existed in the Kentucky and Tennessee area in 1861. Tilghman states, "I repeat again I need reinforcements of every arm. Cavalry first is important, as explained in my former letter. I am not frightened, but only appreciate, as you would do were you in my place, the condition of things here."[19] General Tilghman had sent a message to Colonel Mackall on October 29th explaining conditions at Camp Alcorn (Hopkinsville). The camp had massive illness and poor conditions on every front and was a totally deplorable place.[20]

A letter received by General Tilghman on November 1, 1861, sets the stage for Tilghman's association with then Major [later General] Jeremy Gilmer. Gilmer was the chief

---

[18] Official Records, Series I, Vol. IV, (S# 4), p. 479
[19] Official Records, Series I, Vol. IV, (S# 4), p. 493
[20] Official Records, Series I, Vol. IV, (S# 4), p. 485

engineer of the Western Army. This letter again implies that Tilghman was the chief candidate for command of the river forts of Tennessee. The letter from General Johnston, via Colonel Mackall expressed:

> General Johnson directs you to draw back your command to Clarksville. Let your movement be a well-guarded one. Send your sick and baggage to the rear first, and cover the movement with your effective force. Arrived at Clarksville, employ your men in making the defensive works which have been planned by Major Gilmer.[21]

The letter also discussed the reinforcements that were coming to Clarksville to aid in the defense of the railroad from Clarksville to Bowling Green. Tilghman was also cautioned not to lose sight of the importance of this line of communication. General Tilghman acknowledged Mackall's letter on November 1st, and again requested more troops (200 cavalry).

On November 6th and 7th Tilghman sent telegrams to Colonel Mackall relating conditions about his command. He informed Mackall that his command was improving and that he had sent out a cavalry unit to counter the Union forces in the area that were attacking and destroying property of the local residents. He also related that gunboats were passing near Dover and had likely fired on Fort Donelson. These communications were followed on November 11th with another message stating the conditions at Hopkinsville. A fourth message was sent on November 13th. Tilghman informed the command at Bowling Green that a battalion of Colonel Forrest's cavalry, [later Gen. Nathan B. Forrest] about 300 men, were in his area and that he had made good use of the additional troops. This message, uncommonly, did not contain a request for materials or troops.[22] Of interest, on

---

[21] Official Records, Series I, Vol. IV, (S# 4), p. 495
[22] Official Records, Series I, Vol. IV, (S# 4), p. 527, 535, 550

November 14, Col. N.B. Forrest, in a telegram to Colonel Mackall, requested that his command of eight companies be reunited and allowed to work with General Tilghman, but a negative response was immediately forthcoming. Colonel Forrest was under General Polk's command, and it seems he either had other duties for Forrest, or else he did not consider Hopkinsville-Clarksville area of enough importance for the use of Forrest's command.[23]

After repeated telegrams to the high command, General Tilghman had "ruffled" the wrong feathers too many times. Since he had displayed such an interest in the river forts and their condition, the decision was reached to place him in command of the forts. In a letter from Colonel Mackall, on November 14, General Tilghman was instructed, " Brig. Gen. Lloyd Tilghman will repair to Columbus, Ky., and report to Major-General Polk, by whom, in obedience to instructions from the Secretary of War, he will be assigned to the command of the fortifications at that point."[24] This situation is much like the old adage that exclaims; "he who laughs when things go wrong has just thought of someone to blame it on." Unfortunately, that someone was to be General Lloyd Tilghman, and any and all problems connected with the two river forts, Henry and Donelson, would, from this point forward, be the fault of Tilghman.

In a communication from Colonel Mackall to Tilghman on November 17, Mackall expounds:

> ...You will push forward the completion of the works and their armament with the utmost activity, and to this end will apply to the citizens of the surrounding country for assistance in labor, for which you will give them certificates for amounts due for such labor....The utmost vigilance is enjoined. The general regrets to hear that there has been heretofore gross negligence in this respect—the commander at Fort Donelson away from his

---

[23] Official Records, Series I, Vol. IV, (S# 4), p. 551
[24] Official Records, Series I, Vol. IV, (S# 4), p. 552

post nightly and the officer in charge of the field batteries frequently absent. This cannot be tolerated.... Your command is embraced in the division of Major-General Polk, to whom you will report monthly.[25]

If one is to believe this letter, the conditions at Fort Donelson were far past correction. General Tilghman is, in essence, being told to fix the situation, while the high command knows full well that it is impossible with the current remedies. To complicate matters for General Tilghman, General Polk had no interest whatever in the river forts. North Alabama citizens had appealed to General Polk to strengthen the river defenses, after which he told them to raise a home guard and defend it themselves. This does not sound as if General Polk intended to expend much energy, troops, and money on the river forts and did view them as important.[26]

Gen. Leonidas Polk was to be a "big player" in the career of General Tilghman. Polk was a West Point graduate and the roommate of Gen. Albert S. Johnston while at West Point. Polk was a single minded individual who had grave difficulty in following orders, and he particularly resented taking orders from Johnston. Joseph H. Parks is quoted from his biography of Polk in an article by Steven E. Woodworth as stating, 'Genl. Polk by education and habit is unfitted for executing the plans of others. He will convince himself his own are better and follow them without reflecting on the consequences.'[27] Polk was appointed a Lieutenant-General, and he was second in rank of officers of that grade. General Polk was a man of immense power early in the war, and in

---

[25] Official Records, Series I, Vol. IV, (S# 4) ,p. 560
[26] Thomas L. Connelly, *Army of the Heartland* (Baton Rouge: Louisiana State University Press, 1995), p. 79. Hereinafter cited as Connelly
[27] Steven E. Woodworth, "Leonidas Polk", *The Confederate General* (National Historical Society, 1991), Vol. V, p. 47. Hereinafter cited as The Confederate General

addition, he was a Corps commander in the Army of Tennessee until September of 1863. Polk had a severe dispute with General Braxton Bragg concerning attack orders in the battle of Chickamauga after which Bragg had him transferred to Mississippi. In 1864, he was recalled to help save Atlanta from Sherman and was killed at Pine Mountain, Georgia on June 14, 1864.[28]

Steven Woodworth, in his book *Civil War Generals in Defeat* gives additional insight into General Polk's position:

> Johnston placed too much confidence in Polk. He considered moving Fort Henry from its unfortunate site but finally decided that with time so short before a probable Federal attack and with so much work having been invested at the current location, it would be best to press on, inferior position and all. He thus gave immediate orders to Polk to see to the improvements of the two forts, and particularly to make sure that the hills on the Kentucky side across from Fort Henry were occupied and fortified, since Kentucky neutrality was a thing of the past. Polk simply ignored the order.[29]

There is good evidence that Polk's occupation of Columbus, Kentucky was the chief reason for the loss of Kentucky's neutrality. Polk's Columbus forces were large and for that reason, Johnston instructed Polk to send men to add additional strength to the river forts. He was ordered to send 5,000 troops and he refused, when the order was sent to Polk again, he again refused. Polk's ego stood in the way of what was needed by the Confederate states at that time.[30]

Another key individual in Tilghman's attempts to shore up and strengthen the river forts was Major Jeremy

---

[28] Warner Gray, p. 243; The Confederate General, p. 47
[29] Steven E. Woodworth, editor, *Civil War Generals in Defeat* (Lawrence: University of Kansas Press, 1999), p. 15, 16. Hereinafter cited as Generals in Defeat
[30] Generals in Defeat, p. 16

Gilmer. The quintessential authority on the Confederate Army of Tennessee, Dr. Thomas L. Connelly, gives an insightful sketch of Major Gilmer in 1861:

> When Gilmer came to Bowling Green, he was homesick, unhappy with the assignment, and bored. Nothing seemed to go right for him. He had had an unpleasant trip from Georgia to Kentucky, and complained of the 'common cars' of the railroad and of the poor hotels en route. No sooner had he arrived at Bowling Green than the autumn rains began, and he developed a severe cold. Other occurrences continued to irritate him. His wife did not write often enough and he feared she was ill in Savannah. He was unhappy with his rank as major, and thought he should be promoted to brigadier...Gilmer simply began his assignment with an indifferent, unpleasant attitude....[31]

Gilmer had been ordered to the command of General Johnston for the explicit purpose of working on the two river forts, Henry and Donelson. Even though ordered by Johnston to attend to the defenses of the two forts, Gilmer virtually ignored both forts during the fall of 1861.[32] Gilmer operated much like General Polk, in that he received orders from superior officers, he then calculated and reformulated the information to correspond with his view of the situation and acted accordingly. Since his West Point days as an instructor, he considered himself an expert on what the Union Army would and would not do, due to the weather, mud, etc. He felt no federal advance would occur until April or May of 1862, and with that thought in mind, he was in no hurry to work on the defenses of Henry and Donelson.[33]

Another hindrance was Captain Joseph Dixon; an engineer assigned to work with Gilmer. Dixon felt that the defenses of the Tennessee and Cumberland rivers should not be confined to just Forts Henry and Donelson. His view was

---

[31] Connelly, p. 80,81
[32] Connelly, p. 80
[33] Connelly, p. 81

that several down river points should also be included. Line Port, and Ingram's Shoals were two sites he wanted included in the distribution of manpower, money, and other considerations for the defense of the rivers. He was able to convince Gilmer of the wisdom of this move, after which Gilmer actually expanded the idea to include the blockading of the channel below Fort Donelson. Too many projects, too little time and resources, appears to be the sum of the situation which Tilghman faced. By January of 1862, Donelson and Henry had suffered massive neglect with little hope of any change.[34]

The conflict that ensued between Tilghman and Gilmer occurred due to this neglect of the two river forts. On November 28, 1861, Gilmer telegraphed Colonel Mackall explaining, "... I received a telegram from Mr. T.J. Glenn, civil engineer, employed by me in obstructing the Cumberland River, under the guns of Fort Donelson, with trees and timber, *viz*:

> General Tilghman has ordered me to suspend. Instruct me immediately.
>
> T.J. Glenn

Gilmer replied,

> You will continue the work for obstructing the Cumberland River.

Gilmer continues and closes with the comment that, "I must therefore earnestly request that the general commanding the Western Department hold Brigadier General Tilghman responsible for the act now reported and forbid the repetition of like interference in the future."[35] Gilmer followed up this letter to Colonel Mackall with a letter to Lieutenant Joseph

---

[34] Connelly, p. 82, 83
[35] Official Records, Series I, Vol. VII, (S#7), p. 710

Dixon on December 4th. This letter is somewhat of an apology. Gilmer expounds:

> ... I much regret the interference of General Tilghman with the work trusted to Mr. Glenn. As he has been instructed not to interfere furthur (sic) with our operations, I will expect the agents I employ to execute my orders henceforth. ... Do not let his operations be interfered with by calling off the steamboat for any other purpose.[36]

The constant requests, communications, and complaints by General Tilghman to General Johnston, Assistant Adjutant-General Mackall, and at least one time to President Jefferson Davis, had reached a crisis point with General Polk. He indirectly alludes to the idea that General Tilghman was intruding on his good name:

> ... When General Tilghman was made brigadier-general he was assigned by you to the command of the defenses on the Tennessee and Cumberland. It was at a time when the operations of the enemy had begun to be active on these rivers, and the difficulty of communicating as rapidly as the exigencies of the service required, through the circuitous route to Columbus, made it expedient for him to place himself in direct communication to the general headquarters. Nevertheless, all the support I could give him in answer to his calls was afforded.[37]

On the very next day, General Tilghman sent a telegram to Colonel Mackall expressing his concerns about Polk, Gilmer, and the defense of the forts. He states, "A message from Puducah and Columbus yesterday indicates a movement this way. Will he not let (me) have 1,000 arms from Nashville? I feel discouraged, but will not give up."[38]

---

[36] Official Records, Series I, Vol. VII, (S#7), p. 735
[37] Official Records, Series I, Vol. VII, (S#7), p. 721
[38] Official Records, Series I, Vol. VII, (S#7), p. 719

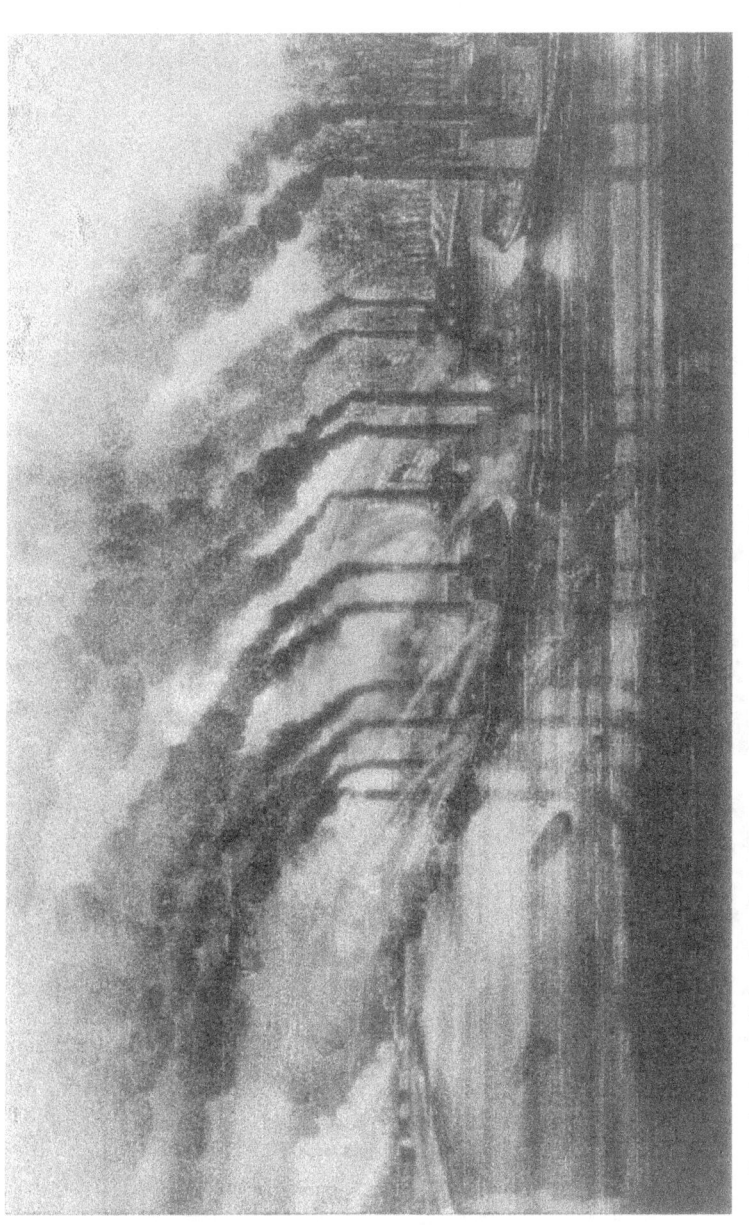

Depiction of the bombardment and capture of Ft. Henry, Tennessee, February 6, 1862

Monument dedicated to General Tilghman
at Vicksburg Battlefield

Historic marker indicating the battle at Champion Hill

153

The warnings issued on the condition of the two river forts by General Tilghman went rather much by the gate, and this was true for several reasons. Since Tilghman was reporting to General Polk, who could hardly have been less concerned, it is easy to see why nothing was done to alter the situation. Secondly, any discussion with Gilmer was a total waste of time for Tilghman. After several disputes with Gilmer, Tilghman realized he had little chance to convince General Johnston about the real conditions at the two river forts.[39]

In early September of 1861, Captain Jesse Taylor had agreed to take command of Fort Henry. Captain Taylor was an experienced artillerist, which Governor Isham G. Harris felt was an essential move to correct conditions at the fort. Captain Taylor made some interesting comments about conditions at the Fort:

> Arriving at the fort, I was convinced by a glance at its surroundings that extraordinarily bad judgment, or worse, had selected the site for its erection. I found it placed on the east bank of the river, and within good rifle range. This circumstance was at once reported to the proper military authorities of the state at Nashville, who replied that the selection had been made by competent engineers and with reference to mutual support with Fort Donelson of the Cumberland, twelve miles away....
>
> ... the accidental observation of a water-mark left on a tree caused me to look carefully for this sign above, below, and in the rear of the fort; and my investigation convinced me that we had a more dangerous force to contend with than the Federals, namely, the river itself.[40]

Captain Taylor reports that local residents confirmed his thinking--- the highest point in the fort would be two feet

---

[39] Connelly, p. 84
[40] *Battles and Leaders of the Civil War*, Vol. I edited by Clarence C. Buel & Robert U. Johnson (New York: The Century Company, 1887), p. 368, 369. Hereinafter cited as Battles and Leaders

under water in an ordinary February rise of the river. Captain Taylor gave this information to the state authorities, and they, in turn, rejected any responsibility and informed him to speak with General Polk at Columbus, who now had authority concerning Fort Henry. The captain immediately followed up on this information, numerous times. He was ultimately referred to General Johnston, and Johnston brought in Major Jeremy Gilmer at that point. Another significant problem at Fort Henry was its armament. The armament of the fort was very low powered at the time Captain Taylor took command in the fall of 1861. By February 1, 1862, Captain Taylor asserts that General Tilghman had significantly increased the firepower of the fort through repeated requests to the high command.[41]

There is a small island about one mile distance from the location of Fort Henry. In the winter of 1861 and 1862, the Federal gunboats, *Lexington* and *Conestoga* made frequent trips to the area near the fort and used the small island as cover. "They frequently", reports Captain Taylor, "fired on the fort, attempting to determine the gun positions within the fort." Captain Taylor again comments that, "On the 4th of February the Federal fleet of gunboats, followed by countless transports, appeared below the fort. Far as [the] eye could see, the course of the river could be traced by the dense volumes of smoke…indicating that the long threatened attempt to break our lines was to be made in earnest."[42]

The 5th of February was a day of continued landing of troops and supplies. By late afternoon, Captain Taylor states that three of the gunboats opened fire on the fort. The Confederates within the fort suffered one death and several wounded. The Columbiad and rifle each fired three rounds and the gunboats pulled away. General Tilghman met with his officers that night. After which the officers variously

---

[41] Battles and Leaders, Vol. I, p. 369
[42] Battles and Leaders, Vol. I, p. 369

estimated that the Federal force was about 25,000. General Tilghman had less than four thousand men under his command, and the men under General Tilghman's command were raw, untried troops, poorly armed with civilian type weapons. The agreed upon decision of the officers and General Tilghman was unanimous, the army had to attempt to withdraw to Fort Donelson. Captain Taylor relates that he was asked by General Tilghman if he could last an hour under a sustained attack, and his answer was that he could. Part of the 1st Tennessee Artillery, one officer, and fifty-four men were assigned to remain at the fort to cover the withdrawal of the troops. General Tilghman returned to the fort after the withdrawal of the army. At that point, none of the fort's guns were operational. The Federal commander, upon noting this fact, renewed the attack with gusto. Captain Taylor relates that General Tilghman conferred with him and Major Gilmer as to whether or not continued resistance was practical, and the decision was made to surrender the fort.[43]

During all this time, from February 4th, until February 6th, the day of the attack, General Tilghman was attempting to procure reinforcements from General Polk. On February 4th, at 5 P.M. Tilghman sent a telegram to Polk stating:

> The enemy is landing troops in large forces on this side of the river, within 3 miles of the fort. Their advance cavalry is at Boyd's, 3 miles from here. I have sent the Dunbar to the mouth of Sandy after two regiments there and the Appleton Belle is gone to the bridge after the remaining companies. There are eight gunboats and nine transports in the river. ... I will await your orders, or what I would more desire, your presence. Come not without a large escort....[44]

General Tilghman sent a similar request to Colonel Mackall:

---

[43] Battles and Leaders, Vol. I, p. 371
[44] Official Records, Series I, Vol. VII, (S#7), p. 858

> If you can reinforce strongly and quickly we have a glorious chance to overwhelm the enemy. Move by Clarksville to Donelson and across, and to Danville, where transport ill be waiting. Enemy said to be entrenching below. My plans are to concentrate closely in and under Henry.[45]

In a final telegram to General Polk at 12 midnight on February 6, General Tilghman has desperation in his tone. He writes, " I must have two regiments, thoroughly armed and equipped, from you... Don't trust to Johnston's re-enforcing me, we need all. I don't want raw troops who are just organized; they are in my way. Act promptly, and don't trust to anyone."[46]

Gilmer, who had been promoted to Lieutenant Colonel, gave an account of the battle. In most aspects, it is very much in congruence with the report of Captain Taylor; however, there are several important differences. Gilmer praises General Tilghman, saying he did "everything it was possible to do to encourage and urge his men to further efforts." Gilmer also contended that, "all was lost unless he could replace the men at the guns by others who were not exhausted. He [Tilghman] replied, 'I shall not give up the works,' and then made an effort to get men from the outer lines to continue the struggle." Gilmer implies that this caused mass confusion among the men in the ranks, and he also appraised the Federal strength at 9,000, a number far below that estimated by the officers at a meeting on February 5th with General Tilghman. Gilmer concludes by proposing that the Federal movement to cut communication with Fort Donelson would have failed if the forces at Fort Henry could have held out a few hours longer.[47]

It has been estimated that on the day of the battle for Fort Henry, the flagpole inside Fort Henry, on the parade

---

[45] Official Records, Series I, Vol. VII, (S#7), p. 858
[46] Official Records, Series I, Vol. VII, (S#7), p. 859
[47] Official Records, Series I, Vol. VII, (S#7), p. 134,135

ground, stood in two feet of water.[48] It is also worth noting that Lieutenant Colonel Gilmer was not part of the group of officers and men who remained with General Tilghman to surrender Fort Henry. Gilmer escaped on foot.[49]

General Tilghman stated in his report of the battle, that General Grant had a force of 12,000 men, confirmed after the surrender of the fort. Tilghman explained that he attempted several techniques to avoid surrender of the fort. He raised a flag of truce, which was to no avail, seemingly not noticed by the Federals. Tilghman acknowledged the courtesy and consideration of Flag-Officer Foote, of the Federal Navy, Captain Stembel and the other naval officers.[50] A final tribute was paid to General Tilghman's efforts at Fort Henry by Lieutenant Colonel Milton A. Hayes, Chief of the Tennessee Corps of Artillery. The Lt. Colonel states," Throughout the action, General Tilghman displayed cool and manly courage, which commanded admiration and inspired our men with noble enthusiasm, which made them scorn the dangers by which they were surrounded."[51]

On February 16th, Fort Donelson surrendered to the Federal authorities and Confederate General Buckner [he was commander of the fort due to fact that Generals Floyd and Pillow had fled] was taken prisoner. As fate would have it, General Buckner surrendered the fort to his West Point classmate, Gen. Ulysses Grant. Bruckner served five months of solitary confinement at Fort Warren in the Boston Harbor.[52] General Johnston's command was crumbling, and unfortunately his view of the situation went from extreme optimism to absolute despair. General Johnston was also

---

[48] Connelly, p. 197
[49] Official Records, Series I, Vol. VII, (S#7), p. 146
[50] Official Records, Series I, Vol. VII, (S#7), p. 144
[51] Official Records, Series I, Vol. VII, (S#7), p. 147
[52] Lawrence L. Hewitt, Confederate General, Vol. I, p. 140

forced to evacuate his position at Bowling Green, since events had taken such an ominous turn.

General Tilghman, along with General Buckner, was also taken to Fort Warren, in the Boston Harbor. In a letter to Confederate Secretary of War G. W. Randolph, H. C. Burnett expressed concern about the treatment he felt that Generals Tilghman and Buckner were receiving at Fort Warren. Burnett was a four-term member of Congress and was expelled in 1861 because of his secessionist views. Burnett claimed that a Captain Chipley, recently paroled from Fort Warren, related to him that Buckner and Tilghman were being held in solitary confinement, and were denied any contact with other prisoners, even while exercising. In addition, they were denied the privilege of writing letters, all of which Burnett felt was the result of members of Congress from Kentucky attempting to punish the generals because of their position on the war. He requested that the Confederate government conduct an investigation, and was reinforced by the Richmond newspaper, *The Examiner*, which also made this claim in an editorial.[53] Tilghman remained at Fort Warren for about six months and on or about August 16th 1862, Tilghman was exchanged and placed in command of about 10,000 exchanged Confederate prisoners at Jackson, Mississippi. The plan of operation under General Tilghman's command was to re-organize and mold these men into companies, regiment, etc., since the majority of these troops had been captured at Fort Donelson and Island Ten. To accomplish the task given to General Tilghman would require exceptional executive ability, given the financial and supply situation that existed in the Confederacy.[54]

Again, Tilghman was presented with a command that was besieged with problems, not unlike Fort Henry in its

---

[53] Official Records, Series II, Vol. IV, (S#17), p. 803; Official Records, Series II, Vol. VII (S#17),p. 804
[54] History of Talbot County, p. 453

159

difficulty. In Special Order # 153, Tilghman was ordered to establish a camp that would be near Vicksburg, and also near the railroad. Not only was he to align the men into regiments, divisions, etc. but these new units were suppose to be the original companies, regiments, etc. from which these men were originally a part. This impossible order came from General Braxton Bragg, a new nemesis in Tilghman's life and career.[55] In a letter to the Secretary of War, General Tilghman asked the Secretary to work on the placement problems, stating, "I can organize men promptly and more efficiently. Can you not give me full and sole control? I cannot communicate with Bragg and matters are at cross purposes."[56] Tilghman also expressed his embarrassment at having to deal with Bragg's staff officer, since he was denied a face to face meeting with Bragg for some undisclosed reason. The Secretary replied saying," If General Bragg has given no instructions about the prisoners, as I hoped he had, the duty of reorganizing them devolves upon Gen. Earl Van Dorn as the senior officer present."[57]

The Prisoner Exchange duty ended around October 24, 1862, at least for General Tilghman. In a lengthy letter to his replacement, Gen. John Gregg, Tilghman explained the duties of the command as well as the past problems and accomplishments. As specified in Special Order # 155, General Tilghman would now report to, and become part of, the command of Gen. Earl Van Dorn.[58]

Earl Van Dorn was a very promising officer in 1861, and was promoted to Major General, to rank from September 19, 1861. He took part in the battle of Bull Run, under Gen. Joseph Johnston's command. In January of 1862, he took charge of the Trans-Mississippi District, and led that army in

---

[55] Official Records, Series II, Vol. IV, (S#17),p. 825
[56] Official Records, Series II, Vol. IV, (S#17),p. 888
[57] Official Records, Series II, Vol. IV, (S#17),p. 889
[58] Official Records, Series II, Vol. IV, (S#17),p. 926, 853,854

the battle of Pea Ridge, Arkansas in March of 1862. This turned out to be a dismal defeat for Van Dorn after which he joined the Army of the Mississippi, under the command of General Beauregard, and was place in command of a reinforcement unit. In June of 1862, he was named to command the Department of Southern Mississippi and East Louisiana, with command headquarters in Vicksburg, Mississippi.

Van Dorn made several critical errors in Mississippi, paramount of which was a declaration of martial law in several Mississippi and Louisiana counties. Due to the political fall out in Richmond, Van Dorn was replaced by Gen. John Pemberton, who named Van Dorn as his cavalry commander. Van Dorn was an excellent cavalry officer who did major damage to Grant's supply lines in his initial attempt to take Vicksburg. General Van Dorn met an untimely death in a lover's triangle at Spring Hill, Tennessee in 1863, by an irate husband.[59]

It was this army which General Tilghman joined in November of 1862. Tilghman's period of acclamation and orientation to his new setting would be short lived. The armies of Grant and Van Dorn clashed in Mississippi, and Van Dorn needed more time and provisions for the completion of his movement and retreat to Granada, Mississippi. On December 5th, 1862, Tilghman collided with Grant's advance unit at Coffeeville, Mississippi at which time Colonels Dickey, Hatch, and Lee were attempting to remove Tilghman's division from its position, blocking the advance unit. At this point, General Tilghman was commanding the 1st Division of the 1st Corps of the Army of West Tennessee, under the direct command of General Lovell, commander of the 1st Corps.

---

[59] Edwin C. Bearss, "Earl Van Dorn", *The Confederate General* (National Historical Society, 1991), Vol. VI, p. 74, 75, hereinafter cited as Van Dorn; Warner Gray, p. 315

The engagement occurred about a mile or so from Coffeeville in the afternoon of December 5th. The Federals, much to their sorrow, miscalculated Tilghman's resolve and strength, and after a rather brief encounter, Tilghman ordered a charge directly into the Federal position. The 9th Arkansas and the 8th Kentucky Infantry regiments made short time of the struggle, pushing the Federals back into mud, undergrowth, and dense trees.

The Federal forces were forced back several miles from Coffeeville, which gave Van Dorn the time he needed to move his troops into Grenada. The engagement also gave General Grant time to pause and rethink his position, which he probably had not expected to happen. Tilghman reported seven killed, forty-three wounded, and ten missing. Federal losses were thirty-four killed, among them Lt. Colonel McCollough, 234 wounded, and thirty-five men taken as prisoners. Tilghman reported the engagement as a complete success, which may be have been somewhat of an overstatement in that it simply delayed the Federal advance.[60]

General Van Dorn had taken on General William Rosecrans in the savage battle of Corinth in October of 1862. The two-day battle ended in a Confederate defeat, even though Van Dorn's army was numerically superior. General Tilghman commanded the 1st Brigade in General William Loring's division, which was the beginning of a long association between the two men. The battle and the retreat of Van Dorn's army set off a whirlwind of criticism and charges against Van Dorn by Gen. John S. Bowen and others. A Court of Inquiry was held, however, nothing came of the charges at least outwardly and publicly, but

---

[60] Official Records, Series I, Vol. XVII/1(S#24), p. 503, 504,505,506,507; Robert G. Hartje, *Van Dorn: The Life and Times of a Confederate General* (Nashville: Vanderbilt University Press, 1967),p. 252

nevertheless, Van Dorn was unceremoniously replaced by Gen. James C. Pemberton on October 14, 1862.[61] Pemberton was now the commander of the Department of Mississippi and Eastern Louisiana and was responsible for the all-important city and stronghold of Vicksburg. Lloyd Tilghman would serve the remainder of his military career, and his life, under General Pemberton's command, where he would command William Baldwin's brigade in Loring's division. The relationship between the two men, Tilghman and Pemberton, would not be smooth nor cooperative. Who exactly, was James C. Pemberton?

Pemberton was born of Quaker parents in Philadelphia, which was in itself a strike against him to many military commanders in the South, the result being that he was never fully trusted nor accepted by many Southern officers. Pemberton went through the same channels as most officers on both sides of the war: West Point, Mexican War, etc. Pemberton's wife, Martha Thompson, was a native of Virginia and this was a deciding factor in Pemberton's decision to commit to service with the Confederacy.

When R.E. Lee was ordered from South Carolina to Richmond in March of 1862, Pemberton was given command of the Department of South Carolina, Georgia, and Florida. Many people in the Confederate government felt this was a" backhanded publicity stunt" on the part of Jefferson Davis. Pemberton was immediately unpopular in South Carolina, and in fact, Governor Pickens of South Carolina demanded his removal for assorted reasons, but primarily because Pemberton wanted to abandon Fort Sumter. The political fall out was tremendous and Pemberton was soon replaced by General Beauregard. The change of command did not occur until late September and by October of 1862, Pemberton was transferred to the western front.

---

[61] Van Dorn, p. 75; Warner Gray, 315

General Pemberton was immediately caught up in a command dispute between Gen. Joseph Johnston and Jefferson Davis about what should be done concerning Vicksburg. Johnston pressured him to abandon Vicksburg to prevent Grant from isolating his army, yet Davis felt Vicksburg should be defended at all cost. Johnston was Pemberton's immediate superior, but Jefferson Davis was the president of the Confederacy, hence, Pemberton chose Davis.[62]

Grant's campaign to take Vicksburg began in December of 1862. To a degree, General Tilghman was a factor, at the least, in slowing down this campaign with his Coffeeville Expedition mentioned previously. Grant sent Sherman to Chickasaw Bluffs, where Sherman made his famous declaration, "I reached Vicksburg at the time appointed, landed, assaulted, and failed." A canal was attempted at Duckport to connect various roads and trails in an attempt to reach Vicksburg, this also failed.

Grant next attempted to open a 400-mile corridor from Lake Providence, Louisiana to a point below Vicksburg. By the end of March 1863, the attempt was given up in favor of a more promising project, which would become known as the Yazoo Pass Expedition. Since Grant could not attack Vicksburg in the conventional fashion, the Federals blasted a hole in the levee to open the Yazoo Pass. The army would then be sent on a circuitous route to reach Vicksburg, across from Millikens Bend, which would also allow for transports in the Tallahatchie River. General Pemberton ordered Loring's division to block this passage, where by Loring constructed Fort Pemberton, ninety miles or

---

[62] Lawrence L. Hewitt, "John Clifford Pemberton", *The Confederate General* (National Historical Society, 1991), Vol. V,p. 9 ; Michael B. Ballard, *Pemberton*, (Jackson: University of Mississippi Press, 1991), p. 96-113 for a complete discussion of the controversy, hereinafter cited as Pemberton; Warner Gray, 233

so above Vicksburg, causing The Federals to withdraw.[63] Steele's Bayou Expedition was another attempt to capture Vicksburg which also failed, however this was more of a naval operation than past attempts to take the city. Admiral Porter and eleven vessels steamed up the bayou while Sherman followed with his Corps. Porter's fleet was nearly captured at Rolling Fork, saved only by a night march with candles by Sherman's forces.[64] On April 17th, Colonel Benjamin Grierson led a raid from La Grange, Tennessee to near Baton Rouge, Louisiana in an attempt to divert attention away from Grant's crossing of the river below Vicksburg. The raid went on for about sixteen days and stirred up considerable consternation and aggravation for the Confederate forces in Mississippi[65]. General Pemberton seemed somewhat baffled as to what should be done next, and at last decided to send Loring to Meridian to take command of all troops in the area and to stop Grierson. General Tilghman was ordered to send troops from Canton to Carthage to block a northwest escape, and in a telegram to General Pemberton, Tilghman reports," Messenger from Carthage again reports regiment of cavalry [at] that place. I have started Fifty-fourth Alabama and a section of artillery, with orders to move rapidly. I have Eighth Kentucky, about 100 strong.... Might effect something if I had more force. Please send it if practicable. I need a few cavalry."[66]

Major Samuel Lockett, Chief Engineer of the defenses of Vicksburg offers a very exact and precise

---

[63] Ulysses Simpson Grant, *Personal Memoirs of U.S. Grant*, (New York: Dover Publications, Inc, 1995), p. 175-178, hereinafter cited as Memoirs; Battles and Leaders, Vol. III, p. 493 (see Grant's discussion on the Vicksburg Campaign in Battles and Leaders, Vol. III, p 493-539 for a more detailed account)
[64] Memoirs, p. 177
[65] Memoirs, p. 192
[66] Official Records, Series I, Vol. XXIV/1 (S#36), p. 553

account of events concerning the defense and ultimate fall of Vicksburg. Major Lockett explains:

> At last General Pemberton became convinced that General Grant's intention was to march up the east bank of the Big Black River, to strike the railroad at or near Edward's Depot, and thus cut his communications with Jackson.... On the 12th of May, under the orders of General Pemberton, I went to Edward's Depot to put the Confederate forces in position upon the ground, selected for them to occupy, covering all approaches from the south and east....The army remained at Edward's depot from the 13th to the 15th. During this time General Pemberton received numerous dispatches from President Davis, and from General J.E. Johnston.... He then made the capital mistake of trying to harmonize instructions diametrically opposed to each other, and at the same time to bring them into accord with his own judgment, which was adverse to the plans to both. Mr Davis' idea was to hold Vicksburg at all hazard...Johnson's plan was to cut loose from Vicksburg altogether....[67]

Major Lockett continues with his account of events leading to the Battle of Champion Hill and events that followed the battle:

> Pemberton moved out from Edward's depot in obedience to a dispatch from General Johnston, ordering him to attack in the rear a force which he supposed General Johnston was going to engage in front. Under all the circumstances the Confederates made a gallant fight, but they were driven from the field with heavy loss in killed, wounded, and captured.... Stevenson's division bore the brunt of this battle and suffered the heaviest losses.... Loring's division did not cooperate with the other two, through some misunderstanding or misconception, and was scarcely engaged at all during the fight.[68]

General Pemberton's behavior in preparation for this battle that occurred on May 16 was bizarre and encumbered

---

[67] Battles and Leaders, Vol. I, p. 487
[68] Battles and Leaders, Vol. I, p. 487

with indecision, and it was the only battle in the western theater in which General Pemberton was the commander. Grant and Pemberton's leadership style is an exhibition of opposites: while Grant made use of his subordinates and his supply personnel, Pemberton's preparation gives no hint of order or logic. Initially, Pemberton planned to attack Grant's supply lines and troops were put into motion to carry out this attack. Conflicting orders from General Johnston directed that Pemberton's army meet Johnston north of the Southern Railroad. This order had been previously rejected by Pemberton, and he [Pemberton] now gave the order to reverse march and return to Edward's Depot.

General Loring questioned this command, and urged Pemberton to establish a battle line, and General Pemberton more or less acquiesced and Loring was ordered to deploy his division along a high ridge that contained the Coker house. General Stevenson was commanded to move the supply train along as rapidly as possible. Bowen's division moved into position on a ridge near the Ratliff house.[69]

On the march back to Edward's Depot, Pemberton's command encountered the troops of Carr's and Osterhaus' divisions. Colonel J.E.B. Jackson and a regiment of Georgians established a roadblock to enable the Confederates under Pemberton's command to reach Edward's Depot. During the return march General S.D. Lee's brigade came into contact with McPherson's XVII Corps and General Alvin Hovey's division of McClernand's XIII Corps about one-half mile from Champion Hill. Grant was with McPherson's Corps, and meanwhile Logan's

---

[69] Edwin Bearss, "Grant Marches West: The Battle of Champion Hill and Big Black Bridge", *Blue and Gray* (Columbus, Ohio), Vol. XVIII, May 2001, p. 9, 10. Hereinafter cites as Bearss, Blue and Gray. Dr. Bearss is the leading acknowledged authority on the Battle of Vicksburg. Much of this discussion is from his articles and his monumental three-volume work on this battle.

division of the XVII Corps, along with Hovey's division, formed a line of battle. General Stevenson, Lee's division commander, rushed two brigades and several batteries to assist Lee, and before noon, the battle was in progress.[70]

The Confederates were soon overwhelmed by the divisions of Hovey and Logan and the situation was at a desperate juncture. Pemberton ordered Bowen to support Stevenson's brigades, and as usual Bowen was outstanding and heroic. Hovey's division was smashed and Bowen was now within about one-half mile of Grant's headquarters. General Marcellus Crocker's division of the XVII Corps reached the battle scene at the crucial minute. Sixteen cannons enfiladed the Confederates of Bowen's division.[71] Loring would be problematic in this conflict, which was not unusual, since he had a history of bad relations with most superior officers.

General Pemberton and General Loring lacked mutual respect for each other; in fact, they disliked each other significantly. Loring was a Wilmington, North Carolina native who spent most of his life in Florida. He was a troublesome personality who was constantly engaged in disputes with superior officers for the slightest aspect of any disagreement. Loring's first major duty of the war occurred in West Virginia. Following the Romney Campaign, Loring opposed the stationing of his troops in the exposed town during the extreme winter conditions. He requested, and obtained permission from Secretary of War Benjamin to move to Winchester. Jackson ["Stonewall"] exploded with

---

[70] Bearss, Blue and Gray, p. 16-20
[71] Edwin Bearss, "The Vicksburg Campaign", *Civil War: Official Magazine of the Civil War Society (* out of print), No. 64, October 1997, p. 38,39. Hereinafter cited as Bearss, Vicksburg. Sylvanus Cadwallader, *Three Years With Grant*, edited by Benjamin P. Thomas (Lincoln: University of Nebraska Press, 1955), p. 79. Hereinafter cited as Cadwallander.

angry and threatened to resign, resulting in Loring's transfer to Southwestern Virginia and his promotion to major general. Shortly afterward, he was transferred to a command in Mississippi.[72]

Pemberton tended to anger Loring by ignoring his constant request for more troops, guns, etc., mainly because Pemberton simply did not have the supplies nor the manpower that Loring requested. General Loring tended to be aggressive and seemed to lack an overall appreciation of the prevailing conditions in the Western Theater of the war. In contrast, General Tilghman and Loring seemed to get along smashingly, although they were of very different temperaments. Loring's influence on Tilghman brought about a feeling of antipathy toward Pemberton. Added to Loring's influence on Tilghman was an old grievance held against him [Pemberton] by Tilghman from a dispute in North Mississippi. This hostility toward Pemberton was contagious and grew into a serious situation for the commander who, unfortunately, never really addressed the problem.[73]

As a demonstration of the lack of respect and understanding that existed between Loring and Pemberton, Loring was order by Pemberton to come up with his division on the left to assist Bowen on the march back to Edward's Depot. He refused and was given a second request and ultimately came to the center of the battle line. As mentioned earlier by Major Lockett, Loring's division never *fully* took part in the Battle of Champion Hill. At any rate, General Tilghman's brigade was left to protect the Raymond-Edward's Depot road, allowing Loring to arrive in time to cover Bowen's escape, even though the valiant effort of General Bowen's division was for naught. The Federals had

---

[72] Stewart Sifakis, *Who was Who in the Confederacy* (New York: Facts on File, 1988), p. 176,177
[73] Generals in Defeat, p. 156

fresh troops brought in and led by Col. G.B. Boomer, the result being that McPherson's Corps now had control of Champion Hill.[74]

General Tilghman had to hold the Raymond-Edward's Depot road or else Pemberton's army faced total destruction with no escape route. L.S. Flatan, a member of Cowan's Battery gives an account of the final hours of Tilghman's life:

> I was the gunner directing and sighting the gun at the time by the advice of General Tilghman, who had a perfect knowledge of the situation of the enemy through his field glasses. His last words to any one were in the highest compliment to me, praising my excellent marksmanship, except the words he spoke as he fell from his horse after a three inch rifle shot had cut him nearly in two, and as he careened and fell he said to his son who caught him: ' Tell your mother, God Bless her.' He was at that time near my gun, but had turned to ride down the line and was fully exposed to the fire of the enemy from small arms as well as a splendid battery that we had been dueling with for at least an hour, and under his direction, we had silenced it.[75]

There seems to be some dispute as to the exact hour of General Tilghman's death. One source states the general died at 1:30 P.M. while another source states his death occurred at 5: 30 P.M. Flatan proclaims that General Tilghman was on horseback when he died, another eyewitness declares that the general was standing when death occurred. While this seems like small and insignificant details, it raises questions about the overall progress of the battle, times, places, etc.[76]

---

[74] Bearss, Vicksburg, p. 42
[75] L.S. Flatan, "Tribute to General Lloyd Tilghman", *The Confederate Veteran*, September, 1910,p. 423
[76] See the *Confederate Veteran*, September 1893, p. 274-275; October 1896, p. 350-352 article by Y.J.V. Greif

Praise for General Tilghman was universal within the Confederate army. General Loring's report of the battle laments:

> It is befitting that I should speak of the death of the gallant and accomplished (Lloyd) Tilghman. Quick and bold in the execution of his plans, he fell in the midst of a brigade that loved him well, after repulsing a powerful enemy in deadly fight, struck by a cannon-shot. A brigade wept over the dying hero; alike beautiful as it was touching.[77]

General Tilghman's death dictated that the second in command assume the command of the brigade. Colonel A.E. Reynolds of the 26th Mississippi Infantry took command. In his report, Colonel Reynolds plaintively writes:

> I cannot here refrain from paying a slight tribute to the memory of my late commander. As a man, a soldier, and a general, he had few if any superiors. Always at his post, he devoted himself day and night to the interest of his command. Upon the battlefield cool, collected, and observant, he commanded the entire respect and confidence of every officer and soldier under him and the only censure ever cast upon him was that he always exposed himself too recklessly. At the time he was struck down he was standing in the rear of a battery, directing a change in the elevation of one of the guns. The tears shed by his men on the occasion and the grief felt by his entire Brigade, are the proudest tribute that can be given the gallant dead.[78]

The Milwaukee *Sentinel* reported General Tilghman's death via the Mobile *Advertiser*, "There was a very heavy and indecisive battle near Edward's Depot Saturday. We fell back to our entrenchments, loss heavy on both sides. General Tilghman killed."[79] In a sense this was a compliment, in that few Confederate brigade commanders received an obituary

---

[77] Official Records, Series I, Vol. XXIV/2 (S#37), p. 80
[78] Official Records, Series I, Vol. XXIV/2 (S#37), p. 81
[79] Milwaukee *Sentinel*, May 23, 1863

in a newspaper as far north as Milwaukee, it certainly was not typical.

General Tilghman's effort to secure the retreat of General Loring's division was at least partially successful. As Loring's Division was wading Baker's Creek, which had receded somewhat, Gen. Eugene Carr's division of McClernand XIII Corps had crossed the creek and was moving down the west side. Loring quickly regrouped and headed down the east side of the creek, intending to rejoin Pemberton at some point. Later he saw flames and realized that Edward's Depot had been abandoned, and rejoined General Johnston on May 19th.[80] By a quirk of battle and Loring's habit of ignoring the orders of his superiors, his division escaped the Vicksburg siege.

A point of interest concerns how the battle obtained the name Champion Hill. Since the history of battles is most frequently written by the winners, the Union army normally would have named the battle after the nearest stream, mountain---something which was well known and not subject to change. General Grant had already selected the name Baker's Creek, and the battle is frequently referred to by this name. However, Champion Hill is more frequently mentioned as a marker for this battle. Sylvanus Cadwallader, a war correspondent for the Chicago *Times,* and later the New York *Herald* and Joseph B. McCullagh of the Cincinnati *Commercial* conferred in writing their account of the battle. They both agreed that the battle should be called Champion Hill. Grant said he felt he should have some say about it [in a very good-natured fashion].[81] Nonetheless, the battle is known by both names, and to add additional confusion, Champion Hill and Champion's Hill are both frequently cited as the proper name. By whatever name one cares to use, as Dr. Terrence Winschel stated in his work,

---

[80] Bearss, Vickburg, p. 44
[81] Cadwallader, p. 81

Vicksburg: Fall of the Confederate Gibraltar, "Champion Hill was the largest, bloodiest, and most significant battle of the Vicksburg campaign."[82] There is no doubt that this is a totally accurate statement.

Gen. Lloyd Tilghman was buried in the cemetery at Vicksburg. His wife lived to the age of 80, moving from Clarksville, Tennessee to New York to be with her sons. Upon her death, the general's body was moved to New York City and placed beside his wife. His sons placed a life size bronze statue of the general in full uniform in Puducah, Kentucky, and they also marked the area of his death near Edward's Depot with a huge granite boulder, with a bronze tablet with the inscription:

Lloyd Tilghman
Brigadier General C.S.A.
Commanding First Brigade
Loring's Division
Killed here the afternoon of May 16, 1863, near
the close of the Battle of Champion's Hill.[83]

Dead at forty-seven, a human life far from its potential, Lloyd Tilghman was not the greatest brigadier general in the Confederate army - far from it. In fact, he led his brigade in only a few engagements and campaigns. Tilghman was, for want of a better term, a "throw away" general. From the outset of his career in the Confederate army in 1861, he was given commands which others could not handle or had given up any hope of improving. The two river forts, for example, were never viewed as vitally important until it was too late to save them. General Tilghman realized their importance long before others and

---

[82] Terrence J. Winschel, *Vicksburg: Fall of the Confederate Gibraltar* (Abilene: McWhiney Foundation Press, 1999), p. 75
[83] History of Talbot County p. 455

earnestly requested supplies, arms, men, etc. to bring about their improvement. In virtually every instance he was ignored or neglected because of another supposed priority elsewhere. General Tilghman seems to have been frequently commanded to hold his position so that other brigades, divisions, etc. could have an escape or retreat route. Tilghman may actually have viewed this as praise and honor for his brigade and in fact, it may have been. Considering Tilghman's lack of political savvy, he was probably simply being used by the likes of Loring, Polk, and others.

Lloyd Tilghman was an accomplished engineer who had experience with the railroad, canals, cities, and the military. Yet, he was under the control of a major [Gilmer] who probably had less practical experience, and certainly less interest in the improvement and fortification of the river forts. Even the most inexperienced military strategist could easily have determined that control of the Mississippi River was essential for the Confederacy to win the war. Yet, opportunities were ignored to gain this control, even though Tilghman pressed those in command and presented what he felt was necessary to preserve the forts. His requests were passed over as unimportant and irrelevant by General Polk, and to a degree, by Gen. Albert. Sidney Johnston.

When the end came for Fort Henry, those who were opposed to Tilghman's position were not to be found. Major Gilmer left the fort on foot rather than surrender with General Tilghman; yet, Gilmer was to a large degree responsible for what happened to Fort Henry and Fort Donelson. Gilmer made many condescending remarks about General Tilghman, and since he had the ear of Polk and Johnston, his views prevailed. Polk seemed to have been offended by General Tilghman's constant requests for basic military hardware, supplies and other needed items, and General Polk could have made a difference but he elected to do nothing.

The measure of a man, military or civilian, is the opinion held about him by his peers and equals, especially after his death. Lloyd Tilghman was held in the highest esteem by generals, as well as the men in the ranks. Proof of this is as simple as examining publications such as the *Confederate Veteran*. The number of General Lloyd Tilghman Confederate Veteran Associations is extraordinary. An astute comment from Dr. Terrence J. Winschel, historian at the Vicksburg National Military Park defines the life and efforts of General Tilghman, " The death of Lloyd Tilghman on May 16, 1863, epitomized the Confederate tragedy that was Champion Hill as the courage, bravery, and determination of the Southern soldiers, exemplified by Tilghman, was not enough to save Vicksburg and establish an independent nation."[84]

"He hath borne himself beyond the promise of his age, doing, in the figure of a lamb, the feats of a lion."[85] Such a man was Gen. Lloyd Tilghman, General in the Confederate army.

---

[84] A requested comment given to this writer via letter on September 10, 2001
[85] Shakespeare, *Much Ado About Nothing*

General George Stoneman

GEN. GEORGE STONEMAN

He has been characterized as somewhat taciturn, a little ascetic, doe-eyed, and very reserved. George Stoneman, aside from all of these descriptions is one of the most enduring figures of the Civil War, yet considering all of the many and varied military commands held by Stoneman, little is really known about him. Truly, Stoneman is without doubt one of the little known *important* personalities of the Civil War era.

Richard Stoneman, the grandfather of George Stoneman, came to the United States soon after the American Revolution and settled in the town of New Berlin, New York. His future wife, Mary Perkins, and her family had recently moved to New York from Rhode Island. This was a period in American history of families migrating westward, and George Stoneman, the father of future General Stoneman, was no exception. He moved to western New York's Chatauqua County, and took up residence in Busti, near Jamestown New York, about 1810. Soon afterwards, he married Catherine Cheney, and the young family ultimately had ten children; young George, born on August 8, 1822, was their first born. The Stoneman family was typical of pioneer families of that period of history, in that they involved themselves in many activities in order to survive, such as farming, lumbering, herding, etc. Even though it may have built character, this was certainly not an easy life.[1]

---

[1] *Twenty-sixth Annual Reunion of the Association of Graduates of the United States Military Academy* (Saginaw: Seemann & Peters, Printers

Stoneman received his basic education at the Jamestown Academy, where he proved to be a competent student. As is still the case today in many congressional districts, George had to compete for the cadetship that existed in the congressional district of New York where the Stonemans lived. Young George received his appointment to West Point from Representative Staly N. Clarke, a Whig who represented New York's 27th district. Stoneman entered West Point on July 1, 1842, graduating thirty-third in a class of fifty-nine students. At West Point, Stoneman was a serious student who received few demerits, with the exception of his senior year.[2] His roommate was Thomas Jackson ("Stonewall"), and as John Waugh explains in his book, *Class of 1846,* "The two shared what may have been the most becalmed quarters in West Point history, a noiseless room on the first floor of the south barracks. Nobody ever heard from them. Their neighbor in the next room said he "scarcely knew they were there."[3] Future Union general Darius Couch, expressed the opinion that, "they were thinkers rather than talkers." Jackson neither sought nor received much companionship, however Stoneman seemed to have had more social graces, was a more open person, hence had more friends and social relationships, according to Waugh.[4]

After graduation in 1846, Stoneman's career followed the same sequential pattern as most graduates of the 1840s. From 1846 until 1848, Stoneman was involved with the Mexican War. He served as Acting Assistant

---

and Binders, 1895), p. 25; hereinafter cited as Association of Graduates; John C. Waugh, *The Class of 1846* (New York: Warner Books, 1994), p. 46; hereinafter cited as Waugh
[2] *Official Register of the Officers and Cadets of the U. S. Military Academy, June 1843-1846*
[3] Waugh, p. 46
[4] Waugh, p. 46

Quartermaster of the Mormon Battalion from October 1, 1846, until February 1, 1847, and on the march from Fort Leavenworth, Kansas to San Diego, where there were skirmishes with hostile Indians as well. The young lieutenant served on frontier duty at the Presidio of San Francisco in 1848 and 1849, then at Sonoma during 1850 and 1851, and as a scout in 1851, against the Coquille Indians. In 1851-1852, he was entangled in skirmishes with the Yuma Indians. The young soldier served at Ft. Orford, Oregon in 1852, and performed escort duty for a topographical party through the Sierra Nevada Mountains, and for a railroad surveying party through Arizona and Texas during 1853 and 1854.[5] The future general served as the Aide-de-Camp to General Wool from January 4 until May 2, 1855; he then was assigned to garrison duty at the Jefferson Barracks in Missouri during 1855, and did frontier duty at Camp Cooper, Texas from the end of 1855 until 1858. He requested and received a leave of absence in 1858, and returned to frontier duty serving as commander of the Pecos Expedition in 1859. Stoneman took part in various skirmishes and combat in and around Fort Brown, Texas from December 1859 until 1861, ultimately serving another tour of garrison duty at the Cavalry School for Practice at Carlisle, Pennsylvania in 1861, until the outbreak of the Civil War. During this nine-year period of frontier duty, Stoneman achieved a reputation as a first class cavalry officer.[6] Additionally, he received a degree of notoriety due to his escape by steamer with a portion of his

---

[5] General George W. Cullum, *Biographical Register of the Officers and Cadets of the U.S. Military Academy,* Vol. II (Boston: Houghton, Mifflin and Company, 1891), p. 280; hereinafter cited as Biographical Register; Letter written to Captain George W. Cullum by General Stoneman on September 28, 1860, outlining his military service prior to the Civil War; hereinafter cited as Stoneman Letter no. 1
[6] Association of Graduates, p. 28

company to New York, refusing to surrender his command to Confederate Gen. David Twiggs.[7]

Stoneman was a Major in the First Cavalry at the outbreak of the war. He was summoned to Washington shortly after his return from Texas to aid in the defense of Washington, taking part in the occupation of Alexandria, Virginia. Maj. Stoneman led an advance into Virginia on May 24, 1861, over Long Bridge, which was successful, but Stoneman is not mentioned in the four reports recorded in the *Official Records of the War of the Rebellion*.[8] In what he considered a lucky break, he joined General George McClellan's staff on June 20, 1861, in West Virginia,[9] serving until August 3, 1861, after which he was transferred to the 4th U.S. Cavalry and promoted to Brigadier-General of Volunteers ten days later. He commanded the cavalry reserve from August 14, until October of 1861,[10] and played a role in McClellan's operations in West Virginia, the result being he later became the Chief of Cavalry, Army of the Potomac. This was largely an advisory position with little real decision making power, plus the dates vary somewhat on this promotion. Van Noppen [Dr. Ina Van Noppen, foremost authority on Stoneman's raids in Western North Carolina and Southwestern Virginia, past professor of history at Appalachian State University] relates this promotion as dating from October 16, 1861, until January, 1862---- but with a different title: Stoneman's Cavalry, Army of the Potomac, which implies he may have commanded only a segment of the Army of the Potomac's cavalry. Cullum

---

[7] Association of Graduates, p. 28
[8] Letter written to General George W. Cullum by General Stoneman on February 5, 1866, outlining his military service in the Civil War, p. 1; hereinafter cited as Stoneman Letter no. 2
[9] Stoneman Letter no. 2, p. 1
[10] Ina Van Noppen, *Stoneman's Last Raid* (Raleigh: North Carolina State University Print Shop, 1966), Van Noppen traces Stoneman's career in the first 25 pages of her book; hereinafter cited as Van Noppen

[military biographer] dates this promotion from August 14, 1861, until March 10, 1862. Stoneman was engaged in Cavalry reconnaissance's toward the Rappahannock River and Gordonsville, Virginia from February through March of 1862.[11]

During the Peninsula Campaign, Stoneman was in command of the reserve cavalry division at Yorktown, Williamsburg, and operations concerning Richmond, and on May 4 and 5, he commanded the advance guard of the Army of the Potomac. General McClellan's first step in the Peninsula Campaign was to take Yorktown, which would serve as the beginning point from where he hoped to launch his campaign toward Richmond. McClellan had major problems to contend with at Yorktown, the two outstanding ones being maps that were incorrect, and the fact that he miscalculated the importance of the Warwick River in planning the campaign. Another problem was his inability to obtain McDowell's Corps when needed, and if this was not enough, the Federal Navy did feel they could silence the batteries at Yorktown and Gloucester, permitting an amphibious attack. McClellan felt that given these express circumstances, a siege was his best, and maybe his only, option to take the city, and in view of these impediments he decided to proceed, placing Gen. Fitz-John Porter in charge of the siege operations. Between seventy-five and one hundred Parrotts, mortars, and Howitzers were brought in for the siege, which began on May 1, with an artillery attack. Confederate Gen. John Magruder wanted to delay his retreat as long as possible, hoping that this delay would give the Confederate forces in Richmond more time to prepare for an attack. On the night of May 3, Magruder quietly slipped out of Yorktown. Stoneman was in command of the pursuit, or

---

[11]Van Noopen, p. 1-25; Biographical Register, p. 281

advance guard force. In his account of the ensuing skirmishes near Williamsburg he relates:

> ...My instructions were to pursue and harass the rear guard of the retreating enemy, and if possible to cut off his rear guard, or that portion of it which had taken the Lee's Mill and Yorktown road. In harassing the enemy, I was to be supported by Hooker's division, which was to follow us by a forced march along the Yorktown and Williamsburg road, and in cutting off the rear guard, I was to cooperate with the division of General Smith, which was to march on the other, or Lee's Mill, road. Six miles from Yorktown we came upon the enemy's pickets. Two miles farther we came up with the rear of his guard, consisting of a regiment of cavalry, with a deep ravine and bad crossing between us and him.[12]

Stoneman continues his report stating that he had word that General Hooker was close behind with supporting divisions. General Cooke [J E B Stuart's father-in-law] led the advance and suddenly found his small force facing a regiment of cavalry, a battery of artillery, and three regiments of infantry. The situation all of a sudden turned grim. Stoneman continues:

> ...Owing to the limited space of cleared ground in which we could possibly operate with cavalry or artillery, I was unable to bring into action more than one battery and about 300 cavalry. The remainder of the force I directed formed in a clearing half a mile to our rear to cover our retreat, which I saw must necessarily soon be made unless the infantry support, 2 miles behind at last accounts, should come to our assistance.[13]

To make bad matters even worse, the Confederates were reinforced and in the process of turning Stoneman's

---

[12] *A Compilation of the Official Records of the Union and Confederate Armies* (Washington: Government Printing Office, 1881), Vol. XI/1, p. 424; hereinafter cited as OR
[13] OR, Vol. XI/1, p. 424

command, and were about to cut it off. The Confederates were firing from Fort Magruder, and taking a toll on men and animals. After forty-five minutes, Stoneman received word that Hooker was behind Smith's division and could not get around him. In the face of all these negatives, Stoneman made the wise decision to retreat. Confederate General Longstreet's forces were about to overwhelm the Federal left, but at the critical moment, General Kearny's division arrived and the situation stabilized somewhat. Stoneman ends his report with a rather strange comment, "During the 5th, my command was split up into fragments by the commanders, and I remained an idle spectator until the arrival of the general commanding."[14] Several thoughts can be drawn from this statement: a lack of leadership existed on Stoneman's part, he was too modest, he lacked the ability to perceive events taking place, etc. still one must make his own determination as to which is most nearly correct. Nevertheless, the Confederates managed to complete their withdrawal during the night of May 5.

In the afternoon of May 9, the Federal cavalry of General Stoneman encountered the Confederate cavalry near the village of Slatersville. This small village could actually be more accurately deemed a crossroads about two or three miles from New Kent Court House, Virginia. Stoneman was holding point for the Army of the Potomac as it moved ever closer to Richmond. The 6th U.S. Cavalry was leading Stoneman's forces, and Major Williams of the 6th Cavalry believed that the Confederates were in large numbers ahead of his column, so he hesitated until the troops behind him closed up. General Stoneman sent word to encircle the small detachment of Confederates that seemed to be cut off from the main force. He wanted to surround them and force an easy surrender, and Major Williams complied with the

---

[14] OR, Vol. XI/1, p. 425

command immediately, but a trap had been laid for the Federals. A single trooper appeared to be signaling his company of the arrival of the Union forces. The Federal troopers then began their pursuit, at which point the cavalry force sent by Major Williams was almost immediately overwhelmed, and withdrawal was the only option available to the Union cavalrymen at that point. Upon the arrival of Stoneman's infantry, the Confederates moved out of the woods in force, with artillery. Even though they were outnumbered, the Confederates continued the fight for about two hours. Losses were small on both sides, probably less than twenty. By 9:30 P.M. on May 9, the Union forces were in control of New Kent Court House.[15]

General McClellan was in need of intelligence about the movements, strength, and intent of the Confederate army in the Spring of 1862. He was receiving a degree of scrutiny and criticism from many sources, and most of them felt he was too slow and not aggressive enough in his campaign against the Confederates to capture Richmond. For this reason, he push General Stoneman toward Richmond with main force effort. Complicating matters even more so was the arrival of many regiments of raw troops that had to be inculcated into his command. While still an asset, untried recruits were frequently too haughty and unaware of the fatal dangers at hand, seemingly showing a sense of baneful immortality, and a refusal to follow orders---McClellan desperately needed experienced soldiers.

On May 13, General Stoneman and his forces took control of White House Landing. The name "White House" was given to the house, which was once owned by Martha Washington. During Stoneman's visit, the house was owned by "Rooney" Lee, Robert E. Lee's son. The house was

---

[15] Robert F. O'Neill, "Cavalry on the Peninsula", *Blue & Gray*, Vol. XIX, no. 5, June, 2002, p. 40; also see OR, Vol. XI/2, p. 247; O'Neill's account of this battle is the most complete source available

situated near the Richmond and York River Railroad, making it a prime location for Union activity and a good central location; therefore, McClellan elected to use White House Landing as his central base. General McClellan made an observation about the cavalry at his disposal, which was less than complimentary, "The cavalry organization remained unchanged, and we were sadly deficient in that important arm, as many of the regiments belonging to the Army of the Potomac were among those which had been retained near Washington."[16] His evaluation concerning the cavalry was more accurate than he realized. His forces were now, and would be in the future, confronted with great difficulty in crossing the Chickahominy River due to presence of the Confederate cavalry, which the Union cavalry seemed unable to stop or contend with in any supportive manner. McClellan was compelled to supply General McDowell's forces from White House Landing supply depot, and he later states that this was the cause, in large part, for the failure of the Peninsula Campaign. McDowell was on the opposite side of the Chickahominy, and having to supply McDowell's army was a constant drain on available resources, from McClellan's viewpoint.[17] In essence, McClellan was astride the Chickahominy, supplying troops he might not be able to use, with resources he felt he could not spare.

General Stoneman continued the drive toward Richmond, and was engaged on May 23, 1862, in a skirmish at New Bridge. Lt. Colonel William Hays, commanding a brigade of Horse Artillery explains, "On the 23rd of May Captains Robertson's and Tidball's batteries were placed in positions to drive the enemy's troops from New Bridge and

---

[16] Robert U. Johnson and Clarence C. Buel, editors, *Battles and Leaders of the Civil War* (New York: The Century Company, 1887), Vol. 1, p. 173; hereinafter cited as Battles and Leaders

[17] Battles and Leaders Vol. I, p. 173-174; Stoneman Letter, no. 2, p. 2

the banks of the Chickahominy, which service they succeeded in accomplishing in a very short time. The command on the same afternoon marched in the direction of Mechanicsville." Captain James M. Robertson, of Lieutenant Colonel Hays brigade relates, "On the evening of the 6th, I was detached…and reported to General Stoneman for duty with the advanced brigade of the army, and remained on duty until the 31st of May, 1862… On the 23rd of May the battery was put in position at Hogan's near New Bridge, and opened fire upon some cavalry… Fifty-one shells were fired, when the enemy retired."[18] General Stoneman was on the north side of the Chickahominy, hoping to link his cavalry with General McDowell's corps, coming overland from Fredericksburg. The weather was very restrictive for any military operations during the first two weeks of June. Torrential rains gummed up the roads, washed out the bridges, and generally made any large scale movements impossible. General McClellan was also on the north side of the Chickahominy with Porter's Fifth Corps near Boatswain's Swamp, on June 25, where plans were composed until after midnight on the 26th. This was a very dangerous situation for McClellan, of which General Lee took note and hoped to take full advantage.

In the last week of June 1862, General McClellan's army was in the following configuration: Porter's V Corps on the right of the line [North side of the river] facing toward Richmond, Franklin's VI Corps, and Sumner's II Corps, and finally Heintzelman's III Corps, with General Keyes IV Corps held in reserve [on the South side of the Chickahominy River]. McClellan commanded 92,500 effective troops. On the other side of the Chickahominy, on the extreme right, McCall and the Pennsylvania Reserve Division had taken a position at Mechanicsville about June

---

[18] OR, Vol. XI/2, p. 242, 247

19, in support of the V Corps.[19] McClellan and his army were still astride the Chickahominy and the Seven Days battles would be the result of this situation.

General Lee planned to hit the Federal army south of the Chickahominy with Maguder's forces. Longstreet, D.H. Hill, A.P. Hill, and Jackson would hit Porter's Fifth Corps with Lee's 60,000 troops. After Porter was defeated, the Confederates would then attempt to cut off McClellan's rail line to White House. On June 23, Lee held a war council with Longstreet, both of the Hills, and Jackson. It was decided that Jackson and D.H. Hill would hit Porter's right flank, while Longstreet and A.P. Hill made a frontal attack on Porter's corps, and Huger and Magruder pinned down McClellan's major force on the south side of the river. A. P. Hill would then advance on Mechanicsville, clearing the bridge over the Chickahominy for Daniel Hill and Longstreet, after which the combined forces would then reestablish contact.[20] This was the plan of action for what has came to be known as the battle of Mechanicsville on June 26, 1862. Confusion reigned, as often happens in war. Jackson was instructed to leave Ashland, Virginia and march toward Beaver Dam, where he would then communicate with General Branch at Half Sink, seven miles north of Meadow Bridges, upon his arrival. [Jackson did not arrive until 3:00 P.M.] A. P. Hill was then to communicate with Jackson and then with D.H. Hill and Longstreet before he launched his attack. A.P. Hill became impatient since no word had been received from General Branch about Jackson's arrival. When Jackson finally arrived, no one was available to brief him and he therefore bivouacked his forces for the night. A.P.

---

[19] Alexander S. Webb, *The Peninsula: McClellan's Campaign of 1862*, (Edison ,NJ: Castle Books, 2002, from the original published in 1881), p. 119-120; hereinafter cited as The Peninsula
[20] OR, Vol. XI/2, p. 498-499

Hill's division thus engaged McClellan's entire right wing in a battle that continued until 9 P.M.[21]

Where was General Stoneman during this encounter? Stoneman, quite by chance, played no real role in the battle of Mechanicsville. General Webb, in his book, *The Peninsula: McClellan's Campaign of 1862* states:

> On the morning of the 25, General Porter ordered General Morell to detail two regiments of not less than 500 men each, to serve under General Stoneman with the cavalry...Colonel Lansing who reported to Stoneman immediately, marched with him to White House—were transported by water to the James River and rejoined Morell at Westover, and thus were not engaged in the six days battles.[22] (The General is referring to the Seven Days battles)

General Stoneman, in his letter to General Cullum, confirms Webb's statement, and explains, "From that time [battle of Mechanicsville] until after the battle of Gaines Mill June 27[I] was in command of the cavalry on the right of the A of P."[23]

On July 5, 1862, Stoneman was given command of all the cavalry serving in the Army of the Potomac, with the exception of 2nd U.S. Cavalry, and McIntyre's squadron of the 4th Cavalry. Stoneman was ordered to report directly to McClellan and receive his orders from the commanding officer. On July 8, Stoneman reorganized the cavalry of the Army of the Potomac, and the general had his problems early on with this new position. It seems that many in the Army of the Potomac did not take the cavalry seriously. An example is expressed in a letter to McClellan on July 10, 1862, in

---

[21] William W. Hassler, *A.P. Hill: Lee's Forgotten General* (Chapel Hill: University of North Carolina, 1962),p. 45-51;hereinafter cited as A.P. Hill; this is a very fine analysis of the battle, primarily from the Confederate viewpoint

[22] The Peninsula, p. 130 (note)

[23] Stoneman letter no. 2, p. 3

which he informs," ...Commanding officers of scouting parties and brigade commanders complain that the men of their commands are taken away by generals, colonels, and other officers to act as orderlies, & etc. I have the honor to request that the general commanding give directions that this be stopped in (the) future."[24] It seems from this request that the cavalry was not taken seriously by officers not only in the infantry and artillery, but perhaps, even the cavalry officers themselves.

It is a well-known fact that General Stoneman had a serious hemorrhoid condition. It is difficult to determine, for this reason, if he was ill or simply not involved in the action of the cavalry during the Seven Days battles. As stated earlier, General Webb writes that he was taken back to White House, by order of General Porter to support General Casey. Stoneman says in his letter to General Cullum that from May 27, until June 27, he commanded the cavalry; he makes no mention of any other assignment or duty until September 10, 1862. Another source simply explains that he was ill during the battles of the Seven Days.[25] A correspondence from General McClellan on August 22, 1862, Special Orders No. 241, offers some insight into Stoneman's health and mental attitude during this period, " At his own request, Brig. Gen. George Stoneman is relieved from duty with the Army of the Potomac, and will proceed to Washington and report to the Adjutant-General of the Army for orders..."[26]

On September 10, Stoneman was appointed to command the 1st Division, III Corps. He held this position until November 15, 1862. On October 11, General McClellan sent the following message to Stoneman:

---

[24] OR, Vol. LI/1, p. 716; OR XI/2, p. 930
[25] The Peninsula, p. 130; David Gerleman, "George Stoneman," *Encyclopedia of the Civil War*, Vol. IV, p. 1874; hereinafter cited as Gerleman
[26] OR, Vol. LI/1, p. 754

> A force of rebel cavalry, supposed to be about 2,000 strong crossed into Maryland yesterday, at McCoy's Ferry, above Williamsport, stayed at Chambersburg last night, and left this morning at 9 o clock, in the direction of Gettysburg. It is possible they may attempt to recross the river at Leesburg. The commanding general directs that you keep your cavalry well out on the approaches in the direction of Frederick, so as to give you time to mass your troops at any point where they attempt to cross....[27]

General Stoneman replied to McClellan that he had sent out cavalry on all the roads, in all, about 1,200 troops. Stoneman was guarding about a thirty-mile area along a river, which was fordable. Stoneman further explains that he was given information by Colonel Ruggles, obtained from paroled prisoners stating that Stuart would probably recross the river at the mouth of the Monocacy River. At about 2:45 A.M. and again at 4:30 A.M., Stoneman received reliable information that Stuart was recrossing at the mouth of the Monocacy,[28] still General Stuart made good his escape, in part, due to Stoneman's excessive and conservative caution. Even though cavalry was sent to the designated area, delay and overall tardiness had precluded any hope of engaging the enemy. This would be a nagging problem for General Stoneman in many future situations.

The Chambersburg Raid, as this exploit is often called, was truly an extraordinary accomplishment. Stuart traveled about 125 miles in less than thirty-six hours. He captured 1,200 horses, took the war to the enemy, and made a fool of George McClellan and the Army of the Potomac. To say that McClellan was embarrassed is an understatement, at the very least. McClellan made every excuse he could muster to override and cover up this

---

[27] OR, Vol. XIX/2, p. 43
[28] OR, Vol. XIX/2, p. 43-44

blunder. He claimed he was deficient in cavalry, and that his orders had been disobeyed, among other reasons. This bad press may have contributed to Lincoln's dismissal of McClellan, and rightfully Stoneman was concerned enough to ask that a Court of Inquiry to assess blame be convened. Nonetheless, Stuart's success was berated by many military authorities, some of which were Confederates, "Pointless, not worth the risk, no military objective completed", are examples of the comments made. As for George Stoneman, the Chambersburg Raid was a mark against him in the high command's book.[29]

Douglas S. Freeman, a knowledgeable authority on the Army of Northern Virginia and Gen. Robert E. Lee, states in his account of the Chambersburg Raid that Lee wanted information and reconnaissance on McClellan's army, no doubt this is an accurate statement. McClellan acted with dispatch to arrange his army to combat whatever Lee had in mind for him. In a message from McClellan, Stoneman was directed to," …cross tomorrow (Monday) morning at Edwards Ferry… and to hold Leesburg… You will establish a cavalry picket of some strength at Aldie and one at Waterford, scouting out to Purcellville, and, if possible, to Snicker's Gap.[30] The date of this message is October 25 or 26, a short time after Stuart's ride around the army. Without doubt, McClellan was mending his defensive political walls.

On September 1, 1862, General Philip Kearny was killed at the Battle of Chantilly. Kearny was the commander of the 1st Division, III Corps of the Army of the Potomac.

---

[29] Emory M. Thomas, *Bold Dragoon: The Life of J.E.B. Stuart* (New York: Vintage Books, 1986), p. 179-180; also see Douglas Southall Freeman, *Lee's Lieutenants: A study in Command*, One-Volume Abridgment by Stephen W. Sears (New York: Scribner, 1998), p.388-390; hereinafter cited as Lee's Lieutenants
[30] OR, Vol. XIX/2, p. 496

General Stoneman was given this division on September 10, and held the position until November 15, 1862. This was a period of enormous changes in the Army of the Potomac, not only for Stoneman, but also for other notable individuals, in particular Gen. George McClellan. On November 7, 1862, McClellan was relieved of command, after which Gen. Ambrose E. Burnside took command of the Army of the Potomac on November 9, 1862.[31] On October 30, Gen. Samuel Heintzelman, commander of the III Corps of the Army of the Potomac, was transferred to other duties, the result being that General Stoneman was appointed Corps commander of the III Corps on November 15, 1862. [32]

In less than a month after receiving command of the III Corps, Stoneman was promoted to Major-General of Volunteers [November 29, 1862]. While General Stoneman gloried in this good fortune, within the same one-month time period, he would be in the middle of one of the war's greatest and most savage battles.

After General McClellan was relieved of command on November 7, he was ordered to report to Trenton, New Jersey to await orders for a new assignment, but no orders were ever issued. After General Burnside took command of the Army of the Potomac, there was a considerable range of feelings about the new commander. The generals of the Army of the Potomac felt that Burnside was a good man, loyal, and dependable, but too inexperienced to assume such an important command. They also immediately gathered that change was imminent, and would occur soon.

The first major change explained to Burnside's lieutenants concerned the size of the corps. General Burnside enlarged the corps to double that of their former size. He

---

[31] OR, Vol. XIX/2, p. 557
[32] Biographical Register, p. 281; Stoneman letter, no. 2, p. 3; Stewart Sifakis, *Who was Who in the Union* (New York: Facts on File, 1988), p. 191

gave them new names: Grand Divisions. General Couch's II Corps and Willcox's IX Corps would form the Right Grand Division, under the command of General Sumner. The Center Grand Division was made up of the III Army Corps of General Stoneman and the V Army Corps under the command of General Daniel Butterfield. The Center Grand Division was commanded by General Hooker. The Left Grand Division was composed of the I Corps led by General John Reynolds, and the VI Corps, commanded by General William Smith. The Left Grand Division was commanded by General William Franklin.[33]

General Burnside changed the entire plan for the upcoming campaign, often referred to as the Rappahannock Campaign and the battle of Fredericksburg would become a major part of this campaign. Burnside called a meeting with his staff on December 9, at which he reveled that he was aware of the Confederate defense arrangements at Fredericksburg, where Longstreet commanded about 38,000 troops and Jackson about 30,000. The Confederate forces extended some five miles along the range of hills surrounding the city, and Marye's Heights, the lowest of these hills, was under the control of Longstreet's forces. At the foot of Marye's Heights was a stone wall about four feet high, which would afford an extraordinary defense for the Confederates. Jackson and Longstreet were separated by quite a distance, convincing Burnside that a three point landing and attack after crossing the river would allow his forces to get between the two Confederate corps. Franklin would land below the city, Sumner would cross the river at two points, directly in front of the city, while The Center Grand Division of General Hooker would be held in reserve.

The Federals were under constant attack by Confederate sharpshooters, called "Hornets". This delayed

---

[33] Battles and Leaders, Vol. III, p. 145-147

the federal forces crossing the river, which was about 500 feet wide at the city of Fredericksburg. There seems to have been considerable animosity against the Army of the Potomac at this particular battle, far more than was usually the case. During the last weeks of November, the Federal Army had demanded the surrender of the city, informing the mayor, Montgomery Slaughter, that unless surrender occurred, the city would be shelled within sixteen hours. Most of the residences left Fredericksburg, but nonetheless, the shelling of the city simply reinforced the negative view held by most Southerners that all "Yankees" wanted death and desolation for the South. This view and its collateral feelings probably contributed to the unusually heavy slaughter at Fredericksburg.[34]

On December 11, five pontoon bridges were constructed across the Rappahannock River by the federal engineers. This in itself, was no easy task, considering the cold, the "Hornets'", and the time element. On the 12th of December, federal troops began crossing the river. The "Hornets" were active, making this a much longer and more formidable task. What should have taken a few hours, at most, took many hours. General Barksdale's 17th and 18th Regiments of Mississippians [the "Hornets] laid down deadly fire until men of the 7th Michigan from General Howard's division, took pontoon boats and rowed across the river and finally silenced the "Hornets" [they were also ordered to cease by General Longstreet]. Afterwards, the

---

[34] *Civil War*, February 1998, Issue no. 66, (formerly the magazine of the Civil War Society) the entire issue is devoted to the Battle of Fredericksburg see pages 24-48 for detailed information; *Photographic History of the Civil War*, Vol. I (Secaucus, NY: Blue and Gray Press, 1987 reprint of the 1911 edition), p. 82-102; hereinafter cited as Blue and Gray

engineers finished their work and the crossing commenced on the 12th of December.[35]

December 13 was on a Saturday, and the weather was absolutely frightful, extremely cold, a fog was in place, and was very heavy. The attack took place at 8:A.M., but it was at least 11 A.M. before any real fighting occurred. This battle was an absolute disaster for the federals, exemplified by the fact that by 2:30 in the afternoon, the Left Grand Division was in major trouble, and by 3:30 P.M., this Division was more or less defeated. Sumner's Right Grand Division was in a "lead snowstorm" at Marye's Heights where General Winfield Hancock's Irish Brigade lost 900 of its1, 200-man attack. General Longstreet gives his account of this advance:

> ...Hancock, coming speedily with his division, was better organized and in time to take up the fight as French was obliged to retire. This advance was handsomely maintained, but the galling fire they encountered forced them to open fire. Under this delay, their ranks were cut up as rapidly as they had collected at the canal, and when within a hundred yards of the stone wall they were so thinned that they could do nothing but surrender, even if they could leap to the road-bed. But they turned, and the fire naturally slackened, as their hurried steps took them away to their partial cover.[36]

The stonewall was a death trap for many Union soldiers. Gen. John Ames gives an account of the conditions at the stonewall: ["In front of the Stone wall at Fredericksburg"]

> On Saturday, December 13th, our brigade had been held in reserve, but late in the day we were hurried to the battle only to see a field full of flying men and the sun low in the west shining red through columns of smoke... Almost an army lay about us scattered back over the plain toward the town. Not only corpses, but many of the badly wounded, hardly distinguishable from the

---

[35] Battles and Leaders, Vol. III, p. 108
[36] James Longstreet, *From Manassas to Appomattox* (New York: Mallard Press, 1991), p. 310; Hereinafter cited as Longstreet

dead, were here too. To die groveling on the ground or fallen in the mire, is dreadful indeed…

The enemy riddled every moving thing in sight: horses tied to the wheels of a broken gun-carriage behind us; pigs that incautiously came grunting from across the road; even chickens were brought down with an accuracy of aim that told of a fatally short range, and a better practice than it would have been wise for our numbers to face. They applauded their own success with a hilarity we could hardly share in….[37]

General Stoneman's Corps was ordered to be ready to move on December 11 at a minute's notice. He had his corps ready and bivouacked in the area where they assembled, due to the fact that they were unable to cross the river because of the delay of the pontoon bridge construction. On December 12, the III Corps moved to the vicinity of the bridges. The corps was crossing the river to support Sumner's Right Grand Division, but Sumner did not cross the river until about 2 o'clock, hence Fredericksburg was extremely crowded with military units from Sumner's Right Grand Division, so much so that Whipple's Division could not find room, and were directed to bivouac at the foot of the pontoon bridges. Whipple, Stoneman's 3rd Division commander, had been sent to join Sumner's Right Grand Division for this battle. At sundown, Stoneman took his remaining two divisions, Birney's [1st Division] and Sickles' [2nd Division] about three miles and bivouacked them at the two bridges over which the Left Grand Division had crossed the river earlier on the 12th, after which Stoneman then discussed strategy with General Franklin until about 10 P.M.

At daybreak on the 13th of December all was in readiness. Stoneman sent about half a regiment to support DeRussy's batteries, who was in support of General Reynolds' Division. At 11:30 A.M. a division was sent to

---

[37] Battle and Leaders, Vol. III, p. 122-123 (General Ames was in the Second Brigade, Sykes' Division, V Corps

support General Reynolds and Stoneman continued his discussion with General Franklin. Franklin ordered Stoneman to hold one division in immediate readiness to move, so Stoneman sent General Birney's 1st Division and held back Sickles' Division. Later in the day Stoneman made his way to the 1st Division front with Birney. Meade's and Gibbons' divisions occupied the Bowling Green road, which was near the river and the Fredericksburg and Richmond Railroad. Meade and Gibbons had made some inroads into Jackson's defense and driven some of his forces beyond the railroad. Birney's Division was in support of Meade and Gibbons, but both divisions soon retired under great duress. The Confederates were now advancing in force, and Stoneman sent word for Sickles' 2nd Division to advance for additional support. Sickles arrived, formed his division, and the Confederates immediately opened a strong fire on Sickles' right. Both Birney and Sickles were under an intense attack, whereby Birney's division soon faced a deadly barrage from ten or more guns. At long last his and Doubleday's artillery were able to silence the Confederate guns.

After sundown, General Stoneman withdrew his batteries to the other side of Bowling Green Road, strengthened the pickets and supplied rations and ammunition to his men. Stoneman expressed the view that Birney's and Sickles' arrival may very well have save the entire left wing of the army from possible disaster, and he also stated, " But in doing this valuable and important service, the first Division lost upward of 1,000 of as brave men as ever pulled a trigger." The general also made an observation about the division, saying that it was composed of men from the whole country, from Mississippi to Maine. He also alluded to the fact that Kearny would have been proud of his old corps---- they were brave men who did their duty and did not disgrace the Kearny badge.[38]

Another statement which expresses the gravity of this battle, and is expressed in several sources assails, " Later in the day, the dead bodies, which had become frozen from the extreme cold, were stood up in front of the soldiers as a protection against the awful fire to shield the living, and at night were set up as dummy sentinels."[39] Important generals were lost on both sides; Union generals Jackson and Bayard, and Confederate general Maxey Gregg died at Fredericksburg. On December 15, General Burnside ended the attack, after some persuasion, and crossed the river. This battle essentially ended Burnside's role as the leader of the Army of the Potomac, and later at his own request, he was relieved as commander on January 25, 1863. Dead, wounded, and missing in this battle approached 24,000 men.

Before his request for reassignment, relinquishing his command of the Army of the Potomac, Burnside attempting a final crossing of the Rappahannock River at Fredericksburg. A number of possible sites were considered, but Burnside's staff and even the President vetoed some of the sites. It was decided that Bank's Ford was the optimal site for success, which got the movement under way on January 20, 1863. General Stoneman writes:

> "January 20, the corps broke camp and proceeded up the Rappahannock to Bank's Ford. Bivouacked for the night, and remained in the same position the next day waiting for the pontoons, which were delayed by bad roads. January 23, the pontoons being still delayed by muddy roads, the troops received orders to march back to old camp, where they remained that night." *

---

[38] OR, Vol. XXI, p. 358-361
[39] Blue and Gray, Vol. I, p. 96, 102; Battles and Leaders, Vol. III, p. 116

At 8: 40 P.M. Stoneman received a message to march his command to within a half mile of the Rappahannock River, mass his forces out of sight, and make way for the V Corps to come through.* General R. E. Lee stated in his report concerning the "Mud March":

> About dark that evening the rain, which had been threatening during the day, commenced to fall, and continued all night and the following two days. Whether the storm or other causes frustrated the designs of the enemy I do not know; but no attempt as yet has been made to cross the Rappahannock, and some of the enemy's forces have apparently resumed their former positions.[40]

General Burnside's final attempt to cross the river held a modicum of hope for success, but nature intervened, and all was lost. Facing these developments, Burnside requested removal as commander of the Army of the Potomac. No doubt, it would soon have been demanded by the President and others, in and out of the military.

On February 25, 1863, in an accidental meeting of Confederate and Union reconnaissance forces, General Stoneman states in his report that General Averell informed him that the enemy was in force at his lines in the vicinity of Hartwood Church. Stoneman continues, explaining that it appeared that in fact the enemy was in "considerable force". Hartwood Church is about five to ten miles from the Rappahannock River on the Warrenton-Fredericksburg Road. Confederate General Fitzhugh Lee details in his report:

> On the 25, I drove in the enemy's pickets near Hartwood Church, and attacked his reserve and main body. Routed them,

---

[40] OR, Vol. XXI, p. 754 (Stoneman's first statement), p. 985 (second statement), p. 755 (General Lee) the stared footnotes on page 196 and 197 are General Stoneman's, {pages 754 and 985}; page 755 is General Lee's

and pursued them within 5 miles of Falmouth, to their infantry lines. Killed and wounded many of them. Captured 150 prisoners, including 5 commissioned officers, with all their horses, arms, and equipments. I then withdrew my command slowly, retiring by detachments. Encamped at Morrisville that night, and on the 26th recrossed the river, and returned to camp with my prisoners.*

Colonel Benajah Bailey, 86th New York Infantry, in a very different version, claims the Confederates were driven back. This claim is also made by Lt. Colonel Cummins of the 124th New York, included in General Dan Sickles', III Corps report. General Averell, 2nd Cavalry Division commander, reports only thirty-six killed, wounded and missing on February 26.[41] Dyer reports the Union killed wounded and captured at Hartwood Church Skirmish as 150.[42]

The Skirmish at Hartwood Church involved a surveillance mission by the Confederate Army to determine the strength of the Union forces on the Rappahannock River, near Fredericksburg. The Federal Army then determined to assess the Confederate strength and movement in the same area. There is a sense of urgency in the report filed by General Stoneman, a fear that this was to be an all out conflict, thus infantry and cavalry were put into motion to cover any contingency. This skirmish was simply one of many precursory situations leading to the battle of Chancellorsville.

How could a simple crossroads, which could hardly be considered even a village become one of the major battlefields of the Civil War? To make sense of this, an examination of Hooker's campaign plan is necessary. The

---

[41] OR, Vol. XXV/1, p. 22 (Averell's report); p. 25, General F. Lee's report; p. 25, General Sickles' report [* denotes General Lee's reports]
[42] Frederick H. Dyer, *A Compendium of the War of the Rebellion,* Vol. I, (Dayton: Broadfoot Publishing Company & Morningside Press, 1994), p. 913; hereinafter cited as Dyer

Federal Army desired to get its forces below the Rappahannock River and make an advance on Richmond. They had tried and failed at Fredericksburg on two separate occasions. Hooker determined that he could come up with a plan to achieve this goal. He reasoned that the Rappahannock and Rapidan River come together above the United States Ford and at the conjunction, the two rivers form a loop. If the Federal cavalry crossed the upper fords of the Rappahannock, then took a northern loop, and then a southwestern swing, they would cross the railroads north of Richmond, creating havoc for the Army of Northern Virginia. The Federal infantry would cross the Rappahannock River at Kelley's Ford, and the Rapidan at Germanna and Ely's Fords, go down river and open Banks' Ford, getting in the rear of Lee's army, while a smaller secondary force [the VI Corps and Gibbon's division] would attack at Fredericksburg and draw the Confederates away from the main goal of the campaign. This plan had problems; below the Rapidan River, where it converges with the Rappahannock, an area referred to as the Wilderness exist, and Chancellorsville is on the edge of this area. This was an intensely thick growth of vines, trees, brush and brambles, with few roads and even less cleared space, making artillery near useless in this place. To make the task Herculean, Hooker had to get his army in place before the Confederates were aware of his presence, and Chancellorsville is located about ten miles behind what was General Lee's extreme left lines. Hooker reasoned that he could then exit the Wilderness southwest of Fredericksburg, and move on Richmond. He later stated, [after the battle of Chancellorsville] "I felt confident when I reached it [the battlefield] that I had eighty chances in a hundred to win."[43]

---

[43] Battles and Leaders, Vol. III, p. 218; see Battles and Leaders Vol. III, p. 154-243 for a full and complete analysis of this great battle; also

What was General Stoneman's role in this great battle? Stoneman writes, "On April 27, I, then being in Warrenton Junction, with the corps encamped along the Orange and Alexandria Railroad, received a telegram directing me with my commanders to meet some persons from headquarters Army of the Potomac at Morrisville on the following day at 2 p.m.". On April 28, 1863, Stoneman received new orders and instructions. Orders given to Stoneman on April 12 were modified. The original orders stated that Stoneman was to march at 7 A.M. on April 13, cross the river with his entire command and, with whatever means possible, deny Lee his needed supplies. The raiders were to inflict maximum damage in the process. Stoneman ordered the march for April 13. One brigade would cross the river at midnight, and the divisions would later cross at two different fords. Stoneman had command of about 10,000 troops, four batteries of horse artillery [427 men], and twenty-two rifled guns, and each rider had six days rations--- everything looked good. Then the rain began to fall. It rained for three days. The raid was halted at the river's edge due to mud, floods, and the inability of man and horse to travel.[44] New orders were issued to Stoneman, as stated above, on April 28. General Stoneman was instructed to cross the Rappahannock River somewhere, of his determination, between Kelly's and Rappahannock Fords. He was then ordered to send part of his force toward Raccoon Ford and Louisa Court House, and the remaining part of his cavalry was to destroy the Orange and Alexandria, and the Aquia and Richmond Railroads. At some point, his forces would reunite, hopefully at the Pamunkey River, so as to cut off the enemy's retreat. In his orders of the 12th, he was instructed to

---

Ernest B. Furguson, *Chancellorsville: 1863* { New York: Vintage Books, 1993), p.65 [n] gives a very good account of Hooker's plan of battle

[44] Waugh, p. 408-410; Waugh offers a very clear and concise account of Stoneman's problems at the beginning of the raid

note that the primary objective of his mission was to cut the enemy's connections with Richmond by the Fredericksburg route. This order was strongly reiterated again.[45] Stoneman commanded the 2nd and 3rd Cavalry Divisions, Davis' Brigade of Pleasonton's First Division, and Tidball's and Robertson's batteries. He therefore, had the entire cavalry, with the exception of the remainder of General Pleasonton's Division, minus Davis' Brigade.[46]

This cavalry assignment given to General Stoneman has come to be known as "Stoneman's Raid", one of several such raids by this name. The events of this raid are:

1. April 29- Skirmishes at Kellysville, Brandy Station, and Stevensburg
2. April 30- Skirmish at Raccoon Run
3. May 1- Skirmish at Rapidan Station
4. May 2- Skirmish near Louisa Court-House
5. May 3- Skirmish at South Anna Bridge, near Ashland
6. May 4- Skirmishes at Flemmings' (Shannon's) Cross-roads, Tunstall's Station, and Ashland Church
7. May 5- Skirmish at Thompson's Cross-roads
8. May 7- Stoneman's command recrosses Raccoon Ford [47]

The skirmishes around Brandy Station consisted of mainly artillery exchanges between General Averell and the 13th Virginia Cavalry. The 6th Cavalry also saw action on the road toward Stevensburg. The night of April 29th was absolutely dreadful. No fires were built, so as to avoid enemy detection of the command's whereabouts,

---

[45] OR, Vol. XXV/1, p. 1058, 1065, 1066
[46] OR, Vol. XXV/1, p. 1058, Battles and Leaders, Vol. III, p. 236-237
[47] OR, Vol. XXV/1, p. 1057

nonetheless, there was a cold rain falling most of the night. At 4 A.M. the cavalry force moved out with about 3,500 soldiers, and were basically unencumbered with any extra accouterments.

On April 30, General Stoneman received a note found by General Averell's division directed to Colonel Chambliss of the Confederate army. The note discussed the need to determine what type, and the number of troops in the area on the other side of Kelly's Ford, and of course General Stoneman's whereabouts were in question.[48]

Stoneman's Cavalry crossed at Raccoon Ford, on the Rapidan, April 30, early in the day. It was determined that Stuart had crossed at Somerville Ford, a mere five miles above Raccoon Ford, heading toward Fredericksburg. Stoneman ordered a 2 A.M. departure for May 1, and although Stuart's trail was found, he had eluded Stoneman, headed toward Fredericksburg. General Gregg was sent to Louisa Court House, on the Virginia Central Railroad, to destroy tracks, telegraph lines, etc. while Buford's brigade camped on the south bank of the North Anna River.

At 10 A.M. on May 2, Stoneman's cavalry force united at Louisa Court House. A regiment was sent to the area near Gordonsville to determine where six or more trainloads of Confederate troops were destined. A skirmish occurred with the 9th Virginia cavalry when their pickets were driven in by the Maine squadron determining the train's destination. A raiding party was sent to destroy Carr's Bridge, on the main road leading from Spotsylvania to Goochland on the James River. After destruction of eighteen miles of track, water tanks, telegraph lines, and depots, Stoneman moved to Yanceyville, on the South Anna River. From Yanceyville, the unit traveled to Thompson's Cross

---

[48] OR, Vol. XXV/1, p. 1059

Roads, ten miles down the river, arriving at 10 P.M. on May 2.[49]

At Thompson's Cross Roads, the James and the South Anna Rivers are only about twelve miles apart, obviously a very important location. General Stoneman called a meeting of his regimental commanders and explained exactly what he hoped to accomplish for the remainder of the raid. At this meeting, he made his famous "bursting shell" speech. The General said, "... we had dropped in that region of country like a shell, and that I intended to burst it in every direction, expecting each piece or fragment would do as much harm and create nearly as much terror as would result from sending the whole shell, and thus magnify our small force into overwhelming numbers...."[50] Three raiding parties were sent out to reek havoc and carry out the "bursting shell" philosophy. One party went to the James River to destroy the large canal aqueduct over the Rivanna River, and were then to proceed toward Richmond, doing as much damage as possible. A second party, led by then Colonel [later General] Judson Kilpatrick, was to destroy railroad bridges over the Chickahominy, then move on toward Richmond. The third raiding party was to strike the railroads at Ashland, the Fredericksburg, Atlee's, and the Virginia Central, doing maximum damage in all cases. The 5th Cavalry was to backtrack the last group and insure that the destruction was complete. Finally, Capt. Wesley Merritt [later General] was sent out to generate all the destruction he could possibly accomplish. All three raiding parties left camp at Thompson's Cross Roads at 3 A.M. on May 3.[51]

General Stoneman planned for the raiding parties to strike simultaneously hoping to prevent the enemy from

---

[49] OR, Vol. XXV/1, p. 1060
[50] OR, Vol. XXV/1, p. 1060
[51] OR, Vol. XXV/1, p. 1061

communicating information that would prepare them at points where they might otherwise be vulnerable. Some of the raiders returned on the 4th, some on the 5th. Colonels Kilpatrick and Davis pushed on to Gloucester Point, where afterwards Kilpatrick attacked Hungary Station, a main depot on the Fredericksburg & Richmond Railroad on May 4, and encountered no real resistance. Kilpatrick and his command were within two miles of Richmond, closer than any Federal troops, up to that point. In five days, Kilpatrick had ridden two hundred plus miles, taken three hundred prisoners, torched railroad bridges, sunk ferries, burned depots, and wrecked a number of locomotives.[52] Nevertheless, General Stoneman expressed some anxiety about what was occurring with his cavalry. Much was at stake, much more than he realized at that point. Stoneman sent a part of the 5th Cavalry and some of Buford's brigade to Shannon's Cross Roads to check the movement of the enemy forces. Before the main contingent of Stoneman's party reached Shannon's Cross Roads, Lee's and Hampton's cavalry units appeared in the area. Captain Harrison [of Stoneman's command] pulled in his pickets and charged the enemy of 1,200 cavalrymen, losing only a few men. Before Stoneman's cavalry arrived, the Confederates had moved rapidly toward Charlottesville; for that reason Stoneman remained at Shannon's Crossroads the rest of the day and night of May 4. On May 5, the general returned to Yanceyville, on the South Anna River and the remainder of the command also returned to report the progress made on their assignments.[53] Of interest, while at Yanceyville, Stoneman and his men engaged in Divine services, held in the St. James Church at Yanceyville. The services were conducted by the Rev. A. O. Brickman, Chaplain of the 1st

---

[52] Samuel J. Martin, *The life of Union General Hugh Judson Kilpatrick* (Mechanicsburg [PA]: Stackpole Books, 2000), p. 72, 75
[53] OR, Vol. XXV/1, p. 1062

Maryland Cavalry. The service was very patriotic, with a closing prayer by Major C.H. Russell of the 1st Maryland.[54]

General Stoneman had heard nothing from General Hooker, nor had any retreating Confederates been detected. Nothing was known of the Federal army's plight in and near Fredericksburg, with the exception of rumors of its defeat, also food and supplies were now limited. Hooker had promised communication, but six days had passed and all that could be done, had been done, Stoneman reasoned. In light of all these negative factors, it was time to assess accomplishments, pull in all pickets and depart, but this was to prove much easier said than done. Lee and Hampton were nearby, but thought that Stoneman was headed to Charlottesville. Stoneman suspected a major force was in Gordonsville and another at the Louisa Court House, and possibly a smaller force at Tolersville. Buford was then sent out with 650 cavalrymen to threaten any force in Gordonsville, and another detachment was sent out toward Bowling Green to disrupt Confederate communications. After dark, the main body took the middle road between Gordonsville and Bowling Green leading through Tolersville, crossing the North Anna River near the Victoria Iron Works, and from there they traveled to Orange Springs for a later rendezvous with the remainder of the command. The whole command assembled at Orange Springs on May 6, where rumors were circulating of the withdrawal of the federal forces to the north of the Rappahannock. Apprehension was mounting among Stoneman's command, and not without just cause.

Stoneman's cavalry made its way to Raccoon Ford on the Rapidan, and as of daybreak on May 7, the raiding cavalrymen were somewhat out of Confederate reach and felt reasonably safe. After feeding and watering the horses,

---

[54] New York *Times*, May 8, 1863, by way of the Milwaukee *Sentinel*, May 14, 1863

cooking food, and resting, the command made its way toward Kelly's Ford, leaving at about 10 A.M. The head of the column arrived at the ford around 9 P.M. The Rappahonnock was foaming and swollen; not until May 8, the next day, were the raiders able to cross the river. The crossing took the life of one cavalryman and some few horses, but was finally completed by nightfall. Stoneman moved to Bealton Station on the Orange and Alexandria Railroad where supplies and food were located. On the 10th of May, the troops marched to Deep Run, and on the 11th, what remained of Gregg's division also reached Deep Run.[55]

Stoneman received much criticism for his efforts in the Chancellorsville raid toward Richmond. Much of this fall out came due to the actions, or more correctly, the lack of action, of General Averell. Stoneman writes in his report that Averell, "had gone into camp near where I left him... I also sent word back to General Averell that I had not time to concern myself with the enemy in his front."[56] The historian Bruce Catton had this to say about Averell's inaction, " He [Stoneman] sent half his command off under Averell to keep rebel cavalry at a distance, and Averell wondered over to Rapidan Station and went into bivouac there, confused and inert, as much out of the war as if he had been in Cuba."[57] Upon learning of this poor judgment on Averell's part, Hooker summarily relieved him of his command. Much had been expected from the cavalry, in fact, Stoneman and the cavalry, without realizing it, were the main players in the campaign involving Chancellorsville. Stanton, Secretary of War, felt that Stoneman's Raid was a brilliant success, but Hooker scoffed at this assessment of his cavalry.[58] As a

---

[55] OR, Vol. XXV/1, p. 1062-1063 [Stoneman's Report]
[56] OR, Vol. XXV/1, p. 1058
[57] Bruce Catton, *The Army of the Potomac: Glory Road* (New York: Doubleday, 1952), p. 209; hereinafter cited as Glory Road
[58] OR, Vol. XXV/2, p. 452, 438

result of poor performance, and failure to carry out the orders given to him by Hooker, Stoneman also was relieved of command.

The historian Douglas Southall Freeman defines what he felt were Hooker's mistakes in the Battle of Chancellorsville," Hooker did not have a staff capable of conducting an attack in the Wilderness and Fredericksburg simultaneously. His initial blunder was made in sending off virtually all his cavalry for operations against Lee's lines of communication. The absence of the cavalry simplified the march of the Second Corps to the Federal Right." Freeman goes on to say that, "Hooker could have argued that the cavalry did not do its duty, if so, they could have destroyed Lee's lines of supply. Such an argument establishes the path for blaming the cavalry for the failure of the campaign."[59] Unfortunately, this is exactly what happened. Equally regrettable is the fact that Hooker was simply too impatient, and did not give Stoneman's command enough time to complete their assignment before sending his entire command toward Chancellorsville.

General Hooker was to suffer a similar fate as that which befell General Burnside. Hooker probably saw the handwriting on the wall after the Chancellorsville defeat. Not even his champion in the government, Solomon P. Chase could save him. The control of the garrison at Harper's Ferry was the primary issue that brought about Hooker's resignation. Hooker wanted the use of these troops elsewhere and Halleck refused to allow this to take place. Hooker then sent a letter of resignation to the War Department, probably in a fit of anger and rage, but it was immediately accepted. Later, an official representative from the War Department entered General Meade's tent in the

---

[59] Douglas Southall Freeman *Lee's Lieutenants: A study in Command* [One-Volume Abridgment by Stephen W. Sears] (New York: Scribners, 1998), p. 508

early morning hours of June 28, 1863. Meade was sleeping and upon waking, was informed that he was the new commander of the Army of the Potomac. Meade, at first, thought he was under arrest and he immediately tried to decline the promotion but was informed that could not be done. He was the commander----like it or not.[60] Leadership of the Army of the Potomac was much like car racing: if you lose a race, you race in a different car next time; if you lose the next race, there might be a new driver in the next race.

From June 10, until July 20, 1863, Stoneman was absent from duty due to illness. As is widely known, Stoneman had chronic hemorrhoids, which would be a very disabling illness for one who must ride horses for long periods of time. On July 28, Stoneman was assigned to duty as Chief of the Cavalry Bureau in Washington. This was more or less an administrative job, with marginal importance and little decision making power. The bureau was formed in July of 1863, in large part, as a position for General Stoneman and labeled as General Orders No. 236. The Cavalry Bureau Chief had the following responsibilities: to organize and equip the cavalry forces, to purchase all of the necessary horses and other animals, to establish cavalry depots, to organize and discipline cavalry recruits, to receive and take action on reports concerning cavalry troops, and finally, to demand proper upkeep of horses and cavalry equipment[61] In reality, this position was ideal for General Stoneman. He had the necessary experience and background for the position, and he did an outstanding job with the assignment. Given his health and leadership ability, he probably should have considered remaining permanently in this position.

In May of 1864, one of the major campaigns of the war began in the South. The Atlanta Campaign would be one

---

[60] Glory Road, p. 256
[61] OR, Series III, Vol. III, p. 580

of the major determinants of the Confederacy's defeat in the Civil War. This campaign was immense, with hundreds of skirmishes, many engagements, and a number of large battles. The Confederacy and the Union would lose a number of important generals in this campaign. Generals Leonidas Polk, James McPherson, and Charles Harker are three prime examples. Gen. George Stoneman would play a role in this campaign, although not a major role, yet this campaign would come very close to ending his career as a cavalry officer and he would not redeem himself until the last few months of the war.

At the beginning of the campaign, Stoneman was in Lexington, Kentucky involved in replenishing his supply of cavalry horses. Stoneman joined the 23rd Corps before Dalton on May 10 but at that point, he did not have his entire cavalry command present for duty. When he arrived at Dalton there were only, 1,697 cavalrymen present for duty. However, his entire command [an additional 1,493 cavalrymen] joined him later, making a force 3,190 men. Stoneman operated with the IV Corps, commanded by General Howard for a portion of the campaign.[62] Aside from an entry in General Schofield's report, Stoneman was however, engaged in skirmishes around Tunnel Hill and Varnell's Station on May 7. A large Confederate infantry unit attacked General Stoneman on the Dalton & Cleveland Pike, driving in his pickets. The general commanded a force of about 2,000, with a contingent of 1,000 men arriving later. According to General Stoneman, the Confederates were on their way to Ringgold when General Sherman decided that the IV Corps, in addition to the cavalry of Stoneman and McCook should remain at Buzzard's Roost, or Mill Creek Gap and feint an attack against the Confederates, while the main body of the army would move toward Snake Creek

---

[62] OR, Vol. XXXVIII/2, p. 510 [Schofield's Report no. 296]

Gap. Combat occurred at both Mill Creek and Snake Creek Gaps between May 8 and May 13.[63]

On May 17, General Sherman sent Stoneman the following order:

> I send my aide, Captain Audenried, to you, who will tell you all you wish to know. I fear you have got your cavalry too far east to do much good at this time. Instead of going up the Salequa, the Pine Log would have been better. I want you to-morrow night to strike the enemy flank between Cassville and Cartersville or Etowah bridge (railroad). A small section of the road should be broken, enough to take a couple of days to mend...If you need it General Schofield will give you McCook's cavalry, but whatever is done, should be done tomorrow.[64]

This order to Stoneman by General Sherman led to a very unintended situation. In carrying out this order, Stoneman and McCook came upon, quite unexpectedly, General Johnston's army east of Cassville. Johnston was very much surprised to encounter the Federal army in this position, yet this chance meeting of Stoneman and General Johnston's army, may well have saved the Union column moving down the Adairsville's road from a overwhelming, if not fatal attack. According to Albert Castel, the foremost authority on the Atlanta Campaign," this was the most valuable service performed by Sherman's cavalry during the entire campaign."[65]

On May 22, Stoneman was ordered to advance to Milam's Bridge on the Etowah River. The Cassville & Cartersville Road to Stilesbourgh crossed the Etowah River over Milam's Bridge. The Etowah Iron Works and

---

[63] OR, Vol. XXXVIII/1, p. 852-853
[64] OR, Vol. XXXVIII/4, p. 224
[65] Albert Castel, *Decision in the West: The Atlanta Campaign of 1864* (Lawrence: University Press of Kansas, 1992), p. 202; hereinafter cited as Castel

The famous pontoon bridges built at Fredericksburg, depicted by Edwin Forbes

Library of Congress

General Schofield, Stoneman's commanding
general for a large part of the war

General Stoneman and his staff during
the Seven Days' Battles

Grave of General James Martin, confederate general commanding forces in Western North Carolina at the time of General Stoneman's last raid in April of 1865

Confederate flourmills were also destroyed on this raid. The Confederates had burned the bridge, forcing Stoneman to cross at a ford above the mouth of Raccoon Creek, but luckily, he was ultimately able to lay two pontoon bridges the following morning allowing General Schofield to cross the Etowah on May 23, to relieve Geary's Division of Hooker's Corps.[66] On May 25, General Stoneman was ordered to move toward New Hope Church and scour the roads to the left and front of Burnt Hickory. This movement was made in an effort to offer cover for the left and rear of Schofield's XXIII Corps, relieving Geary's division

The month of May was difficult for Sherman. The work required of the men had been long and hard and the army was more or less under constant fire. Sherman lost about 9,000 men, killed, wounded, and captured during May and Johnston's losses were a little over 9,000 in the same categories. Sherman hoped to seize Alatoona Pass and to establish a new railroad base. On June 1, Stoneman's cavalry occupied Alatoona offering cover with his cavalry to allow repairs to be made to the railroad from Kingston to the Etowah.[67] Alatoona Pass would be an important area throughout the Atlanta Campaign, accounting for why the Union forces later fortified the pass to protect the crossing at the Etowah River. On June 3, Stoneman and McCook reached Ackworth, and found the town abandoned. Hooker had extended Geary's and Butterfield's divisions, forcing Johnston to move away from the New Hope Church line he had previously held. Johnston's new line ran from Brush Mountain to Lost Mountain.[68] On June 17, General Stoneman received a message from General Schofield

---

[66] Battles and Leaders, Vol. IV, p. 306; Jacob D. Cox, *Campaigns of the Civil War: Atlanta* (Edison [NJ]: Castle Books, 2002 [reprint of the 1882 edition]), p. 66-67, hereinafter cited as Cox
[67] Cox, p. 88-89
[68] Battles and Leaders, Vol. IV, p. 309

instructing him to, "Hold Lost Mountain and favorable points on the ridges toward the east. ...Push the enemy until you find his new position. I think he will meet us again behind Noyes' Creek."[69] On June 22, Stoneman was somewhat "dressed down" by Schofield for inactivity, " I hear nothing of your cavalry between Cox [commander of the 3rd Division, XXIII Corps] and Hascall [2nd Division commander, XXIII Corps] except the small party [which] just came through from you. Please put in a sufficient force to cover the flank of this position and connect with the brigade left at the cross-roads."[70]

On June 23, the Federal army was four days away from Sherman's most disastrous and costly defeat of the Atlanta Campaign, Kenesaw Mountain. On June 22, the Confederates, under General Hood, made a gallant stand at the Battle of Culp's Farm. He surprised both McPherson and Schofield after a forced night march, appearing on a flank fronting Schofield. After a difficult battle, Hood was forced to retreat. Schofield sent Stoneman a message on the 23 of June to "watch the gap" between Reilly [1st Brigade, 3rd Division] and Hascall [2nd Division]. Schofield also warns Stoneman that," the enemy is in force in their front", to which Stoneman replied that he had information that a Texas brigade was moving toward their rear, via Powder Springs. Stoneman asked for additional support, if Schofield felt it necessary. Mix-ups occurred. The support [the 12th Kentucky Infantry] left with General Cox before Schofield's need for them ended and Stoneman was ordered to recall them. General Joe Johnston was making life tense for the Federals in late June.[71]

The outcome of the battle of Kenesaw Mountain was probably unexpected by Sherman. One might liken it to

---

[69] OR, Vol. XXXVIII/4, p. 503
[70] OR, Vol. XXXVIII/4, p. 569
[71] OR, Vol. XXXVIII/4, p. 577; Battles and Leaders, Vol. IV, p. 310-311

Lee's astonishment on the third day at Gettysburg, when Pickett's Charge failed. General Lee at least acknowledged the failure. Sherman never bothered to comment or elucidate in any proper way, the failure of a frontal charge which most of his subordinates opposed from the outset. Many worthy men died needlessly in that battle, which accomplished nothing. After the battle, Sherman sent McPherson to follow up the right wing of the army under Schofield, across Olley's Creek. The cavalry under General Stoneman was sent to Sandtown and toward the Chattahoochee River, far below General Johnston's lines. All this movement had set the Confederates in motion causing Sherman to conclude that the strong emplacements on Kenesaw Mountain were vacant. Johnston had moved six miles south and established new works at Smyrna Camp Ground and also at the Chattahoochee.[72]

By July 1, Stoneman and McCook had crossed Sweet Water Creek, with cavalry and had moved down the south bank searching for a crossing near the Sweet Water Crossing so that they might pose a threat to the Chattahoochee at Campbellton. The plan was to force Johnston to move from his position north of Kenesaw. The Federal infantry was five miles in the rear of the Confederate Army, ten miles from Kenesaw, four miles from the railroad, and six miles from the Cattahoochee River. The Federals controlled the Sandtown Road presenting Johnson the dilemma of leaving his position north of Kenesaw, or allow the Union to continue to reinforce in his rear near the Chattahoochee River. Stoneman, McPherson and Thomas would then continue to feign an attack while the remainder of the army crossed the river and threatened the Confederates on many fronts. Stoneman met little resistance as he moved down

---

[72] Battles and Leaders, Vol. IV, p. 311; OR, Vol. XXXVIII/2, p. 683

Sweet Water Creek, leading both Stoneman and Schofield to conclude that only state militia controlled the crossings.[73]

On July 5, General Stoneman sent a message to General Sherman from Sandtown Ferry requesting ammunition and a four-gun battery. General Sherman replied with a very praiseworthy message for Stoneman. Important in his message was the statement, "Keep up the delusion of our crossing below Sandtown as long as possible, and I have reason to believe the enemy expects it. We have a nice game of war and must make no mistakes. We ought to have caught Johnston on his retreat, but he had prepared the way too well."[74] The entire month of July up to the 18th had been spent in an attempt to lure Johnston into a series of battles, engagements, skirmishes, etc. which would end the Atlanta campaign. So far, this had been unsuccessful. Stoneman reported to Sherman and Thomas that the Confederates holding much of Atlanta were militia based on his observations down Sweet Water Creek. On July 4, Sherman paid a visit to General Howard stating that he was certain that Johnston would not make another stand north of the river. General Howard ordered General Stanley to double his skirmishers and press the Confederates. Unseen batteries replied, prisoners were taken, and torrents of lead came from hidden places. Sherman admitted he was incorrect. In a letter to General Thomas, Sherman exclaimed, "I have just read General Stoneman's letter, with your endorsement. We have seen enough to-day to convince us that all of Stoneman's information is incorrect. Something more than militia remains at Atlanta, and they are not demoralized. They have fought hard and persistently all day…"[75] This letter was written on the 20th of July. Sherman's reference is to events of that day, reported by Thomas and General Palmer.

---

[73] OR, Vol. XXXVIII/2, p. 514-515 [Schofield"s Report No. 296]
[74] OR, Vol. XXXVIII/5, p. 61-62
[75] OR, Vol. XXXVIII/5, p. 197

Stoneman had given information on troops, etc. since July 1. Also, the Confederate command had change in Georgia when General John B. Hood superseded General Johnston on July 18. The Confederate approach to the defense of Atlanta would soon undergo vast changes as well. General Stoneman's message to Sherman of July 20, repeated the " no force in Atlanta but "new issue" militia; ...the army is utterly demoralized", stating that the information came from a Negro who was taken prisoner by General Nathan Forrest, claiming that he had seen General Johnston often. Stoneman requested that the man be sent back to him after Sherman questioned him, so that he might use him as a guide.[76] No doubt Stoneman was assuredly, too trusting of information which should have been received with a degree of doubt. General Sherman was often exceedingly too exacting in situations involving his subordinates. A brilliant soldier to be sure, he seemed at times, to forget that information is just that, information, and not truth.

On July 25, General Stoneman was given orders that granted him his most important role in the Atlanta Campaign. Special Orders No. 42 directed Generals Stoneman and Gerrard to," call in all detachments and send to-morrow to Roswell or in rear of the infantry all crippled stock and encumbrances, prepared to move at daylight the next morning by a circuit to the left, so as to reach the railroad below McDonough."[77] Stoneman was to command the cavalry force. Gen. Edward M. McCook would also be a part of the raid, commanding his own forces, plus Colonel Harrison's cavalry as a reserve force. The railroad was to be destroyed for a distance of at least two to five miles. The telegraph wires were to be pulled down, carried away or hidden in water.[78]

---

[76] OR, Vol. XXXVIII/5, p. 208
[77] OR, Vol. XXXVIII/5, p. 255
[78] OR, Vol. XXXVIII/5, p. 255

On July 26, Stoneman sent a message to General Sherman requesting:

> In case we succeed in carrying out your wishes will it meet your approbation, should I see a good opening, if I should with a portion of the command make a dash on Macon and by a vigorous stroke release the prisoners (officers) now at that point, and afterwards go on to Americus and release those (privates) there. I would like to try it, and am willing to run any risks, and I can vouch for my little command....[79]

General Sherman replied to Stoneman's request on July 26, saying, "I see many difficulties, but as you say, even a chance of success will warrant the effort, and I consent to it. You may, after having fulfilled my present orders, send General Garrard back to the left flank of the army, and proceed with your command proper to accomplish both or either of the objects named."[80]

General Stoneman and his command began crossing the Chattahoochee on the night of July 27, 1864. The Adjutant General of the cavalry division, protecting the Confederate headquarters on Sand Town Road, Colonel E.T. Sykes, gives his impressions of Stoneman's Raid:

> Stoneman was attempting to turn our right in the direction of Flat Rock, with the supposed aim of making a junction with McCook, and cutting or interrupting our main line of communications, the Macon and Western railroad at or just south Of Jonesboro...On the evening of [July] the 28 Gen. Wheeler reported that he had intercepted and checked Stoneman's raiders at Latimer's, and was then awaiting developments. McCook succeeded for a time in eluding Jackson by skirmishing with our main body, while his main force moved around to the rear and cut the telegraph lines at Fairburn and Palmetto... Gen. Wheeler, taking in the situation, sent Gen., Iverson in pursuit of Stoneman, going in the direction of

---

[79] OR, Vol. XXXVIII/5, p. 265
[80] OR, Vol. XXXVIII/5, p. 265

Macon... forcing Gen. Garrard, who was at Flat Rock for the purpose of covering Stoneman's movements, to return to his infantry's left.[81]

General Wheeler intercepted and turned back McCook, surrounded his command south of Newnan, and captured his cavalrymen who did not cross the river. General Iverson, with the help of General Cobb, broke up Stoneman's command, capturing five hundred of his officers and men near Clinton.[82] There are a number of mitigating circumstances involved with Stoneman's capture and failure to complete his assignment. Gen. Alfred Iverson was a native of Clinton, Georgia and had served as a brigade commander in the Army of Northern Virginia at Gettysburg. On July 1, his brigade was destroyed by the Union 1st Corps. Iverson was a broken man and could no longer serve in a command position. He returned to Georgia and served as commander of state forces at Rome. He was later transferred to Martin's division, Wheeler's cavalry Corps.[83] Without doubt, General Iverson had a distinct advantage over the federal forces; he was familiar with the territory, they were not. In addition, Sherman must be considered as an annulling factor also, in that he did not take into account the strength of the Confederate cavalry in the area south of Atlanta. Stoneman and McCook were opposed, and forced to deal with two strong Confederate forces which prevented them from aligning their combined forces as planned, assuring defeat and capture of well over 1,000 men.

General Stoneman wrote from his prison cell in Macon, under a flag of truce to General Sherman:

---

[81] E.T. Sykes, *The Confederate Veteran*, September, 1897, p. 453-454; hereinafter cited as Sykes

[82] Sykes, p. 454

[83] Lawrence L. Hewitt, "Alfred Iverson, Jr.", *The Confederate General*, Vol. III, (Harrisburg: Historical Society, 1991), p. 143; hereinafter cited as The General

... Before I had completed what I desired to accomplish, I learned that a force of the enemy's cavalry was close upon my rear, and the only course for me to pursue and get out was to turn upon and if possible, whip this force... the officers with me protested that being without ammunition and surrounded, our escape was next to impossible; that there was no use fighting any longer; that we had accomplished our object in covering the retreat of the rest of the command until it was well under way, and that in justice to all concerned we should surrender... I feel better satisfied with myself to be a prisoner of war, much as I hate it, than to be amongst those who owe their escape to considerations of self-preservation.[84]

General Stoneman was a broken man for sometime after this fiasco in South Georgia; he was even moved to tears after being taken prisoner and many historians feel that he should have been, given his performance.[85] General Sherman said afterwards, "The damage done by them scarcely compensated for the loss sustained by Gens. Stoneman and McCook, amounting to upward of fifteen hundred of their men."[86] In a report filed by General Schofield on September 10, 1864, he writes, "On the 27th of July, Major-General Stoneman started, under the immediate orders of the general-in-chief, to make a raid upon the Macon railroad. He succeeded in destroying a large amount of property and doing much damage to the road below Macon.... General Stoneman was captured with about 600 of his command, about 220 were killed and wounded, and the remainder made their escape, but many of them without arms or horses."[87] In justification to General Stoneman, and as a further mitigating

---

[84] John P. Dyer, *From Shiloh to San Juan: The Life of "Fightin Joe" Wheeler* (Baton Rouge: Louisiana State University Press, 1941), p.141 Association of Graduates, p. 33-34
[85] Castel, p. 440
[86] Sykes, p. 454
[87] OR, Vol. XXXVIII/2, p. 517

circumstance, his Provost Marshall, Major Tompkins, wrote on August 12, 1864, " At Monticello, July 28, the General received the first intimation that there were no bridges over the Ocmulgee River. His information, and on which his movements were based, was that there were three bridges North of Macon over this river. His plans were now changed."[88] Aside from all of these factors, General Sherman was livid with anger about the results of Stoneman's Raid. He did not take any blame for having underestimated Hood's capabilities of assembling a cavalry force under the command of General Joe Wheeler, which nearly wiped out 2,000 cavalrymen. Sherman stated in his *Memoirs* that Stoneman had disobeyed his orders to attack the railroad first, before going to Macon and Andersonville.[89] This statement is not surprising, in that General Sherman rarely had anything positive to say about his cavalry. His praise was reserved for the infantry, to be sure, greatly deserved. Yet, Sherman may actually have indirectly given Stoneman a hint that he could go straight for Andersonville. In a telegram to General Halleck on August 3, Sherman writes, "… I think Stoneman has a chance of rescuing those prisoners. It was a bold and rash adventure, but I sanctioned it, and hope for its success from its very rashness."[90] Both Schofield and Howard had reasonably high praise for General Stoneman's attempts and efforts, even though he had failed to accomplish his mission.[91] General Stoneman was held as a prisoner of war until October 27, 1864, however there is some dispute about his release date. Stoneman's release from Camp Oglethorpe [prison of war

---

[88] Association of Graduates, p. 33
[89] William T. Sherman, *Memoirs of Gen. W. T. Sherman, Written by Himself*, [2 Vols.] (New York: Charles L. Webster & Company, 1891), Vol. 2, p. 98-99
[90] OR, Vol. XXXVIII/5, p. 340
[91] Association of Graduates, p. 33

camp where he was held] was in exchange for the release of Gen. Daniel Govan, who had been captured at Jonesborough, Georgia on September 1. Govan was held for three weeks and released at Rough and Ready, Georgia, near September 25, 1864, at least one month before the *official* date given for Stoneman's release.[92]

After his release from Camp Oglethorpe, General Stoneman was ordered to temporarily assume command of the 17th Corps, at the request of Gen. O. O. Howard on October 22, 1864, but this command was never carried out.[93] Gen. T. G. Ransom turned over command of the 17th Corps to Gen. M. D. Leggett on October 10, 1864, and Gen. Leggett held the position until October 31, 1864.[94] On the same day, October 22, General Schofield issued Special Field Order No.135 which assigned General Stoneman to duty as second in command of the Department of the Ohio.[95] This assignment created a tense situation for both General Stoneman and General Schofield for a period of time. Gen. Stephen Burbridge had previously held this position and was informed by the Assistant Adjutant-General Maj. J. A. Campbell on November 19, that he had been replaced by General Stoneman. Burbridge immediately set into motion requests to overturn Stoneman's command assignment. Burbridge was a native of Georgetown, Virginia and likely had political contacts within the government, which he felt would be able to restore his position. On November 28, 1864, Special Orders No. 422 stated, " Maj. Gen. George Stoneman, U. S. Volunteers, is relieved from duty in the Military District of the Mississippi, and will repair to Cincinnati, Ohio, and there await orders…"[96] On the same

---

[92] Edwin C. Bearss, " Daniel C. Govan", The General, Vol. III, P. 18
[93] OR, Vol. XXXIX/2, p. 395
[94] Dyer, Vol. I, p. 517
[95] OR, Vol. XXXIX/2, p. 401
[96] OR, Vol. XLV/1, p. 1106

day, Burbridge received a message from the War Department stating, in essence, that the president had conferred his position of command and that no subordinate could overturn that position, furthermore he also was informed that Stoneman was relieved of duty.[97] On December 5, 1864, General Schofield received a message from the Adjutant General's Office stating that Stoneman had been relieved by an order from General Grant, which was temporarily suspended by Stanton, but later renewed. The matter was referred again to General Grant, who felt that if Schofield felt Stoneman was competent to hold this command, he was authorized to assign him to that position. Schofield immediately wired the Adjutant General's office stating that Stoneman had also been approved by General Sherman, and therefore he intended to assign Stoneman to the position of second in command.[98] Ironically, General Grant had sent a message to Stanton on December 2, in which he concurred that Burbridge "should not be retained."[99] Special Field Orders No. 171, was revoked and General Stoneman was officially reinstated to his appointment as second in command of the Department of the Ohio, ending the command dispute with General Burbridge.[100]

During the month of November 1864, Confederate Gen. John Breckinridge engaged in an attempt to drive the Union forces out of East Tennessee. It was feared that Breckinridge might push his forces into Middle Tennessee or even into Kentucky or West Tennessee. For that reason, Stoneman directed General Burbridge to concentrate as much manpower as possible and push toward Cumberland Gap. Stoneman then made his way to Knoxville to take command of the assembled forces and determine the

---

[97] OR, Vol.XLV/1, p. 1130
[98] OR, Vol. XLV/2, p. 59 for both messages
[99] OR, Vol. XLV/2, p. 16
[100] OR, Vol. XLV/2, p. 73

direction the pursuit of Breckinridge should take. He also conferred with General Thomas and received his thoughts and instructions on what should be done as he passed through Nashville.[101] On November 26, he sent a message to General Schofield seeking his permission to march toward Rogersville, Tennessee, and then to Bristol, in an attempt to reach Bristol before Breckinridge could evade capture or combat; cut off his escape to Saltville, and force him back into Western North Carolina. This would remove any threat of an invasion into Kentucky and allow Federal forces to operate in North Carolina and even into South Carolina. In this message, Stoneman made his famous statement, "...I owe the Southern Confederacy a debt I am anxious to liquidate, and this appears a propitious occasion."[102] General Schofield replied that he approved the plan to push the enemy back and to destroy the salt-works and the railroad. He withheld permission to do anything more until additional information was available.[103] Thus, Stoneman's third raid was now in the works, with a chance of redemption for his failure at Atlanta.

General Stoneman spent the last few days of November 1864, in readying his command for a foray into Southwestern Virginia. General Burbridge was able to assemble an armed and mounted force in Kentucky and General Gillem put together a segment of a Tennessee cavalry brigade. In total, Stoneman had 5, 700 men, excluding a dismounted force. On November 26, the General sent his proposal to General Schofield, as stated earlier, and received official sanction to begin the raid.

Stoneman estimated that the Confederates had from three to six thousand men, a command not significantly smaller than his unit. On December 10, Stoneman's raiders

---

[101] OR, Vol. XLV/1, p. 809
[102] OR, Vol. XLV/1, p. 809
[103] OR, Vol. XLV/1, p. 810

left Knoxville. Prior to his departure, Stoneman had ordered the 4th Tennessee cavalry and the 3rd North Carolina mounted infantry to Sevierville, Tennessee to hold and guard the passes over the mountains into North Carolina. The North Carolina 3rd mounted infantry was to also scour the mountain region between Tennessee and North Carolina and clear it of rebels. Col. George W. Kirk commanded the NC 3rd mounted infantry, and was a steady soldier, totally fearless in carrying out his duties. Two regiments of Ohio heavy artillery were sent to Knoxville from Strawberry Plains, Tennessee, and on December 10, Gen. Alvan Gilliam's command and Stoneman arrived in Knoxville. From there the command went to Bean's Station, where General Burbridge joined the force on December 11. Up to this point, Stoneman had not disclosed the purpose of the raid, or the location of the target to his officers, and did not reveal the details until the third day of the raid.[104]

On December 12, the raiders arrived at Kingsport, Tennessee, opposite the North Fork of the Holston River. Early the next day, Stoneman's troops, under Gillem's command collided with the remains of Confederate Gen. John Morgan's command, led by Gen. Basil Duke, Morgan's brother-in-law. Morgan's younger brother, Col. Richard Morgan, commanded the unit at this point, as Duke was on leave. Gillem made short work of the Confederates and Morgan was captured. Later in the day of the 13th, Burbridge was sent to Bristol, Tennessee to intercept General Vaughn at Greeneville. Gen. John C. Vaughn deserves a comment for his tenacious soldiering, if for no other reason. Vaughn was born in Roane County, Tennessee, served in the Mexican War, returning to East Tennessee in the late 1840s. He served in East Tennessee with Gen. E. Kirby Smith, with Gen. John Pemberton in Mississippi, and with Gen.

---

[104] OR, Vol. XLV/1, p. 810

Longstreet and the Army of Northern Virginia. Ultimately, Vaughn's brigade became a "wild & rogue cavalry" unit. Vaughn succeeded Gen. John H. Morgan after his death as Commander of Western Virginia. His most famous venture was an attempt to usher Jefferson Davis to the Trans-Mississippi, which failed.[105] Burbridge later sent word asking for reinforcements, but upon arrival in Bristol, Stoneman discovered that only picket firing had taken place. A dense fog covered the area and Stoneman feared that Vaughn might escape during the night and link up with General Breckinridge at Saltville. Thus, Burbridge was ordered on to Abingdon, Virginia with instructions to send a regiment to destroy the railroad between Saltville and Wytheville to prevent reinforcements from Lynchburg, preventing an attack on the salt mines.[106]

Stoneman arrived in Abingdon with General Gillem's command on the 15th about daybreak, and learned that Vaughn was only eight to ten miles away on a parallel road. Gillem was ordered to Glade Springs, and Burbridge followed a short time later, where the entire command spent the hours before midnight. At 2 A.M., the command moved and Stoneman was informed that the 12th Kentucky cavalry was advancing toward the salt works, after having destroyed two trains, which prompted Breckinridge to bring a battery down from Wytheville. Stoneman faced a dilemma: should he move on the salt works and capture them, or send a brigade to hold them, and send his main command to attempt the capture of Vaughn and his command, destroy the railroad, Wytheville, and the lead works on the New River, and attack the salt works later? He decided to go after Vaughn and deal with the salt works later; Gillem was sent after Vaughn and was reinforced with two regiments from

---

[105] William A. Blair, "John C. Vaughn", The Confederate General, Vol. VI, p.80-81
[106] OR, Vol. XLV/1, p. 810

Burbridge, and Wade's brigade was detached to threaten the salt works, while Gillem pushed on to Marion, Virginia.[107]

Marion is a small village in Smyth County, Virginia, where on the morning of the 16th, Gillem attacked General Vaughn, which resulted in a rout, and pursued him on to Wytheville, but due to the late hour of the day, the elusive Vaughn escaped with about 200 troops, leaving all his artillery and materials behind. Gillem captured about 200 prisoners, which denied Breckinridge any support he might have received from Vaughn at Saltville.[108]

Stoneman and Burbridge's command moved toward Mount Airy, North Carolina about 11 P.M., arriving there about dawn on the 17th. Stoneman sent Colonel Buckley's brigade to the lead works, about twenty-five miles away to reek total destruction, if possible, and return to Seven-Mile Ford, near Marion and await further orders. By this time, Gillem had destroyed Wytheville, sent part of his command to Reedy Creek, destroyed all the railroad bridges over that body of water, and rejoined Stoneman at Mount Airy around noon of the 17th. The next and major target was the salt works, destruction of which would make the mission a total success.

Breckinridge was rapidly attempting to gather a force to face Stoneman's onslaught, which was very near. Three commands of Confederate infantry still remained in Tazewell County, hoping to unite with Gen. Nathan B. Forrest, were recalled by Breckinridge to combine forces with Duke's command and whatever home guard that might be available. This was the force that Stoneman would face at Saltville. Breckinridge made a major military blunder at this stage of the campaign; he left his strong fortification at Saltville, which in Stoneman's view would have been difficult to subdue. Breckinridge followed the Federal

---

[107] OR, Vol. XLV/1, p. 811
[108] OR, Vol. XLV/1, p. 811

command, and was discovered near Marion. Stoneman took command of Burbridge's troops and led the attack until nightfall, at which time he called off the offensive until morning, due to the disarray of Burbridge's command.[109]

Skirmishing continued for much of the day on the 18th, with many losses on both sides. Breckinridge took stock of his situation and determined that he was nearly surrounded on all sides, and wisely withdrew toward North Carolina to evade capture. Pursuit was attempted the next day, wagons were captured, but trees and obstacles of all types hindered the progress, and for that reason Stoneman recalled all of his command to Glade Springs to plan the attack on Saltville to take place the next day, December 20. Burbridge would enter the town from the north, Gillem would take a roundabout circuitous route and enter the town from the south, making destruction as total as possible before any reinforcements could arrive from Lynchburg. Burbridge was instructed to attack when he heard cannon fire coming from Gillem, but night came and the attack was delayed until the 21st. At this point [night of the 20th] Stoneman sent the 13th Tennessee Cavalry to burn and destroy the town, causing mass confusion, and by 11 P.M. the town was in flames, and what was left of the Confederate command was captured. The day and night of December 21 was devoted to the total destruction of the town and the salt works. General Burbridge was sent back to Kentucky and Gillem back to Knoxville. By December 29, all of the forces of Stoneman's third raid had returned to their home base and were accounted for, reports had been filed, and honors received; Stoneman was vindicated for his disgrace in Atlanta.[110]

In his second letter to Gen. George Cullum, Stoneman states that January and February of 1865 were taken up with the organization of another mounted force for

---

[109] OR, Vol. XLV/1, p. 811
[110] OR., Vol. XLV/1, p. 812-13

a final raid into Southwestern Virginia and Western North Carolina. As a result of his successful raid in December of 1864, Stoneman was assigned to command the District of East Tennessee, Department of the Cumberland, the command which would lead to his final, and most successful raid into Confederate territory, and would end his career as a Civil War general.[111]

On January 31, General Grant sent a message to General Thomas that expressed his desire for General Stoneman to make a final raid:

> I think, however, an expedition from East Tennessee under General Stoneman might penetrate South Carolina well down toward Columbia, destroying the railroad and military resources of the country, thus visiting a portion of the state which will not be reached by Sherman's forces. He might also be able to return to East Tennessee by way of Salisbury, NC, thus releasing some of our prisoners of war in rebel hands. Of the practicability of doing this General Stoneman will have to be the judge, making up his mind from information obtained whilst executing the first part of his instructions... Three thousand cavalry would be a sufficient force to take.[112]

The Cavalry division in East Tennessee was commanded by Gen. Alvan Gillem, a very reputable soldier already known to General Stoneman from his previous raid into Southwestern Virginia. General Gillem tended to be somewhat overly exorbitant about the activities of war, and particularly the death of the Confederate enemy. A comment from the famous Union scout in East Tennessee and Western North Carolina, Daniel Ellis, serves as an example, "The entire brigade had now moved up, and when General Gillem saw the body of Morgan [Gen. John Morgan, killed at

---

[111] Stoneman letter no. 2, p. 4; OR, Vol. XLIV/1, p. 2 [Stoneman's assignment as Commander of East Tennessee; also see OR, Vol. XLIX/1, p. 710, Special Order No. 39
[112] OR, Vol. XLIX/1, p. 616-617

Greeneville, Tennessee] he waved his hat around and cheered the 13th Tennessee Cavalry with the greatest enthusiasm, while the soldiers, as they passed along, seemed to be perfectly wild with delight."[113] This reputation would surface again during Stoneman's last raid.

The cavalry division comprised three brigades, commanded by Colonels Palmer, Miller, and General Brown. The three brigades were made up of nine regiments: 1st brigade, Col. William J. Palmer, 10th Michigan, 12th Ohio, 15th Pennsylvania; 2nd brigade, Gen. Simeon Brown, 11th Kentucky, 12th Kentucky, 11th Michigan; 3rd brigade, Col. John Miller, 8th Tennessee, 9th Tennessee, 13th Tennessee. The three brigades comprised about 6,000 troopers. In addition, the 4th Division, Department of the Cumberland served in carrying out the raid. This division was commanded by Gen. Davis Tillson, and was comprised of two brigades: 1st brigade, Col. Chauncey Hawley, 2nd & 3rd North Carolina Mounted Infantry, 4th Tennessee, 1st Ohio Artillery, Indiana light Artillery, 1st U.S. Colored Heavy Artillery; 2nd brigade, Col. Horatio Gibson, 34th Kentucky, 1st & 2nd Tennessee, 7th Tennessee Mounted Infantry, 2nd Ohio Heavy Artillery.[114] A number of these units were part of the December raid, in particular Col. George Kirk of the 3rd NC Mounted Infantry, who would play a major behind the scenes role in this raid. The mention of his name struck mortal fear in the hearts of the mountain people of Western North Carolina and Eastern Tennessee. It would be late March before the division actually concentrated at Mossy Creek in Tennessee. General Grant had become somewhat impatient while awaiting Stoneman's movement into North Carolina, and sent a second communication to General Thomas:

---

[113] Daniel Ellis, *The Thrilling Adventures of Daniel Ellis* (New York: Harper & Brothers, Publishers, 1867), p. 309-310
[114] OR, Vol. XLIX/1, p. 325-326

General Stoneman being so late in making his start from East Tennessee, and Sherman having passed out of the state of South Carolina, I think now his course had better be changed. It is not impossible that in the event of the enemy being driven from Richmond they may fall back to Lynchburg with a part of their force and attempt a raid into East Tennessee. It will be better, therefore, to keep Stoneman between our garrisons in East Tennessee and the enemy. Direct him to repeat his raid of last fall, destroying the railroad as far toward Lynchburg as he can. Sheridan starts today from Winchester to Lynchburg. This will vastly favor Stoneman.[115]

General Grant's thinking was that General Lee might make a western movement as he became encased between Sherman's army moving north and Grant's army moving south. General Lee might then moved toward Lynchburg and combine forces with Gen. John Echols, who commanded about 7,000 troops in that area, and possibly move on Knoxville.[116]

As previously stated, on March 22, the division assembled at Mossy Creek, moving to Morristown on the 23rd. At Morristown, each man received five days rations, one day's forage, four horseshoes and nails. At daybreak on the 24th, Colonel Miller left with his brigade, taking the north road, and with a rapid march, attempted to get in the rear of the enemy in the vicinity of Jonesborough, while the other two brigades took the Babb's Mill Road, and General Tillson and the infantry moved toward Greeneville. Due to the size of the command, it was necessary to scatter in order to procure forage. Nothing of military significance happened on the 24th or 25th of March, and on the 27th the command

---

[115] OR, Vol. XLIX/1, p. 777
[116] Thomas B. Van Horne, *Army of the Cumberland* (New York: Konecky & Konecky, no date given), p. 547 [this book is a reprint of the 1876 version]; hereinafter cited as Van Horne

moved up the Watauga River, marched until noon, and bivouacked on Iron Mountain until daybreak.[117]

On March 28, the command approached Boone, North Carolina where it was learned that the Home Guard was holding a meeting that day. General Stoneman sent Major Keogh with a detachment of the 12th Kentucky Cavalry, who routed the Confederates, killing nine and capturing sixty-eight. Keogh was an Irishman who had served in the French Foreign Legion, and elsewhere, and had no hesitation about shooting anything in sight. The Home Guard, Confederate soldiers on leave, and local citizens attempted to fight back, and some Federal troops were injured, but the outcome was certain. After the contest ended, the Federal troops burned and destroyed homes, and also the local jail. Since the jail was located in the county courthouse, all of the town of Boone and the Watauga County public records were destroyed. It is a matter of dispute as to exactly who ordered this mishap. Some authorities declare that General Gillem was responsible, while others maintain that Major Keogh instituted this action of his own volition, but regardless of how it occurred, General Gillem received a firm reprimand from General Stoneman for this senseless act of needless destruction.[118] Gillem is purported to have told the people of Boone that, "If you think this is bad, just wait until Kirk [Col. George Kirk of the NC 3rd Mounted Infantry] arrives."[119]

After reaching Boone, the command separated, Colonel Palmer's brigade traveled to Deep Gap, on their way

---

[117] OR, Vol. XLIX/1, p. 332
[118] OR, Vol. XLIX/1, p. 332; Chris Hartley, "George Stoneman's 1865 Cavalry Raid", *Civil War Regiments,* Vol. VI, No. 1, p 77, hereinafter cited as Hartley; John Barrett, *The Civil War in North Carolina* (Chapel Hill: University of North Carolina Press, 1963), p. 351, hereinafter cited as Barrett; each source cites additional information about this incident
[119] This is not an exact quotation, but expresses the intent of Gillem's remark, reported by Van Noppen, p. 39-44

to Wilkesboro, North Carolina and General Brown's brigade and the artillery went by way of Flat Gap Road toward Wilksboro, followed by Miller's brigade. About 9 P.M. Brown's brigade reached Patterson's Factory, on the edge of the Blue Ridge near Lenior, North Carolina which had ample supplies of corn, bacon, and other food items, even though it was actually a cotton mill. Gillem remained to ensure the proper destruction of the mill after any and all needed food items had been confiscated. The artillery did not arrive at the factory until 7 A.M. on the 29th. By nightfall, the 12th Ohio Cavalry had driven the Confederate forces from Wilksboro, after which a large number of horses and other materials were collected.[120] In an attempt to supply forage to the animals, it was necessary to move North of the Yadkin River, but due to heavy rains, it was not possible to ford the river. After several attempts, an area was found on the South side of the Yadkin with plenty of forage, and the division remained encamped there until April 1.General Gillem seized the Augustus Finley house in Wilkesboro for his headquarters, and paraded a horse around which belonged to Gen. John B. Gordon, of Stuart's command, which did little for public relations concerning the division.[121]

On April 1, the division [minus Colonel Palmer who had crossed the river on the 30th] crossed the Yadkin at Jonesville, and by way of Dobson, reached Mount Airy, North Carolina, arriving about 10 P.M. Gillem learned that a wagon train had left Mount Airy at 3 P.M. headed toward Hillsville, Virginia. He immediately sent a pursuit unit from Colonel Palmer's brigade to overtake the train. The detachment sent by Palmer halted at the summit of the Blue Ridge and remained there until the residuum of the division arrived the next morning. After learning of the failure of the pursuit party, another unit was sent with instructions to

---

[120] Hartley, p. 79; OR, Vol. XLIX/1, p. 331
[121] Barrett, p. 352-353

capture the wagons at all cost. Within hours, a report was received by Gillem stating that the wagons were in Federal possession. There were seventeen wagons in the train carrying forage, which General Brown fed to his horses, and then collected the animals and burned the wagons.[122]

The command left Mount Airy on April 3, at daybreak, and arrived at Hillsville, Virginia at about 1 P.M. From Hillsville Colonel Miller was ordered to select 500 men and proceed by way of Porter's Ford on the New River, to Wytheville and destroy the bridges over the Reedy River and at Max Meadows. At Wytheville, Miller ran afoul of the elusive Confederate Gen. John Vaughn of Saltville fame. Vaughn and Colonel Giltner attacked Miller's force, prompting over thirty-five casualties, and serious delays for the mission. Miller was able to complete his assignment, but at a cost in manpower.[123]

Leaving Hillsville, the division continued toward Jacksonville, where at about dark, they encountered a small Confederate force. The Confederates were put to retreat, and near midnight the command bivouacked near a supply of hay in order to feed the animals. Early on April 4, the Federals reached Jacksonville where more hay and corn were available to supply the animals, and after a short rest, Major Wagner of the 15th Pennsylvania selected 250 men and made his way toward Salem to destroy railroad bridges as far east as possible, and rejoin the command later. An interesting fable came into legend after the war ended concerning Wagner's Salem raid. His men contended that General Lee mistakenly thought that their unit was an additional command from the west, which was sent to block any escape toward Lynchburg and General John Echols. Since Sherman was moving in a northward direction and Grant was making his way toward Richmond, they proposed that General Lee

---

[122] Barrett, p. 353, OR, Vol. XLIX/1, p. 331
[123] Hartley, p. 80; OR, Vol. XLIX/1 p. 331

saw no escape and surrendered his army. One must draw personal conclusions as to the validity of this fable.[124]

At about 2 P.M the command moved in the direction of Christiansburg, arriving there at 12 P.M. Colonel Palmer was ordered to destroy the railroad tracks to the east of Christiansburg, while General Brown did the same to the west of the town. Other commands were sent to take control of railroad bridges and ferries over the New and Roanoke Rivers, which was done expediently, giving the Union forces control of at least ninety miles of the Virginia & Tennessee Railroad from Wytheville to Salem, North Carolina. On April 6, the division moved out of Christiansburg toward Jacksonville, arriving there on the morning of April 7, signaling a return toward North Carolina and the final objective of Salisbury. The unit left Jacksonville in the afternoon and headed toward Taylorsville, Virginia, arriving there at 10 P.M., where they remained through the 8th. Colonel Palmer was ordered to make haste toward Danbury, North Carolina, joining the 10th Michigan Cavalry, returning from Martinsville after an skirmish with 250 cavalrymen of Gen. Joe Wheeler's division.[125]

By April 10, the division was back in North Carolina, and a potential problem was developing with the large number of Negroes following the command. This would be a hazard, it was reasoned, if the division encountered a large Confederate force, therefore a large number of the group was sent to East Tennessee, where they joined the Union army, becoming members of the 119th U.S. Colored Troops. The division arrived in Germantown on April 10, remaining but a

---

[124] Charles H. Kirk, editor, *History of the Pennsylvania Volunteer Cavalry* (Philadelphia: [unknown], 1906, 492-493; this incident is reported in a number of sources, both Hartley and Barrett make note of the idea. Kirk's book is a notable source for Stoneman's Raid into western North Carolina and southwestern Virginia
[125] OR, Vol. XLIX/1, p. 332

short while, after which they moved out toward Bethania, another Moravian town. At Bethania, Barrett relates that," ... the troopers broke up the Easter week religious services, ate everything in site, and then moved on to Shallow Ford, on the Yadkin west of Winston."[126] Colonel Palmer's brigade was dispatched to Salem to destroy the clothing factories supplying the Confederacy, and from there to Greensboro to waste and destroy the railroad south of the city, the intent being to disrupt rail traffic between Greensboro and Danville. The remainder of the division moved out and arrived at Shallow Ford at daybreak on April 11. Confederate forces guarding the ford put up little resistance, and fled the area, leaving over 100 new muskets.

An interesting situation developed in Salem, North Carolina concerning the rank and file behavior of Colonel Palmer's brigade. Toward the afternoon of April 10, the brigade arrived in Salem. The day by day records of the Moravians give details:

> ... they appeared all a once in our midst. Before we could realize it, soldiers were seen at every corner of the streets, had taken possession of the post office, and secured our whole town. Some of our brethren had gone out to meet ... Colonel Palmer ... our mayor addressed him personally... the General [Colonel Palmer] assured him that persons and property should be safe and that no destruction of any kind would be allowed, and that we might feel perfectly secure from harm during their stay with us.

The record continues:

> The strictest discipline was enforced, guards rode up and down every street and very few indeed, comparatively were the violations of proper and becoming conduct on the part of the soldiers... During the afternoon of the eleventh a large number of the federals came back from the railroad which they had tapped in several places, they brought 50 prisoners. By some

---

[126] Barrett, p. 356

> mistake they came into the graveyard avenue and passed through the graveyard part of the cemetery, having shifted their camp to a place above town, but passing through those hallowed grounds almost all of them dismounted and led their horses, some even uncovered their heads.[127]

The division was again on the move southward, ever closer to Salisbury, the ultimate goal of the raid. The troopers were now in the vicinity of Mocksville, remaining in that village only long enough to water and tend to the animals, and by nightfall, they bivouacked twelve miles from the city of Salisbury. On April 12, the raiders came to the South Yadkin River, a deep and dangerous river with few fords. A strong rebel resistance was expected, but never occurred, and the crossing took place with no challenge by the Confederates. About a quarter mile from the South Yadkin, the road forked, both forks leading to Salisbury. The main column of the division took the west road, as it was in superior condition. The 12th Kentucky Cavalry took the old or eastern road, and was instructed to make a large and noisy demonstration at Grant's Creek, two miles from Salisbury and possibly attack the upper bridge on the creek. Just before daybreak, the advanced guard of the main column came into contact with the enemy's pickets, which they pushed back across the creek. They were pounded by the Confederate artillery and infantry numbering about 500 assorted reserves, recruited prisoners from the Salisbury prison, etc. on the Salisbury side of the creek. The Federals were close enough to Salisbury to hear the trains coming and going to and from Salisbury on both the South Carolina and Morganton Railroads. This skirmish represented the most intense fighting of the entire raid. [128]

---

[127] *North Carolina Civil War Documentary*, edited by Buck Yearns and John C. Barrett (Chapel Hill: University of North Carolina Press, 1980) , p. 116-117; hereinafter cited as Yearns and Barrett
[128] OR, Vol. XLIX/1, p. 334; Hartley, p.83

General Gillem reported that he received a order from General Stoneman to send 100 men to Grant's Creek, cut the railroad, capture a train, and get in the rear of Salisbury if possible, causing as much confusion as they could muster. The 11th Kentucky was assigned this duty, crossing about two and one half miles above the bridge on Grant's Creek. The 13th Kentucky was ordered to cross the creek at a lower level, and Colonel Smith, one of Stoneman's aides, was sent with a command of dismounted infantry to cross the creek at an even lower level. The 11th Kentucky shortly carried out their assignment, and turned the Confederate's left, at which point Colonel Miller was ordered to advance on the main road. His men repaired the bridge weakened by the Confederates, crossed over, followed by Brown's brigade in support, pursuing the Confederates retreating toward the town. It has been estimated from sources available that the Confederate force at Salisbury numbered about 3,000 men, under the command of General W. M. Gardener. Former Lt. Gen. John Pemberton, of Vicksburg fame had just arrived in Salisbury shortly after the resignation of his commission as a Lieutenant General in 1864, and now as a Lieutenant Colonel of artillery, was most likely in charge of the artillery at Salisbury.[129]

The Confederate retreat had now turned into a rout. The pursuit continued until as most sources report, "the enemy's troops lost any semblance of organization, and all who had escaped capture, hid themselves in the woods."[130] The raiders made a considerable "haul of materials" as a result of this victory. As General Gillem reported, " the fruits of this victory were: 18 pieces of artillery, with caissons, forges, and battery wagons, 17 stands of colors, 1,200-1,300

---

[129] OR, Vol. XLIX/1, p. 334; Hartley, p. 83-84; Barrett, p.357 [Barrett states that General Pemberton was an ordnance instructor]
[130] Van Horne, p. 550; OR, Vol. XLIX/1, p. 334

prisoners, possession of the town, with its immense depots and arsenals, [and] the Salisbury Prison."[131] Later in the day, Colonel Palmer reported that he had successfully destroyed two large factories, 7,000 bales of cotton, cut the railroad once north of Greensboro, and in three places between Greensboro and the Yadkin River, plus the capture of over 400 prisoners. Major Wagner also reported the destruction of all bridges on the Tennessee and Virginia Railroad within four miles of Lynchburg. At 2 P.M. on April 13, Major Barnes reported the destruction of all supplies completed, which consisted of the follow items: 10,000 stand of arms, 1,000,000 rounds of ammunition [small type], 10,000 rounds of artillery, 6,000 pounds of powder, 3 magazines, 6 depots, 10,000 bushels of corn, 75,000 uniforms, 250,000 blankets, 20,000 pounds of leather, 6,000 pounds of bacon, 100,000 pounds of salt, 20,000 pounds of sugar, 27,000 pounds of rice, 10,000 pounds of saltpeter, 50, 000 bushels of wheat, 80 barrels of turpentine, $15,000,000 Confederate money, $100,000 value in gold of medical supplies.[132]

General Stoneman proved to be a gentleman even in the midst of such violence and mayhem. On April 12, the following event is reported to have occurred in Salisbury:

> ... Together we looked out onto Innis Street along which our house fronted. The roadway was jammed with a surging mass of mounted soldiers. It was frightening, curiously thrilling to see the capless cavalrymen standing erect in their stirrups as the rode. Almost at once we heard the sound of voices... their emphatic demand for liquor sounded as if they had come for strong drink rather than conquest... A small wooden keg rewarded a successful search... Thirty troopers filled their canteens with liquor drawn from the wooden keg.... How dreadful the sounded in our ears the shouts of 'Fire'! 'Fire'! [the barn had been torched by the troopers] 'This outrage has gone far enough,' she [Mamma] said. 'I'll ask General Stoneman for

---

[131] OR, Vol. XLIX/1, p. 334
[132] OR, Vol. XLIX/1, p. 334-335

protection; it's the only way.' [Mrs. Bradshaw, "Mamma" went to General Stoneman's headquarters] Mamma accosted a fine upstanding orderly. 'I wish to speak to the gentleman who is in authority here', she said. [General Stoneman talked with the lady] ' Madame', the General replied, 'Your request for the protection of your dwelling is granted. A guard will be detailed immediately to attend to your home.' [As the division departed Salisbury, Ms. Bradshaw states] ... General Stoneman and his officers rode into view. I noticed they checked their horses as they passed our house.[133]

The division left Salisbury on April 13 at 3 P.M. The only prize that was not obtained on the raid was the destruction of the railroad bridge over the Yadkin River, some six miles from Salisbury. General Beauregard had dispatched about 1,000 men, home guard, "galvanized Yankees" [soldiers formerly in the Union Army] etc. to defend the bridge, under the command of Gen. Zebulon York, a native of Maine. The Confederates were on a high rise and shelled the Union troops profusely as they attempted to cross and destroy the bridge. By nightfall of April 12, the Federals gave up and returned to Salisbury.[134] On the trek back to Knoxville, captured artillery and approximately 1,000 prisoners accompanied the division, reaching the city of Lenoir on the 15th. The 16th of April was spent in refitting artillery and returning prisoners to East Tennessee. On April 17, General Stoneman left the command and all movements and decisions were cleared with him, and General Gillem now commanded the division. Colonel Palmer, presently in Statesville, was ordered to establish his headquarters in Lincolnton, North Carolina where he could maintain a watch on the Catawba River. General Gillem moved, with Brown's and Miller's brigades toward Morganton, where they ran into Confederate infantry, commanded by General McCown

---

[133] Yearns and Barrett, p. 118-120
[134] Hartley, p. 85; Barrett, p. 358

about two and one half miles from the Catawba River. The bridge over the river was torn up, the fords were blockaded, and any passage over the river was disputed by General McCown. After getting in the rear of the Confederates, using artillery and dismounted troops, the Confederates were driven away, and fifty prisoners were taken. Morganton [near the Catawba River] produced large supplies of corn and bacon for the Confederate army, as well as other useful items, now were in the hands of Gillem's command.[135]

On April 19, Gillem moved toward Asheville by way of Swannanoa Gap, but on reaching the gap on the 20th, it was too secure, with both infantry and four pieces of artillery, to pass. Colonel Miller made several feints to throw the enemy off course, while Gillem moved toward Rutherfordton, North Carolina, forty miles south of the gap, on the April 21, and by dark on the 22, Gillem had cleared the Blue Ridge via Howard's Gap with little resistance. At daybreak on the 23rd, the advance guard entered Hendersonville, about twenty miles south of Asheville, deceiving the Confederates into believing they [Gillem] were established there, the Confederates returned to Asheville. The 11th Kentucky Cavalry supported by the 11th Michigan was ordered to pursue the Confederates, attack, and take the artillery they controlled. This was accomplished, along with seventy prisoners taken by the two regiments. Colonel Palmer had been ordered to move his command to Rutherfordton, but sent a message to Gillem stating that General John Echols of the Confederate army had informed him that a truce had been agreed upon, and therefore, he remained in Lincolnton. Palmer was instructed to move to Rutherfordton, because the possession of a gap through the Blue Ridge was essential. Gillem left Hendersonville at

---

[135] OR, Vol. XLIX/1, p. 335

midnight on April 23, with intentions of attacking Asheville at some point the next day.[136]

At around 3 P.M. on April 24, General James Martin sent General Gillem a flag of truce from Asheville, explaining that he had been notified of a truce; a second flag of truce later in the day requested a meeting with Gillem. The Federal troops arrived in Asheville the next morning April 25. General Martin was a native of the area, born in Elizabeth City, North Carolina. He was a West Point graduate, and had served in the Army of Northern Virginia, in Hoke's division. Martin lost his arm in the Mexican War and suffered somewhat from this for the remainder of his life. Later, he was transferred to the command of the District of North Carolina, with headquarters at Asheville. General Martin was a creditable leader, with few resources, and was more or less at the mercy of General Gillem's division.[137] Asheville was the foremost city in Western North Carolina, in terms of support of the Confederacy. The city had about 1,200 residents in 1865, and by all accounts, it was a rough frontier town. In many regards, it was a small country village with no basic amenities such as a water and sewer system, lights, telegraph service, railroad service, or any real connection with the outside world. Asheville did have one sterling and important aspect, dear to the Confederacy---- the finest Enfield-pattern musket factory in the Confederacy.[138]

At 11 P. M. on April 23, General Gillem received a message from General Sherman that the truce existed, and that General Stoneman should report to the railroad station at Durham's Station or Hillsborough. Sherman was unaware that General Stoneman was 200 miles away from Salisbury,

---

[136] OR, Vol. XLIX/1, p. 335; Van Horne, p. 551-552; Hartley, p. 86
[137] OR, Vol. XLIX/1, p. 335-336; Edwin Bearss, "James Green Martin", *The Confederate General,* Vol. IV, p. 160-161
[138] F. A. Sondley, *A History of Buncombe County North Carolina* (Spartanburg: The Reprint Company Publishers, 1977), p. 691

whereas the division under General Gillem's command was a mere sixty miles from his base at Greeneville, Tennessee. Because of these facts, Gillem decided to march to Greeneville, and during the meeting with General Martin on the 24th, he requested a supply of rations for his men for the trip, avoiding confiscation of the local citizens foods, etc. General Martin agreed, and supplied three days rations to General Gillem's division. Gillem felt that since the town of Asheville would have been a simple conquest, he refused any demands and terms suggested by Martin.[139]

On April 25, General Brown and Colonel Martin began the march toward Greeneville, Colonel Palmer was ordered to proceed to Waynesville and Quallatown, down the Little Tennessee. Gillem concludes his report of the raid by stating the division had taken forty-six pieces of artillery, 6,000 prisoners, and seventeen battle flags. He was given a leave of absence to travel to Nashville to attend the session of the state Legislature by General Thomas, dated April 24. Gillem left the division in the hands of General Brown. On the night of April 26, General Brown returned to Asheville with his brigade and sacked the town. General Martin explained:

> .... I believe no one escaped entirely--- I was arrested and taken to Genl. Brown and after an absence of less than one hour I returned to my house in charge of a United States Officer. When we reached the house I found Mrs. Martin and my daughters going over the house with a squad of Federal soldiers holding candles for them to examine all the trunks and for such things as the fancied and to such things they helped themselves. The officer ordered them out of the house immediately, and they obeyed. The same men had been before, or were immediately after detained as a guard for my house, but the officer remained

---

[139] OR, Vol. XLIX/1, p. 336

also until the troops left.... Some very hard stories were told of Genl. Brown, but I think I had better say nothing more.[140]

One cannot but wonder why such an event occurred; was the word of a general in the Federal army worthless, did General Brown carry out this deed without the consent of General Gillem? Several thoughts have been suggested over the last 138 years as to why this dastardly and unprovoked attack occurred. The most likely reason is that the terms of the surrender offered to General Johnston by General Sherman were disapproved by President Lincoln and orders went to all generals in the field to do all in their power to bring the Confederates to better terms. In a letter to General Stoneman from General Thomas on April 24, this is, in essence, what was suggested. Dr. Ina Van Noppen advanced this theory in her text *Stoneman's Raid*, and states that she felt that General Gillem left Asheville with no knowledge that such an event was in the works. Also, General Brown was, in all probability, simple carrying out orders from General Stoneman, and would otherwise not have committed such a breach of trust. [141]

At the end of the war, General Stoneman found time for romance and in 1865, he married Mary Oliver Hardisty of Baltimore, Maryland, with whom he had four children. On June 27, Stoneman became the commander of the Department of Tennessee, a position that he held until June 5, 1866. Also, for a short time, August 13-31, Stoneman

---

[140] Barrett, p. 364; General Martin's quotation is from a letter written to C. P. Spencer by General Martin on June 11, 1866, from the Southern Historical Collection, University of North Carolina, Chapel Hill

[141] Ina Van Noppen, "The Significance of Stoneman's Last Raid", *North Carolina Historical Review*, January - October, No. I-4, see specifically p. 520-521; OR, Vol. XLIX/2, p. 457 for General Thomas' letter to General Stoneman * Dr. Van Noppen give much of the same information in her book ,*Stoneman's Last Raid* (Raleigh: North Carolina State University Print Shop, 1964)

commanded the District of the Cumberland, and during September, and much of October, the general awaited new orders that came on December 17, 1866, when he was assigned to command the District of Petersburg. Stoneman held this position until March 31, 1870. Early in May of the same year, he was transferred to the west to command the Department of Arizona from May 3, 1870, until June 4, 1871. At this point, the old soldier requested retirement, which was granted on August 16, 1871, for disability contracted in the line of duty. No doubt, this disability was the perennial problem Stoneman had suffered since the early days of the war, that of hemorrhoids.

After retirement, the Stoneman family settled at *Los Robles*, in what is today San Marino, California. In 1879, Stoneman was asked to serve, and accepted, a position on the Railroad Commission of California. At this point, the former soldier turned politician when he opposed the accelerating power of the Pacific railroads in the affairs of state in California. In 1883, Stoneman accepted the nomination of the Democratic Party to seek the governor's office, and ultimately was elected governor of California. Stoneman served the state well, and stated his philosophy in his inaugural address in 1883, "The people are sovereigns and we are the servants." Stoneman is frequently cited as one of California's foremost governors in the last three decades of the 19th century. General Stoneman had taken an interest in politics immediately after the war in his support for President Johnson's leniency toward the Southern people. This was likely not a popular position in the view of many public officials who held major positions in the Republican Radical Congress during Reconstruction. By the early 1890s, Stoneman's health began to fail and he more or less took up residence in his native state of New York, living with his youngest sister, Catherine [Mrs. Benjamin H. Williams] in Buffalo. On September 5, 1894, the "Great Raider" departed this life with the dignity and respect he so richly deserved.[142] General George Stoneman is buried in the Lakewood-Bentley Cemetery, at Busti, New York. The cemetery is older than the Civil War, and reports state that the cemetery may soon be abandoned for lack of care and interest.[143]

George Stoneman probably held more commands than any general officer in the Union or Confederate armies, at the very least, fifteen different command assignments. George Stoneman was the quintessential, *all-purpose* general, commanding corps, divisions, armies, and everything in between, in the eastern and western theaters of the war.

How should General Stoneman's ability as a soldier and leader be remembered by the American people? Some comments by his peers might give an insight. From General Robert McAllister, who served under General Stoneman, "General Stoneman commands our corps, in which is Carr's Brigade, Sickles's Division. You recollect that I was with Stoneman in the advance for several days when on the Peninsula until we reached the Chickahominy. He is a good officer, and this review was splendid."[144] From General Darius N. Couch, a West Point peer and fellow soldier serving with General Stoneman: "The success of this Expedition, which had been projected by the Lieutenant-General with so much confidence in the capacity of its leader, was one of the finishing strokes of a War wherein

---

[142] General Stoneman's postwar career materials came from: Biographical Register, p. 282; Lenora A. Snedeker,"Busti Boy Became Civil War General, California Governor", undated and unknown newspaper article furnished by the Fenton History Center, Jamestown, NY; Gerleman, p. 1875

[143] Jean Moore, " Taps Will Sound on Memorial Day", Jamestown *Journal,* March 29, 1971

[144] *The Civil War Letters of General Robert McAllister*, edited by James I. Robertson, Jr.(Baton Rouge: Louisiana State University Press,1998), p.253

General Stoneman had filled with capability more positions of trust perhaps than any other general officer engaged.[145] This comment was in reference to General Stoneman's last raid into Virginia and North Carolina in 1865. The historian, Thomas B. Van Horne, a contemporary of General Stoneman's career, had this to say about the final raid, "This expedition was ably conducted and eminently successful. General Stoneman's strategy put the enemy under positive disadvantage, at each objective, in receiving the intended blow."[146] Roy P. Stonesifer, in his article on General Stoneman in the *Biographical Dictionary of the Union: Northern Leaders of the Civil War,* "Troubled by hemorrhoids and possessing only modest ability, he achieved limited success as an aggressive cavalry commander."[147] As previously stated, Secretary of War, Edwin Stanton felt that Stoneman was perhaps the most inept general in the Union Army. General Thomas, while often in praise of General Stoneman, at times made condescending remarks about him, such as " It seems that when twenty-five of the enemy are seen anywhere, they are considered in force," [OR, Vol. XXXVIII/5, p. 196]. From the many statements, reports, and comments filed by General Schofield mentioned in this work, it is obvious that Schofield held Stoneman in high regard. Still, it appears that the views on General Stoneman's military abilities are very much a mix of opinions, some very competent soldiers felt he was exceptional, while others viewed him as below average as a soldier and leader.

Perhaps the most authentic and credible single fact that attests to the probability that Stoneman was held in respect as a soldier with ability and competence is the many

---

[145] Association of Graduates, p. 35
[146] Van Horne, p. 552
[147] Roy P. Stonesifer, "George Stoneman", *Biographical Dictionary of the Union: Northern Leaders of the Civil War,* edited by John T. Hubbell & James W. Geary (Westport, CT: Greenwood Press, ?) p. 510

commands given to him. No general with the ability, judgment, and leadership of Grant would have allowed a person under his command to lead a corps, an entire department, division, etc. or any of the other positions of trust given to Stoneman if he was incompetent or inept. Another very telling piece of evidence to support the view that Stoneman was competent and had leadership is the fact that he was in the Federal army for twenty-five years. Again, no person could remain in the military, operating at that level, for that length of time and be less than competent, and have little leadership ability. If this is not the case, then many historians have been under some very great illusions for a very long time about the ability of generals like Grant, Schofield, and even Sherman, who approved Stoneman for command of the Department of East Tennessee. [See footnote # 98]

What constraints limited George Stoneman's performance and leadership as a general commanding a corps, cavalry division, and other position of responsibility? No doubt, Stoneman lacked the vainglorious attitude of many Civil War generals on both sides, the Sheridans, Custers, Picketts, and Stuarts, for example. An example of this is his report on the final raid in Western North Carolina. Stoneman's report is a mere two pages of "bare bones" information stating that General Alvan Gillem should receive much of the credit for the success of the raid. General Gillem's report extended to eight pages, mentioning General Stoneman at various points, acknowledging that he was in command, yet in a rather vague fashion, as if Stoneman was off, somewhere else. General Stoneman was somewhat more lenient than other commanders about the behavior of his men, and their deviation from standard military deportment were. Rumor has persisted for a century about the amount of drinking which is purported to have occurred on the raid south of Atlanta, and both raids into

Western North Carolina and Southwestern Virginia. For a fact, the troopers consumed alcohol and created havoc in Salisbury [see footnote # 133], but in fairness, this behavior pales in comparison to the behavior of Sherman's "Bummers", and for that matter, much of his entire command on the "March to the Sea".

Another constraint, which would be considered a positive trait to some observers, was the *naivete* that often appears to have influenced General Stoneman's thinking. A prime example of this attitude or point of view is Stoneman's lack of concern about General Averell's behavior on the raid during the Chancellorsville Campaign. Averell took a large part of Stoneman's command out of action, yet Stoneman said something to the effect that he could not be bothered with Averell's situation [see footnote # 56]. Another example is Stoneman absolute disregard of what would occur when he requested to attempt a release of prisoners at Andersonville. It is difficult to believe that he felt the Confederates would simply not react to his threat far into their lines [see footnote # 79]. Such behavior undermined Stoneman's reputation as a field commander, and easily could have prevented him from holding a command again. A final example of this behavior is Stoneman's neglect, and seeming lack of appreciation for the good will and many favors shown to him by General Schofield. General Schofield saved Stoneman from absolute oblivion on a number of occasions, two examples are the situation which came about when Stoneman was appointed Assistant Commander of the Department of Ohio, and Stoneman's failure to communicate with Schofield during the first raid into Southwestern Virginia and Western North Carolina. Schofield could easily have allowed Stoneman to return to some dustbin job, but he came to his aid, and rescued his position from an attack by General Burbridge. On the first raid, he sent reports to everyone except General Schofield, and Schofield reminded him of his neglect, and all was forgiven. One would think that Stoneman would have shown a little more appreciation for this kindness, yet he probably simply took it for his due, and may silently have felt some gratitude.

George Stoneman seems to have been a man of great kindness. This comes over in many aspects of his career, but the best example occurred in Salisbury on April 13, 1865, when Stoneman, on the word of a single citizen, Mrs. Bradshaw, placed a guard at her home to ensure it would not be molested. This was not unheard of and other commanders probably also extended this protection, few would have done so on the request of a lone civilian in a defeated town in 1865. In addition, Stoneman never failed to give credit to his subordinate officers, many times giving them more credit than he allowed for himself. The General was overly cautious, which may have been a reason for his lack of success at times, yet it was probably also a factor of concern for his men. It has been said that courage does not abhor caution, which certainly applies to General Stoneman. As Samuel Butler, the English essayist once said, "Belief follows the path of least resistance," and the "taciturn, ascetic, doe-eyed cadet" of the 1840s, was never able to offer enough resistance to change the belief which that label branded into his career as a soldier.

Darlington County, South Carolina Historical Commission

A turn of the century photograph of General Law

GEN. EVANDER MCIVOR LAW

The last Confederate Major-General died on October 31, 1920. He was a native South Carolinian, born in Darlington, a Citadel graduate and a military man through and through, having played a leadership role in over forty-five Civil War battles. As a soldier, educator, and the founder of the Tuskegee Military High School in Alabama, Evander McIvor Law represented the best military prototype the South had to offer in 1861. This heritage extends back to the Revolution, where his forefathers had proudly served as a part of General Francis Marion's regiment. Law was twenty-six at the beginning of the Civil War and was viewed by most of people who knew him as a very personable and capable individual who possessed a great many of the qualities that endear one person to another, such as honesty, loyalty, dependability, and good judgment. By all accounts, a handsome man, arrow straight, jet-black hair and beard. He would need all this and more to survive the entanglements he would undergo with his "South Carolina Cousins", let alone the Federal troops, during the Great War.

Law was the son of Ezekiel Augustus and Elizabeth M. Law, a very prominent family in South Carolina, where E. Augustus was a highly respected member of the Darlington Bar. Evander's family was rather large, even for the period in which they lived, as the large number of siblings confirms: his brother Julius Augustus, who was the Darlington County Treasurer, and John K. and Thomas C. Law, both, successful attorneys in California, Edwin Augustus Law, who served in the Confederate army and gave his life for the cause, John Bradley Law, a Darlington planter, and Samuel Fulton, and William Cowan Law, who both died early in life. Evander's sister Mary Elma was the wife of a doctor, his sister Elizabeth Evans was also married to a distinguished local gentleman, and his sister Eliza died very early in life.[1]

Law entered The South Carolina Military Academy [Citadel] in 1853 and was doubtless a serious student, who excelled academically in his early years as well as at the Citadel. Born on August 7, 1836, Law was almost seventeen when he entered the Citadel, which was slightly older than most cadets. The Citadel was, and is today, an outstanding military school very similar to West Point in many aspects, and assuredly during the 1850s, the work was equally as challenging as that at West Point. In his final year at the Citadel, Law was an assistant instructor in *Belles Lettres*, graduating in 1856, number three in a class of fifteen students.[2]

Teaching appears to have been Law's calling in his prewar years and he would spend the next five years of his life as a teacher. Law's first professional teaching position was at the Kings Mountain Military Academy at Yorkville, [York] South Carolina. Micah Jenkins [and others] founded this school, and was also a Citadel graduate and would become Law's major antagonist during the war. The problems of Law and Jenkins concerning command during the Civil War would become a military clinic in what not to do in the midst of a war. The two young generals competed for an important military position [division commander] until well into the war. After a tour at Kings Mountain, Law moved to Tuskegee, Alabama and established the Tuskegee Military High School, along with Robert Parks at some point in 1860, the exact date is unclear and sources vary somewhat

---

[1] Information supplied by the Darlington County Historical Commission by letter, September 19, 2002
[2] Information supplied by the Citadel Archives

concerning the date. Law taught *belles llettres* and history at Tuskegee, and also served as the principal of the school. Some sources also claim that Law studied, and actually practiced, law before the war. This would seem to have been rather unlikely, given the time frame. He graduated from the Citadel in 1856, taught at Kings Mountain Academy, and founded his own school in Alabama during a five year period from 1856, until 1860. There simply would have been no time available for the study and practice of law before the war.[3]

When the Civil War began, Law recruited a company of soldiers, largely from the Tuskegee Military High School. These recruits would later become part of the 4th Alabama Infantry and assisted the state of Florida upon its secession, in the capture of Pensacola and the nearby forts. When the students officially became a part of the 4th Alabama Infantry, Law's recruits proceeded to Virginia. The 4th had been organized at Dalton, Georgia on May 2, 1861, and mustered into service for twelve months at Lynchburg, Virginia on May 7. From Lynchburg, the regiment went to Harpers Ferry, but withdrew to Winchester, Virginia and became part of Gen. Barnard E. Bee's Brigade. The 2nd, and 6th Mississippi, the 1st Tennessee, and the 6th North Carolina made up the rest of the brigade. Due to his military education and background, it comes as no surprise that Law became the regiment's Lieutenant Colonel.[4]

---

[3] Lawrence L. Hewitt, "Evander McIvor Law", *The Confederate General*, William C. Davis, editor (Harrisburg National Historical Society, 1991), Vol. IV, p. 22-25; hereinafter cited as the General; The Pensacola *Journal* obituary supplied by Darlington Historical Commission, identified as the *News and Press*; hereinafter cited as Obituary; Evander McIvor Law, *Dictionary of American Biography* (New York: Charles Scribner's Sons, 1961), Vol. VI, p. 38-39; hereinafter cited as the Dictionary of American Biography

[4] Http://www.archives.state.al.us/agis.html; hereinafter cited as Alabama Archives

The 4th Alabama, as a part of Bee's Brigade, saw combat in the first major land battle of the war. On July 16, 1861, The Army of the Potomac under the command of Gen. Irvin McDowell left Washington to confront the Confederate army, which was beyond Centreville at Bull Run. On July 21, McDowell attacked the Confederate left flank at Matthews Hill, in what would be a day of ultimate disappointment for the Union troops. It was a long day of intense fighting and the Confederate army was driven back to Henry Hill, but later in the day Confederate reinforcements arrived, some of which came from the Shenandoah Valley under the command of Gen. Thomas Jackson. The Confederates, with new vigor and reinforcements, were able to break through the Union's right flank forcing a Union retreat that became a near rout. Even in victory, the Confederates were not much better organized than the Federals, in that no real pursuit occurred after the battle. General Bee, the brigade commander of the 4th Alabama, was killed in the action of the battle, yet his fame lives on as the general who anointed Gen. Thomas Jackson with the name "Stonewall", because he and his troops were "standing like a stonewall" as Bee urged his brigade to fall in behind Jackson and move forward. Gen. Joseph Johnston, the Confederate commander in reference to Jackson's stance and Bee's actions said:

> General Bee moving towards the enemy, guided by firing, had with a soldier's eye selected the position near Henry house, and formed his troops upon it. They were the Seventh and Eighth Georgia, Fourth Alabama, Second Mississippi, and two companies of the Eleventh Mississippi, with Imboden's battery. Being compelled, however, to sustain Colonel Evans, he crossed the valley and formed on the right and somewhat in advance of his position. Here the joint force, little exceeding five regiments, with six field pieces, held the ground against fifteen thousand United States troops for an hour, finding themselves outflanked by the continually arriving troops they fell back to General

Bee's first position, upon the line of which Jackson, just arriving, formed his brigade and Stanard's battery.[5]

With the death of General Bee, the 4th Alabama Infantry transferred to the Peninsula and became part of Gen. William H. C. Whiting's Brigade. The battle of First Manassas, or First Bull Run took a heavy toll on the regiment which sustained thirty-eight killed, and 208 wounded out of a total of 750 men taking part in the battle. Among those wounded was Evander Law who suffered severe injury, but recovered enough to return to duty, and was promoted to Colonel in October of 1861. The regiment spent the winter of 1862, in Dumfries, Virginia where most of the men, during the month of January, signed re-enlistment papers for three years, after which the regiment underwent reorganization in April of 1862, and moved toward the action on the Virginia coast.[6]

After the battle of First Manassas, the 15th Alabama Infantry, which would later be a part of Law's Brigade, took part in the battles of Front Royal and First Winchester, as a part of Jackson's Shenandoah Valley Campaign. Col. William Oates was in command of the 15th Alabama and would be an important officer in Law's brigade throughout most of the war.

The first action after Manassas for Colonel Law occurred at Seven Pines, or Fair Oaks. On May 31, General Joseph Johnston realized that the IV Corps of the Union army, under the command of General Keyes was isolated, in a sense, at Seven Pines, south of the Chickahominy River. Johnston determined that this would be an easy target to destroy and ordered A P. Hill and Magruder to ferret out any Federals along the line of the river north of their position. Longstreet, along with General Whiting's Division, would

---

[5] *Official Records of the War of the Rebellion*, Series 1, Vol. II, p. 474; hereinafter cited as OR (all records are Series 1, unless otherwise noted)
[6] Alabama Archives; Confederate General, Vol. IV, p. 23

take the Nine Mile Road and complete the same order. Hill was ordered to make a secondary attack, in conjunction with General Huger, who would make a foray along the Charles City Road. Longstreet miscued and took his army along the route assigned to Hill and Huger. This error caused a general slow down of the entire operation; the result being that a battle designed to begin at dawn was delayed until 1 P.M. The repercussion was that Hill made a lone attack, and the Confederate casualties were very high.

About 4 P.M., Whiting's Division was ordered to move toward Fair Oaks down Nine Mile Road to reinforce D. H. Hill. Sedgwick, the Union general, arrived with his division just as Whiting's attack began, resulting in Whiting's repulse and forced retreat. General Johnston was severely wounded and Gen. G. W. Smith assumed command of the army. Longstreet was ordered to attack the following day [June 1] at dawn. Even though the orders were completed, Longstreet's attack was too tame to be effective. Gen. R. E. Lee arrived in the afternoon of June 1 and assumed command of the army and ordered a withdrawal of the combat forces to the original Confederate positions.

Colonel Law commanded General Whiting's Brigade and Whiting commanded Gen. G.W. Smith's Division, while Smith led the Left Wing of the Army in the attack, and took command when General Johnston was severely wounded. *Battles and Leaders* states that, " The leading brigade, commanded by Colonel Law... advanced, and so much strength was developed by the enemy that General Smith brought his other brigades into action on the left of Law's."[7]

---

[7] *Battles and Leaders of the Civil War*, edited by Clarence C. Buel and Robert U. Johnson, 4 Vols. (New York: The Century Company, 1887), p. 202-218 [quotation on page 214]; hereinafter cited as Battles and Leaders; also see Alexander Webb, *Campaigns of the Civil War: The Peninsula* (Edison, NJ: Castle Books, 2002), pages 97-117 [Reprint of the original 1881 edition], hereinafter cited as Webb; for a discussion of

The battle of Seven Pines was inconclusive, for the most part, but still some very important inferences can be drawn from the results. Douglas S. Freeman, a noted historian of the Army of Northern Virginia as well as a biographer of General Lee, cites the Confederates "mentioned in dispatches" as the probable leaders of the army in future battles. He notes that seven men were singled out for praise in dispatches, but Evander Law is not in the group. The most important outcome of the battle was R. E. Lee's rise to leadership, and in a sense, Joseph Johnston's decline from leadership. Law would ultimately become a *protégé* of General Hood as Hood gained rapid acclaim in the formation of the 4th Texas Infantry. This regiment would be a part of Hood's Brigade, which was in Whiting's Division. Hood was already a brigadier and developed an immediate fondness for Law. Hood mentions Law's role in his autobiography *Advance and Retreat* and states that his brigade was ordered to move to the right flank and support Longstreet. Law's brigade [actually Whiting's Brigade, Law commanding] then came into contact with the Federal forces involving Law in fierce combat, for which he received little credit or mention. The connection between Micah Jenkins, Law's old "boss" at the Kings Mountain Military School, and General Longstreet, began to take shape during this battle. Freeman notes that Jenkins, of the Palmetto Sharpshooters, "had prepared himself for that day and the honors that awaited him", and Longstreet would be a part of the chorus extolling his honors.[8] A factor detracting from Law's fame was the unfortunate truth that he did not write a

---

this battle, also Douglas Southall Freeman, *Lee's Lieutenants: A Study in Command,* abridged by Stephen Sears (New York: Scribner, 1998), pages 123-144; hereinafter cited as Freeman
[8] Freeman, p. 138-139; Gen. John Bell Hood, *Advance and Retreat* (New York: Konecky & Konecky, no date given), p. 23; hereinafter cited as Hood [General Hood's autobiography]

brigade report for this battle, nor for many others in which he took part. Whiting was not commanding the brigade, and therefore he did not write a brigade report. In the battle of First Manassas, General Bee was killed, and no report was written for the brigade, hence nothing about the 4th Alabama Infantry's role surfaced in that battle. Consequently, Law did not "get mentioned in the dispatches" as Freeman so succinctly phased it, but neither did Hood.

The battle of Seven Pines was, without doubt, poorly managed, perhaps, one of the most mismanaged battles of the war. The Confederate army did little that was in their interest, mistakes caused generals to get lost, regiments not follow the order of battle, but follow their own plan of battle, and brigades to lose all sense of accountability. The artillery was unable to take position because the road was jammed with troops who were idle due to a lack of orders. The battle ended at sunset, nothing had changed except the Confederacy had 11,000 dead and wounded.

While the 15th Alabama Infantry was not yet a part of Law's brigade, it is worth noting the activity of this brigade. The 15th was a part of Jackson's Shenandoah Valley Campaign, taking part in the Cross Keys engagement on June 8, 1862, and the Port Republic engagement of June 9, 1862. Cross Keys involved an encounter between Ewell's Division and Gen. John C. Fremont's forces. Fremont withdrew after a jolt given to Gen. Julius Stahel's brigade by General Trimble. The Port Republic encounter occurred as a result of the isolation of two brigades of Gen. Erastus Tyler's command. Confederate casualties were high, but finally Jackson's forces turned the Union's left flank. Forces from Cross Keys and those of Port Republic forced the Union troops to retreat, leaving Jackson in control of the Shenandoah Valley, for the most part. [9]

---

[9] Battles and Leaders, Vol. II, p. 291-293

Gaines' Mill was the third of the Seven Days' battles. This battle was largely a confrontation between Gen. Fitz-John Porter's V Corps and Gen. Robert E. Lee's Army of Northern Virginia. Gaines' Mill was an important battle for a number of reasons, paramount being that the defeat of Porter's V Corps signaled to McClellan that his attempt to capture Richmond would be unsuccessful at that point in time. This led McClellan to issue the command for a retreat toward the James River.

When the battle of Seven Pines ended, Lee began to plan for the means to free Richmond from the grips of the Union forces. Whiting's Division was sent to Staunton, as a feint. Whiting joined Jackson, and marched down the Chickahominy River toward Richmond. When Jackson neared McClellan, the Confederate army would then cross the river and attack in force. At dawn on June 27, Whiting's Division moved, later in the day, to support Longstreet's attack on Cold Harbor. The V Corps held its own against various Confederate attacks until late in the day, but General Lee determined that the Federal line had to be broken or the day was lost. Whiting's Division came on the battlefield in front of Turkey Hill and General Lee directed Whiting to press the enemy with his division. Whiting's position was about in the center of Porter's line, which was the key location to the battle. Hood's Brigade was on the left, and Whiting's Brigade, led by Evander Law, was on the right. Hood detected a break in the Federal line between Law's command and the other brigades, the result being that he was able to lead about 500 men of the 4th Texas through a maze of lines and terrain. Hood dismounted and led his men against the Union rifle pits instructing his Texas "shock troops" to hold their fire until he gave the order----about ten yards from the enemy. As the Federal forces, weary from a long period of intense battle, began to fall away, Hood opened fire. The Federals were decimated, and torn with sheer panic. Hood's Texans pursued the fleeing troops, followed by Colonel Laws' 4th Alabamians. As a result of the Federal line in retreat, Law, in a post war letter to the editors of *Battles and Leaders* explains:

> Whiting's division covered the ground on which J.R. Anderson's, Archer's, and Field's brigades had previously attacked. We passed some of these men as we advanced to the assault. We carried the Federal line in our front, and Longstreet on our right, bringing up his reserves, again attacked and carried his front. At the last and successful advance the line from left to right was: Longstreet (Anderson, Pickett, Whiting {Hood and Law}, Jackson (Winder and Lawton), Ewell (one or two brigades), and D.H. Hill (Rodes, Anderson, and Garland)....[10]

This letter was written to correct statements made by others in the account of the battle. Law's article, "On the Confederate Right at Gaines' Mill", in *Battles and Leaders* gives a good account of the battle, but unfortunately, it was written two decades after the battle occurred, when in reality it should have been Law's battle report in the *Official Records*.[11]

General Whiting praised both Hood and Law for their service in the battle, however, Whiting's report was written for the division, not his old brigade, led by Law in the Gaines' Mill battle. As stated earlier, Law did not see fit, or else was not asked, to submit a written report, the result being that unfortunately his brigade received few of the accolades they should by all rights have received.[12]

---

[10] Battles and Leaders, Vol. II, p. 335; also see Hood, p. 24-29; see Webb, p. 128-136 for a discussion of the Battle of Gaines Mill; Richard M. McMurry, *John Bell Hood and The War For Southern Independence* (Lincoln: University of Nebraska Press,1982), p. 46-48; hereinafter cited as McMurry
[11] Battles and Leaders, Vol. II, p. 363-365
[12] OR, Vol. XI/ 2, p. 564

The Confederate army was in fighting trim after the battle of Gaines' Mill, except for A. P. Hill's "Light Brigade". Hill had sent in his troops about 2 o'clock and was engaged in an extremely vicious and deadly battle of lengthy duration. Finally, after about two hours, Longstreet and Jackson came to his aid. In fairness, Porter's V Corps gave about as good as it received, nonetheless, about 7 P.M., after at least five hours of continuous battle, the Confederates had established a solid front line. The Confederates lost about 8,000 killed, wounded, and captured in the battle of Gaines' Mill and the Federal army's losses numbered about 7,000 killed, wounded, and captured.[13]

The battle of Gaines' Mill ended on June 27, 1862 and a mere four days later, the final battle of the Seven Days occurred, the battle of Malvern Hill. If possible, Malvern Hill was even more of a disaster than Seven Pines. The Federal army was in control of Malvern Hill, which rises to about sixty feet in height and is about one-half mile wide. Located on the north bank of the James River, Malvern Hill was an extremely difficult, if not impregnable, position for the infantry of either army to have held. On July 1, 1862, General Lee commenced a series of very unconnected assaults on the Union position at Malvern Hill.

The Confederate battle plan was to begin the advance on a signal, given by General Armistead's Brigade, which was designated to be the lead brigade. Plans went awry as they often do in battle, and Generals Huger and Magruder somehow managed to cut off Amistead's Brigade. The shouting of the lead brigade was not heard along the line because of the roar of cannons and gunfire. The battle began with a Confederate advance against Porter's and Couch's positions, on the left and center of the line. The Confederate attack was quickly quelled by blistering artillery fire. The

---

[13] Webb, p. 150

intensity of the battle fell upon Morell's (Porter's Corps) and Couch's (Keyes' Corps) divisions when at about 3 P.M. Anderson, of D. H. Hill's Division charged against Couch's right. The charge was met with intense musket fire, followed by stringent artillery fire. Later in the afternoon, (5:30 P.M.) on hearing a loud commotion, Hill thought this was the attack signal and gave the order to advance, personally leading the charge. Hill's troops were able to advance, but were forced to retreat after little progress. Magruder, who was awaiting rifled artillery, became impatient, and ordered his division (Wright, Mahone, and Cobb) to advance, however, they were forced to recoiled time after time due to the intense artillery fire. Magruder's charge, while unsuccessful, was perhaps the most famous of the entire battle but nonetheless, the struggle continued until 9 P.M., at which time the Confederates withdrew. [14]

> D. H. Hill had this to say about the battle of Malvern Hill:

…The battle of Malvern Hill might have been a complete and glorious success had not our artillery and infantry been fought in detail. My division, having been three times engaged, had exhausted all their ammunition and had been sent back for a fresh supply. If I had had them with me with a good supply of ammunition I feel confident that we could have beaten the force immediately in front of us. Again, the want of concert with the infantry divisions was most painful. Whiting's division [Colonel Law] did not engage at all, neither did Holmes. My division fought an hour or more the whole Yankee force without assistance from a single Confederate soldier….

The actual loss in battle was, in my opinion, greater on our side than on that of the Yankees, though most persons differ

---

[14] Webb, p. 153-167; also see Gen. Porter's account of the battle in Battles and Leaders, p. 406-427; also James Longstreet, *From Manassas to Appomattox: Memoirs of the Civil War in America* (New York: Mallard Press, 1991 edition of the original), p. 141-145; hereinafter cited as Longstreet

with me. The advantage in position, range, caliber, and number of guns was with them....[15]

Gen. Alexander Webb, who was the Chief of Staff, Army of the Potomac, made this statement about the conclusion of the battle, "... as an eye witness [I] can assert that never for one instant was the Union line broken or their guns in danger. During the night, the troops were withdrawn from the hill and put in motion toward Harrison's Landing." The reason for this movement, according to General Webb, was that the Federal navy affirmed that they were unable to protect the movement of supplies from an attack from the opposite bank of the James River.[16]

General Webb asserts that General Lee offered the following as reasons for the Confederate army's loss at Malvern Hill, "Ignorance of the country, difficulty of communication, [and] the density of the forest, which hindered the movement of artillery and made it impossible to bring up a sufficient force of that arm to oppose successfully the extraordinary strength in that regard opposed." Webb seems to have felt that none of these reasons really explained the true cause for the defeat, which was, in his view, poor organization and a lack of command direction.[17]

From statements made by General Whiting, it also appears that General Hill was correct in his analysis of the battle when he proclaimed that Whiting's Division never really took part in the battle. General Whiting, in his report on the battle explains, "After the attack commenced on the right my division, with the exception of two regiments on the right of my line, which was near the center, and some of the Texas skirmishers, had nothing to do with the battle except to suffer a murderous artillery fire, which they did un-

---

[15] OR, Vol. XI/2, p. 629
[16] Webb, p. 167
[17] Webb, p. 157

flinchingly.... From my point of view the enemy appeared to fight with great stubbornness, and our attack [seemed] to have made but little impression upon him."[18] The Seven Days battles were an overall disappointment for the Confederacy, in that while most viewed the withdrawal of the Union forces as a good sign, it was the view of many others that the Federal forces should have been crushed.[19] As for Malvern Hill, this was a battle of Confederate infantry versus Union artillery, and given the location of the Union forces and the superior artillery at their disposal, the outcome was never in doubt.

After the battle of Malvern Hill, Colonel Law was given a brigade command and became part of Hood's Division. Hood writes in *Advance and Retreat*, on August 15, 1862, "My command had been increased by the addition of two or more batteries and a splendid brigade, under Colonel E.M. Law, an able and efficient officer."[20] The date mentioned in this statement is not confirmed by other sources, which place Law's command as a part of Hood's Division at a later date.[21] The first engagement of Law's Brigade under Hood's command was a skirmish at Hazel River, Virginia on August 22, 1862. This skirmish occurred as part of the Campaign in Northern Virginia leading to the battle of Second Manassas, or Second Bull Run. General Lee gives an account of the skirmish, "On the 22, Jackson crossed Hazel River at Welford's Mill and proceeded up the Rappahannock, leaving Trimble's brigade near Freeman's Ford to protect his trains". Later in the afternoon, Hood was dispatched by Longstreet, along with Whiting's Brigade (Law commanding) to relieve Trimble. As Hood arrived,

---

[18] OR, Vol. XI/2, p. 157
[19] OR, Vol. XI/2, p. 498
[20] Hood, p. 31
[21] Stewart Sifakis, *Who Was Who in the Confederacy* (New York: Facts on File, 1988), p.165; hereinafter cited as Sifakis, Confederacy

Trimble was attacked by a large force, but with Hood's arrival the Federals were forced to retreat, with heavy losses. Hood's account of the battle gives all the credit to Jackson [Trimble's brigade], and barely mentions the role played by his and Law's commands.[22]

Gen. John Pope came to Washington, D.C. in late June of 1862, after a rather successful tour of duty in the Mississippi area. Pope arrived in Washington as a "hero", and everyone seemed to recognize him, still, Pope could not fully understand why he had been summoned to the East at this time, given his success in Mississippi. It would later be reveled to him that he was to confront Gen. "Stonewall" Jackson in an attempt to force Lee to enlarge the defense of the Virginia Central Railroad, allowing McClellan to attack Richmond. Pope was not happy with this new assignment, and for many valid reasons. Pope asserted that he was also assigned the insurmountable task of uniting the armies of McDowell, Fremont, and Banks, all three of whom were senior to Pope in rank. In addition, Pope would be in command of this new army and acknowledged that any hope of success in this situation was a "forlorn-hope", as he described it. General Pope requested to be relieved from this assignment, but this was not to be the case. The new army was organized and was to be referred to as the Army of Virginia, Gen. John Pope commanding. [23]

On June 27, 1862, General Pope assumed command of the Army of Virginia, consisting of three corps, with a total of about 38,000 men. In early July Jackson's Corps was detached from Lee's army and concentrated at Gordonsville, Virginia while Stuart's cavalry was on the march observing the movements of the new army. On August 13, Longstreet's corps linked with Jackson at Gordonsville and General Lee commanded the combined army on that particular day

---

[22] OR, Vol. XVI, p. 553; Hood, p. 32
[23] Battles and Leaders, Vol. II, p. 450

[August 15, 1862]. D. H. Hill's Corps was the only Confederate military force confronting McClellan at Harrison's Landing, hardly enough to stop McClellan from attacking Richmond.

In an attempt to draw Pope's army into battle, Jackson attacked a Federal detachment crossing his lines on the Warrenton Turnpike on August 28. General Pope was now convinced that he had somehow trapped Jackson, and thus concentrated his entire army against him. On August 29, a series of assaults were set in motion against Jackson, all of which were failures, and with heavy Federal casualties.[24] On August 29, Longstreet's Corps arrived about 12 P.M. and took position on Jackson's right flank. The next day, August 30, Pope took up the attacks again, seemingly unaware that Longstreet had entered the fray, whilst Fitz John Porter also attempted an attack which was severely put down. Longstreet then launched a counterattack thought to have been the largest mass assault of the war. Second Manassas was very nearly a repeat of First Manassas. Colonel Law's report describes the events:

> Leaving Thoroughfare Gap at sunrise on the 29th, the brigade marched in the direction of Manassas Junction. At Gainesville, on the Warrenton turnpike, the line of march changed abruptly to the left, along the turnpike, in the direction of Centreville. ...I was ordered by Brigadier-General Hood, commanding the division, to form the brigade in line of battle to the left of the turnpike and almost at right angles with it, the right resting on the road, and the left connecting with General Jackson's line.... At this point, a severe artillery fire was opened by the enemy's batteries. A halt was ordered, and the troops remained in position until our artillery could be brought forward. Our batteries took position on a ridge to my left and rear, and opened fire, with marked effect upon the enemy.[25]

---

[24] Battles and Leaders, Vol. II, p. 461-472
[25] OR, Vol. XVI, p. 622-623

Law continued his report stating that the artillery attack went on until nearly 4 P.M. at which time Jackson ordered an attack, driving the Federals to Groveton. Law explains that he then moved his command to Groveton, aligning with the troops on his left. About 6 o'clock, a Federal battery moved to within about 400 yards of Law's position, and when the battery prepared to open fire Law was ordered by Hood to attack, the result being that he was subjected to fire from artillery and enemy infantry. Fortunately, he was able to subdue the artillery before they found the range. The infantry fire was put down by the 2nd Mississippi, and later with the Texas Brigade, they cleared the field of the Federal forces. The remainder of Law's brigade also challenged and defeated the forces before them, but the battle continued until well after dark. At Hood's command, Law's brigade returned to the position they held earlier, to the rear of Groveton.[26]

On August 30, at daybreak, the Federal army advanced a heavy line of skirmishers toward Groveton, and a very diligent and determined exchange of fire continued until 3 o'clock, at which point the main attack of the Federals began. The attack, made by General Morell's Division on Jackson's right, was soon repulsed, and the entire Confederate line was ordered forward. Law's Brigade was ordered to advance to Groveton and support a battery at that location. For over one-half hour, the brigade was under intense artillery fire when Hood ordered the brigade to move across the turnpike to the left of the Texas Brigade. Law immediately detected a strong Union force moving toward a ravine, with the obvious intent of placing a battery in the area. He then ordered three regiments, the 6th North Carolina, 4th Alabama, and the 2nd Mississippi, forward to the ravine, and specifically to a pine thicket near the ravine from which

---

[26] OR, Vol. XVI, p. 623

he intended to hit the battery on both sides, the 11th Mississippi having been ordered previously to attack the battery. After awhile, when the 11th Mississippi did not come forth, Law combined the 6th North Carolina, the 4th Alabama, and the 2nd Mississippi and moved on the battery. The battery force escaped, but many of the infantrymen were captured, in addition intense pursuit of the enemy continued until well past dark, when General Longstreet gave the order to halt for the night.[27]

The 31 of August gave no sight of the Federal army and it was now evident that a massive retreat had occurred. Law later discovered that his orders for the 11th Mississippi had been incorrectly received and as a result, the regiment moved to the left of the Chinn house instead of to the right. It was detached from the brigade for awhile, advancing with the troops in that part of the battlefield, and fighting superbly. Law continued his report by commending all the officers and men in the brigade for their courage under fire. The brigade suffered the loss of fifty-six killed, and 264 wounded.[28]

General Pope was in a very misinformed position due to the fact that he believed that the Confederates were retreating toward the mountains. He sent word to Washington to this effect, and explained how he was preparing to begin his pursuit. What had actually occurred was that Longstreet had made a reconnaissance mission, which Pope misread as a battle, and when Longstreet withdrew, Pope accounted this as a retreat. He had furthermore informed Washington that Generals Hooker and Kearny were certain that Confederate losses were heavy. By the morning of August 30, Pope also believed that the Confederate army was in full retreat, and on that assumption, an attack was ordered against Jackson about one o'clock

---

[27] OR, Vol. XVI, p. 624
[28] OR, Vol. XVI, p. 624-625

forcing Jackson to later call for reinforcements. Artillery was sent in by Longstreet and after several valiant attempts to regroup, the Federals had to withdraw. [29] On September 1, pursuit by Jackson and Stuart began in earnest. Jackson reached Ox Hill late in the afternoon and combat took place (Chantilly or Ox Hill) as the Federals were in position upon the arrival of the Confederate pursuit, and even though Jackson was attacked, the Federals were repulsed without any considerable assistance by Longstreet or Stuart, Longstreet having arrived later. The weather was horrid, high wind, rain, thunder, etc., and some of Jackson's men were disorganized by the conditions and both armies were in disarray as a result of the weather. Gen. Philip Kearny was attempting to regroup his division when he ran into Confederate forces that were determined to capture him. After repeated challenges, he continued his attempt to escape and was killed by a rain of rifle fire, as was Union Gen. Isaac Stevens.[30]

Union losses at Second Manassas, including Chantilly, and Bristoe Station, were 1747 killed, wounded, 8, 452, and missing, 4,263, for a total of 14, 468 men. Confederate losses were 1,481 killed, 7, 627 wounded, and 89 missing, for a total of 9,197 men. The total for the two armies exceeds 23,000 killed, wounded, and missing, ranking this battle as the sixth most deadly battle of the war for the Union army, and the ninth most costly for the Confederate army.[31]

After the battle of Second Manassas, the army moved in the direction of Frederick, Maryland where General Hood, blamelessly, found himself confronted with a rather unusual

---

[29] Longstreet, p. 185-186
[30] OR, Vol. XVI, p. 566; Longstreet, p. 185-186
[31] William F. Fox, *Regimental Losses in the American Civil War: 1861-1865* (Dayton: Morningside Bookshop Press, 1985 { reprint of the 1888 edition], p. 541, 550; hereinafter cited as Fox

situation. Some members of Hood's Texas Brigade had captured a number of new Federal ambulances and Hood intended to use them for the benefit of his troops. General Nathan Evans, ["Shanks"] demanded that the ambulances be turned over to him, for use by the Carolina troops, to which Hood declined, whereby Evans became enraged and illogical, and placed Hood under arrest. General Lee decided that Hood should remain with his command, but in limbo at the tail of his division. In the interim time, Longstreet's Corps had massed at Hagerstown, Maryland. Hood relates that his division had become "restive... somewhat inclined to insubordination on account of my suspension."[32] About this time [September 13] intelligence affirmed that the Army of the Potomac was moving toward South Mountain, Maryland inciting Longstreet's Corps to move toward Boonsboro Gap on September 14. Boonsboro Gap is a narrow and winding pass, through which the turnpike from Washington to Hagerstown passed. Hood's Division [Law's Brigade] reached South Mountain about 3:30 P.M. and Hood [Law] was directed to go right, as some of the Confederate forces had already been overrun. The pathway toward the right flank was overgrown and thick with brush, a difficult passage, at best. Hood ordered his brigade commanders, Colonels Law, and Wofford, to have their men fix their bayonets. When the Federal troops came to within a distance of seventy-five to one hundred yards the order to charge was given, which totally astounded the Federals, resulting in their retreat back beyond the mountain. As the day and the battle ended, the Confederates had gained control of South Mountain. Hood later returned to Boonsboro Gap, to find Gen. D. H. Hill and others at a tavern discussing the events of the battle, at which point Hood made inquiries and was immediately given a sign to be silent, because the enemy was

---

[32] Hood, p. 39

nearby, and had driven the Confederates back. Lee and Longstreet were immediately informed of this situation and a decision was made to fall back to Sharpsburg, Maryland.[33]

There is disagreement about the role played by Hood [Law] in the battle of Boonsboro, or South Mountain. Gen. D. H. Hill had this to say about the battle and Hood's comments:

> The battle of South Mountain was one of extraordinary illusions and delusions. The Federals were under the self-imposed illusion that there was a very large force opposed to them, whereas there was only one weak division until late afternoon...
>
> The Confederates, with more than half of Lee's army at Harpers Ferry, a distant march of two days, and with the remainder divided into two parts, thirteen miles from each other, were in good condition to be beaten in detail, scattered, and captured.

Hill continues his comments relating to Hood's version of the battle:

> ...General Hood who came up a short time before this advance, with the brigades of Wofford and Law, claims that he checked and drove back the Federals. G.T. Anderson reports that only his skirmishers were engaged. The surviving officers under G.T. Anderson ... say that the same thing was true of their brigades in the afternoon. Ripley's brigade was not involved at all...
>
> Hood was mistaken, then, in thinking that he had driven back the Federal advance. The opposing lines were close together at nightfall, and the firing between the skirmishers was kept up till a late hour.[34]

On September 13, Longstreet and Lee met to discuss the Maryland campaign. Longstreet wanted D. H. Hill's troops

---

[33] Hood, p. 40-41
[34] Battles and Leaders, Vol. II, p. 559-560, 571

and his Corps to unite at Sharpsburg, rather than South Mountain, presuming that such a march would exhaust his men and probably detract from their ability to combat the Federals. Lee listened, but refused to make any change in his plans, and on the morning of September 14, Longstreet set out to reach South Mountain, arriving there at about 3 o'clock in the afternoon. The Federals were heavily entrenched; still Longstreet and Hill were able to hold out until Lee ordered the withdrawal to Sharpsburg. On the afternoon of September 15, Hill and Longstreet took up a position in front of Sharpsburg, with Longstreet on the right of the Sharpsburg and Boonsboro turnpike, and Hill on the left side. It was discovered that the left side was the weaker of the two at the Dunker Church, therefore Hood's two brigades took up position at the church. After the fall of Harpers Ferry, General Jackson was ordered to march to Sharpsburg.[35] Longstreet made a somewhat stayed comment about the Maryland campaign, "Then it was that we should have retired from Sharpsburg and gone to the Virginia side of the Potomac. The moral effect of our move into Maryland had been lost by our discomfiture at South Mountain, and it was then evident that we could not hope to concentrate in time to do more than a respectable retreat, whereas by retiring before the battle, we could have claimed a very successful campaign."[36]

General Hood was very displeased with the situation of his men, claiming that they were in dire need of food, clothing and shoes. In addition they had been issued no meat and very little bread for several days, living on green corn and apples. Unfortunately, Hood's division came into immediate combat, which went on into the night. At last, Hood was able to request relief for his men to cook their small rations but General Lee could spare no one, and

---

[35] Battles and Leaders, Vol. II, p. 665-666
[36] Battles and Leaders, Vol. II, p. 666-667

suggested Jackson might be of help. Jackson ordered Lawton's and Trimble's brigades to relieve Hood, with the promise that he would come to his [Jackson's] aid if the situation required. Shortly, Hood had to make good on that promise, when a member of Lawton's staff came to request Hood's support. Upon arriving at the battle site, Hood discovered that the two brigades were out of ammunition, and they were contending with possibly two infantry Corps. Hood had only about 2,000 men in his command and stated, "… with the trusty Law on my right, in the edge of the wood, and the gallant Colonel Wofford in command of the Texas Brigade on the left, near the pike, we moved forward to the assault."[37]

Colonel Law's account of the battle is both brief and concise:

> Soon after daylight on the 17th, the attack of the enemy commenced. The battle had lasted about an hour and a half, when I was ordered to move forward in the open field across the turnpike. On reaching the road, I found but few of our troops on the field, and these seemed to be in much confusion, but still opposing the advance of the enemy's dense masses with determination. Throwing the brigade at once into line of battle, facing northward, I gave the order to advance. The Texas brigade, Colonel Wofford, had in the mean time come into line on my left, and the two brigades now moved forward together… So far we had been entirely successful and everything promised a decisive victory. It is true that strong support was needed to follow up our success, but this I expected every moment.[38]

Law continues his report, explaining that, "a large Federal force (ten times our number) of fresh troops was thrown in our front. Our losses up to this time had been very heavy; the troops now confronting the enemy were insufficient to cover properly one-fourth of the line of battle; our ammunition was

---

[37] Hood, p. 41-43 [quotation on p. 43]
[38] OR, Vol. XIX/1, p. 937

expended; the men had been fighting long and desperately, and were exhausted from want of food and rest."[39] At this point, the Confederates were using ammunition from the dead bodies of their own troops as well as Federal troops. No support seemed to be forth coming and unfortunately, if the brigade remained in place, or if they attempted to advance without support, either choice would result in massive deaths. Law regrouped the brigade behind the Dunker Chapel, along with the Texas Brigade, with General Hood's assistance. In the meantime, reinforcement arrived and the brigade was relieved to obtain ammunition.[40] This account of Law's brigade is verified by General Palfrey in his book, *The Antietam and Fredericksburg*. Palfrey's account claims that, " It seems to be certain that Law's and Wofford's brigades had almost 'been annihilated', [Wofford states], by their fight with the I and XII Corps, and they were withdrawn just before Sedgwick reached them."[41] Law's brigade after awhile, returned to battle, where they were under cannon fire until nightfall.

At about 4 P.M. Burnside reached Sharpsburg and his men were actually in the streets of the city, but Lee had no units left to challenge him. At about the same point in time, Gen. A. P. Hill reached Sharpsburg from his tour at Harpers Ferry, seventeen miles away and fell upon Burnside, wearing his red battle shirt, screaming and encouraging his division onward, driving him back to Antietam Creek. The battle of Antietam, or Sharpsburg was over, but not everyone was aware of the fact.

General Longstreet made several poignant comments about the battle of Antietam or Sharpsburg. In relation to the fresh troops brought in by General McClellan, toward the

---

[39] OR, Vol. XIX/1, p. 938
[40] OR, Vol. XIX/1, p. 938
[41] Francis W. Palfrey, *The Antietam and Fredericksburg* (New York: Castle Books, 2002), p. 85 [a reprint of the 1882 edition]

end of the battle, Longstreet commented, "The fresh troops of McClellan literally tore into shreds the already ragged army of Lee, but the Confederates never gave in." Concerning the failure of the Confederate army to successfully move into Maryland, Longstreet felt, "The great mistake of the campaign was the division of Lee's army. If General Lee had kept his forces together, he could not have suffered defeat."[42] On September 18, after dark, the Confederate army crossed the Potomac at Shepherdstown, after a less than spectacular offensive into Maryland.

Some pursuit did in fact occur after the battle of Antietam, despite the criticism, which McClellan endured, from the president and others. On September 19, a detachment from the Union V Corps crossed the Potomac at Boteler's Ford and attacked the rearguard of the withdrawing Confederate forces, commanded by Gen. William Pendleton, and was able to capture four guns. Federal operations on the 20th were not as successful for General Porter, who sent out parts of two divisions and attempted to establish a bridge position. This contingent was counterattacked by Gen. A. P. Hill's division as they were crossing the Potomac, nearly destroying the 118th Pennsylvania, causing nearly 300 casualties of the regiment's 737 men Captain Donaldson of the 118th was overheard to have said, " God! Just think of it! -- sending such troops to fight the veterans of A. P. Hill and Stonewall Jackson". The captain made reference to the fact that many of his men were unable to load their weapons [Belgian made]. As a result, no further pursuit was attempted by the Union forces.[43]

---

[42] Battles and Leaders, Vol. II, p. 668, 673
[43] Longstreet, p. 263-265; Francis A. Donaldson, *Inside the Army of the Potomac: The Civil War Experience of Captain Francis A. Donaldson,* edited by J. Gregory Acken (Mechanicburg, PA: Stackpole Books, 1998), p. 138, 133, hereinafter cited as Donaldson

The month or so after the battle of Antietam or Sharpsburg was one of much needed rest for both armies. The Confederate army reposed between the lines of the Potomac and Winchester Rivers until late October. The army used the time to re-supply their infantry with shoes, clothing, and other necessities, from whatever was available. They also involved the troops in improved drill and discipline techniques, and during the month of October 1862, promotions were forthcoming for officers in the Army of Northern Virginia. Evander Law was promoted to Brigadier-General on October 15, ranking from October 3, and was given permanent command of the brigade, which he had actually been commanding since General Whiting moved to division command. Longstreet was promoted to Lieutenant-General, and would shortly be given command of the I Corps, Army of Northern Virginia.

After the October respite, both armies resumed "the war" and began to make decisions about their next campaign. Things had changed dramatically in the Federal army – Gen. Ambrose Burnside was given command of the Army of the Potomac, and General McClellan was from that point, no longer a part of that army. The goals and campaigns of the army would be subject to change, which would not please many of the private soldiers as well as others outside the army in the United States. Strangely enough, General Lee was aware of this change within twenty four hours of the time the news reached the Union command in Warrenton, Virginia, but needless to say this information was not sent to General Lee as a courtesy notice, but came through other channels.

On the 19th of November, the Confederate command got word that the Federal forces were moving toward Fredericksburg by corps and divisions, therefore, Longstreet sent two divisions to Fredericksburg to intercept this tide of Union troops. The Confederate command determined that the Federals intended to cross the Rappahannock River, hopefully, before any serious interception could occur. To counteract this crossing, the Confederates made a forced march and arrived at Fredericksburg about 3 o'clock on November 21st. General Sumner's Grand division had already arrived and was encamped on Stafford Heights, overlooking the town of Fredericksburg. A General Statement had been delivered to the people of the city, in essence stating that unless the city was surrendered to Federal forces within sixteen hours, the Federal army would begin shelling the city. Longstreet conferred with the city authorities explaining that the Confederate army had no intention of occupying the city and were there to protect against the advancement of the enemy. The mayor of the city convinced Sumner that this was the case, and the shelling order was canceled. Nonetheless, by November 27, it was evident to both the Confederate and Union armies that a major battle was about to take place and the local people were advised to evacuate the city. The Confederate command made the following assignment of its forces: Anderson's division was placed next to the river on Taylor's Hill, Ransom and McLaws were positioned on Marye's Hill, [Marye' Heights] Pickett's division was on Telegraph Hill, and Hood's division [General Law] was located on Deep Run Creek.[44]

On the hill position occupied by General Jackson, the divisions of A. P. Hill, Early, and Taliaferro, were entrenched, with D. H. Hill held in reserve. The Washington Artillery was situated on Marye's Hill and assigned the task of alerting the army of any Federal advance, while General Barksdale and his Mississippi brigade were serving as pickets in front of Fredericksburg. On December 11, immediately before daybreak, a lone cannon blast was sent

---

[44] Battles and Leaders, Vol. III, p. 70-73

from Marye's Hill, this was the signal --- the Federal army was about to attempt to cross the Rappahannock. The Federal forces came to the water's edge and began construction of pontoon bridges to send troops across the river. General Barksdale and his "Mississippi Hornets" gave them a blast of galling lead that forced them to run for cover. Repeatedly, the attempt to construct a bridge was made, with the same result, blistering fire from Barksdale's brigade. This continued until pass noon, when in desperation the Federals turned their artillery on the town of Fredericksburg, forcing Longstreet to issued an order to cease the picket fire, with which Barksdale immediately complied. The Federal forces completed their bridge and by morning most of Sumner's troops had crossed the river. About a mile down river, below the town, General Franklin had been allowed to construct pontoon bridges and send his Grand division over the river.[45]

The main event of the battle of Fredericksburg occurred on December 13, 1862. Longstreet checked his corps, aware that the fog was heavy and the air misty, and even though it obscured the view, it also carried every sound to the Confederate positions. Hood's division was ordered to make a flank attack if Jackson was overrun, and Pickett was to assist Hood. General Franklin made a rapid advance toward Jackson's position and immediately Confederate Major Pelham turned his artillery on Franklin. Jackson held his fire until the Federals were close, then opened with a mighty blast of musket fire, sending the Federal troops into panic and confusion. A second attempt was made on Jackson's position, due to the Federals having found a gap between the brigades of Archer and Lane. The Union troops poured through this gap and fell upon Gregg's brigade, and the general was soon mortally wounded. Reinforcements

---

[45] Battles and Leaders, Vol. III, p. 75

arrived, allowing Archer and Lane to recovered and regain the lost ground.

    Law's brigade formed a part of the second, or the reserve line, extending from Hamilton's Crossing to Dr. Reynold's house. Law was ordered to support A. P. Hill's division if needed, resulting in his support of Pender's brigade which made up part of the first line on Law's left. Law detected a Federal battle line forming to advance on Latimer's battery, and he ordered the 57th and the 54th North Carolina regiments to attack the enemy, who had control of the railroad crossing in front of the battery. The Federals were driven and checked by the two North Carolina regiments. The North Carolinians then took a position on the railroad, and with the support of the 4th Alabama, they held the position until after dark.[46] This position was held by Hood's division until the end of the battle, and graciously, Hood gives a more detailed account of Law's brigade at the battle of Fredericksburg. Hood concludes his statements concerning Law's action by stating, "As usual, Brigadier-General Law was conspicuous upon the field, acting with great gallantry, and had his horse killed under him while personally directing the movements of his brigade."[47] Law's brigade sustained fifty killed, 164 wounded, and five missing at Fredericksburg,[48] the majority of these losses having been incurred by the 57th North Carolina regiment. The extent and severity of this battle to the Federal troops is well expressed by Capt. Francis A. Donaldson of the 118th Pennsylvania, a participant in the battle, " It was, without doubt, the grossest of all gross mismanagement of this shocking battle, or slaughter, for at no time during the day did it rise to the dignity of a battle. The Confederates themselves actually stopped the fight because they were too tired to kill

---

[46] OR, Vol. XXI, p. 624
[47] OR, Vol. XXI, p. 622
[48] OR, Vol. XXI, p. 624

anymore."[49] Captain Donaldson was making reference to the stone wall or fence, from which the Confederates were sending torrents of lead and conveying death and injury to untold numbers of Union troops.

Law's brigade remained in the Fredericksburg area during the Winter months of 1863, there being little military activity until April. General Law took this opportunity to get married to Jane Elizabeth Latta on March 9, 1863. After his marriage in March, General Law engaged in a campaign that has come to be known as Longstreet's Tidewater Operations that occurred from April 11, until May 4, 1863. By late March, Longstreet had convinced General Lee that a movement against the city of Suffolk to raid its vast food stores of bacon, fish, and other necessary items was a viable risk. It was decided that Longstreet's Corps and the Department of Southern Virginia, commanded by Gen. Samuel French would launch the campaign. Longstreet commenced the drive in early April, into an area much like the "low country" of South Carolina, flat, sandy, and somewhat high in humidity and moisture.[50] The "Record of Events" from the <u>Federal Department</u> of Virginia for April 11 - May 4, 1863, cites the order of events which occurred at Suffolk:

April 11 - [Confederates] advanced on Suffolk, from Blackwater, drove in the pickets, capturing the cavalry outpost on South Quay Road
April 12 - [Confederates] advanced on Somerton Road, were repulsed,
April 13 - [Confederates] concentrated along the Nansemond River, erected heavy batteries and blockaded the river, but were unable to cross, gunboats were involved constantly

---

[49] Donaldson, p. 187
[50] McMurry, p. 69

April 19 - [Confederates] opened fire on the gunboats from Fort Huger, Federal infantry crossed the river on the gunboat *Stepping Stones* and stormed the fort, capturing five pieces of artillery and taking 129 prisoners[51]

An account of Capt. Robert M. Stribling [CSA] commanding the Fauquier Artillery gives a vivid description of the fall of Fort Huger:

> About 2 o'clock on the night of April 16th, the pickets stationed up the river fell back to the fort, reporting that the enemy had landed in force above. Notice was immediately sent through one of my sergeants to General Law. In the mean time Lieutenant-Colonel Coleman advanced his skirmishers up the river and found no enemy at the points indicated... My sergeant returned and reported that a regiment was in the woods, about three-quarters of a mile distant, having been sent down to our support. When the enemy landed on the evening of the 19th, there was no picket or lookout up the river; no gun was fired or no notice whatever served of their approach... The construction of the fort was such a nature that I could not use my guns with full effect against a land force....[52]

The 48th Alabama arrived too late to be of any help to Fort Huger but also Capt. L. R. Terrell, of the 48th Alabama, commanding two companies, discussed with Col. John K. Connally of the 55th North Carolina the possibility of storming and recapturing the fort. Terrell advised against it, explaining that the fort was surrounded by marshes and deep ravines, which were very steep. About 1 A.M., General Law appeared and suggested that Connally was too far out and that he should fall back about one-quarter of a mile to the woods. At about daybreak, General Hood arrived and was in agreement with General Law about the capture of Fort

---

[51] OR, Vol. XVIII, p. 271[this is not an exact quotation, but was shortened for easier reading]
[52] OR, Vol. XVIII, p. 337

Huger; thus no attempt to retake the fort was made on the 20th.[53]

There seems to have been some confusion about the role of General French and that of General Hood in this campaign. Longstreet writes:

> ... General French seems to be under the impression that General Hood's command was expected to protect the batteries. Such was not the expectation, and his conclusion that General Hood's command was expected to protect them seems strange, as the batteries were under his control exclusively, and he was twice ordered to take the fifty-fifth North Carolina, the largest regiment in this army, for that purpose...
>
> The command at the fort [Capt. Robert Stribling] seems to have been completely surprised, and is probably less excusable than other parties in the affair.[54]

General French replied that, "Inasmuch as the troops of General Hood extended to Hill's Point, I did not think that the watching of the movements of the enemy devolved on me."[55] This affair led to bloodshed among Confederate enlisted men and officers. Officers of the 55th North Carolina reported that General Law had accused them of poor behavior in the struggle for Fort Huger, and before it ended, two officers of the 55th North Carolina and two officers of General Law's brigade were involved in a duel. There were no fatal injuries and the two elements reached a reasonable solution, but some questions arose as to General Hood's action, or lack of action concerning this unfortunate situation.[56]

Hood was never happy about the entire campaign and states in his autobiography, "... When General Longstreet marched back to Petersburg, and thence towards Suffolk --- a

---

[53] OR, Vol. XVIII, p. 339
[54] OR, Vol. XVIII, p. 326-327
[55] OR, Vol. XVIII, p. 1010
[56] McMurry, p. 70

movement I never could satisfactorily account for, and which proved unfortunate, since it allowed General Hooker, who had superseded Burnside the latter part of April, to cross the Rappahannock and attack General Lee in the absence of one-half of his Army."[57] Hood continues, "Nothing was achieved against the enemy on the expedition to Suffolk, at which point he possessed a safe place of refuge within his strong fortifications, protected by an impenetrable abatis."[58] All this aside, Hood was probably most disgruntled about the fact that his division did not take part in, or share in the spectacular victory at Chancellorsville.

In January of 1863, General Law's brigade was reorganized, becoming an all Alabama unit; the 4th, 15th, 44th, 47th, and 48th Alabama regiments made up Law's Brigade from this point onward. Both Law and Hood were saddened by the lose of the 6th North Carolina and the 9th and 11th Mississippi regiments but on the other hand, they were proud to be associated with the regiments gained from Alabama. Hood's Texas troops had developed a sense of comradeship with the departing troops, which often develops during combat when soldiers are in immediate peril and mortal danger.

The historic victories at Fredericksburg and Chancellorsville raised Confederate confidence to an exorbitant level and there was some justification for this feeling of superiority of the Confederate army, if the records are examined. This in no way reflects on the ability of the Federal soldier who was both competent and courageous, at a level equal to the Confederate soldier, but unfortunately, he was frequently not given the opportunity to demonstrate this competence, as a result of decisions made by his superior officers. This situation prompted the Confederate high command to lose sight of the ability of the Federal soldiers,

---

[57] Hood, p. 51
[58] Hood, p. 51

and why the battles were seemingly so one sided. It was the old adage come to life, "the Confederates didn't necessarily win, the Federals just lost". General Lee was convinced by June of 1863, that he should launch an offensive campaign, and determined that to remain in a strictly defensive stance would ultimately relegate his army to a position of defending Richmond, and little more. Furthermore, Lee reasoned that if the Federal army could not be drawn into battle in Virginia, he would move northward, with the goal of occupying Washington or Baltimore. The decision was made to use the Shenandoah Valley as an avenue to achieve the desired goal and if the Confederate government refused to allow the offensive campaign, nothing would actually be lost. Thus, General Ewell was given the task of clearing the Shenandoah Valley of Federal troops.[59]

Anticipating the possible campaign, the Confederate Army of Northern Virginia was reorganized into three Corps, with three divisions in each Corps, and four brigades in each division, but the divisions of Rodes and Anderson had five, and Pickett's had three at Gettysburg. This made up thirty-seven brigades of infantry and a division of cavalry, under the command of General J.E.B. Stuart, with six brigades. General Imboden commanded 2,000 horsemen and a battery of horse artillery. In addition to reorganization, troop strength had increased and nearly all of the Confederate officers were experienced under combat conditions, and as well, the private soldiers were nearly all veterans of long standing.[60]

By June 8, Longstreet and Ewell had joined Stuart at Culpeper, Virginia and General A. P. Hill was still in Fredericksburg, all of this occurring without Hooker's knowledge. Hooker ordered his cavalry under General Pleasonton to attack Stuart at Culpeper resulting in a

---

[59] Battles and Leaders, Vol. III, p. 257-258
[60] Battles and Leaders, Vol. III, p. 258

significant cavalry battle at Brandy Station, which is usually regarded as the first true cavalry battle of the war. Both sides lost about an equal number of killed and wounded. Another battle leading to the Gettysburg campaign occurred at Winchester on June 14 in which General Milroy was caught up in a sudden and swift attack by Confederate General Early and decided that withdrawal was his best defense. Pursuit occurred and after reinforcement, a severe battle took place, with large federal losses. The retreat continued until the Federal force split up, some going to Harpers Ferry, and others crossing the river at Hancock.[61]

On June 14, A. P. Hill left Fredericksburg, and Longstreet left Culpeper on the 15th, however, Hill's Corps arrived ahead of Longstreet at Shepherdson on the 23 of June due to the fact that Longstreet was holding the Blue Ridge gaps supporting Stuart. On June 21, Ewell was ordered to take Harrisburg, and by the 23rd, Ewell's Corps was en route, Gordon's brigade having been ordered to take control of the bridge across the Susquehanna. Everything looked positive for the Army of Northern Virginia, which had suffered no real problems concerning this offensive up to this point. Lee was unaware that Gen. George Meade had replaced Hooker as commanding general of the Army of the Potomac. Having heard nothing from Stuart, Lee's actions were guided by the impression that Hooker was still south of the Potomac and consequently, Longstreet and A. P. Hill were ordered to join Ewell at Harrisburg. Late on the 28th of June, a Longstreet scout reported that the Federals had crossed the river, and Hooker had been replaced by Meade, who was presently at Frederick, Maryland. The Confederate rendezvous point was then changed from Harrisburg to Cashtown. Gen. Henry Heth's division reached Cashtown on the 29th of June and on June 30, Heth sent Pettigrew's brigade to Gettysburg, about

---

[61] Battles and Leaders, Vol. III, p. 261, 264-265

nine miles away, to procure a supply of shoes and other goods. Pettigrew encountered a substantial federal force [Merritt's brigade] and immediately returned to Cashtown. Hill sent word to the high command that he would advance on Gettysburg the next day, July 1. Meade's headquarters was at Tarrytown, from which he commanded seven corps of infantry, plus cavalry and artillery. Lee's entire army was moving toward Gettysburg, while Meade's was scattered, giving Lee a slight edge, and for that reason he instructed Ewell, who was moving to assist Hill on his movement toward Gettysburg, that a general battle was to be avoided until the entire army arrived.[62] Conditions and events were now in place for the upcoming battle at Gettysburg, the major and decisive battle in the eastern theater of the war, if not the entire war.

On July 1, Longstreet sent word to Hood and the brigade commanders to rejoin the I Corps at Gettysburg. Law had his brigade prepare three days of rations, when shortly a courier arrived with instructions to join Hood. The brigade was eighteen miles from Gettysburg; still Law was unable to get the brigade in motion until 4 A.M. and arrived at Cashtown about dawn on July 2. Around noon, the brigade joined Hood at Herr's Tavern on the Chambersburg Road where the brigade rested awhile, and a search for water was undertaken but with little success.[63]

On July 2, General Lee designed a plan of attack whereby two divisions of Longstreet's Corps would travel via the Emmitsburg Road, and seize the Peach Orchard, as well as the high ground west of Little Round Top. Colonel Alexander's artillery could use the Little Round Top

---

[62] Battles and Leaders, Vol. III, p. 267, 271, 272, 273, 279
[63] Morris M. Penny and J. Gary Laine, *Struggle for the Round Tops: Law's Alabama Brigade at the Battle of* Gettysburg, *July 2-3, 1863* (Shippensburg, PA: Burd Street Press, 1999), p. 26; hereinafter cited as Round Tops

elevation to assist in an infantry attack against Cemetery Ridge. Ewell would then attack the Federal right and A. P. Hill would assault the center, preventing Meade from gaining reinforcements. Longstreet was opposed to the plan from the beginning and offered an alternate plan, which Lee rejected. Lee ordered an attack for 11 A.M., however, Longstreet requested, and obtained a delay until Law's Brigade arrived. By 1 P.M. Longstreet's Corps was in motion, showing little enthusiasm, and making frequent stops. All this movement was supposed to be conducted in such a way as to avoid detection, but as frequently was the case, Longstreet took roundabout routes, retraced his path, and generally meandered. It was decided that Gen. Joseph Kershaw's brigade would attack the Federal left, but upon sighting the Federal infantry's position, Kershaw realized their alignment now made his charge a frontal attack, making it evident that General Lee's attack plan would not suffice under these new conditions. General Hood sent out his Texas scouts and attempted to determine the exact positions of the Federal forces, reasoning that if his division attacked along the Emmitsburg Road as ordered, he would face extreme and destructive fire from the flank and the rear. Due to the concave form of the Federal lines, Hood concluded that it would be a suicide mission, and he immediately informed Longstreet of the situation he faced, but Longstreet refused to change the battle plan saying simply, "General Lee's orders are to attack up the Emmitsburg Road." Hood sent a second request to delay the attack order, and again, he received the same reply. A third attempt was made, whereby Longstreet was asked to come and appraise the situation personally, still Longstreet refused and restated the same order as before. In the interim time before the actual attack, Longstreet finally appeared and Hood again requested a change of orders, and Longstreet replied, "We must obey the orders of General Lee." The attack occurred, and about the time Hood reached the Peach Orchard, he was severely wounded by an exploding incoming shell fragment. At this point General Law, by order, acquired command of the division.[64] Hood had hoped to send a brigade around Round Top and attack the Federals from the rear, but the plan was countermanded, resulting in Hood's wound, which took him out of the battle. Hood even appealed to General Lee, who was present on the battlefield immediately before the attack, but Lee replied, "I cannot take the chance of losing a brigade. We must do the best we can."[65] It is significant to note that Hood's Texas scouts informed him that there was no military presence on top of Round Top, but behind this two mile long rock structure lay massive artillery that would be exposed to any artillery atop of Round Top.

Law's brigade was ordered to make for the Federal left flank, which Hood felt rested at the end of Houck's Ridge, or extended to the base of Big Round Top. Robertson was to remain close to Law's left, at all cost. The long march to reach the battlefield had taken a toll on the men of the division, the fighting force having dropped nearly twenty percent due to stragglers falling out from heat and exhaustion. Law was very meticulous in the arrangement of his officers, the most senior colonel was placed on the extreme right and the junior colonel in the center of the brigade, and by 3:30 P.M. Law's brigade was ready for combat.[66] Around 4 P.M. the most severe action of the second day occurred. Part of the division, under Robertson, crossed Plum Run and crashed into Devil's Den, while another part of the division moved to approach Big Round Top [the 47th and 48th Alabama move toward the eastern side of Big

---

[64] Hood, p. 56-60; Round Tops, p. 30
[65] William G. Piston, *Lee's Tarnished Lieutenant: John Longstreet and his Place in Southern History* (Athens: University of Georgia Press, 1987), p.58; hereinafter cited as Tarnished Lieutenant
[66] Round Tops, p. 34

Round Top]. The 4th and 5th Texas and the 4th Alabama regiments crossed Plum Run and moved in the direction of Little Round Top for the assault.[67]

Gen. Gouverneur Warren, a member of General Meade's staff, had progressed to the signal station atop Little Round Top to try and get a better overall view of the battlefield. He immediately surveyed that Ward's (Federal) left flank was about to be overrun by the Confederates, and unless immediate reinforcement arrived, Little Round Top would pass into Confederate hands. Warren realized the Confederates would then be able to flank the entire Union line and establish batteries to drive the Federal troops from the ridge. In reality, Warren correctly surmised that Little Round Top was the key to entire battlefield. This was the position toward which General Law was moving in the late afternoon of July 2. General Warren rushed down from Little Round Top searching for a regiment, brigade, or some fighting force to prevent the Confederate army from capturing and occupying Little Round Top. Warren found his brigade in a roundabout fashion due to the fact that Colonel Strong Vincent, V Corps, 3rd Division, 3rd Brigade was in the right place at the right time to fill this demand. Gen. George Sykes, V Corps commander, ordered Gen. James Barnes, 1st Division commander to send a brigade to Little Round Top. Since Vincent's brigade was leading the division, which was part of the forces on the move to oppose Longstreet's attack, he was the logical choice. Vincent immediately responded. The brigade had four regiments: 44th New York, 83rd Pennsylvania, 16th Michigan, and the 20th Maine. After making his way to the eastern slope of Little Round Top, Vincent put out skirmishers on the lower slopes of Little

---

[67] Abner Doubleday, *Campaigns of the Civil War: Chancellorsville and Gettysburg* (Edison, NJ: Castle Books, 2002), p. 166-168 [Reprint of the original 1882 edition], hereinafter cited as Doubleday; Round Tops, p. 47

Round Top. As events unfolded, the 20th Maine became the anchor of the Federal left, the direction from which the most active combat would occur. Lt. Col. Joshua Chamberlain commanded the 20th Maine, little knowing that on July 2, he would step into historical immortality as a Civil War officer. Vincent's 3rd brigade arrived to take their position on Little Round Top, a scant fifteen or so minutes before General Law's [Hood's] division made its way to the "valley of the shadow of death" which is at the base of Little Round Top. [68]

General Law has left the student of the Civil War a dearth of written material by which to ascertain his role in the greatest battle of the war. Law's lengthy article in *Battles and Leaders* should have been his report in the *Official Records,* yet fortunately, much can be gained from the account Law presents in *Battles and Leaders*. The time of the division's action on July 2 is confirmed as 4 o'clock. Law's [Hood's] division was on a ridge above the valley [lower level of Little Round Top] separating it from Big Round Top. It seems to have been impossible for the Confederates to determine the extent of the Federal left's ascent up Round Top. Law captured a few medical support workers who revealed that the Federals had no fear of attacks at that point [behind Big Round Top] and consequently the area had only minimal security. Scouts were immediately sent to determine the Federal troop support in the area, and they confirmed that the Federals had no military presence on the summit, which validated the information given by prisoners. It was immediately determined that Round Top was the *point d'appui* as Law termed it, from which the Confederate right wing could be extended toward the Taneytown and Baltimore roads, on the Federal left.

Law conferred with Hood before the start of the battle and suggested a right flank movement. Hood was in

---

[68] Doubleday, p. 168-170; Round Tops, 72, 79; Longstreet, p. 370-373

full agreement but informed Law that he had received orders to make a frontal attack. Law immediately lodged a formal protest, to which Hood concurred, and directed Captain Hamilton of his staff to deliver the protest to General Longstreet. As stated earlier, Longstreet denied the protest several times, which led Law to question whether Lee was ever made aware of the protest, but he seems to have concluded that Longstreet felt it was hopeless to suggest a change to Lee. Law makes a very serious observation on this issue:

> Just here the battle of Gettysburg was lost to the Confederate arms. It is useless To speculate upon the turn affairs might have taken if the Confederate cavalry had Been in communication with the rest of the army, and if General Stuart had kept General Lee informed, as he should have done, of the movements of the Federal Army… The whole matter then resolves itself into this: General Lee failed at Gettysburg on the 2d and 3d of July because he made his attack precisely where His enemy wanted him to make it and was most fully prepared to receive it.[69]

Law states that the order of attack was to begin on his right, his brigade leading, and the remaining brigades taking position successively toward the left; by 5 o'clock the attack had begun. The Confederates came up on the Union's first line of battle, Devil's Den, separated from Little Round Top by Plum Run valley. The fighting at this point became severe, the division being exposed to artillery fire from the heights in front and from the left, plus infantry rifle fire. The advance continued until the Union forces faded, yet appearing still to be constantly reinforced. Law emphasized that the terrain made advancement much more difficult, so much so that many soldiers took unnecessary risks attempting to be more effective, ending in their death. By 6

---

[69] Battles and Leaders, Vol. III, p. 322

P.M. Devil's Den was in Confederate hands. The 4th Alabama had sweep over the northern slope of Round Top and cleared it of Federals, and within minutes advanced toward Little Round Top. General Law felt that Meade was aware of the importance of Little Round Top, and he therefore constantly sent reinforcements to threatened points, as they appeared to be near collapse. At this point [6:30 P.M.], McLaws' division united with Law's to offset the constant reinforcement of the Federal troops. A "back and forth" battle occurred, neither side being able to gain advantage. This continued until dark, after which both sides refurbished their lines with rocks, logs, or whatever was available, in audible range of each other.[70] When night finally and mercifully arrived, Law's division, and Longstreet's Corps occupied and controlled Devil's Den, the Peach Orchard, the Wheat Field, and the ground in front of the Round Tops. On the minus side of the Confederate effort, the Federal army's lines were still in place and intact from Cemetery Ridge to the Round Tops, and they were still in control of Little Round Top. There was much concern that a difference in thought denied the Confederate divisions and corps the unity and cohesion necessary for greater success which they otherwise might have obtained. There was no real cooperation and concerted action among the three corps, which some historians feel, was the fault of General Lee.[71]

Success seemed unobtainable with the current plan of attack in place on the 2nd of July, so General Lee decided to assault Cemetery Ridge directly with Longstreet's corps. Two of Law's batteries were sent to assist General E. P. Alexander in the cannonade of the Federal position south of Cemetery Hill, in preparation for General Pickett's charge. Law confirms that Longstreet came to his position and instructed him to prepare for a renewed attack in the

---

[70] Battles and Leaders, Vol. III, p. 323-326
[71] Tarnished Lieutenant, p. 58

Confederate front. Law was shocked, in that the battle plan on July 2 had already resulted in about a twenty five percent loss of the men in his division. More than 2,000 men had been killed and wounded, among them Generals Anderson and Robertson, both of whom sustained wounds, and McLaws' division was in no better shape. Nevertheless, the cannonade began before noon on July 3, 300 guns strong, creating dense smoke, and loud noise for miles in the valley. During this confusion, a new menace appeared, in the form of General Kilpatrick's division of cavalry. Immediately before noon Kilpatrick massed his cavalry in the timbers, which extended from the base of Big Round Top to Kern's house. Colonel Merritt's cavalry brigade moved across the Emmittsburg Road and deployed a line of dismounted cavalrymen, bringing about much of the Confederate cavalry. Confrontation with Merritt's cavalry continued until about 3:30 P.M., the result being that two of Law's regiments were forced to act almost like skirmishers. Two additional regiments [11th and 59th Georgia] were detached from the main line and soon doubled up the dismounted cavalry. At about this time [5 P.M.], Gen. Elon Farnsworth's cavalry charged the line held by the 1st Texas. The charge continued for sometime, the Federal cavalry making a more or less circuitous ride. Some of the general's troopers broke away finally, leaving General Farnsworth with but a few loyal followers. Fransworth boldly rode up to the 15th Alabama and demanded that they surrender, forthwith, he was fired upon by the regiment, and his horse was killed, and shortly, the general was mortally wounded.[72] There is a degree of confusion as to which of Law's regiments actually was responsible for General Farnsworth's death. Mr. J. O. Bradfield writes in the *Confederate Veteran,* "I am sure that

---

[72] For a more complete account of General Farnsworth charge, see Battles and Leaders, Vol. III, p. 393-396, which is the account given by Captain H.C. Parsons, 1st Vermont Cavalry

no member of the 4th Alabama Regiment, who was at Gettysburg, will claim that he was within a mile of where this fight occurred [Farnsworth's charge]. I was a member of Company E, 1st Texas Regiment." Bradfield goes on to say that his regiment should be given credit for this aspect of the battle of Gettysburg.[73] Late in the day of July 3, Law was ordered to withdraw from his position, moving to a new position across the Emmittsburg Road, remaining there until the 5th, after which the march began toward Fairfield Gap.[74]

Law did not escape criticism for his role as acting division commander at Gettysburg. It has been suggested that when he was designated as division commander he failed to appoint an officer to command his brigade, however this was not the case. Col. James L. Sheffield, commander of the 48th Alabama was appointed to command the regiment, performing exceptionally well, dealing with the Farnsworth charge, and remaining in command until the division left the battlefield.[75] It has also been suggested that that neither general Anderson, Robertson, or Benning mentioned receiving any orders from General Law during the afternoon of July 2. This is understandable given the fact that the battle did not get fully underway until pass 3 P.M. Also, Robertson was somehow separated from the rest of the division due to the heat of the battle. Additionally, General Robertson was wounded and for a time was completely out of the battle. Adding to the confusion, two of his regiments [4th and 5th Texas] became entangled with Law's brigade, and he [Robertson] requested that Law "look after them". Anderson was also wounded in the battle, and had to leave the field of battle, command falling to Lt. Col. William Luffman.

---

[73] J. O. Bradfield, "At Gettysburg, July 3", *The Confederate Veteran*, Vol. 30, 1922, p. 225-226
[74] Battles and Leaders, Vol. III, p. 323-330 [taken from Law's "Struggle for 'Round Top']
[75] OR, Vol. XXVII/2, p. 396

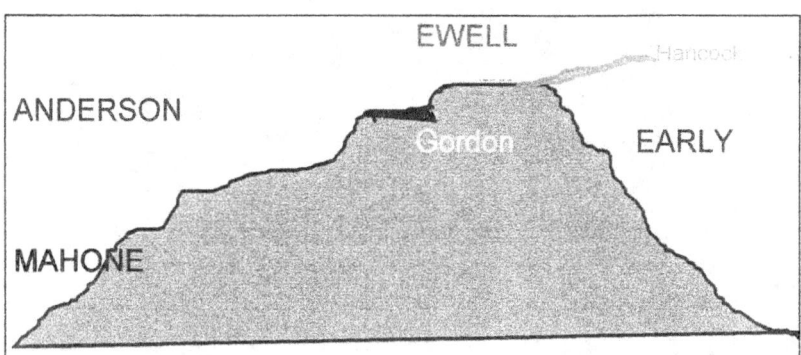

THE MULE SHOE AT SPOTSYLVANIA

Grant ordered Hancock to ready the II Corps for an attack against the "Mule Shoe" held by Ewell's Corps. Hancock led 20,000 troops into battle, and within fifteen minutes, poured through the gaps in the line held by Gordon. Gordon countered and attacked with the help of Rodes' and Early's divisions. By late afternoon, Hancock had regained his earlier position at the "Bloody Angle", or the "Salient".

Conditions faced by General Law and the Army of Northern Virginia in the widlerness, depicted by Edwin Forbes

General Benning was instructed to follow General Law when the attack began, and remain about 400 yards behind Law's brigade. In the madness of the battle, he somehow mistakenly thought that Robertson's brigade was Law's and followed the Texans instead of Law's brigade. Given the intensity of the battle, the loss of General Hood, and the sudden command situation that was thrust upon him, Law probably performed as well as could have been expected.[76] Any number of sources stress that Law was also unaware of his new command position for some time, probably not until 4:30 P.M., at the earliest.[77] It is of interest that Longstreet praised Law's command behavior at Gettysburg in his official report, but this praise would change to abject criticism when the I Corps moved to Tennessee.[78]

The losses at Gettysburg are astronomical, by any standard of battle calculation, passed or present. Hood's division lost 2, 268 men in killed, wounded, and missing. This is from a total of 7,392 men present for duty at Gettysburg. The total Confederate casualties [killed, wounded, and missing] at Gettysburg are 22,968, for the Union army, 23,001 [killed, wounded, and missing]. These numbers do not really express the post war suffering that the wounded endured for the remainder of their lives, the anguish of their families, and the economic deprivation they must have experienced.[79]

At the end of the day on July 3, Lee held a war council with his subordinates to determine the best move the

---

[76] Larry Tagg, *The Generals of Gettysburg: The Leaders of America's Greatest Battle* (Mason City, Iowa: Savas Publishing Company, 1998), p. 228, 231, 233

[77] Noah Andre Trudeau, *Gettysburg: A Testing of Courage* (New York: Harper Collins Publishers, 2002), p. 341

[78] OR, Vol. XXVII/2, p. 363

[79] William F. Fox, *Regimental Losses in the American Civil War:1861-1865* (Dayton: Morningside Bookshop Press, 1985), p. 541, 550 [reprint of the original 1888 edition]

Army of Northern Virginia should consider. The options were few, perhaps nonexistent; however, it was decided that if General Meade did not attack on the morning of July 4, the army would begin the retreat march back to Virginia. The army was moved to Seminary and Snyder ridges, orders were issued, and materials were being readied for the march, at which point Lee suggested a prisoner exchange, but Meade declined, probably because he was in a position to do so, although other reasons have been suggested for his decision.[80] The weather was absolutely frightful, rain continued into a deluge delaying the army's return to Virginia. Only after darkness did the rain subside enough to allow the Confederate army to begin the slow dismal march back to Virginia, minus 23,000 comrades. Longstreet's Corps marched South along the eastern side of the mountains, toward Hagerstown on July 6, commenting that the troops were exhausted, he reached Hagerstown at about 5 P.M. The command sought out a proper campsite and after securing a decent site, remained there until July 10th. Some skirmishing took place during the return march, which added to the overall difficulty, not withstanding the rain, mud, and additional flooding.[81] On July 11, General Lee established a defense line protecting the river crossings at Williamsport and waited for the Union forces to arrive. On July 12, the Federals reached Williamsport [or Falling Waters] and tested Lee's the defense line. On July 13, skirmishing was severe, as Meade attempted to overrun the Confederate defense. A new bridge was constructed and the Confederate army began crossing the river until past dark on July 13. Kilpatrick's and Buford's cavalry arrived and attacked Heth who was still on the Maryland side of the withdrawal. Gen. James Pettigrew

---

[80] Lee's request, OR, Vol. XXVII/2, p. 299; Meade's decline, OR, Vol. XXVII/1, p. 79
[81] OR, Vol. XXVII/2, p. 363

was mortally wounded in this rear guard action, and 500 of Heth's men were taken as prisoners.[82]

The wagon train conveying the wounded, which was seventeen miles long, was under the command of Gen. John D. Imboden. The wagons were moving by way of the Chambersburg Pike, [Cashtown Road] westward to avoid Chambersburg. The wounded suffered extreme hardships on the retreat to Virginia, even more so, as some of the suffering wounded had not received any medical attention since the battle. In addition, others had not received medical attention, or food for thirty-six hours. Gen. William D. Pender was among the wounded in transport back to Virginia and unfortunately, the return trip to the Confederate lines took his life.[83]

It was late in July when the Confederate Army of Northern Virginia finally completed the long, exhausting, and depressive return to Virginia. After all, the most significant battle of the war to date was a disaster, with over 23,000 men dead, wounded, or missing. After a period of rest and recovery, Longstreet, for reasons open to speculation, requested that the I Corps go to the western theater of the war to reinforce the Army of Tennessee. The reason most often suggested for this request was a desire by Longstreet to obtain an independent command, possibly Braxton Bragg's. General Lee approved the request, with some reservations, and Longstreet submitted the request to the Confederate Secretary of War [the request to the

---

[82] OR, Vol. XXVII/1, p. 937 [report no. 338 of Col. William Gamble, 8th Illinois Cavalry] ; also see Battles and Leaders, Vol. III, p. 429 [photograph]
[83] W.C. Storrick, *Gettysburg: Battle and Battlefield* (New York: Barnes and Noble, 1993), p.82-83 ; [Storrick was an eyewitness to the battle of Gettysburg who later became a guide at the Gettysburg battlefield]; also see Battles and Leaders, Vol. III, p-420-429 for General Imboden's account of the trip back to Virginia

Secretary of War actually preceded Lee's approval].[84] The request was approved and arrangements for the trip west were put into place. There was only one rail track westward, via Augusta to Chattanooga, and it was decided that two days should be adequate for the trip. The first train arrived at Orange Court-House on September 9, for the long and arduous trip to Chattanooga, but Instead of two days, the trip required more than two weeks, before the last of the artillery finally arrived in the Chattanooga area. In addition to the I Corps, Gen. Micah Jenkins' South Carolina Brigade was transferred to Hood's division, which was to be the beginning of a long and difficult ordeal for General Law. As early as June 8, 1863, Jenkins was writing requests for transfer to the Army of Northern Virginia, from his current post as brigade commander in the Department of North Carolina, Gen. D. H. Hill commanding, and on July 8, General Hill endorsed Jenkins' request for transfer. Jenkins had been a part of General Pickett's Division when Longstreet embarked on the Suffolk Campaign, but when Longstreet was recalled by General Lee, Jenkins and his brigade remained on the Blackwater and did not take part in the battle of Gettysburg. Jenkins again requested a transfer back to Pickett's Division on July 14, and this request was endorsed by Gen. Robert Ransom, then commander of the Department of North Carolina and Southern Virginia. On September 11, 1863, Jenkins' Brigade was transferred to Hood's Division, Longstreet's I Corps.[85] Longstreet had, and would in the future, take Jenkins "under his wing", and would make every attempt to promote and advance Jenkins, by whatever means necessary. The two men had little in common, other than birth in the state of South Carolina. Jenkins was "an aristocrat", and beyond that, his father-in-

---

[84] Longstreet, p. 433
[85] OR, Vol. XXVII/3, p. 908; OR, Vol. XXVII/3, p. 984; OR, Vol. XXVII/3, p. 1004; OR, Vol. XXVII/3,p. 1005; OR, Vol. XXIX/2,p. 713

law, David Jamieson, was the president of the South Carolina Secession Convention. Longstreet had no such connections in South Carolina, his adopted state of Georgia, or elsewhere.[86] Some claims have been made that Hood requested that Jenkins' brigade be assigned to his division, but from the available evidence this appears to be doubtful.

Gens. Braxton Bragg and William Rosecrans would engaged in battle a number of times during the war, the recent being the Murfreesboro campaign at the end of 1862, which was a Federal victory, yet somewhat indecisive. The two armies would not be engaged again until the Spring of 1863, in the Tullahoma campaign. In September of 1863, General Rosecrans wanted to drive Bragg and the Army of Tennessee out of the region, and especially Chattanooga. Bragg, in fact, was forced out of Chattanooga, but not out of the region, he simply moved South into Georgia. Bragg was equally determined to regain his position at Chattanooga. Thus, on September 17, 1863, Bragg began his movement toward Chattanooga, facing a determined foe, better armed [Spencer rifles], with cavalry and mounted infantry.

Longstreet arrived in the Chattanooga area on September 19, and immediately set out for General Bragg's headquarters, arriving there at 11 P.M. Bragg informed Longstreet that the attack was set for early morning the following day [September 20]. Longstreet was assigned the left wing of the Army of Tennessee, and at daylight on September 20, began to search for Hood's brigades, which had arrived earlier. General Hood, although still recovering, had arrived in the Chickamauga area on the 18th, and proceeded to Ried's Bridge where he encountered Federal troops. A skirmish ensued before the Federals were driven six or seven miles, and the bridge taken.[87] Longstreet having

---

[86] Longstreet, p. 436-437; Bruce S. Allardice, *More Generals in Gray* (Baton Rouge: Louisiana State University Press, 1995), p. 249
[87] Hood, p. 61

just arrived, did not know the area, let alone the men and officers under his command. The plan that Bragg designed was to cross the Chickamauga, hit the enemy's left, and block his route to Chattanooga. Longstreet was given a map and some basic instructions as to his role in the operations. Kershaw's and Humphrey's brigades were place with Hood's brigades to act as an assault unit, each brigade separated by about a hundred paces. The Union XIV, XX, and XXI Corps were assembled for battle under the overall command of Gen. William Rosecrans. Bragg's plan of battle had somehow leaked out to Rosecrans and he aligned and adjusted his army accordingly.[88]

The battle of Chickamauga actually got under way on the morning of September 19, and since Bragg gave no specific orders, things began to go downhill rapidly. Hood was without any real orders, especially as to his movements with Gen. Simon Buckner. The results of this faulty planning wasted Bragg's forces and allowed Rosecrans to locate Confederate positions. Compounding the problem, Bragg's vague and indecisive orders left half of the army uninvolved in the battle, and those that were involved, were in a state of utter frustration, a prime example being Gen. A. P. Stewart. Stewart was pulled from the line and ordered to go around Hood, with no further orders once he had completed this move. Finally unable to locate General Polk, now in " semi-command ", Stewart took matters into his own hands and finally got involved in the battle at mid afternoon.

More specific orders might have won the battle for the Confederates on September 19. Hood and Buckner probably could have cut Rosecrans' movements to Chattanooga via the La Fayette and Dry Valley roads, had Bragg made a more detailed battle plan, involving all components of the army. Opportunities for the Confederates

---

[88] Longstreet, p. 439-442

fell by the wayside "to the tenth power". Hood's division attacked without Buckner, Hindman's division was uninvolved behind Hood, and remained as a reserve division, since he had no orders. The foremost authority on the Army of Tennessee, Thomas Connelly, describes the key event of the battle:

> ...Longstreet ordered Hood and Hindman to advance in a mass offensive.
> About 11:30 A.M., Hood's lead division, that of General Bushrod Johnson, roared across the La Fayette Road, swarmed around the Brotherton house, and then continued toward the west through the fields around the house. Immediately, Johnson discovered a gap in the Union line. Because of an obvious error in the shifting of troops, the Federals had left a division-wide gap, a quarter of a mile wide, in Johnson's front. Supported by Law and Kershaw, Johnson smashed the the Federal line.[89]

General Rosecrans was a very nervous and excitable soldier who wanted all aspects of battle covered in detail, with no loose ends. He received a report early in the day on September 20 concerning battle line positions, leading him to believe that there was a gap in his defense. Captain Stanford Kellogg, General Thomas' aide-de-camp, observed what he though was a hole in the Federal line, after which he rushed to Rosecrans explaining that General Brannon was off line and that General Reynolds' right was exposed. Major Bond, a member of Rosecrans' staff, was directed to write a dispatch to General Wood to fill in General Brannon's position when he moved to support General Thomas. Wood received the dispatch, and even though he was certain that no gap existed, he followed the order as written, after conferring with General Thomas who agreed that he should do so. The

---

[89] Thomas L. Connelly, *Autumn of Glory: The Army of Tennessee, 1862-1865* (Baton Rouge: Louisiana State University Press, 1971), p. 223, see pages 201-234 for a discussion of this battle; hereinafter cited as Connelly

order was incorrect, and so were Wood and Rosecrans for their hasty judgment which was a major factor that greatly contributed to the loss of the battle for the Federal forces.[90] By 1 P.M. the Federal right was in retreat on Dry Valley Road. If the Confederates had taken, and they could have, McFarland's Gap, the Federals would have had no escape except toward the Bragg's army, in their attempt to reach Rossville Gap. Not only would the Confederates have simply won the battle of Chickamauga, they would most likely have destroyed Rosecrans' army, and regained control of a vital area.

    As often occurred, General Law did not write a division or brigade report for the battle of Chickamauga, and in order to account for Law's movements in the battle, one must look to the brigade commanders within the division. General Benning of Law's [Hood's] division states his brigade was under intense fire for most of the day, in addition he explains that the brigade was in dire need of artillery. Benning was supposed to follow Law's brigade on the 20th, but somehow got separated and was faced with a formidable Union force, which after an intense fight withdrew. He reported an exceptional number of killed, wounded, and missing in the two-day battle. General Robertson fared not much better as he also bemoaned the lack of artillery. Robertson states, "I sent three messengers for a battery, all of whom returned without any. I then went myself, but could not get the officer in command of the only one I could find to bring his battery up." Robertson also declared that he was attacked by friendly fire. He writes that he had asked the units on his right and left to join in an attack after he discovered a hole in the Federal line, but they did not respond. He seemed to have concluded that they were

---

[90] William M. Lamers, *The Edge of Glory: Biography of General William S. Rosecrans, USA* (Baton Rouge: Louisiana State University, 1961), p. 342-345.

the origin of the "friendly fire". He, like Benning, had considerable loss of men and officers in the two-day battle.[91] A final comment by Col. Van H. Manning also expresses discontent with not only the arrangement of the battle line, but more importantly, with the use of the available manpower. He felt that his regiment was fatigued, due to the great distance the men had to travel in order to engage the enemy. In addition, Manning felt that the regiments were "boxed" too closely, which prohibited movement and led to confusion in the ranks.[92]

Even though the Confederates won the battle of Chickamauga, they also suffered extreme losses. On September 20, Bragg reported 59, 242 men under his command, and this included Longstreet's I Corps, Army of Northern Virginia. General Rosecrans reports 60, 867 men in his three corps, on September 20. Longstreet places the Confederate losses at 17, 800 [estimate], and Union losses at 16,550. Twelve Confederates regiments lost over fifty percent of their forces in killed, wounded, and missing. Another six regiments lost forty five to fifty percent of their numbers. In two hours, Longstreet's corps lost forty four percent of its strength.[93] Chickamauga has been called, "one of the greatest battles ever fought on the American continent… a near repeat of Shiloh."[94]

After the defeat at Chickamauga, the Federal army was now somewhat besieged in Chattanooga, in that food supplies were limited and becoming more so by the day. Chattanooga was, in 1863, not an easy place to maneuver military supplies and food for a large army. It was rather desolate and isolated due to its location, plus the roads were few and in extremely poor condition. Faced with this

---

[91] OR, Vol. XXX/2, p.518-519; OR, Vol. XXX/2, p. 511-512
[92] OR, Vol. XXX/2, p.513
[93] Longstreet, 458-459
[94] Connelly, p. 201

situation, General Grant, with the assistance of General Thomas, conceived the now famous "Cracker line Operation "on October 26. This operation was established to serve as a supply line for Rosecrans' army from the Federal depot at Bridgeport, Alabama to Chattanooga. A road would have to be opened on the Tennessee River from Brown's Ferry to Chattanooga. Also, an advance through Lookout Valley, and the securing of Kelley's Ferry Road would be required for the successful completion of the "Cracker Line". Gens. "Baldy" Smith, John B. Turchin, and William B. Hazen were assigned the task of establishing and securing a proper bridge location. General Hooker left Bridgeport with three divisions heading toward Brown's Ferry. When Hooker reached Lookout Valley, on October 28, he detached Gen. John Geary's division at Wauhatchie, a depot on the Nashville & Chattanooga Railroad, to make certain that the line from Bridgeport would remain secure. Longstreet and Bragg, taking note of the movement, decided that a night attack [extremely unusual in the Civil War] might be successful, and set the attack for 10 P.M.[95] From this point, confusion reigned in the Confederate ranks. Gen. Micah Jenkins, Longstreet's *protégé,* had taken command of Hood's division, due to Hood's leg wound at Chickamauga. Jenkins had been imported into Hood's division, at Longstreet's urging, passing over General Law, who had led the division in two of the major battles of the war. Jenkins was Law's senior by one month, and the situation was approaching disruptive levels. This battle, Wauhatchie, would be a decisive turning point in General Law's military career.

  Jenkins, along with Longstreet, was called in to confer with Bragg and to observe the positions occupied by

---

[95] Wiley Sword, *Mountains Touched With Fire: Chattanooga Besieged, 1863* (New York: St. Martin's Press, 1995), p.115-116, hereinafter cited as Sword; OR, Vol. XXXI/1, p. 217

the Federal forces. He was then ordered to concentrate at the base of the mountain with the three brigades that were on the east side, and be ready to cross the river as soon as it was dark enough to conceal his men from enemy fire. Law was ordered to advance his brigade when it was dark and occupy the heights in his front. These heights commanded the road that extended between the Federal forces. Jenkins arranged for two brigades under Law's command to hold the position between the Federal forces, while his brigade, commanded by Col. John Bratton, was sent to make the attack on the rear guard. Bennings' brigade was held on the left of Law's two brigades in order to reinforce Bratton. Bratton implied that all was going well until he was commanded to abandon his position when he was recalled, because his safety depended upon Law's brigades being in position. This is essentially Longstreet's account of the events that occurred on October 28, 1863.[96]

General Law relates the following account concerning the battle of Wauhatchie:

> Just before night I met Brigadier-General Jenkins, commanding division, who informed me that three other brigades of the division were then moving across the mountain with the view of crossing Lookout Creek to cut off the enemy's trains and capture the rear guard and stragglers. He requested information regarding the roads, &., as I was familiar with the locality. After giving all the information in my power, I ventured to remark to him that in my opinion the enemy had a large force at the point upon which we intended to move, and that one division was insufficient for the accomplishment of the end in view; that a failure would result, and the troops engaged in it would be seriously injured. I was satisfied, from close and constant observation, that not less than 6,000 or 8,000 troops had been thrown across the river from Moccasin Bend; that one corps (6,000-7,000 more) had passed my position going toward Brown's Ferry, and that another of the same strength was

---

[96] OR, Vol. XXXI/1, p. 218

following. General Jenkins replied that he had positive orders to proceed on the expedition.[97]

Shortly thereafter, Law captured a prisoner who was from Gen. O.O. Howard's XI Corps. It was ascertained from the prisoner that Howard's Corps had passed the point toward which Law's command was directed [junction of the Chattanooga and Brown's Ferry roads], and that a division and a half of Gen. Henry Slocum's XII Corps was following. Law advanced his force to a clearing where the river, the Chattanooga road, and the hills converged into a sort of triangle. At this point, General Robertson reported to Law, by order of Jenkins. Robertson informed Law that Colonel Bratton was crossing the creek, and that General Benning would follow, and take up a line on Law's left, and the combined force would then take command of the Brown's Ferry road. Bratton would then push forward and if he encountered a small force, he would deal with it, if the force was large, he would withdraw back across the creek and attempt to communicate with Benning. Law would attempt to prevent Federal reinforcements from moving toward the railroad, and hold his position in case Bratton had to withdraw his troops. Law was informed that Bratton was moving, at which point he ordered his command forward to a position overlooking the road. In the interim, Benning had moved up on Law's left, in the rear of Bratton's brigade, which was advancing toward the Federal position. A column of Federal troops began moving up the road on Law's right, [Gen. Hector Tyndale] and Law determined to call in his skirmishers. The column was fired upon and they immediately scattered but they soon reformed, and a second volley again dispersed them. Additional Federal troops appeared [Gen. Adolph von Steinwehr] and in unison, they attacked Law's position. The fighting was repulsed after a

---

[97] OR, Vol. XXXI/1, p. 225-226

time, but not before Law received a message from Jenkins that Bratton had run into heavy fighting, possibly a corps, and that Jenkins was withdrawing and Law should hold his position until he was clear.[98]

Law sent a courier to Jenkins, shortly *before* Jenkins' message reached him. He explained to Jenkins that he was under frontal attack, and that the Federals might be able to send troops to the rear of those attacking him, and engaged Bratton, placing him in grave danger. While all this was in progress, General Robertson reported to Law that a strong force was moving over the hill on their right. A second attack began, after which Law returned his line to its original location, and then into a hollow below the hill. As clarification, Law states that, "When the order for my command to retire was given I had already received information that Colonel Bratton had been withdrawn, and that he was actually at the bridge, and the firing on the left had ceased for nearly, if not quite half an hour. Believing that the object for which my position was occupied had accomplished, I withdrew."[99] Col. John Bratton, commanding Jenkins' brigade had this to say about his withdrawal:

> First at the point, Second Rifles [part of Bratton's Brigade] on the left, [and] behind the railroad. The enemy, with his left driven, crowded and huddled upon his center, occupied the base. His line of fire at this time certainly was not more than 300 or 400 yards in length, and but from 50 to 150 yards in breath, and the sparkling fire making a splendid pyrotechnic display and encouraging the hope that the balls intended for us were lodging on themselves. At this juncture I received orders to withdraw and move back in good order, as the enemy were pressing in the rear.[100]

---

[98] OR, Vol. XXXI/1, p. 227-228
[99] OR, Vol. XXXI/1, p. 228
[100] OR, Vol. XXXI/1, p. 232

This does not sound like a commanding officer who has "run into a corps" and must immediately withdraw. Something else must be placed in the mix up in orders to make any sense of this situation. One of the leading authorities on this battle, Wiley Sword, states that, "Bratton believed he had the Yankees at a serious disadvantage. His situation seemed favorable, and as he was about to charge, the turning point occurred, not Rickards' [General Geary's officer of the day] clearing of the railroad embankment, but an order to withdraw issued by division commander Micah Jenkins."[101] Another interesting account of the battle is given by Maj. J. L. Coker, who was the Assistant Adjutant-General on Colonel Bratton's staff. Major Coker relates:

> ...General Geary's Federal division was not attacked by Longstreet's corps, but by Jenkins' South Carolina brigade, commanded by Colonel [afterwards General] John Bratton... General Howard was opposed by a small force, and made such progress that Jenkins' brigade was in danger of being cut off from the crossing over Lookout Creek. They were ordered out when they seemed to be getting the better of General Geary, who was surprised by the night attack, and no doubt thought himself greatly outnumbered, and reported himself attacked by a corps instead of a brigade.[102]

Longstreet attempted to place the blame for the failed mission at Brown's Ferry on the head of General Law, and he also claimed that Law had withdrawn prematurely, and that his cavalry was inept and derelict in their duty. Longstreet also, by implication, said that the ill feeling that existed between the two men, Law and Jenkins, was Law's fault and was due to his poor judgment. Wiley Sword, states,

---

[101] Sword, p. 137 [not an exact quotation but certainly Dr. Sword's words and meaning]
[102] Battles and Leaders, Vol. III, p. 690 [note]

"Law's withdrawal was the reason for pulling back Bratton, claimed Jenkins. On the contrary, it is certain that Jenkins ordered Bratton's retreat prior to Law falling back, based upon the appearance of Tyndale's brigade and the almost unopposed occupation of Tyndale Hill, formerly held by Benning."[103] This difference between the accounts of Law and Jenkins about what occurred at Wauhatchie became an out and out battle of opinions and criticism that ultimately led to Longstreet's official charges against Law. Wiley Sword concludes, "Jenkins simply hadn't committed enough troops for an effective night action. Law burdened with the blame for his belated pullback, had been ill served by both Longstreet's carelessness and Jenkins's animosity."[104]

In early November of 1863, Bragg called a high level meeting with Longstreet and the other corps commanders of his staff at which he announced to the generals that he intended to send Longstreet corps, with Alexander's and Leydon's artillery, and Wheeler's cavalry, into East Tennessee. Longstreet had already intimated that he could strike Burnside, and possibly return to Chattanooga before Sherman could reach that city. Although shrouded, Bragg and Longstreet had developed an intense dislike for each other, and Bragg wanted to be rid of Longstreet. By November 5 the trains were available and ready, and by November 10 the majority of the corps had reached Sweetwater, Tennessee.[105]

General Burnside had been ordered to hold Knoxville, and as a result of Longstreet's movement, he [Burnside] decided to assume a defensive posture. All of his pontoon bridges were removed and the railroad bridge destroyed. When Longstreet moved his corps on the 12th, the bridge was repaired with little interference at Huff's Ferry.

---

[103] Sword, p. 143
[104] Sword, p. 144
[105] Longstreet, p. 481-483

The 13th and 14th of November were spent in shoring up and securing the bridge and working on a bridge defense plan in the likely event of an attack. Late in the afternoon of November 14, a large contingent of Federal troops appeared and combat resulted, after which, pursuit was ordered by Longstreet on the 15th. Col. E. P. Alexander, Longstreet's artillery commander, remarked about this pursuit:

> On the 15th, the corps marched to Lenior's Station, the batteries being distributed along the column. On arriving near the station the enemy were found in line of battle awaiting us, and although the sun was already setting, an attack was ordered by General Longstreet, and the disposition for it commenced. Darkness, however fell before one-half of the column could be deployed into line, and the night being rainy and the ground rough, wooded, and unknown, the attack was postponed until dawn.[106]

Burnside immediately headed, with all speed, to Campbell's Station, a small village, where the road to Knoxville [Kingston Road] and Concord Road intersected. Burnside hoped to arrived at Campbell's Station before Longstreet, and then take Kingston Road into Knoxville and safety. Longstreet, naturally, hoped to reach the area first, deny Burnside his route to Knoxville, and force a battle outside the earthworks that had been constructed previously. Burnside reached the intersection around noon, ahead of Longstreet, whose forces arrived within the hour. Colonel Alexander continues his report:

> The pursuit was immediately ordered on two roads, General Jenkins on the right, General McLaws on the left (the two roads uniting at Campbell's Station), half the artillery accompanying each column. The right column arrived at 12 m at Campbell's Station, the left at about 2 P.M, and the enemy was found in line in a strong position. General Jenkins being sent around his right

---

[106] OR, Vol. XXXI/1, p. 478

flank, I was ordered to attack him in front with artillery, which I did with seventeen pieces of my battalion and Major Leyden's. After a sharp fight of a half hour the enemy fell back so rapidly as to avoid the flank attack of General Jenkins.[107]

General Jenkins made this" proclamation" about the attack at Campbell's Station:

> Brigadier-General Law, being on the right, was ordered to move, followed by Anderson's brigade, far enough along the hills upon the enemy's left to bring the next to last of Anderson's regiments opposite the enemy's guns, so that not only the guns but their supporting lines might be struck in flank and rear by an attack in line by the two brigades. ...Upon reaching Law's brigade I found that he had not gone far enough to the right to put Anderson in position, but his own brigade by advancing would strike the battery and enemy's flank. Sending to stop Anderson, I directed in person General Law to make the attack with his brigade independently of Anderson... In a few minutes, greatly to my surprise, I received a message from General Law that in advancing his brigade had obliqued so much to the left as to have gotten out of its line of attack. This causeless and inexcusable movement lost us the few moments in which success from this point could be obtained.[108]

Burnside ordered his two divisions on Kingston Road to withdraw about a mile to a ridge behind their line, forthwith Longstreet for reasons unknown, suspended the attack and Burnside moved as rapidly as possible to Knoxville. Another account by J. A. H. Granberry, of Waverly, Georgia, a soldier who was a part of Longstreet's corps alleged that, "We followed the retreating enemy to within a mile of so of Knoxville. On the way we came upon a collection of about a hundred wagons, from which our teamsters selected the best in exchange for their own... If our army had followed the

---

[107] OR, Vol. XXXI/1, p. 478
[108] OR, Vol. XXXI/1, p. 526

enemy right into the city without giving him time to fortify, it was believed by many that the city with the force that held it, would have been taken...".[109]

Longstreet, in his relentless pursuit of General Law, claimed that Law made a statement to a staff officer, who spoke to Longstreet saying, "I know at the time it was currently reported that General Law said he might have made the attack successfully, but that Jenkins would have reaped the credit of it, and hence he delayed until the enemy got out of the way." Longstreet, as expected, does not identify the staff officer who made this claim.[110]

By November 17, Burnside and his army were safely in Knoxville, and by noon of the same day, McLaws' division had reached the suburbs of Knoxville. As the night of November 17 approached, the Confederate lines were well established and in place. Fort Loudon just northwest of Knoxville, later called Fort Sanders after the general who defended it, was a series of earthworks, partially surrounded by a twelve feet wide, and seven to eight feet deep, ditch. The ground around the fort sloped upward, where trees had been cut, and wire established and stretched between the stumps. Even with all of these negative factors, which would make negotiation of this formidable ditch very difficult, it was decided by Longstreet that Fort Sanders was the only practicable place through which Knoxville could be entered. The general concluded that a night attack might be the key to overwhelming the fort, thus, three Confederate brigades of McLaws' division attempted the attack, with three brigades of Jenkins' division in reserve to also follow up after McLaws made his attack. This doomed attack lasted about twenty minutes, and was totally unsuccessful because the deep ditch and the defensive fire from the fort prevented the

---

[109] J. A. H. Granberry, "Longstreet before Knoxville, *The Confederate Veteran*, Vol. 31, p. 372, 1923

[110] Longstreet, p. 495

Confederates from reaching their objective. Shortly thereafter, Longstreet received word of Bragg's defeat at Chattanooga, with a plea to return to Ringgold, if possible. This was "another fine mess" in which Longstreet had entangled himself, and he decided after some contemplation, to remain in Knoxville.[111] In his haste to shift the blame, and take another swipe at Law, Longstreet implied that had Jenkins been able to make his attack at Wauhatchie, the Confederate army would most likely have destroyed the Federals and recovered East Tennessee. He claimed that Jenkins attributed his failure to Law's mismanagement at Wauhatchie and as well at Campbell's Station.[112] In essence, it was Longstreet's and Jenkins' view that Law was the reason for the loss of East Tennessee by the Confederate forces.

If all this was not enough to mortify and strip the morale out of the most loyal soldier in the Army of Northern Virginia's I Corps; Longstreet [at Jenkins' request] arrested Gen. James Robertson. Jenkins attested that Robertson made statements to his regimental commanders that the war was lost, and he was immediately arrested by Jenkins and charged with "conduct prejudicial to good order and military discipline." Longstreet concurred with the arrest and endorsed Jenkins' charges.[113] The Jenkins and Law controversy was greatly accelerated by Robertson's arrest, plus the fact that Jefferson Davis refused to name a successor for Hood's division. By the middle of December, Law concluded that he could no longer endure the abusive and shabby treatment he was receiving at the hands of Jenkins and Longstreet, and he therefore decided to resign his position in Longstreet's corps, and possibly the Confederate army. Longstreet must have had a pang of consciousness,

---

[111] Longstreet, p. 502-507
[112] OR, Vol. XXXI/1, p. 458
[113] OR, Vol. XXXI/1, p. 467

and attempted to patch things up, so to speak, suggesting that an outsider be named to replace Hood as division commander, and recommended Gen. William Whiting, but no action was taken on this proposal by the Confederate War Department.[114] Longstreet seemed to be in a state of moral depression about what was happening to his command. He seems to have finally realized that he was responsible, at least indirectly, and that much of the low morale was a reflection of his less than admirable command abilities. He requested that the Confederate War Department transfer him, or send another officer to take command of the I Corps. They did neither of these things, but they did grant Longstreet the powers of an independent commander. Longstreet also had serious differences with General McLaws, and attempted to remove him from command, convening a court martial board in February of 1864. McLaws sent letters to friendly commanders attesting that Longstreet was searching for a scapegoat for the Knoxville defeat. This confrontation between Longstreet and McLaws made allies of Law and McLaws. As stated earlier, Law decided to resign, and did in fact tender his resignation on December 19. He made the decision to personally carry the resignation to Richmond, with Longstreet's knowledge. Law returned to Tennessee, after changing his mind, and circulated a petition requesting that his brigade be transferred to Virginia or Mobile. He then sent the petition to Longstreet, who forthwith went into orbital rage and had Law arrested for obtaining leave under false pretense, creating dissension, and destruction of government [he destroyed the letter of resignation] property. Law returned to Richmond, partly to assist McLaws with his court martial [Longstreet removed McLaws from command on the charge that he was derelict in his duty as a commanding officer at the battle of Fort Sanders]. He [Law]

---

[114] Tarnished Lieutenant, p. 78-79

attempted to get a feel as to who would and would not support Longstreet's charges. In April, the Confederate government refused to support Longstreet's claims and returned Law to duty. Longstreet immediately had him arrested, claiming that if Law was to be released, then he felt that he could no longer serve as the corps commander.[115]

All of these charges came to nothing, as far as consequences, for Law and McLaws. In April of 1864, McLaws was more or less cleared of all charges and found guilty of only a minor infraction. President Davis refused to allow any of the charges against General Law, even in the face of General Lee's intervention. Davis rebuked Longstreet, especially for the second arrest, in light of the fact that the charges had been dismissed by Richmond. Law and McLaws were in a state of jubilation because of Longstreet's censure and the disregard of his claims in Richmond.[116]

The Knoxville campaign offered little in the way of success for Longstreet, Law, and the I Corps. On December 4, Longstreet was making his way toward Rogersville, Tennessee after a very disappointing failure at Knoxville, reaching Rogersville on December 9, after a less than aggressive pursuit by Gen. John Parke. Gen. J. M. Shackleford, of Parke's command was sent out to locate Longstreet, and was near Bean's Station on December 13, which infuriated Longstreet so that he made the decision to return to Bean's Station and make an attack. The battle with General Shackelford continued for most of the day, [beginning at about 2 P.M.] ending at dusk when the Federals retreated toward Blain's Cross Roads. Longstreet blamed General Law and General McLaws for not acting quickly

---

[115] Tarnished Lieutenant, p. 79-80; OR Vol. XXXI/1, p. 472; Longstreet, p. 548

[116] Law to McLaws, p. 9, April 29, 1864, McLaws Papers, Southern Historical Collection, University of North Carolina

enough to prevent the Federal cavalry's escape.[117] This failure, as Longstreet viewed it, was another of the reasons leading to McLaws removal from his command. The Blain's Cross Roads attack effectively ended the Knoxville Campaign, after which Longstreet set up winter camp at Russellville, Tennessee.[118] The move to the western front of the war had proven to be a decisive failure for Longstreet, and had alienated two of his best commanders, beyond repair. He attempted to set things "right" with McLaws, who was also from Augusta, Georgia where Longstreet had grown up. He [Longstreet] left Edgefield County, South Carolina to attend school at Richmond Academy in Augusta, Georgia where his uncle was an instructor. McLaws and Longstreet were classmates at West Point, as well as childhood friends. General Law's brigade [Hood's division] was singled out by Douglas S. Freeman as, "all in all, probably the finest combat force in the Army of Northern Virginia". [119]

Longstreet and the I corps would have one more encounter with the Federal forces before leaving Tennessee in January of 1864. Gen. John Parke sent his command to Danridge on January 14, a hamlet near the East Tennessee and Virginia Railroad, on the right bank of the French Broad River and about thirty miles from Knoxville. The corps commanders of the Union forces were Gens. Burnside and Gordon Granger. Longstreet was able to bring up additional troops on January 15, threatening the town of New Market, which was the Union base of operations. The Union forces attempted to occupy the town of Kimbrough's Crossroads with cavalry under the command of Gen. Samuel Sturgis, but

---

[117] Mark Boatner, *The Civil War Dictionary* (New York: David McKay Company, Inc. 1961), p. 53
[118] Longstreet, p. 513-514
[119] Freeman, p. 640

were repelled by Confederate infantry and artillery.[120] Forced to withdraw, Sturgis' cavalry forces made their way to Danridge, where a battle occurred on January 17, continuing until past dark with no real change in the Federal position. The Federals withdrew to New Market and Strawberry Plains during the night, with no pursuit by the Confederates due to a lack of ammunition and artillery.[121] This operation is considered a Confederate victory, with failure to follow through, destroy, and capture the Union forces, as should have been the case. Longstreet describes this segment of his tenure in East Tennessee as a "succession of small engagements". This is an accurate description of the post Knoxville campaign that wrought no changes for the Confederate forces in East Tennessee. A very insightful statement is included in William G. Piston's work on Longstreet, *Lee's Tarnished Lieutenant*, concerning his relationship with General Law and other members of the I Corps, "The causes of his difficulties with McLaws, Robertson, and Law were complex. The problems did originate with him, and such disharmony did not characterize his command over the course of the war. Nevertheless, his handling of the situation was poor. He was too partisan toward proteges like Jenkins and Kershaw and downright petty and vindictive toward those who opposed him."[122]

On April 7, 1864, Longstreet and the I Corps were ordered back to Virginia by General Lee, and doubtless, Longstreet was very happy at the prospect of leaving Tennessee and General Bragg. On April 22, the corps arrived

---

[120] General Sturgis commanded the cavalry of the XXIII Corps Army of the Ohio, the IX Corps, and other Union cavalry; General Parke was Burnside's Chief of Staff, and had commanded the IX Corps in the past; General Granger commanded the IV Corps, Army of the Cumberland; it was General Grant's orders that this occur in this manner
[121] Longstreet, p. 527-528; Or Vol. XXXII/1, p.85; Or, Vol. XXXII/2, p. 116
[122] Tarnished Lieutenant, p. 81

at Mechanicsville, about five miles from Gordonsville. Within three weeks, Longstreet and the first corps would be involved in one of the major battles of the war. The Wilderness Campaign was conducted on the same ground as the battle of Chancellorsville, a year before and it would also have some of the same unfortunate consequences --- the loss of some key Confederate generals. Longstreet, for a time, would be one of the generals lost to the army.

As was frequently the case, General Law either did not, or was not allowed to compose an official report for the battle of the Wilderness, but he did write a lengthy report for *Battles and Leaders*. As Law points out, there was a new ingredient in this battle, General Grant. Previously, Grant had commanded forces in the west, but Lincoln had seen fit to promote Grant to commander of all Union forces in the war. Grant would prove to be a different type of opponent than had previously been faced by the Army of Northern Virginia. The Army of the Potomac crossed the Rappahannock River on May 4, but was so far in advance of the supply trains, that the army was forced to wait for the trains to catch up. Gen. Winfield S. Hancock's II Corps bivouacked at Chancellorsville, the V Corps, commanded by General Warren, remained at the Old Wilderness Tavern, and the Union cavalry at Parker's Store. On May 2, the Confederate Army's three corps were located: Longstreet and the I Corps at Gordonsville, Ewell and the II Corps near the Rapidan River, and A. P. Hill and the III Corps farther up the Rapidan. About noon on the 4th of May, Ewell was deployed to the Orange Turnpike, and Hill's Corps was paralleled with him on the Orange Plank Road, while Longstreet was ordered to move rapidly and follow Hill on the Plank Road. Ewell's Corps was the first to encounter the Federal forces. Grant had issued orders to continue the march at 5 A.M. on May 5, and Ewell detected the Federals crossing the turnpike from the direction of Germanna Ford.

General Meade felt that Lee was attempting to deceive him, and planned to force the battle at the North Anna River. Lee had selected the Wilderness as the battle site because: he knew the area, it would prevent large masses of troops in formation, and limit the Federal artillery's effectiveness. [123] The Wilderness was forest land, about fifteen miles square, and is located about half way between Orange Courthouse and Fredericksburg, and certainly not an inviting place to have a major battle if the use of artillery and large troop numbers are to be used effectively. This battle, like most of the post 1863 battles, would be one of flanking movements.

General Hill came into conflict with the Federal forces on the Plank Road at Parker's Store. The battle began between Getty's division of the Union VI Corps and Heth's division of the Confederate III Corps and would required Hancock's recall at 4 o'clock in the afternoon to help remove Hill from the Wilderness. Gen. Cadmus Wilcox's division came to support Heth's division, resulting in a fierce battle of small units and regiments, not corps. This was a battle of immense grit, pain, and suffering, which did not end until about 8 P.M. Lee, in the interim period, sent a message to Longstreet to make an all out march to reach the battlefield by daylight. Longstreet began his march at 1 A.M. on May 6, but would be required to travel about thirty-six miles to reach the battlefield where Hill and the III Corps were involved in an intense battle. Longstreet did not reach Parker's Store until after daylight, and was still about three miles in the rear of Hill's forces. Since the divisions of Heth and Wilcox were worn down from battle, and assumed that they would be relieved on the 6th, they made no preparations for battle, no lines, no defense, nothing. Later, they explained that they could hear the Federals moving and talking, but had been ordered to give the men rest.

---

[123] *Battles and Leaders*, Vol. IV, p. 119-122[this is General Law's account of the battle, *From the Wilderness to Cold Harbor*]

Longstreet was extremely critical of Hill for this ill-advised order to his division commanders. At first light, Hancock's troops attacked and things looked grim for a time, but fortunately Longstreet arrived in the middle of this attack. Kershaw's division took the right of Plank Road and Field's division [Hood's replacement] the left, with Gregg's brigade in front, and Benning's behind it, with Law's brigade next, and Jenkins following. By 9:45 Hancock had been pushed back to his original point of departure. The battle changed hands several times in a short span of time. About 10 A.M. it was determined that the Federal left flank was only a short distance south from the Orange Plank Road, and Longstreet immediately moved the brigades of Mahone, Wofford, Anderson and Davis, under Mahone's command, around that end of the Federal line. Mahone's attack hurled the men of Hancock's II Corps back, and put mortal fear into their eyes, while Jenkins' brigade was moved forward to renew the attack. Longstreet and Kershaw rode forward with Jenkins and his brigade when suddenly, Mahone's command, not recognizing Jenkins' brigade [they were wearing new dark gray uniforms, which may have appeared blue in the brush] opened fire and summarily Jenkins was killed, and Longstreet was badly wounded. Kershaw rushed out and screamed, "They are friends", and the firing stopped. It took several hours to remove the dead and wounded, and to assign a new commander, General Field, for the I Corps. The battle see-sawed, but when Hill's III Corps rallied in their rear, the battle shifted and ended as a Confederate victory, even though General Grant continued his offensive.[124] The battle of the Wilderness, for all intents and purposes, was over but Grant's Overland Campaign was not.

The night of May 7 was consumed with both armies making a mad dash for Spotsylvania. General Meade ordered

---

[124] Battles and Leaders, Vol. IV, p. 123-126; Longstreet, p. 564-566

General Warren and the V Corps to begin the march down Brock Road toward Spotslyvania at about 5 P.M. on May 7. Hancock was to follow with the II Corps, and Sheridan was to cover the south flank. Meade seems to have been unaware that Gen. Fitz Lee's cavalry was patrolling Brock Road and it would appears that he thought that the road was empty. General Lee ordered General Anderson, now in command of the I Corps due to Longstreet's injury, to begin the march toward Spotsylvania before 3 A.M. on May 8, assisted by Kershaw's and Field's divisions. Anderson, thinking ahead, concluded that his command would be unable to get any rest due to the smoke, battle noises, and other distractions, and began his movement at 11 P.M. His thinking was that he could rest his troops after they arrived near the area of Spotsylvania. General Pendleton had been ordered by General Lee to cut a road to shorten the distance, thus Anderson arrived at Spotsylvania at 8 o'clock on the morning of May 8. General Stuart's cavalry had blocked the Federal cavalry's approach on Brock Road with the assistance of General Law's and several other brigades. The few Federal troops that were holding Spotsylvania Courthouse were easily dislodged, giving the Confederates a decided edge in the early stage of the upcoming battle.[125] General Warren got a very unpleasant and unexpected surprise at Spotsylvania. When the combat began, Warren thought that he was contested by a cavalry brigade, at most, unaware that he was facing Anderson's [Longstreet's] I Corps. Both armies were exhausted from the march and continuous fighting, and since the Federals were attacking, the Confederates enjoyed a slight edge in this particular action. By 10:30 A.M., Warren informed Meade of his defeat, and also apprised him of the fact that he could not take Spotsylvania with the force at his command. By 3 o'clock in

---

[125] Battles and Leaders, Vol. IV, p. 128

the afternoon of May 8, Ewell had come up to assist Anderson, making an assault by Warren useless. Sedgwick's corps did not arrive to reinforce Warren until 5 P.M., and by dusk dark, it was all over for Warren's V Corps.[126]

On May 9, the Confederate army was aligned in the following formation at Spotsylvania: [note the illustration following this page]

---

[126] Battles and Leaders, Vol. IV, p. 128; Bruce Catton, *Grant Takes Command* (New York: Castle Books, 2000), p. 213-214, hereinafter cited as Catton's Grant

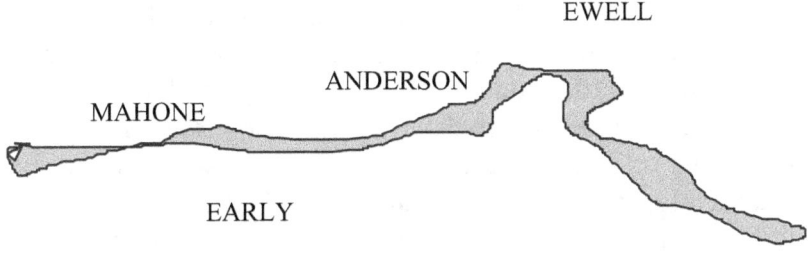

The famous "Mule Shoe" salient was formed by the dome shaped spread of Ewell's command between Anderson's and Early's forces. The salient was about three-quarters of a mile deep and a half mile wide. General Law states that no important engagements occurred on May 9, but that May 10 was a "field day". Grant attempted to break the Confederate lines on May 10, the first unsuccessful assault being made on Field's Division. Again at about 3 o'clock in the afternoon, another attack was made with more or less the same result. Law also confirms that the Confederate soldiers went out from the breastworks and collected additional weapons, and other useful items. There were no Confederate reserves, and for this reason, the men decided to arm themselves as fully as possible --- "two or three weapons are better than one." After several hours since the second unsuccessful attack, a torrent of Federal troops appeared, moving toward the Confederate lines of Field's division. In a bloody repulse, the Federals troops were cut down by companies and regiments until only a few soldiers remained.[127]

May 11 was a rainy and disagreeable day, and no real engagements occurred. Lee directed that artillery on the left and center of the line should be withdrawn, if it was "difficult of access". General Long, Ewell's chief of

---

[127] Catton's Grant, p. 225; Battles and Leaders, Vol. IV, p. 129

artillery, removed all but two batteries from the position of Gen. Edward "Allegheny" Johnson, who was on the now famous "Mule Shoe". On the night of May 11, Johnson became aware that the Federals were massing on his front and requested the return of the artillery, feeling that he would be attacked before dawn. General Johnson was right--- at dawn on May 12, the attack occurred --- the guns were returned just in time to be captured. The Federals overran the "Mule Shoe" and captured not only the guns, but also General Johnson, twenty pieces of artillery, and 2,800 men, practically the entire division. Hancock's II Corps was the major force in this attack, although Burnside and IX Corps were also suppose to take part in the May 12 attack. By 10 A.M., Lee had put ever man available into the battle, which went on into the night with abject horror occurring in and around the salient, by the hour. Field's division [Law] was attacked by the VI Corps, but severely repulsed the attack. Early, engaged and defeated Burnside's IX Corps on the other side of the "Mule Shoe".[128] From the end of the day of May 12, until May 18, the troops rested and no engagements of major importance occurred. The time was spent in realignment of the commands, rest, and refurbishment. Nonetheless, the battle of May 12 at Spotsylvania is regarded by many Civil War historians as the fiercest sustained combat of the entire war.

    A final attempt was made to attack the Confederate lines at Spotsylvania on the morning of May 18. The attack was aimed at the only area of the salient where any glimmer of success had occurred, but it turned out to be less successful than any of the previous attempts. The II and VI Corps comprised the Federal troops involved in the approach toward Ewell's corps. The attacking force, "was broken and driven back in disorder before it came well within reach of

---

[128] Battles and Leaders, Vol. IV, p. 131-134; Catton's Grant, p.226

the muskets of the infantry."[129] On the afternoon of May 19, the attack began anew and Ewell's Corps was "thrown round the Federal left wing to ascertain the extent of this movement." Ewell lost 900 men in a severe engagement, which lasted well into the night. General Law assessed Ewell's situation, "This seemed a heavy price to pay for information that might have been otherwise obtained, but the enemy had suffered more severely, and General Grant was delayed in his turning movement for twenty-four hours."[130]

The Federal army got started first in the race for the North Anna River. On the 20th of May, Hancock's II Corps left Spotsylvania, followed by the rest of Grant's army. Ewell moved out on the morning of May 21, followed by Longstreet's Corps, with Hill following, after a skirmish with the Federal VI Corps. The Army of Northern Virginia took the Telegraph Road, which was the most direct route, as opposed to Grant's route, which was a more circular path to the river. The Confederates arrived on the south side of the river about noon on the 22nd of May, giving Lee and the Confederate army eighteen or more hours advantage over the Federals. Warren's Corps arrived on the north side of the river before noon on May 23, and crossed the river unmolested at Jericho Ford. As the corps moved away from the river, Warren encountered Gen. Cadmus Wilcox's division of Hill's Corps, which resulted in a fierce, but indecisive engagement. Law states that it appeared that Lee intended to offer no real resistance to Grant's crossing of the river, at least for the time being. On May 24, Hancock's Corps crossed the Chesterfield Bridge, came into contact with both Ewell's and Longstreet's Corps in position for battle. The VI Corps crossed the river at Jericho Ford and joined Warren, and a very unusual situation resulted: both wings of Grant's army were across the river, but there was

---

[129] Battles and Leaders, Vol. IV, p. 134 [Law's report]
[130] Battles and Leaders, Vol. IV, p. 134

no connection between the two wings. When Burnside attempted to cross the river and make up the center of the army, he was dealt with very aggressively, and denied any foothold on the south side of the river. Grant had inadvertently separated his army, and neither side could reinforce the other, a stroke of genius on the part of General Lee. The 25th and 26th of May were spent in attempts by Grant to find a weak spot in the Confederate defense. Law's brigade crossed the Richmond and Fredericksburg Railroad and his men built log breastworks, and moved to one side of the works to avoid the constant fire. Law relates that:

> As I was passing that point on one occasion, the men called to me, 'Stoop!' ...
> Turning quickly, I caught a glimpse of something blue disappearing behind a pile of dirt that had been thrown out from the railroad cut some distance in front. Taking one of the muskets leaning against the works I waited for the reappearance of my friend in blue, who had taken such unfair advantage of me. He soon appeared, raising cautiously behind his earthworks, and we both fired at the same moment, neither shot taking effect. This time my friend... commenced reloading rapidly, thinking, I suppose, that I would have to do the same. But he was mistaken; for, taking up another musket, I fired at once, with a result at which both of us were equally surprised, he probably at my being able to load so quickly, and I at hitting the mark. He was found there, wounded, when my skirmishers were pushed forward.[131]

On the morning of May 27, Grant's army had withdrawn and was on its way to Hanover Town. Grant was now closer to Richmond than the Army of Northern Virginia, a somewhat disturbing fact for the Confederacy. An extremely intense cavalry [followed by infantry] battle occurred at Hawes's Shop between the troops of Hampton and Fitz Lee and

---

[131] Battles and Leaders, Vol. IV, p. 137 [previous paragraph, see p. 135-136]

Sheridan's advance forces. The Confederates were too strong for any prospects of success, and another Spotsylvania type battle was now in the making at Cold Harbor.[132]

On May 31, Sheridan was in possession of Cold Harbor, and was reinforced with two corps of infantry. Ernest Furgurson, in his book *Not War But Murder: Cold Harbor 1864*, gives a rather unique account of the place called Cold Harbor:

> Nothing but a mouldering wayside tavern distinguished this obscure crossroads from a hundred others in war-weary Virginia. The name hinted no connection with the first families of the Old Dominion, or the nearest farmer, miller, creek, or swamp. Some soldiers wrote it Coal Harbor, some Cool Arbor… No one seemed to know who named the place, or why. There was no harbor closer than Rocketts Landing, at Richmond…
>
> Nor was anything cold to be had there in the muggy days when the war passed through. … 'an inn which does not provide hot meals'--- is now the accepted explanation for the name of the historic crossroads that lies 9.9 miles east-northeast of the capitol in Richmond.[133]

Longstreet's and a segment of Hill's corps and the divisions of Hoke and Breckinridge were positioned to confront Sheridan's command. The fighting began at Cold Harbor late in the day on June 1, with an attack on Hoke's and Kershaw's divisions, which were in the process of being turned, but the attack was checked and the line restored before nightfall. By dawn of June 2, it seemed that a second Spotsylvania was about to occur. The XVIII Corps of Gen. W.F. Smith was positioned to attack the Confederate right wing. In the afternoon of June 2, Early attacked Burnside's IX Corps, and a part of Warren's V Corps, taking 200 or so prisoners, which prevented Burnside and Smith from

---

[132] Battles and Leaders, Vol. IV, p. 138

[133] Ernest B. Furgurson, *Not War But Murder: Cold Harbor 1864* (New York: Alfred A. Knopf, 2000), p. 76-77; hereinafter cited as Cold Harbor

carrying out a coordinated attack at Cold Harbor on June 3.[134]

In the morning of June 2, Law moved with his brigade, and Anderson's to carry out a discretionary reinforcement on the right of the Confederate line. After an inspection of the battle line, it was determined that Kershaw's division needed support on his right wing. The ever observant Law determined that the line was noticeably bent at almost a right angle, plus it was spread on open ground, and very poorly situated to resist an attack. The defense line was redesigned so that a marshy area that existed near the line would be in front of Law's command, with firepower coming from a slope on the other side of the marsh. This new design would shorten and strengthen the line before the Federal attack, which Law reasoned was inescapable the next day at dawn. He worked much of the night rearranging and actually staking out the position with a bundle of wooden stakes. He then positioned his men on the line, with artillery on both ends, after which Kershaw withdrew his division from that position, and destroyed the works previously built by his men.[135]

The speculation was correct, and at dawn, the attack began. Law states that he actually feared his troops would deplete their ammunition due to the rapid fire and the vast number to targets, and ordered a supply of ammunition be brought forward. The general vowed that he had never witnessed such carnage, not even at Marye's Hill or Second Manassas. He made his now famous statement, "It was not war; it was murder", to accurately express his disgust at the death of such a large number of men. The XVIII Corps alone lost over 3,000 men. Law's Alabamians presented an almost "automatic fire", with the help of General Bryan's Georgians reloading the weapons, and passing them forward. Law

---

[134] Battles and Leaders, Vol. IV, p. 138
[135] Battles and Leaders, Vol. IV, p. 139

sustained a wound as well, one of the few Confederate officers wounded in this battle. A bullet nicked Law above the eye, putting him out of active duty for awhile. General Law concludes his description of the battle at Cold Harbor by commenting, " Before 8 o'clock A.M. on the 3rd of June the battle of Cold Harbor was over, and with it Grant's 'overland campaign' against Richmond."[136]

Law's problems with Longstreet had reached a crisis point before the battle of Cold Harbor, and after long consideration, he decided that the situation was long passed repair. After his recovery from the wound at Cold Harbor, Law made his request to transfer to a cavalry unit in General Johnston's command. On January 7, 1865, General Law was officially relieved from duty with the Army of Northern Virginia. He first received orders to report to General Bragg at Wilmington, NC for assignment and particulars, thankfully, this was revoked shortly and he was reassigned to the cavalry under Gen. Wade Hampton's command.[137] General Law soon received a cavalry command with Gen. Wade Hampton, and was assigned to command the former brigade of Gen. Matthew C. Butler. General Law was in command of the rear guard defending General Beauregard and the Confederate army's evacuation from the city of Columbia [most likely with General Butler still in command], that was captured on February 17, by General Sherman.[138] Gen. Joseph Wheeler's cavalry division was in Columbia at this time, as was General Butler's. There are some rather puzzling aspects about this assignment. In a centennial publication in remembrance of Sherman's burning of the city of Columbia, Law is not mentioned as having served in any capacity. Confederate generals who did receive

---

[136] Cold Harbor, p. 149; Battles and Leaders, Vol. IV, p. 141-142
[137] OR, Vol. XLVI/2, p. 1020; OR, Vol. XLVII/2, p. 1204; OR, Vol. XLVII, p. 1320
[138] OR, Vol. XLVII/2, p. 1193

praise for their efforts to save and assist with the evacuation of Columbia were Gen. Joe Wheeler, Gen. William Hardee, Gen. Lafayette McLaws, and Gen. Matthew C. Butler. Without doubt, all of these commanders made significant contributions. Aside from the fact that General Law was in command of the evacuation, which also is mentioned, little attention or note was given to his actions or presence during the fall of the city.[139] This is extremely daunting, in light of the fact that the general is a native South Carolinian. The publication, *Sack and Destruction of the City of Columbia*, by William G. Simms, is perhaps the most complete account given by an eye witness of Sherman's capture of Columbia. Simms had this to say about General Law's role in the capture of Columbia, "On Wednesday, the 15th, the city was placed under martial law, and the authority confided to General E. M. Law, assisted by Mayor Goodwyn and Captains W. B. Stanley and John McKensie. With characteristic energy, the officer executed his trusts, and was employed day and night in the maintenance of order... there were but few instances of crime and insubordination."[140] Five lines are very meager praise for the general who organized the security and order of the city during its most petrified hours. Law was assigned to command General Butler's cavalry brigade in late February of 1865, and Butler was given a division command under General Hampton, after Hampton's command was sent to South Carolina to confront Sherman as he crossed into South Carolina from Georgia. General Butler was a significant cavalryman who had served with distinction in the Army of Northern Virginia, as a part of General J.E.B. Stuart's cavalry.[141]

---

[139] "The Burning of Columbia: 1865", *The State*, February 16-17, 1965
[140] William Gilmore Simms, *Sack and Destruction of the City of Columbia* (Columbia: Powers Press of Daily Phoenix, 1865), p. 33;
[141] Sifakis, Confederacy

As Sherman's army moved into North Carolina, Gen. Judson Kilpatrick's cavalry division was assigned to protect General Sherman's left flank. On March 9, two of Kilpatrick's brigades camped near the Charles Monroe House in Hoke County, North Carolina. Kilpatrick's command was caught in a rather serious thunderstorm, when due to the glow a lighting bolt, Kilpatrick realized that he was in the middle of one of Hampton's regiments. Moving as cautiously as possible, he made his way toward Monroe's Crossroads. He arrived there about 9 P.M., and with his female companion, Marie Boozer, spent the night in a small cabin. Kilpatrick's men, who had been captured by Hampton's forces, gave up his whereabouts to the Confederates. At dawn, General Butler's command [which included General Law] rushed into the camp and totally surprised Kilpatrick's cavalry. Upon hearing the commotion, Kilpatrick rushed out in his nightclothes, in total shock, narrowly escaping capture by the Confederates.[142]

The Confederate army now faced a difficult dilemma and all of the possibilities were fast tracks to defeat. The forces available to General Johnston were few and far between, plus an additional problem existed because the forces were widely scattered, and it would be difficult to mass them where they could be most effective. Johnston stated in a letter to General Lee on March 18, "The troops will be united to-day, except two divisions of Cheatham's corps not yet arrived. Effective totals, infantry and artillery: Bragg, 6,500, Hardee, 7,500, Army of Tennessee, 4,000. Should Sherman move by Weldon would you prefer my turning to Clarksville? Lieutenant-General Hardee's loss on 16th was 450. Prisoners taken the next day report the enemy's about 3,300."[143] Johnston needed time to position

---

[142] Samuel J. Martin, *The Life of General Hugh Judson Kilpatrick* (Mechanicsburg, PA: Stackpole Books, 2000), p. 220-221
[143] OR, Vol. XLVII/2, p. 1426

his troops [less than 25,000] and position them in the needed specific areas. On March 18, General Hampton gave Johnston complete information on the location and strength of the Federal forces. Due to the fact that General Johnston was unable to examine the terrain personally, Hampton offered his view as to the best positioning of the army. The cavalry would move out at dawn and occupy positions held by them on the previous day. The infantry would deploy across the main road in a one corps, two corps position. Hampton would then take a position on the extreme right, and no offensive action would take place until Hardee, who was camped farther away, was in position.[144] On March 20, Wheeler's Cavalry [General Law] moved to the left of the army and immediately engaged a large force of infantry moving up the Goldsboro and Bentonville road. General Law, in a report on the 20th, explains, "I have found the right of the enemy's line. It is simply an extension of the line in front of our infantry by skirmishers who are stationary…. I have found another country road, above this one, which leads into the Goldsborough road… I have sent a picket to watch it."[145] Later in the engagement, Law reports that the enemy was advancing rapidly, and that a few regiments of infantry might check the advance. He concludes that the cavalry was simply too weak to accomplish much. Wheeler's cavalry was able to check this command and hold them in position until evening, after which his command was relieved by Hoke's infantry division.

On March 21, as Hampton's plan was about to go into action, Law reported at 2 A.M.:

> My scouts have just returned from the right of the enemy's lines. They report no retrograde movements of the enemy; on the

---

[144] Battles and Leaders, Vol. IV, p. 703

[145] OR, Vol. XLVII/1, p. 1131[General Wheeler's comments]; OR, Vol. XLVII/2, p. 1443 [Law's report]

contrary, the indications are that he will fight to-day. The scouts penetrated to the Goldsborough road and conversed with men from the Fifteenth Corps, who stated that their commands were on the line in front. I will keep a few men along Mill Creek on the other side in order to notify me of any movement of enemy from the neighborhood of Cox Bridge across toward Smithfield or Bentonville....[146]

The battle of Bentonville should never have occurred for many reasons. General Johnston could not have defeated Sherman's army regardless of how the battle was planned or directed. Sherman had at least a five to one ratio of troops to his favor, if Schofield's 26,000 men are included. In fact, Johnston had been unable to defeat the XIV and XX Corps of Slocum's left wing. Johnston felt he had to try and delay Sherman's connection with Grant in Virginia, to give Lee breathing room for a possible escape to the west. The battle was fought over a three day period, March 19-21, in a small village about twenty miles west of Goldsboro, the majority of the fighting occurring on the 19th and 20th. However, Wheeler reports that he fought the enemy "warmly" on March 21, shortly after daybreak. The skirmishing continued until at least March 25, at Bentonville, and beyond that date in other areas. Wheeler related in what may have been his last real campaign report:

> April 2, I marched to Raleigh with 2,000 men, but returned immediately. April 10, General Sherman's entire force advanced, driving us back toward Raleigh. April 13. On the morning of the 13th we evacuated the city and the enemy occupied it in large force. General Kilpatrick pushed out after me, charging our rear... At Morrisville Station the enemy again appeared that evening, but after severe skirmishing retired toward Raleigh. April 14 and 15. On the 14th I moved on to Chapel Hill, and on the 15th the enemy approached but after firing a few shots without effect again retired... Thus ended the

---

[146] OR, Vol. XLVII/2, p. 1447

campaign, the war, and the military power of the Confederacy....[147]

On March 20, on the recommendation of Generals Johnston and Hampton, Law was promoted to Major General. This promotion occurred in the heat of the battle of Bentonville, yet still greatly deserved. This promotion most likely occurred, in part, due to General Matthew Butler's illness on the 19th. Johnston immediately appointed Law to command the division vacated by Butler, and by precedent it was customary to have a major general commanding a division. Law was a distinguished general with long service in the Army of Northern Virginia and was serving on Johnston's staff, and was without a command. The command was short lived, because in early April, Johnston's command underwent extensive reorganization and as a result, Law's division no longer existed.[148] On Monday morning of April 17, Sherman and Johnston met at the home of James Bennett to discuss surrender terms, thus ending hostilities in the eastern theater of the war. [149]

General Law officially surrendered his command on April 25, 1865 at Greensboro, North Carolina. As the war ended, most former Confederate officers gave considerable thought to what their next move should be, pondering their options carefully. Conversely, General Law immediately returned to South Carolina and became the administrator of his father-in law, William A. Latta's estate. Law lost no time taking the Oath of Allegiance on September 13, 1865,

---

[147] Nathaniel C. Hughes, Jr., *Bentonville: The final Battle of Sherman and Johnston* (Chapel Hill: University of North Carolina Press, 1996), p. 222, hereinafter cited as Hughes; OR, Vol. XLVII/1, p. 1131-1132 [Wheeler's quotation is from the OR]

[148] Hughes, p. 170, 220

[149] John G. Barrett, *The Civil War in North Carolina* (Chapel Hill: University of North Carolina, 1963), p. 380-381[Barrett's account of the battle of Bentonville is also an excellent source, p. 318-349]

declaring his occupation as farming. William Latta was a wealthy man, with extensive agricultural holdings and railroad interests. As a result, Law became the president of the Kings Mountain Railroad, and later a surveyor. Later still, his interest in newspaper work increased and would ultimately become his occupation. In 1873, Law returned to Tuskegee, Alabama and was instrumental in the founding and organization of the Grange in that area.

In 1881, he returned to the work he had pursued before the war, that of a military school superintendent. He became the superintendent of the Kings Mountain Military Academy, at York South Carolina, the same location where before the war; he and Jenkins had worked. He held this position for two years.

In 1893, Law made his way to Florida, and founded the Florida Military Institute at Bartow in 1894. In 1895, the school became a public institution, and received state support and county scholarships. Law served in this position until 1903, after which he resigned, for political reasons. In 1906, General Law became the editor of the Bartow Courier-*Informant*. He held this position until 1916, and if this was not enough, Law became a Trustee of the Sumerlin Institute, from 1905 until 1912.

On July 3, 1913, General Law took part in the dedication of the 1st Vermont Cavalry's Monument at Gettysburg. The 1st Vermont was part of Kilpatrick's cavalry division, and took part in what is today referred to as Farnsworth's Cavalry Charge, in which General Elon Farnsworth was killed, after a heated dispute with Kilpatrick as to the necessity and military value of the charge. General Law's brigade was involved in the defense against this charge. The 15th Alabama, under Colonel William Oates, was the regiment of Law's brigade that was most closely involved with the defeat of General Farnsworth's charge, however there is dispute about which regiment was most closely involved with this famous charge, as discussed earlier.

Law was elected to serve as a member of the Polk County, Florida Board of Education in 1912, and served in this position until his death in 1920. Many historians feel that Evander Law is, in fact, the "father" of public education in the state of Florida. In addition, Law was extremely active in Confederate veterans' activities, serving as a division commander of Florida from 1899 until 1903. He also helped to establish and organize a chapter of the United Daughters of the Confederacy in the city of Bartow.[150]

Gen. Evander M. Law departed this life on October 31, 1920, the ranking surviving officer of the Confederate army. Law suffered a cerebral stroke, fell into a coma and died a week later. Prior to his death, Law survived six years as the highest ranking, living Confederate officer. All businesses in the city of Bartow closed during General Law's funeral and schools were dismissed throughout Polk County, Florida in respect for his death and for his funeral. General Law was laid to rest in Oak Hill Cemetery in Bartow.[151]

There is an old adage that states, "nothing separates like silence." This certainly can be said, and accurately so, about the military career of General Evander Law. Law has left the historian little of his thoughts, suspicions, military views, praise for his subordinates, or achievements of his

---

[150] The General, Vol. IV, p. 24; Mr. Joe Spann, Manager of the Polk County, Florida Historical and Genealogical Library; Steven A. Cunningham & Beth A. White, "The First West Virginia Cavalry in the Gettysburg Campaign", *Civil War Regiments*, Mark A. Snell, editor, Volume Six, No. 3, Mason City: Savas Publishing Company [Law's post war career material came from the *Confederate General* and Mr. Spann's files and research, and the Darlington Historical Commission] the 1st Vermont's Monument material is from *Civil War Regiments*]

[151] Obituaries for the *News and Press* [location unknown] and the *State*, Columbia, October 31, 1920

troops. With little doubt of contradiction, one could say that no major general in the Confederate or Union army, who held a field command, completed fewer battle reports and dispatches than Evander M. Law. The historian is left to wonder, was this by choice, or was Law simply too occupied with other things, or was his communications disregarded by his superiors? A well trained military specialist, Law was a graduate of one of the best private military institutions in the United States. He had served as a student/graduate assistant professor in English at the Citadel during his senior year, and with this background Law must have had excellent writing and communication skills.

Mr. Joe Spann is the Manager of the Polk County Historical and Genealogical Library in Bartow, Florida. In addition, Mr. Spann is a student of Law's career, as well as an authority on his life. Spann states:

> First and foremost, General Law was tremendously interested in education... We know that he was a clear communicator, both verbally and in written form. His surviving letters testify to an intellect of the first order.... Secondly, General Law was a brilliant strategist. His contemporaries said so many times. Before a battle he was able to quickly comprehend the situation, distill the essential parts and synthesis the best plan of action. When under fire, his perceptions were sharpened and his thinking clarified even further. After years of study, I am left with the impression that he "instinctively" knew the right thing to do and was able to communicate it effectively to his officers.... In the final analysis General Law had a number of character flaws which hampered his military and civilian careers. He was the very essence of a southern gentleman, very conscious of proper manners and social protocol. But he was known to be blunt in his communications. Never crude or demeaning, just painfully honest. He was also quick to take offense, even over trivial matters. We would say that he suffered from "knee-jerk" reactions or was "thin skinned." ...I think that this is the character trait to which General Longstreet most objected. Longstreet readily admitted on a number of occasions that Law was a brilliant strategist, but I believe he also knew that

a great leader of men must be of steady character, unmoved by the trivial matters of everyday command.[152]

Evander Law was also a realist about how he was perceived by other Confederate officers. A prime example of this perception was his long-standing face off with Gen. Micah Jenkins. When Law realized he was not able to counteract Jenkins' influence with Longstreet, he immediately attempted to separate himself from the I Corps of the Army of Northern Virginia. He repeatedly requested transfer to another assignment, which placed him in serious conflict with Longstreet.

Law also exhibited a degree of compassion that was often lacking in the military high command. His famous statement concerning the battle of Cold Harbor, while often quoted and was used as a book title, " Not war, but murder", in a sense defines his total honesty. Law realized that Federal troops were dying in a suicidal charge and without hesitation, expressed his view of the situation, and similar sympathy is put forth concerning events at the battle of Fredericksburg. This certainly is not, and should not be viewed as a sign of weakness. Even the victorious must acknowledge a worthy and valiant opponent. Law seems to have been such a person, never fearful of expressing compassion, respect, or honest opinions.

General Law never gave a satisfactory account of his role and conduct in the war of secession. Any historian would greatly desire an account, from Law's standpoint, of his dispute, first with Gen. Micah Jenkins, and secondly, with Gen. James Longstreet. Why would such a dispute occur between two men, Law and Jenkins, who: worked together at the Kings Mountain Military School, attended the Citadel, were born in the same state, probably were familiar

---

[152] Mr. Joe Spann's views on General Evander M. Law, given by request, via e-mail on October 10, 2002

with the same influential people in South Carolina and the high command of the Confederate Army? Was it simply Jenkins' driving desire to become a major general, and a division commander? Law never gives any real account of this dispute; in fact he left virtually nothing to history at all about the dispute. And what of Longstreet? It appears that Law abhorred Longstreet's very presence and would have gone to any lengths to escape Longstreet's influence and command. As Spann suggested, was this simply a "thinned skin" reaction by Law to a perceived injustice by Longstreet? It has been suggested that Longstreet was displeased with Law's performance at Gettysburg and used Jenkins' exemplary service and career desires to bypass Law as division commander. This could be true, yet as shown earlier, Longstreet praised Law's handling of the division at Gettysburg in Hood's absence. From the period after the battle of Gettysburg and the move of the I Corps of the Army of Northern Virginia to the western theater of the war, the feud between the two men was born. The only new ingredient in the situation was the presence of Gen. Micah Jenkins. Law appears to have concluded that Jenkins somehow "stole" the command that belonged to him, and he never relinquished that point of view. He seems to have also concluded that Longstreet allowed this to happen, and supported Jenkins, which made Longstreet a conspirator as well as Jenkins.

Although the reasons are unfathomable, Evander Law is virtually an unknown person to many people in South Carolina. He is not associated with many of the Confederate heroes from the Civil War that are held in utter reverence by the Palmetto State. General Sherman, who is still at present widely regarded as a vile man in South Carolina, is far better known. One would think that General Law, even though he entered the war from the state of Alabama, would have a degree of recognition in his native state. Law resided in

South Carolina for a time after the war, and married into a distinguished family from South Carolina. He seems to have been highly respected and widely known in his native state from the end of the war in 1865, until the turn of the century. A quotation from C. Vann Woodward, the imminent historian of Southern culture might explain this omission, "The time is coming, if indeed it has not already arrived, when Southerners will begin to ask themselves whether or not there is really any longer very much point in calling themselves Southerners."[153] Perhaps that time is now. To put a modern twist to this omission of General Law, as Southerners we sometimes "talk the talk", but we don't always "walk the talk". A truly honorable person, who is willing to defend his beliefs with words and action, no matter where he is from, should never be forgotten. Somehow we frequently allow fame to constitute character, and as Stephen Holden [essayist] is credited with having stated, "when hype is confused with achievement, lifestyle with work, gossip with history, it becomes difficult to determine the reality of events." This quotation has much relevance to many of the participants in the Civil War, and Evander M. Law was no exception.

---

[153] From his book, *The Burden of Southern History*

Photograph of General Charles Harker
from *Harper's Magazine* about 1863

GEN. CHARLES GARRISON HARKER

The state of New Jersey supplied over 60,000 men to the Union Army during the Civil War, and one of those men was Charles Garrison Harker. Born on December 2, 1835, Harker spent his youth in Swedesboro, Gloucester County, New Jersey. A personal friend and schoolmate of Harker's, a Mr. W.W. Paterson describes him as, "A modest, unassuming and honorable young man, who early in life seriously associated himself with his church and on many occasions expressed a desire that someday he would enter the ministry."[1]

Harker's father, Joseph B. Harker died when Charles was only six years old, leaving a wife, five sons and three daughters. His childhood probably was stressful and hectic, considering the number of children and the economic situation, and with so many siblings, it is extraordinary that the family was able to survive in tact. Nevertheless, Harker managed to received a basic education in the public schools of the town, which was no small accomplishment considering his economic situation and the time period in which he lived. He later moved to the nearby town of Mullica Hill to take a job as a store clerk in the retail business of a Mr. Nathan T. Stratton. This was a stroke of phenomenal luck for young Harker, in that Stratton was more than just a businessman, and Harker was to become more than simply a clerk in Stratton's business

---

[1] Paul Minotty, "Brigadier General Charles G. Harker", *Bulletin of the Gloucester County Historical Society*, Vol. 14, No. 5, September, 1974, p. 17.; hereinafter cited as Gloucester Bulletin

establishment.[2] Stratton was a member of the United States House of Representatives from 1851 to 1855, and as a member of Congress, he was entitled to appoint prospective students to the United States Military Academy at West Point. Stratton was taken by the forthrightness, honesty, and the willingness to work displayed by young Harker, therefore on July 14, 1854, Stratton gave his recommendation for Charles Harker to become a cadet at West Point. By a quirk of fate, the recommendation was sent to Jefferson Davis, a member of President Pierce's cabinet, whose life would indirectly impact momentously on the life and death of Charles Harker. On July 13, 1854, young Harker replied to the appointment in lieu of his brother Joseph, who was away in Philadelphia on business. Harker stated in his letter to Stratton, "An education has always been my great object, but I had little hope of obtaining one until I could procure the means by habit of industry and economy."[3] The appointment was confirmed August 1, 1854, and in hindsight, this was a very appropriate appointment, because Charles Harker is an example of the caliber of young man that is deserving of a publicly financed education.

Harker quite obviously was a serious student at West Point, in light of the fact that he received less than one hundred demerits in each of his years at the Academy, with the exception of his sophomore year. He graduated sixteenth in a class of twenty-seven students in 1858, and his highest proficiency was in the areas of engineering and geography. Future Confederate generals Edward Porter Alexander and Ellison Capers were contemporaries of Harker while he was

---

[2] Andrea J. Hogan, "Brigadier General Charles G. Harker", Salem County *Sampler*, June 21, 1978,p. 8
[3] Archival Records from the Office of Admissions at the United States Military Academy at West Point

at West Point.⁴ It has been stated that no less an important general than O.O. Howard, while an instructor at West Point, singled out Harker as an exemplary cadet. This is notable in light of the fact that General Howard would be Harker's Corps commander on the last day of his life. Gen. Robert Anderson, of Fort Sumter fame while an instructor at West Point, recognized and stated that he felt Harker was destined for greatness as a military officer.⁵ These predictions would prove to be correct, yes, Charles Harker would indeed achieve fame and rise to greatness, but at a very high personal sacrifice.

Upon graduation, Harker was promoted to Second Lieutenant of Infantry on July 1, 1858, and for a brief period served on garrison duty at Governor's Island, New York with the 9th Infantry. From New York, Harker was sent on a tour of frontier duty, where he was assigned to a tour at Fort Dallas, Oregon in 1859. Later during 1859, he was assigned to duty at Colville Depot, Washington from 1859 until 1860, and from Colville Depot, Harker was assigned to the Northwest Boundary Survey for escort duty during 1860, and back to Coville Depot until 1861.⁶

On May 14, 1861, Harker was promoted to First Lieutenant, 15th Infantry, serving from July 1861 until November of 1861, as a drill instructor for recruits from Ohio in what would later be referred to as the Army of the Ohio, commanded by Gen. Don Carlos Buell. During this period of his career, Harker was promoted to Captain on October 24, 1861, in the 15th Infantry. On November 11, 1861, Harker was again promoted, this time to Colonel,

---

⁴ Register of the Officers and Cadets of the U.S. Military Academy, West Point, New York, June 1854-1858
⁵ Gloucester Bulletin, p. 17
⁶ General George W. Cullum, *Biographical Register of the Officers and Graduates of the U.S. Military Academy* (Boston: Houghton, Mifflin and Company, 1891), p. 706; hereinafter cited as Graduates

commanding the 65th Ohio Regiment of Volunteers, which would, from that point, be known as Harker's Regiment for the duration of the war.[7]

Colonel Harker served in Kentucky at the outbreak of the Civil War. Since he was an engineer with past experience, he was involved in the building of military roads in eastern Kentucky with General Buell's Army of the Ohio. This location of Buell's army placed Harker in time and location as part of the Union Army that was involved in the battle of Shiloh, April 6 and 7, 1862. Shiloh was the first large-scale battle of the war, and one of the war's most important battles.[8] When Forts Henry and Donaldson fell in early 1862, Confederate general Albert Sidney Johnston was forced to give up Kentucky and much of western and middle Tennessee. Johnston selected Corinth, Mississippi as the site to stage his attack against General Grant and the Army of the Tennessee, which would ultimately be the battle of Shiloh. It was Johnston's hope and contention that Buell would not be able to reach Grant before an attack could be launched and completed. The attack was supposed to occur on April 4, but was delayed until April 6th, which suggest the reason the Confederate army was unable to conclude the battle successfully before Buell arrived. General Johnston was killed and Gen. G. P. T. Beauregard assumed command of the Confederate forces. The Confederate army numbered about 40,000, but on April 7, it had the strength of only about 30,000, whereas Buell's and Grant's combined forces on April 7 numbered 40,000.[9] This battle resulted in nearly

---

[7] Graduates, p. 706; Thomas Cushing, *History of the Counties of Gloucester, Salem, and Cumberland, New Jersey, with Biographical Sketches of Prominent Citizens* (Everts & Peck, 1883), p. 164

[8] Comment by Shelby Foot, given in a lecture at First Presbyterian, Spartanburg, SC, April 24, 2002

[9] See any standard reference work for complete analysis of this battle, or see WWW.CivilWar.com-battles of Tennessee

25,000 casualties: 13,000 for the Union and 11,000 plus for the Confederacy.[10]

In the battle of Shiloh, Colonel Harker was a member of the 20th Brigade, Gen. James Garfield commanding, 6th Division, Gen. Thomas Wood, commanding, Army of the Ohio. General Garfield is less than explicit in his report of the brigade's activities at Shiloh. He relates only that the brigade arrived at 1:30 P.M. on the 7th of April and was pulled up to the front of Buell's line at about 3 P.M. Garfield also explains that the Confederate army was in retreat and therefore his command was only marginally involved in the battle. General Garfield concludes by simply stating the command suffered no casualties.[11] Gen. Thomas Wood, commanding the 6th Division explains that he accompanied the 20th Brigade [Harker's] and that he led the brigade to the engagement at Shiloh. The 20th Brigade also took part in the pursuit of the Confederate army's retreat, but the distance between the Union and Confederate forces was too great to allow any effective small arms damage. For this reason the brigade bivouacked, with the 21st Brigade, in readiness for an attack on the 8th of April, which did not occur.[12] Colonel Harker received his first close up encounter with war at the battle of Shiloh, which surly must have stunned the sensitive young man. The day of April 7, 1862, must have been an excruciatingly painful one for Colonel Harker, as well as the rest of the men in both armies. Given the number of casualties, and the fact that an extreme thunderstorm occurred the night of April 6, and soldiers were still on the

---

[10] William F. Fox, *Regimental Losses in the American Civil War: 1861-1865* (Dayton: Morningside Bookshop Press, 1985), p. 541; hereinafter cited as Fox Losses

[11] *Official Records of the War of the Rebellion,* Series I, Volume X/1, report no. 131, p. 379; hereinafter cited as OR (all entries are Series I unless otherwise noted)

[12] OR, Vol. X/1, report no. 130, p. 378

battlefield in abject agony, unable to return to their respective armies or receive any medical aid, had to have presented a frightful scene. Colonel Harker was a religious man, and one can only imagine what effect this experience must have had on this young and somewhat inexperienced soldier.

The 65th Ohio Regiment under Harker's command was part of the 20th Brigade, commanded by General Garfield, 6th Division, II Army Corps, Army of the Ohio, until July 10, 1862, when Colonel Harker became the commander of the 20th Brigade. Before Harker took command, the brigade was engaged in the siege of Corinth and was under fire for a time. The siege, and later battle, of Corinth was in a sense, an extension of the Battle of Shiloh. Gen. Earl Van Dorn CSA reached Corinth with his command on April 23, to assist Gen. P.G.T. Beauregard. The siege occurred from April 29 - May 30, 1862. The battle of Corinth, a virtual eruption of military force, occurred later on October 3 - 4, 1862. Beauregard, as mentioned earlier, took command of the Confederate army after the death of General Johnston at Shiloh. Harker's brigade played an insignificant role in the siege, in relation to other battles in which the brigade was involved. [13] Colonel Harker and the 20th Brigade's involvement in the siege of Corinth were part of a massive troop assemblage of 100,000 men under the command of Gen. H.W. Halleck, "Old Brains". After the occupation of Corinth, the Union Army looked toward Chattanooga as its next objective. General Buell and the Army of the Ohio moved into middle Tennessee, and as a result, General Bragg, in late August of 1862, began his

---

[13] Edwin C. Bearss, "Earl Van Dorn", *The Confederate General* (The National Historical Society,1991), Vol. VI, p. 74; Fox Losses, p. 329; Frederick H. Dyer, *A Compendium of the War of the Rebellion* (Dayton :Broadfoot Publishing Company & Morningside Press, 1994), Vol. II, p. 1527, hereinafter cited as Dyer's

famous expedition into Kentucky, with Buell and the Army of the Ohio in pursuit. General Harker and the 20th Brigade would play a minor role, as well, in this campaign.[14]

The battle of Perryville, Kentucky occurred on October 8, 1862. Colonel Harker was part of the Army of the Ohio, General Buell commanding, I Corps, commanded by Gen.Thomas Crittenden, 6th Division, of General Thomas Wood, under which Harker's brigade served. Much has been said about this battle, primarily because it was a public relations failure for both Bragg and Buell. Buell would face a Court of Inquiry as a result of the events of this battle. Colonel David Uequhart, a member of Bragg's staff said about the battle: "The battle of Perryville, a hard - fought fight against many odds, was merely a favorable incident that decided nothing. Our army, however, was elated and did not dream of a retreat, as we had held the field and bivouacked on it. But the commanding general, full of care, summoned his lieutenant-generals to a council and both advised retreat."[15] General Buell also made an astute statement about this battle:

> If the campaign, with no more advantageous results, had been marked by one general and destructive, but not disastrous battle, it would no doubt have been received with more popular favor, and perhaps even have been more easy of professional praise. I shall not insist on that point, but I shall particularly make no apology for not having fought battles where the issue was reasonably doubtful, and where they in fact proved not to have been necessary for the success of my cause. Besides, in an open field, with capable commanders, it takes two parties to inaugurate a battle---one to begin the attack, and another to

---

[14] *The Photographic History of the Civil War* (Secaucus, NJ: The Blue and Gray Press, 1987), Vol. I, part II," The Assault on Corinth", p. 146; hereinafter cited as Photographic History

[15] *Battles and Leaders of the Civil War*, edited by Clarence Buel and Robert U. Johnson (New York: The Century Company, 1887), Vol. III, p. 603; hereinafter cited as Battles and Leaders

stand and receive it. It was much talked of after the event, that Kentucky was known to be the immediate object for which Bragg moved from Chattanooga....[16]

General Buell's headquarters was a mere two miles or so from the battlefield. Quite unbelievably, Buell was not aware that the battle was in progress until 4 P.M., even though it had reached its peak at 2:30 P.M. Corps commanders Crittenden and Gilbert did not realize until late in the day of the 8th that McCook and Sheridan were under heavy attack. In light of the absence of this knowledge, only nine brigades of Buell's army were completely engaged, even though fifteen brigades were in the area and could have supported the battle. Buell lost the opportunity for a major defeat, while Bragg fled the battlefield, leaving his dead and wounded.[17] As stated earlier, Colonel Harker was in Crittenden's I Corps, and as a result, he was only inappreciably involved in the battle of Perryville. Colonel Wagner, of the 21st Brigade, reports that his brigade and Colonel Harker's, "lay on their arms, in order of battle".[18] Bragg, true to form, attempted to fight the battle of Perryville without adequate or even creditable intelligence. The Confederate army fought well, but suffered an important defeat, which greatly affected the morale of the army in future battles.[19]

In November of 1862, Colonel Harker became part of the Army of the Cumberland, under the command of Gen. William Rosecrans. The first major battle undertaken with this new command was Stones River or Murfreesboro. The battle occurred December 31, 1862, and continued until

---

[16] Battles and Leaders, Vol. III, p. 50
[17] Mark Boatner, *The Civil War Dictionary* (New York: David McKay, Inc., 1959), p. 645
[18] OR, Vol. VX/1, p. 1071
[19] Wiley Sword, *Mountains Touched with Fire: Chattanooga Besieged, 1863* (New York: St. Martin's Press, 1995), p. 22; hereinafter cited as Sword

January 2, 1863. Prior to this battle, Colonel Harker was giving testimony as a witness for the defense at General Buell's Court of Inquiry on December 24, 1862.

Bragg's Army of the Mississippi was reorganized into the Army of Tennessee, and following the defeat at Perryville, Bragg moved his army toward Murfreesboro for the Winter. Rosecrans, now in command of the Army of the Cumberland, set out from Nashville to intercept Bragg. The two armies connected on December 29, 1862. Rosecrans' army was nearly 44,000 strong and Bragg's about 37,000 [these numbers represent effective and battle ready soldiers]. The Army of the Cumberland was organized into three wings commanded by Crittenden, Thomas, and McCook. Crittenden's forces made up the left wing of the army at the battle of Stones River. Colonel Harker was given command of the 3rd Brigade, 1st Division, commanded by Gen. Thomas Wood, XIV Army Corps. Crittenden was ordered by the high command to go into the city of Murfreesboro, and he immediately ordered a night march over unknown ground against an indeterminate force by two of his divisions, Wood's and Palmer's. Both division commanders protested and the order was suspended for an hour. General Rosecrans countermanded the order later. Crittenden placed Wood's division flanking the river, Palmer was on his right, and Van Cleve was held in reserve near a ford on Stones River. The opposing forces in this battle were well known to each other and Confederate general Braxton Bragg and Gen. William Rosecrans would engage several more times before both departed to other assignments. The night of December 29 was cold with an abominable horrendous freezing rain taking place. General McCook, the right wing commander, did not arrive at the battle scene until 3A.M. the night of December 30th. McCook was given orders to align his troops for battle and at 4A.M. He reported to Rosecrans that the battle line was complete. Rosecrans was unhappy with the alignment and felt that the line should be facing South. This was important because McCook would most likely receive the Confederate attack, if one occurred. Barring an attack, McCook was to hold all enemy forces possible in his front. Thomas, commanding the center of the army, and Palmer's division were to skirmish the enemy's center, down as far as the river, while Crittenden's major objective was to oppose Breckinridge. Wood's division was to cross the bridges at an upper ford and move toward Murfreesboro. The plan was to dislodge Breckinridge, gain the upper ground and allow Wood's batteries to enfilade the troops fronting Negley and Palmer. It was a complicated plan with many avenues for failure, but without doubt, McCook was the key to the success or failure of the battle plan. It is of interest that Bragg had formulated a battle plan nearly identical to that of Rosecrans. On December 31, Bragg attacked the right flank of the Union Army, driving Rosecrans back toward Nashville until federal reinforcements arrived late in the day at which time he was then able to re-established his line. Both armies marked time on January 1, and no significant combat took place. On January 2, Bragg launched a second offensive and drove Union forces across McFadden's Ford [on the Stones River]. With the help of artillery, the Union army recovered and Bragg was forced back to his original position of December 31. On January 4, 1863, Bragg retreated toward Shelbyville and Tullahoma, Tennessee. Even though Rosecrans did not pursue the Confederates, he immediately claimed he had won a victory, and analogously, Bragg also claimed victory based on his attack of January 2nd.[20] The Army of the Cumberland suffered 13,000 killed, wounded, or captured. The Confederates lost about 10,000.

---

[20] See Battles and Leaders, Vol. III, p. 613-637 for a detailed account of the battle. For a streamlined account see WWW.Civil War.COM-battles, or Mark Boatner, *Civil War Dictionary*, p. 803-808

[21] This was no small battle in terms of numbers or importance for either army, but was of greater importance for Bragg's army and its future battles.

Colonel Harker, in his report to the division commander relates his impressions about the morning of December 31:

> About 8 A.M., December 31, I received orders from General Wood, commanding division, to cross the river with my command. The movement was commenced, in obedience with General Wood's order, but was suspended for a few moments by an order emanating from Major-General Crittenden, commanding the left wing. While awaiting further orders, Major-General Rosecrans passed my command, and gave me direct instructions to proceed immediately to the support of the right wing of our army, which was yielding to the overwhelming force of the enemy at that point. (*Note- this was McCook's Wing*)
>
> ...On approaching the right, much confusion was visible; troops marching in every direction; stragglers to be seen in great numbers, and teamsters in great consternation endeavoring to drive their teams they knew not whither. My progress was impeded by the confusion, while the enemy was pouring shot and shell upon us from at least three directions, wounding several men in my command.[22]

As mentioned earlier, General McCook was commanding the right wing of the army and was the key to the success of the battle plan. Colonel Harker and the 3rd Brigade were moving to his assistance, as directed by General Rosecrans. Colonel Harker continues by stating that his command was in dire peril on the right and center, and that an officer in a command on his left reported a strong force of enemy in his [Harker's] front. Harker continues:

---

[21] Joseph B. Mitchell, *Decisive Battles of the Civil War* (New York: Fawcett Premier, 1955), p. 112-113
[22] OR, Vol. XX/1, p. 501

> At this point, my command was in a precarious situation, with a strong foe in front, which though repulsed, could not be followed up for want of support, my right threatened, and my left already turned. It therefore became necessary to change the disposition of my command and fall back.... The Thirteenth Michigan, from their position, opened upon the enemy with telling effect, and, having caused his ranks to waver, followed up the advantage with a charge, supported by the Fifty-first Illinois Volunteers, who had come to our relief. They completely routed the enemy.[23]

Colonel Harker gives considerable praise to Colonel Shoemaker commanding the 13th Michigan Volunteers. It should be noted that Harker lavishingly praised anyone in his command who made any significant contribution to the success of any battle plan.

Late on the 31st of December, Harker was ordered back to rejoin the 1st Division. The attack on January 2 probably was the most intense Harker had ever experienced. He also relates that the brigade was the unintended victim of "friendly fire" by Captain Stokes' battery, with injury reported. The 3rd Brigade was ordered to cross Stones River under adverse conditions. The Confederates continued to fire and exact pain for every foot of ground taken. On January 4, the Army of the Cumberland occupied the city of Murfreesboro after a difficult and hard fought battle.[24]

General Wood, commanding the 1st Division had this to say about Colonel Harker's role in the battle of Murfreesboro:

> Colonel Harker, was detached early in the day and sent to re-enforce the right. It remained on that part of the field during

---

[23] OR, Vol. XX/1, p. 503

[24] OR, Vol. XX/1, p. 504; for additional information on Colonel Michael Shoemaker and the 13th Michigan's role in the Battle of Stones River (Murfreesboro) see
http://users.aol.com/dlharvey/13thinf.htmCharles+Garrison+Harker

the entire day. (3rd Brigade) I am unable to, consequently, speak of its services from personal observations; but its extremely heavy list of casualties shows how hotly it was engaged and what valuable service it rendered. I am sure it fully met expectations I ever confidently entertained of what would be its bearing in the presence of the foe.[25]

Colonel Harker was recommended to the high command by General Wood for promotion to brigadier for his role in the battle of Murfreesboro. He unquestionably fully deserved the promotion but it would take another battle or two before recognition was finally paid to this exceptional soldier.

As stated earlier, at the conclusion of the battle of Murfreesboro, Bragg moved his army to the Shelbyville and Tullahoma area of Tennessee. From early January until late June of 1863, the Army of Tennessee and the Army of the Cumberland attempted to regain their strength and shore up their respective positions. A statement by Lt. Colonel Kniffin, of General Crittenden's staff, sheds some light on the importance of Tollahoma's location: "…Murfreesboro was Rosecrans' secondary base of supplies, while Tullahoma was Bragg's barrier against Rosecrans' farther advance toward Chattanooga, the strategic importance of which, as controlling Confederate railroad communication between the east and west, had rendered it the objective point of all campaigns of the armies of the Ohio and the Cumberland."[26] Tullahoma was a sprawling town at the convergence of the Nashville & Chattanooga railroad and a branch of the Wartrace and Manchester Railroad. Rosecrans had rather complete accounts of Bragg's materials, troops, defenses, and potential for battle. Bragg's location was formidable and would be difficult to overcome. The strength of the two armies was about equal, Bragg with 45,000 infantry and

---

[25] OR, Vol. XX/1, p. 462
[26] Battles and Leaders, Vol. III, p.635

cavalry, and Rosecrans with 48,000.[27] Rosecrans decided not to attempt a frontal attack, but rather to seize the bridge over the Elk River, south of Tullahoma and then attempt to threaten Bragg's line of retreat and force him to emerge and fight. To accomplish the entire battle plan, Rosecrans would quite literally attempt a magic slight of hand act. He planned to attempt a feint of a feint. He wanted Bragg to think he was going to offer battle in all the locations that would appear to be poor selections as battle sites. He wanted to keep Hardee in Shelbyville, and prevent him from reinforcing Polk, and at the same time threaten Polk's position. Crittenden would all the while march down back roads far to the east of Tallahoma in order to gain Bragg's right and rear. All these attempts at Polk and Hardee, were cover-ups to allow Crittenden to move in a somewhat undetected fashion.[28]

An unexpected continuous rain occurred from June 23 until July 4, 1863, leaving the roads in a state of mush, where animals were nearly lost in the murk of the clay and sandy soil. Even General Rosecrans lent a hand to help move guns and wagons. Crittenden's corps faired far worse than the other two corps, but finally on the morning of June 28, Crittenden's corps was laboriously able to crawl toward Manchester, and needless to say, Rosecrans was already there. It had taken Crittenden four days to move 21 miles while both Thomas and McCook's Corps waited two full days for Crittenden to arrive. General Wood's division, of which Colonel Harker was a part, was exhausted and thus allowed to rest for a time.[29]

The three Federal corps were now assembled and ready for battle, but this was just another attempt to deceive

---

[27] Battles and Leaders, Vol. III, p.636
[28] William M. Lamers, *The Edge of Glory: A Biography of General William S. Rosecrans, USA* (Baton Rouge: Louisiana State University Press, 1999), p. 277-280; hereinafter cited as Lamers
[29] Lamers, p. 281-283

Bragg since Rosecrans had no intention of attacking over such ground. An attack would most likely have been a dismal failure, and by the time Bragg figured out that Rosecrans planned to attack his left and rear, it was too late to do anything except try and protect Chattanooga. Bragg crossed the Tennessee River at Bridgeport, Alabama and Sheridan's division immediately took control of Tullahoma on July 3, 1863.[30]

Tullahoma was a campaign with few battles, with a duration of about two weeks. At most, the only significant battle of the campaign was Hoover's Gap, which occurred between the commands of General Thomas and Gen. Alexander Stewart. General Thomas' Corps attacked Hoover's Gap, which was under the control of the Kentucky 3rd Cavalry (CSA) on June 24. The Federals easily moved them out. Two Confederate brigades from General Stewart's division came to the rescue of the 3rd Kentucky, engaging the Federals in a battle which did not end until noon of June 26. Stewart then wisely commanded his two brigades to withdraw due to superior federal firepower.[31]

Colonel Harker was part of an exhausting march to Manchester, where no real fighting occurred, but such is the lot of a soldier. One of the most important battles of Harker's career was forthcoming and very soon, one in which he would play a major role and would achieve a measure of well-deserved fame. Even though the Tullahoma Campaign coincided with the battles of Vicksburg and Gettysburg, many Americans are unaware that the Tullahoma campaign had occurred. July 4, 1863, was celebrated as a mark of two momentous Federal victories, but it should have marked three important victories.

Colonel Harker was given his only military leave after the battle of Murfreesboro. As mentioned earlier, the

---

[30] Lamers, p. 284; 290; Battles and Leaders, Vol. III, p. 637
[31] WWW.civilwar.com-battles-Tennessee; Lamers, p. 280

Army of the Cumberland took a much needed rest and recruitment break from mid January until the Tullahoma Campaign, and for a period of four plus months, the army was involved in no major battles. An interesting rumor concerning Harker's private life occurred at this point in his career. Colonel Harker was never married, but legend proclaims that the colonel did find a potential bride and companion in Cleveland, Tennessee in 1863. Ezra Warner, in his work, *Generals in Blue*, mentions the rumor in a footnote, and credits the statement to Lloyd Lewis. Lewis is the author of *Sherman, Fighting Prophet*. In this work Lewis states that Harker won the affection of a Tennessee belle while the army was encamped on the estate of her relative, the brother of Confederate general Gideon J. Pillow. No citation for this affair is given and Lewis leaves it to the reader's discretion to decide the truth of the matter.[32]

General Harker spent much of his only military leave of absence in New Jersey. He had always desired and hoped to fight with troops from his home state, but the shy and reticent young man would not hear of anyone intervening on his behalf to bring about a transfer. He took extreme pride in his native state and its role in the war. At the end of his twenty-day leave, the colonel returned to Tennessee and the 3rd Brigade, where his promotion to brigadier was only a short time away.[33]

After Tullahoma, the Union Army of the Cumberland continued its effort to drive the Confederates out of Tennessee and to gain control of the city of Chattanooga. The army was still under the command of General William Rosecrans, who would experience both fame and defeat

---

[32] Ezra J. Warner, *Generals in Blue* (Baton Rouge:Louisiana State University Press, 1964), p. 626

[33] John Y. Foster, *New Jersey and the Rebellion* (Newark: Martin R. Dennis & Co., 1868), p. 853; hereinafter cited as New Jersey and the Rebellion

during this campaign. Chattanooga is situated on a bend in the Tennessee River and General Braxton Bragg well understood that Chattanooga was a major target of the Federal Army, primarily because with the fall of this city, the road to invade Georgia would be wide open. After Murfreesboro, Bragg fled over the Cumberland Mountains, burning the bridge at Bridgeport, Alabama hoping to slow the Federal advance in Tennessee. The federal army was forced to halt at Stevenson, Alabama because they were unable to transport any needed military supplies over the undeveloped roads of eastern Tennessee. It now became a necessity to repair the Nashville and Chattanooga Railroad, which the Confederate army had destroyed. Once the railroad was operational, supplies could then be transported to Bridgeport and Stevenson to supply the army, which was accomplished in mid August of 1863.[34]

The Army of the Cumberland came into the Chattanooga area, divided by corps and via different points. Bragg was again completely deceived, and thus concentrated his troops above Chattanooga. This enabled Rosecrans to cross the Tennessee River unencumbered, but it also divided his strength. Rosecrans, believing Bragg had retreated toward Rome, Georgia, ordered Crittenden to begin pursuit. This division of the Army of the Cumberland was not lost on Bragg, who then decided that he could crush Thomas' advanced divisions with massive force, which failed due a delay in the attack plan. Bragg next turned toward Crittenden, who had also divided his forces. Polk was ordered to attack, but on September 13, Polk, again failed to move his forces as ordered. Crittenden reunited his Corps and was now safe on the west side of Chickamauga Creek.[35]

---

[34] Photographic History, Vol. I, Part III, p. 272-274
[35] Photographic History, Vol. I, Part III, p. 278; http: WWW.CivilWar.com-battlesGeorgia

General Thomas made up the left wing of the Federal army, Crittenden made up the center, and McCook commanded the right wing of the army. The Army of the Cumberland had between 55,000-70,000 troops. The Confederate army had a new ingredient in this upcoming battle, the I Corps of the Army of Northern Virginia commanded by General Longstreet, sent from Virginia to aid General Bragg's Army of Tennessee. By September 19, Longstreet had crossed the Chickamauga and the two armies were now poised to engage in a major battle.

The battle began with a general movement of the Confederates attempting to flank the Union's left wing. The attack was supposed to begin at daybreak with Polk's corps, but as was often the case; it was approaching 10 A.M. when things really got serious. Thomas was reinforced time after time and the Confederates continued to put on an outstanding show of firepower, but nonetheless, the attack was put down. What one hears in the heat of battle does not always translate into the correct action, and such was the case at Chickamauga. Reynolds and Brannon were pressed by Bragg's attack to near their original positions at the start of the battle. Rosecrans ordered General Wood [Colonel Harker's division] to close up on Reynolds, but Wood misunderstood and moved his division from Brannon's right. This created a massive hold in the center of the Union battle line. Longstreet's veterans rushed into the gap and Wood's right side was shattered immediately. All of Sheridan's and part of Davis' and Van Cleve's divisions were driven from the battlefield. McCook and Crittenden were unable to stem the rushing tide of Confederates and thus McCook, Crittenden and Rosecrans fled to Chattanooga like "scalded dogs." [36] The Confederate General St. John Liddell gives his account of the situation:

---

[36] Photographic History, Vol. I, Part III, p. 284

A soup line which General Harker and the Union Forces might have faced at Chattonooga before the "Cracker Line"

General Thomas J. Wood was General Harker's division commander at Chickamauga, and was involved in shifting the Federal line which allowed the Confederates to advance, and ensured their success in this important battle

Library of Congress

Depiction of the Battle of Kenesaw Mountain, June 27, 1864, where General Harker was fatally wounded

The front of Kenesaw Mountain, Georgia

General John Newton was General Harker's division commander at the Battle of Kenesaw Mountain where General Harker was mortally wounded on June 27, 1864

> The enemy force to our front had largely increased. Rosecrans had withdrawn units from his right to maintain his ground on his left and to prevent our turning his rear. I was again forced back about 200 yards. All of our fighting had been done in thick oak and brush woodlands. We could not see each other until close at hand. Rosecrans, in supporting Thomas so heavily, so weakened his right wing that Longstreet's men had a comparatively easy time with the thin line opposed to them.[37]

Given this seeming victory, the Confederate army now zeroed in on General Thomas, located on Horseshoe Ridge. The Confederate army had the smell of victory in their nostrils, and led by Longstreet, assaulted the ridge. They were somehow pushed back while Thomas frantically searched for Sheridan and his brigades for reinforcement. As mentioned earlier, Sheridan had been driven back by Longstreet's assault, but resourcefully, Sheridan moved on Rossville, and came down the Lafayette road on Thomas' left.[38]

Colonel Harker gives a lengthy, detailed account of this aspect of the battle:

> ... from the troops having given way in General Davis' front, there was a wide gap, embracing the distance from the point where my troops first went into action, to the right of General ---; that the rebels were rapidly advancing through this gap; that my brigade by sweeping across this gap checked their progress, and giving the troops on our right time to reform added greatly toward preventing a movement on the part of the rebels similar to that which proved so disastrous to the army on the following day, to wit, breaking through our lines and separating the right from the left.[39]

---

[37] St. John R. Liddell, *Liddell's Record*, edited by Nathaniel C. Hughes (Baton Rouge: Louisiana State University Press, 1985), p. 143
[38] Photographic History, Vol. I, Part III, p. 286
[39] OR, Vol. XXX/1, p. 692

The segment of the battle known as Snodgrass Hill occurred between 1:00 and 7:00 P.M. This was a crucial part of the battle and during the encounter Colonel Harker and his brigade defended an area known as Snodgrass Field. For his role in organizing the Union defense of Snodgrass Hill and the connecting Horseshoe Ridge, Thomas earned the fabled title "Rock of Chickamauga". In his report, Colonel Harker relates, "General Brannon, having rallied a part of his command, it, together with fragments of other commands, formed on the hill at my right, while my brigade formed in two lines to the left of Brannon, fronting to the South and nearly perpendicular to Reynold's division, then on my left."[40] Steven Woodworth, in his book *Chickamauga, A Battlefield Guide*, feels that Harker's defense was a key to the Confederate army failing to completely overrun Thomas' position. Harker formed his brigade into two lines and made good use of the terrain. When the Confederates attacked, one line raised and fired, and when the next attack occurred, the other line fired, while the first line reloaded under cover of the hill. Colonel Harker continues, "From about 1 P.M. until nightfall, this line was repeatedly attacked, but remained unbroken. The enemy, failing to carry our line from the front, gradually worked around our right, and must finally have succeeded but for the timely appearance of a part of Steedman's division of Major General Gordon Granger's corps."[41] Meanwhile, General Thomas maintained calm and complete serenity that had a profound effect on Harker's and other troops. Harker concludes stating that his brigade received orders to fall back to Rossville, and arrived there about 11P.M.[42]

---

[40] OR, Vol. XXX/1, p. 695
[41] OR, Vol. XXX/1, p. 695
[42] OR, Vol. XXX/1, p. 695; also see Steven Woodworth, *Chickamauga: A Battlefield Guide* (Lincoln: University of Nebraska Press, 1999), p. 74-75; also Lamers, chapter 15, p. 325-361

After the battle of Murfreesboro, General Wood had recommended Colonel Harker for promotion to brigadier general. He was denied this promotion and General Wood tried again after Chickamauga. He stated: "In the late campaign he [Harker] has peculiarly distinguished himself. He made two of the most daring and brilliant reconnaissance during the campaign-reconnaissance's almost without parallel in the annals of warfare…I earnestly recommend him for promotion to the rank of brigadier-general." [43] If this was not enough, the XXI Corps commander, Gen. Thomas Crittenden added his praise: "This report of Colonel Harker furnishes another convincing proof of his great value to the service."[44]

The Battle of Chickamauga is one of the major battles of the Civil War. The number of casualities reached nearly 35,000, and unfortunately, this battle more or less ended General Rosecrans' career as the commanding general of a major army, and as well signaled the beginning of the end for Braxton Bragg as a commanding officer of note in the Confederate army. Chickamauga was the beginning of the distinguishing, but brief career of Charles Harker as a noteworthy brigadier general. General Harker at last received this well deserved promotion on September 20, 1863, little realizing that he would be dead within a year.

Chattanooga, in 1863, was a place with a history of violence, loneliness, and desolation, and additionally, this had been the case for at least one hundred years. The area had been a gathering place for outlaw Cherokee, Creek, Shawnee and other Indians whose bands had terrorized the entire southwestern frontier area. Chattanooga was an important railroad town by the 1860s that suggested to Bragg, communication, ordinance, and other necessities of war. Furthermore, Chattanooga was also the gateway to the

---

[43] OR, Vol. XXX/1, p. 640
[44] OR, Vol. XXX/1, p. 687

lower South, which meant all of the needed items to sustain an army during conflict: food, ammunition, and supplies of every description. Chattanooga additionally was also a fortress of a sort, and for that reason, in order for Rosecrans to make any inroads into this fortress; he would have to transverse difficult mountain roads, narrow valleys, and operate with little or no sustenance for his army. To make any respectable attack, Rosecrans would face at least fifty miles of such obstacles. Doubtless, these are not very good odds for any army planning to make an attack in enemy controlled territory.[45]

Bragg was experienced enough to perceive that the Chattanooga situation presented opportunities for his army. The Federal army was, and had been confined to the city for many weeks, additionally, the animals were weak, the men were hungry, and things looked as if they would not be improving any time soon. Bragg expected the Army of the Cumberland to make a run for better conditions elsewhere, but this did not immediately occur. Bragg then surmised an attack was imminent and asked for and received more troops.[46]

During the month of October 1863, the Federal Army underwent a complete reorganization. The Departments of the Ohio, the Cumberland, and the Tennessee were united under a new banner referred to as the Military Division of the Mississippi, with Gen. U.S. Grant as the general commanding. Rosecrans was replaced by Gen. George Thomas as the commander of the Army of the Cumberland, also, Gen. Joseph Hooker brought 15,000 men from the Army of the Potomac to Bridgeport, Ala. Sherman and about 20,000 men under his command were sent to Memphis from

---

[45] Thomas L. Connelly, *Autumn of Glory: The Army of Tennessee*, 1862-1865 (Baton Rouge: Louisiana State University Press, 1998), p. 138; hereinafter cited as Connelly
[46] Sword, p. 68

Vicksburg. Hooker was able to secure a direct line from Kelly's Ferry to Bridgeport, after which he then pushed the Confederates across Lookout Creek, which opened a link between Bridgeport and Brown's Ferry. The Army of the Cumberland was now able to receive needed supplies to avoid starvation and ultimate surrender, by way of the now famous "Cracker Line".[47]

During this period of reorganization, General Harker also changed commands. Harker was now part of the IV Corps, commanded by Gen. Gordon Granger, 2nd Division, under the command of Gen. Phil Sheridan. Harker still commanded the 3rd Brigade, however it was somewhat enlarged.

In 1863, Chattanooga was a much smaller town than exist today, with a population of about 2,000 citizens. Statements about the town from the Federal troops were typically, "Chattanooga is a dirty, nasty irregular town, a shabby little town of few houses, Chattanooga is barren of anything worth having."[48] To the typical infantryman, this probably seemed to be the case. Chattanooga would prove to be a large piece of the puzzle Grant needed to solve the arrangement for his invasion of the states of Georgia and the Carolinas, and no doubt, the fall of Chattanooga would allow this invasion to occur. On November 23, General Harker relates:

> About 12m. on the 23d of November, I received an order from Major-General Sheridan, commanding the division, to march my command with 40 rounds of cartridges, without knapsacks or haversacks, to an eminence known as Brush Knob, about one-half mile to the front of the line of rifle-pits commanded by Forts Wood and Negley, and nearly equidistant from each.... We remained in this position until General Wood

---

[47] Photographic History, Vol. I, Part III, p. 296
[48] Sword, p.83

advanced upon Orchard Knob, which advance was followed by General Wagner's brigade (the Second Brigade).[49]

General Harker further informs us that he was ordered to extend his skirmish line forward, after which his brigade was ordered to remain in place. Food and assorted military gear, plus additional rounds were supplied to each man. The 24 of November was quiet on Harker's immediate front, even though the battle of Lookout Mountain occurred on that day and was won by Union forces on Harker's right. On the morning of November 25, Harker was again ordered to extend his line and after this was completed, the brigade was inactive until about 3 P.M. General Harker continues his account:

> ...Colonels Opdycke and Walworth were order to move forward at the firing of the signal gun from Orchard Knob, and to carry the works at all hazards—were directed to conform to the movements of General Wagner's brigade, which was on my left. The ground on my immediate front was covered with timber for a distance of about one-eighth of a mile; from there to the rifle-pits at the foot of Missionary Ridge, a distance of half a mile, the ground was entirely cleared of timber and comparatively level.[50]

General Harker recounts that a signal was given and the lines moved forward, causing his brigade to be exposed to blazing enemy fire when they reached the open ground. The first line of enemy rifle pits was taken, which totally exhausted the men, after the rapid march they had just completed across an open plain. His advance troops began ascending the ridge and even under galling fire, they reached about one-third of the distance to the summit. Apparently, some confusion and misdirection occurred and the brigade on Harker's left retired, by order of someone who was undetected by

---

[49] OR, Vol. XXX1/2, p. 229
[50] OR, Vol. XXXI/2, p. 230

Harker's command. Harker ordered his brigade to retire and reform, at which point General Sheridan appeared and stated that no order to retire had been given by him and he would order an advance when the troops were rested somewhat.[51] General Harker continues with his account of the Battle of Missionary Ridge:

> The order to again push forward was soon given by General Sheridan, and was obeyed with alacrity by the command. The difficulty and danger with the brave officers and men passed through from the foot of the hill to the summit baffles description. From the nature of the ground it was impossible to move forward with regularity and in line, exposed to the most galling fire of musketry and under a ceaseless storm of grape, canister, and other deadly missiles…The command moved steadily forward taking advantage of every depression in the ground… the crest was being reached to the admiration of all who witnessed it….[52]

The summit was reached by Harker's command, which immediately took control of General Bragg's headquarters, placing the entire ridge in federal hands. The enthusiasm was unparalleled, according to Harker. Sheridan gave the order to pursue the enemy, executing the desire of Union troops to carry out their unrestrained aggression against the Confederates. Harker, Sheridan, and others had difficulty reforming the lines, due to the desire of the troops to reap revenge for the defeat at Chickamauga. At about 1 A.M. on November 26, Harker narrates that he was ordered to cross the Chickamauga and shortly ordered to return to his position at Chattanooga, accounting some 500 prisoners, many small arms, and pieces of artillery captured by his command.[53] The fierceness of this battle is attested to by Captain Edward Bates, of the 125th Ohio who states, "The

---

[51] OR, Vol. XXXI/2, p. 230
[52] OR, Vol. XXXI/2, p. 231
[53] OR, Vol. XXXI/2, p. 231

most fearful tornado of bursting shells had now passed into a more destructive shower of grape... The enemy's fire was now terrific."[54] General Sheridan, in his *Personal Memoirs* relates an interesting occurrence concerning General Harker at the conclusion of battle of Missionary Ridge. Sheridan recounts that to better view the Confederate retreat, he leaped on a Confederate cannon that had been captured only a few minutes earlier. General Harker also vaulted upon one of the cannons, but unfortunately the barrel was still hot, to the extent that Harker scorched his posterior so badly that he could not ride for several weeks.[55]

Many in the Confederate army felt Bragg was the cause of the defeat at Chattanooga, for example Gen. Arthur Manigault who stated, "he was completely out generaled." Manigault felt Bragg was overconfident and as usual, underestimated the enemy.[56] Grant explains in his writings, "Bragg was a remarkably intelligent and well informed man, professionally and otherwise. He was thoroughly upright. But he was possessed of an irascible temper, and was naturally disputatious. A man of the highest moral character and the most correct habits, yet in the old army he was in frequent trouble."[57] From these viewpoints, one may be able to conclude why this massive defeat occurred, although Grant felt that all he [Grant] had ordered to occur, had occurred, and that the outcome was no accident. [58]

General Harker received high praise from General Sheridan for his role in the battle of Chattanooga. General Sheridan proclaimed, "I take great pleasure in

---

[54] OR, Vol. XXXI/2, p. 244
[55] Philip Sheridan, *Personal Memoirs of P.H. Sheridan* (New York: Charles L. Webster & Company, 1888), Vol. II, p. 856
[56] Lockwood R. Tower, editor, *A Carolinian Goes to War* (Columbia: University of South Carolina Press, 1988), p. 142
[57] Ulysses S. Grant, *Personal Memoirs of U.S. Grant* (New York: Dover Press, 1995), p. 260; hereinafter cited as Grant's Memoirs
[58] Grant's Memoirs, p. 260

recommending these officers [Harker & Sherman] for promotion to brigadier-generals, a position which they have fairly won on this and other fields, and which they are fully qualified by ability and long experience to fill."[59] Little did General Sheridan realize, this accolade had already been given to General Harker based on his efforts and leadership at the Battle of Chickamauga.[60]

After Chickamauga, the Federal army's major concern was the continued occupation and control of eastern Tennessee, and to accomplish this, it was necessary to rid the area of Longstreet's troops. A number of small engagements occurred to accomplish this end, causing Longstreet to expressed great frustration about the situation in east Tennessee. Longstreet seemed to think that General Bragg had President Davis' attention and that he did not, which was probably true. On February 22, 1864, Longstreet began his march back to Virginia, happy to be rid of Bragg.[61] No doubt, General Harker and the Army of the Cumberland played a role in the decision of the I Corps of the Army of Northern Virginia to leave the area of Chattanooga and Chickamauga

General Thomas gives an account of the Army's activities from January through April of 1864. The activities of the IV Corps, 2nd Division, 3rd Brigade during the period were as follow [Harker]:

> ...From the 1st until as late as the 20th of January, no movement of any consequence took place. Small scouting parties of both cavalry and infantry were sent out from time to

---

[59] OR, Vol. XXXI/2, p. 192
[60] Graduates, p. 706 (this official record of West Point dates Harker's promotion as September 20, 1863)
[61] James Longstreet, *From Manassas to Appromattox* (New York: Mallard Press, 1991), p. 540

time to watch the movements of the enemy, but failed to find him in any considerable force in our immediate front.[62]

General Thomas continues the account of the IV Corps' activities:

> January 14 and 15, under orders from department commander, the Second and Third Divisions broke up camp near Blain's Cross-Roads and moved, with all trains, toward Dandridge, Tenn, for forage and subsistence...reached Dandridge at night...January 17, slight skirmish with the enemy; under orders fell back to Strawberry Plains at night; ... January 18, encamped at Flat Creek, Tenn., and beyond Holstein River, in vicinity of Strawberry Plains. January 20, moved to Sevierville via Knoxville. January 21, passed through Knoxville and went into camp south of the Holstein. January 23, two brigades of the Second Division ordered to Loudon and one brigade to Kinston...[63]

General Thomas writes that in February of 1864, "Four regiments of the Third Brigade of the Second Division [General Harker's brigade] and [a] section of artillery moved to Sweet Water on the 17th and returned on the 22d. During the absence of Major-General Sheridan Brigadier-General Wagner [was] in command from the 24th instant".[64] Little occurred during the month of March for General Harker and the 2nd Division, since the entire division was engaged in the construction of a railroad bridge over the Tennessee River at Loudon, Tennessee, and additionally the division was also guarding stores of the army.[65] During the month of April, General Thomas reports, "...Second Division marched from Loudon to Cleveland, Tennessee, on the 15th, 16th, 17th, and 18th instant."[66] By the end of April and the beginning of May

---

[62] OR, Vol. XXXII/1, p. 7
[63] OR, Vol. XXXII/1, p. 23
[64] OR, Vol. XXXII/1, p. 23
[65] OR, Vol. XXXII/1, p. 24
[66] OR, Vol. XXXII/1, p. 24

1864, events would accelerate rapidly for the Army of the Cumberland and especially for Gen. Charles Harker.

As the Confederate Army of Tennessee retreated from Tennessee toward Georgia, a series of battles occurred, which involved the Army of the Cumberland, and are collectively known as the Atlanta Campaign. After the 2nd Division of the IV Corps left Cleveland, Tennessee in late April 1864, General Harker found himself involved in major and very intense engagements until his life ended June 27, 1864. The first of these engagements is collectively referred to as Rocky Face Ridge [Georgia].

Rocky Face Ridge is a "catch all" term for the engagements of Buzzard Roost, Mill Creek, Dug Gap, Snake Creek Gap, Tunnel Hill, Varnell's Station, and "action near Dalton". This series of engagements occurred between May 5-11, 1864. General Johnston held a position on the long and high Rocky Face Ridge. General McPherson, commanding the Army of the Tennessee, along with General Thomas and the Army of the Cumberland, were under the command of General Sherman, who had replaced General Grant, now, the leader of the entire Union forces. McPherson would move through Snake Creek Gap, Thomas would attack frontally, and hold the Confederates in position, and Schofield, commanding the Army of the Ohio, would attack via Varnell's Station, on the Confederate right. Sherman's combined force numbered about 100,000 men.[67]

The commanding General of the IV Corps, Army of the Cumberland was now Gen. O.O. Howard. General Howard replaced General Granger, who was transferred to other duties. In addition, Gen. John Newton commanded the 2nd Division, and General Sheridan had been transferred to the Army of the Potomac. A background statement on

---

[67] Thomas B. Van Horne, *Army of the Cumberland* (New York: Konecky &Konecky, (reprint of the 1875 edition), p. 368-378, hereinafter cited as as Van Horne. Also see WWW.civilwar.com-battles

General Newton might be useful for clarification and identity purposes. John Newton was a career soldier, a graduate of West Point, standing second in the class of 1842. Newton was a native Virginian who elected to remain with the Union, and by most accounts was usually thought of as a completely professional soldier by commanders on both sides of the war. He served under Burnsides at Fredericksburg and commanded the 1st Corps at Gettysburg after the death of General Reynolds. He was sent to the western theater in April of 1864, and became the commanding officer of the 2nd division[68]. General Newton explained in his report to General Howard that, "General Harker's brigade was ordered to ascend to the northern extremity of Rocky Face Ridge, the 125th Ohio Volunteer Infantry [Colonel Opdycke] clearing the way as skirmishers, which being effectually done, the whole brigade ascended to the summit."[69] Of course, it was certainly not that simple. In a correspondence from Chief of Staff Gen. William D. Whipple, to the General Command, Whipple states, "Harker's brigade is upon Rocky Face Ridge, but has not entire possession of it. Howard and Palmer have possession close up to the gap at Buzzard Roost…Fifteen wounded in Harker's brigade reported."[70] Later in the day of May 8, 1864 (3.30 P.M.), General Schofield, in a letter to General Sherman relates, " On my arrival at the gap at the end of Rocky Face Ridge I found that Harker's brigade, of General Newton's division, had preceded me. He had occupied the gap and gained a footing on the ridge. I therefore relieved his troops in the gap with one brigade of Judah's division.…" At about 3.50 P.M., General Schofield sent another message to

---

[68] Stewart Sifakis, *Who was Who in the Union* (New York: Facts on File, 1988), p. 289; Stephen Sears, *Controversies and Commanders* (New York: Houghton Mifflin Company, 1999), p. 142
[69] OR, Vol. XXXVIII/1, p. 292
[70] OR, Vol. XXXVIII/4, p. 77

General Sherman," Captain Engle has just returned with your dispatch of 12m, directing me to make a lodgment on the summit, and push on down to Buzzard Roost. My troops are now moving accordingly. I did not make this move before General Harker had preceded me. I asked him to inform me if he wanted help, but none have not been asked for any."[71] On May 9, General Sherman's message to General Thomas stated, "Hold fast all ground you have gained. Have the road built to-night and artillery in position as against the gap, I think Brigadier-General Harker has advanced somewhat."[72]

On May 14, 1864, the 2nd division was ordered to align in reserve behind the XXIII Corps. As the day progressed, the XXIII Corps became engaged at Resaca, a small town, which in 1864, had about 400 inhabitants most of which had fled from the coming battles. The 2nd division was ordered forward by General Newton and General Harker's brigade was ordered to relieve a portion of the XXIII Corps. General Newton explains, "The position just taken by Harker was a short distance in advance of their line of entrenchment's and commanded by them, and it was only by taking advantage of every little inequality of the ground that the brigade could maintain its position."[73]

General Newton gives additional details about the battle at Resaca: "Colonel Sherman's brigade was ordered, toward the close of the afternoon, to relieve General Harker. Our loss was considerable in Harker's and Sherman's brigades. Among the wounded were General Harker and Colonel Opdycke, One hundred and twenty-fifth Ohio Volunteer Infantry, both of whom refused to quit the field and remained on duty till they recovered".[74]

---

[71] OR, Vol. XXXVIII/4, p. 83
[72] OR, Vol. XXXVIII/4, p. 90
[73] OR, Vol. XXXVIII/1, p. 293
[74] OR, Vol. XXXVIII/1, p. 293

General Harker, even though an extremely modest man, wrote a letter to a friend about his experience at Resaca. The letter is dated May 22, 1864:

> You are aware that the great Southwestern campaign under General Sherman is in progress. Thus far, we have had several quite severe engagements, in which we have been entirely victorious. In the battle of Resaca, on the 14th instant, I was wounded, though not dangerously. I was struck on the leg by a shell, which exploded immediately after passing me, wounding General Manson and killing my own horse and that of one of my orderlies. It was quite a narrow escape for me. My leg, though slightly cut and painfully bruised, is doing well. I did not leave the field, though unable to exercise full command for about thirty-six hours. You and my family will be glad to learn that I can walk and ride very well now. I am able to discharge all my duties, and hope to be able to conduct my brave little command, which has so nobly stood by me in so many severe engagements, through the great struggle, or perhaps series of struggles which will doubtless ensue before the fall of Atlanta.[75]

The general concludes his letter with a portent of the future, "The result of the great battle before us cannot be doubted, though all of us cannot hope to witness the great triumph which must crown the efforts [of] our magnificent army."[76] Little did the general know, or even suspect, that he would be one of those who would not witness the fall of Atlanta and the close of the war.

May 15 was a Sunday, during which the two armies exchanged artillery and musketry fire much of the time. On May 16, the Confederate army had evacuated the field and the 2nd division marched into Resaca. The bridge crossing the Oostenaula River was repaired, and the army then moved toward the town of Calhoun, General Harker's brigade leading the way and skirmishing with the Confederates most

---

[75] New Jersey and the Rebellion, p. 854
[76] New Jersey and the Rebellion, p. 854

of the time. The night of May 16 was spent in Calhoun by the army, before marching toward Adairsville on the 17th.

Colonel Sherman's brigade led the march toward Adairsville, which engaged the Confederate cavalry in heavy fighting until late in the day. About two or three miles from Adairsville, the 2nd division confronted the Confederate infantry. Sherman's brigade and several regiments of General Harker's brigade took part in heavy fire, which continued until after sundown, with Sherman's brigade suffering heavy losses. General Howard refused to believe that such a large force of Confederates had engaged Sherman and the 2nd division, primarily because he was under extreme pressure from General Sherman to move forward toward Atlanta. Finally, he realized what was at stake and prepared the IV Corps for battle, however General Thomas convinced him to delay until morning, since the hour was late. General Sherman, in spite of all this information, felt that Johnston did not intend to make a stand at Adairsville, and he was correct.[77]

On May 18, the 2nd division marched into Adairsville, encountering the Confederate entrenchments from the day before. The division remained for a considerable time in Adairsville. From that point, the division, along with General Wood's division marched to within three miles of Kingston and camped for the night. On May 19, about three miles South of Kingston, the divisions engaged with the Confederate army in a confrontation that lasted well into the night. Around noon, General Stanley's division along with the IV Corps approached Cassville and immediately sighted three battle lines on high ground near Two Run Creek. At 3 P.M., General Thomas sent word to General Sherman in Kingston that he had sighted at least one

---

[77] Albert Castel, *Decision in the West: The Atlanta Campaign of 1864* (Lawrence: University of Kansas Press, 1992), p. 193-194; hereinafter cited as The Atlanta Campaign; OR, Vol. XXXVIII/1, p. 293

Confederate division and advised Sherman that with Hooker and Schofield, he could make a huge dent in the Confederate forces. About 5 P. M., the XX Corps, along with the IV Corps and part of the XXIII Corps were in line to open fire on the ridge east of Cassville. Enfilading fire ensued on the Confederates, forcing General Polk to declare that withdrawal was at hand. After consultation with Polk and Hood, Johnston ordered an immediate retreat about 9 P.M.[78] The 2nd division spent May 20 through 22 in regrouping and refitting the troops, even so, after the brutally tough engagement at Cassville, rest was most definitely needed. On May 23, the division crossed the Etowah River, after a 1 P.M. start and camped about three miles beyond the river at 11 P.M. On May 24, the division marched to Burnt Hickory, and on the 25, moved toward New Hope Church, crossing over Pumpkin Vine Creek. The 2nd division then followed the XX Corps, and advanced to the area near New Hope Church but did not take part in the engagement. From May 26, until the withdrawal of the Confederate army on June 4, the 2nd Division was in constant danger from sniper fire, skirmishing, etc. The unit suffered many losses, and general weariness and fatigue with the overall situation. June 5 saw no action, but on June 6, the division moved toward Morris Hill Church. From June 7 through June 9, the 2nd Division was relatively inactive, and from June 10 until the 14th the unit was in the Pine Mountain area and under continual fire from the Confederates. On the 15th, the division led an attack, which, along with intense skirmishing, continued until the 18th resulting in great loss of life by both the division and the corps. The Confederate army then moved to their position at Kenesaw on the night of June 18.[79] From June 19 through June 26, Newton's Division and the IV Corps were engaged in constant skirmishing, yet not moving

---

[78] Atlanta Campaign, p. 200-204; OR, Vol. XXXVIII/1, p. 294
[79] OR, Vol. XXXVIII/1, p. 294-295

to any great extent, seemingly static, and with no real progress in sight. June 26, 1864 was Pentacost Sunday and most of the troops, Confederate and Union, attempted to attend church services brought about by informal truces. A few miles distant, General Sherman drafted an attack order for June 27, all the while, remaining at his headquarters on Signal Hill. The attack order commanded General McPherson to attack south and west of Kenesaw, and for General Thomas to select a site near the center of the Confederate lines for his attack, and all the assaults were ordered for 8 A.M. on June 27. Sherman wrote a letter to his wife explaining what would take place the next day. McPherson spent his time making plans as to where best to launch his forces, and Thomas surveyed the Confederate lines and determined there was little hope of any breakthrough, but finally selected an area just south of the Marietta-Dallas road. Thomas informed Howard and Palmer that a division from each of their Corps would take a major role in the attack. Thomas selected Davis' division from Palmer's Corps, but allowed Howard to make his own selection, which would be Newton's 2nd Division. The rank and file troops picked up on the action to be taken on June 27, noticing signs, such as hospitals being cleared for the wounded, which were sure to be profound in number. The men of the Army of the Tennessee and the Army of the Cumberland expected a flanking attack, not unlike that used at Dalton, Cassville, and other place. They did not learn that this was to be a frontal attack until early on the morning of June 27. They were not happy, but determined that they would make a supreme effort for "Uncle Billy".[80]

    General Newton assembled his division of about 5,000 men behind General Stanley's Division. General Harker assembled his brigade to the left of General Wagner,

---

[80] Atlanta Campaign, p. 304-307; OR, Vol. XXXVIII/1, p. 295

and by 8 A.M. all the preparations were complete, and for the next fifteen minutes all available artillery was unleashed on the point of attack. In the interim, General Harker gave all of his private papers to a staff member, after telling the staff member, "I shall not come out of this charge today alive".[81] About 9 A.M. the attack began in earnest. Col. Dan McCook's brigade experienced extreme musket and artillery fire. From the point of origin of the attack to the Confederate works was about six hundred yards and waiting for the Federal troops were Generals Cheatham and Cleburne's troops. These soldiers may well have been the finest in the Confederate Army of Tennessee. The only weak point in the line was a hill held by Maney's brigade of Cheatham's Division. The loss of men during the advance at Kenesaw was extreme. Colonel Dan McCook was mortally wounded early in the day, and died a month later in Ohio. His next in rank, Colonel Harmon was soon killed, but Newton's Division experienced somewhat different conditions. While less exposed, his division had to deal with obstructions and various entanglements and was exposed to terrific firepower. Newton withdrew his division, realizing that there was no hope of success, but unfortunately in this brief time between withdrawal and a supreme second effort, Gen.Charles Harker was mortally wounded. Harker was still on his white horse, going up and down the lines, attempting to rally his troops, waving his hat and encouraging his men. The bullet tore into his arm and chest, causing him to topple from his saddle immediately. Men in the 3rd brigade risked their lives to recover their beloved general. General Harker was carried back to the Union lines, but sadly the general died later that evening.[82] His last conscious statement was, "did we take the mountain"?

---

[81] Atlanta Campaign, p. 311
[82] Van Horne, p. 405-407; Atlanta Campaign, p. 311, 315-316

The actual combat concerning the Battle of Kenesaw Mountain probably took place within a two hour time period, concluding by 11 A.M. Sherman asked General Thomas at about 2:45 P.M. if there is any hope. General Thomas replied:

> The division commanders report the enemy's works are exceedingly strong; in fact, so strong that they cannot be carried by assault except by immense sacriface, even if they can be carried at all. I think, therefore, the best chance is to approach them by regular saps, and if we can find a favorable position to batter them down. We have already lost heavily today without gaining any material advantage; one or two more such assaults would use up this army.[83]

The battle of Kenesaw Mountain resulted in 4,000 casualties, 3,000 of which were Union soldiers. General Sherman offered no explanation or anything approaching remorse for this colossal failure, yet he could have handled this battle differently. Later, he would revert to his flanking technique, which had served him well in the past. Confederate General Johnston's statement concerning the battle of Kenesaw was sadly accurate," After maintaining the contest for three-quarters of an hour, until more of their soldiers lay dead and wounded than the number of British veterans that fell in General Jackson's celebrated battle of New Orleans, the foremost dead laying against our breastworks, they retired---unsuccessful---because they had encountered *intrenched infantry...*".[84]

What should be remembered about the life and military career of Charles Garrison Harker? He gave his life for his country, and he was an inspiration to his men and a credit to the United States army. Yet, that can all be said for many of the men who fought in the Civil War, on both sides.

---

[83] OR, Vol. XXXVIII/4, p. 609-610

[84] Joseph E. Johnston, *Military Operations During the Civil War* (New York: Da Capo Press, 1990 reprint of the original 1874 edition), p. 343

What makes this soldier any different from the several million men who took part in this conflict? General Harker seems to have been made and created for this role. He grew up in a small New Jersey village, was educated at West Point and almost immediately became a soldier, never really experiencing adult life in any way except in light of a military sentiment. He fought in some intense battles, some of the most severe and deadly which took place during the entire war. He never really experienced a life apart from this conflict, and he never felt real happiness as an adult, only war, death, and grief. There is a haunting sadness in this man's face, which reaches out and compels the viewer's attention. And if that were not enough, he lost his life never knowing if his efforts and supreme sacrifice would count for anything, or even make the slightest difference. The price paid by soldiers in all wars is always high, even the brave man has fears and periods of anxiety, if he is honest about his feelings. Gen. Charles Harker was a brave man and he had fears, and was not ashamed to admit his fears. If one accepts the idea that nobility is the attempt to complete the moral, the proper, and the virtuous actions in this life with no expectation of reward, then General Harker was a noble human being as well. This is not difficult to accept after a little thought: he was educated for war, and he took part in what is perhaps our most important war, and he went into a battle which, by his own words, he would not survive. Yet, he went without complaint, with fears, bravery, and nobility. What more could a soldier have done? The great bard said it well, "He that dies pays all debts."[85] Charles Harker paid the ultimate debt for a nation torn apart in a war which is perhaps the greatest conflict in American History, one which many people cannot forget, and one which others prefer not to remember.

---

[85] William Shakespeare, *The Tempest*

EPITAPHS & NOTES*

Charles Stone-

A victim of conspiracy, yet he remained undaunted

Lloyd Tilghman-

He suffered ingratitude but was never offended

Charles Hamilton

Blind ambition ushered in his military demise

Charles Harker

A hero shot down in the morning of his youth

Evander Law

Valor fell prey to dogmatic favoritism

George Stoneman

Divergent military accomplishments have not profited him identity

*No bibliography is included with this work. All of the sources consulted for this manuscript are included on the various pages and contained within the footnotes. Hopefully, this will enable the reader to more readily determine how any given statement has been determined as factual. In addition, this system eliminates the cumbersome task of having to refer to the end of the manuscript, by chapter and page number to ascertain the source of a quotation, source, or other aspects of the manuscript.

www.ingramcontent.com/pod-product-compliance
Lightning Source LLC
Chambersburg PA
CBHW071015240426
43661CB00073B/2293